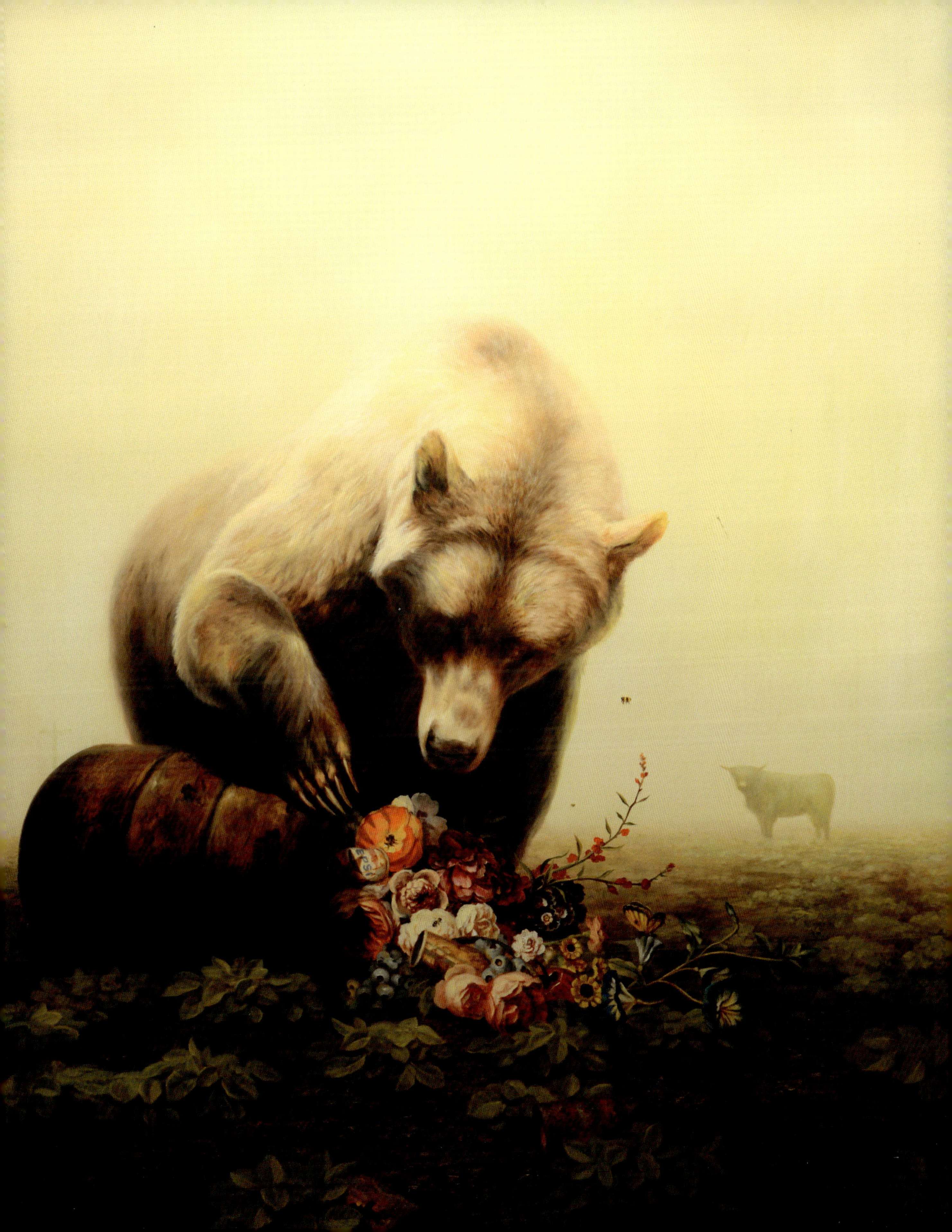

First published in the United States of America in 2016
First edition

Gingko Press, Inc.
1321 Fifth Street
Berkeley, CA 94710
email: books@gingkopress.com
www.gingkopress.com

ISBN: 978-1-58423-594-1

Printed in China

Publisher: Gwynned Vitello

Editor: Evan Pricco
Art Director: Michael Dooling
Contributing Editor: Kristin Farr
Managing Editor: Alex Nicholson

Design and Art Direction: Nisan Perera

FRONT COVER:
TIFFANY BOZIC
SANGUINE (DETAIL)
ACRYLIC ON MAPLE PANEL

BACK COVER:
JOHN PUSATERI
COUNCILLOR III (DETAIL)
COLORED PENCIL, PASTEL, ARCHIVAL DIGITAL PRINT ON RAG PAPER

PREVIOUS:
MARTIN WITTFOOTH
HARVESTER
OIL ON CANVAS

RIGHT:
RYAN McLENNAN
FIT FOR THE TABLE
ACRYLIC AND GRAPHITE ON PAPER

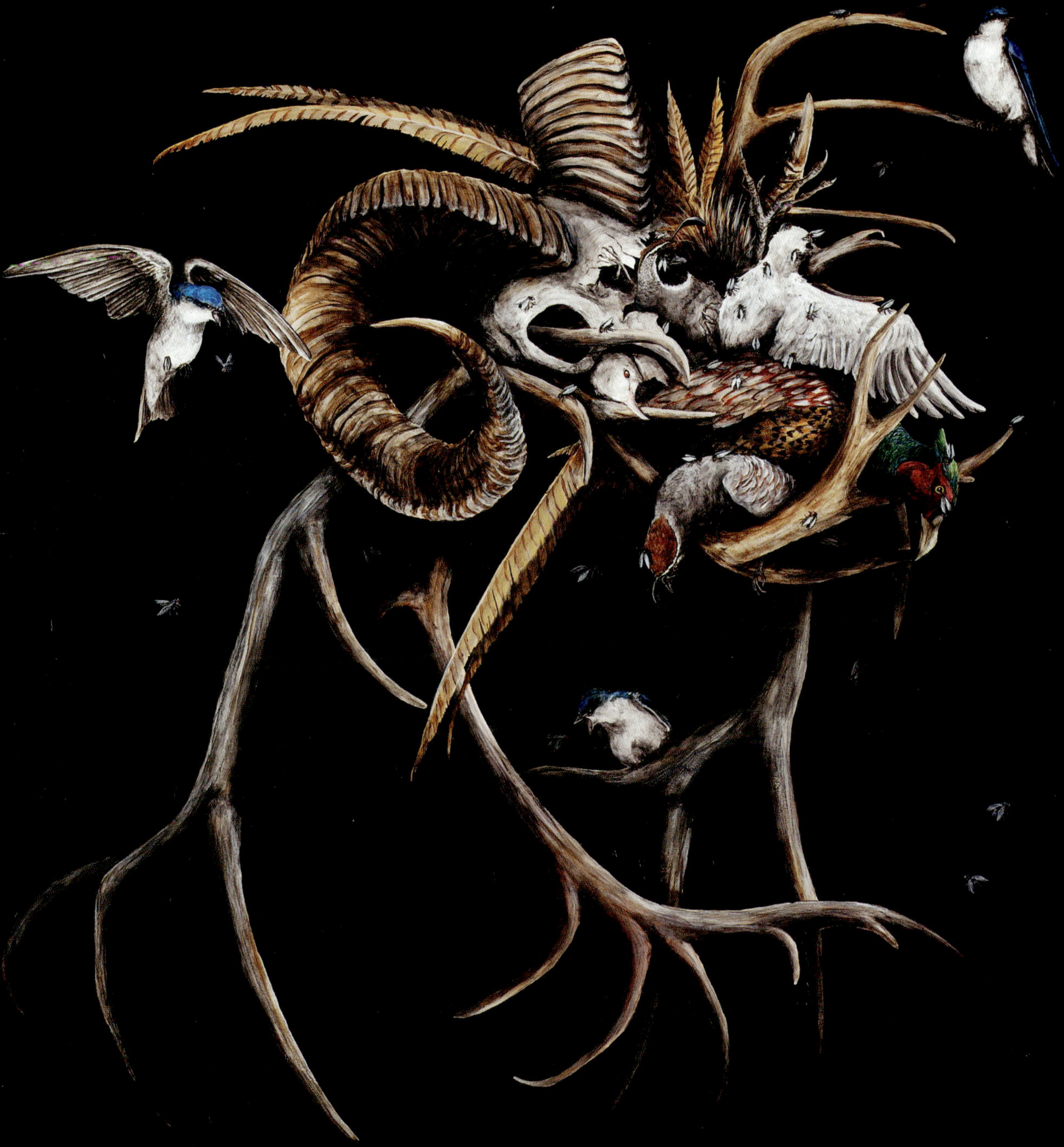

CONTENTS

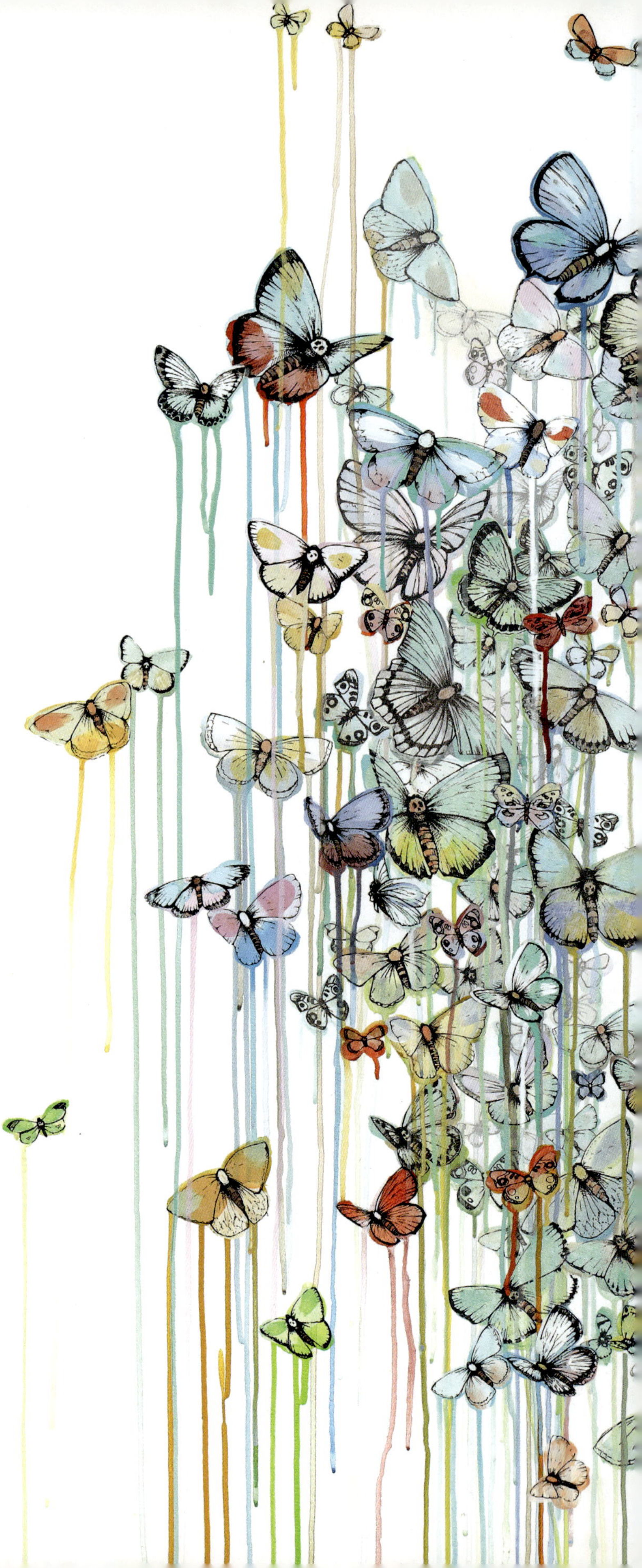

SAGE VAUGHN, *RING CYCLE II*,
60" X 60", OIL ACRYLIC, INK AND VELLUM ON CANVAS

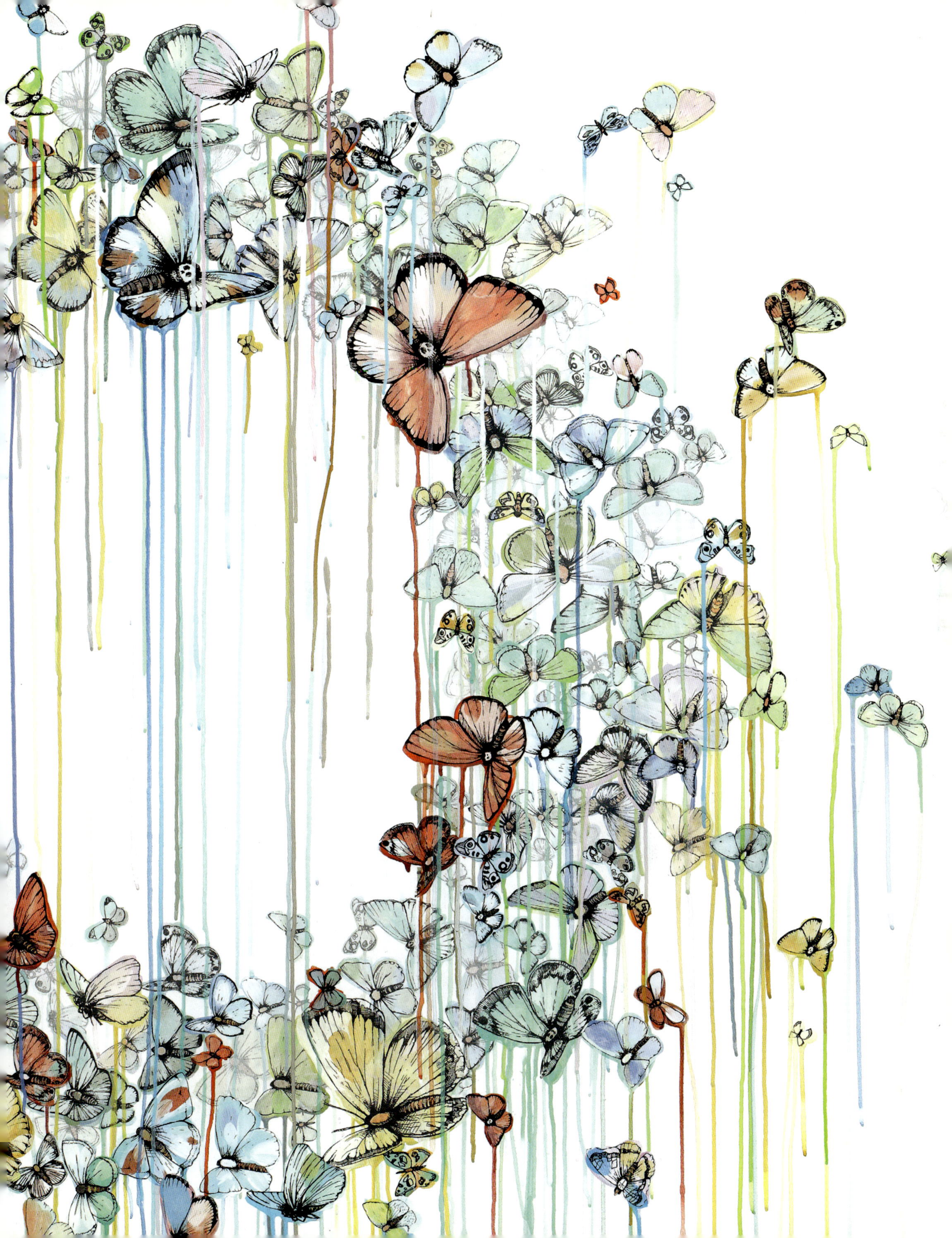

INTRODUCTION

Our Need to Be Wild

"The reason why we're all so drawn to that [animal] imagery is that the caveman buried something down deep in your brain, under that carefully constructed, deathproof box-store shopper, which gets a tiny existential titty twister. It punches you right in that nagging part of your brain that knows it's going to die."
—AJ Fosik

It's hard to find a jumping-off point or the genesis of a particular project. Animals, nature and environmental art are all topics that have filled the pages of *Juxtapoz* over the years, sometimes deliberately and conceptually, but often times organically. Tiffany Bozic, Tara Tucker, Corey Arnold and others in this book have been featured in the pages of our magazine. In recent years, Jane Kim, Josh Keyes and Sage Vaughn have appeared as we have made a conscious effort to examine the relationship between artists and their thematic representations of human impact on the environment.

This effort has borne itself in our desire to focus on the idea of animals in art, or as we put it, the genre of Wild. From sculpture to painting, muralism to photography, *Juxtapoz Wild* is a contemporary examination of why and how artists use the natural world in their work. In some instances, like Keyes, Ryan McLennan, and Lara Ball, the work speaks to nature's balance in the absence of humans. AJ Fosik, Laurel Roth and Dennis McNett all find strength and symbolic power in transforming animals into almost folklorish heroes. And there are muralists like Jane Kim, ROA, Faith47 and DALeast who use the public arena to remind us of the destruction of other species with which we share the Earth.

Not everything in this book is meant to be a politically-charged or environmental statement. Our scope was broadened to include the absurd and the supernatural. However, each artist has been asked to confront environmental themes, and to present their work under the guise that our need to be wild is perhaps a reaction to our abuse of what makes the Earth so special to begin with. As Carlo McCormick notes so eloquently in his foreword, "It's no wonder then that we consistently return to nature as metaphor and allegory for the human condition." May we tread a little lighter, and let our wild side break free.

—Evan Pricco
Juxtapoz *Editor-in-Chief*
August 2015

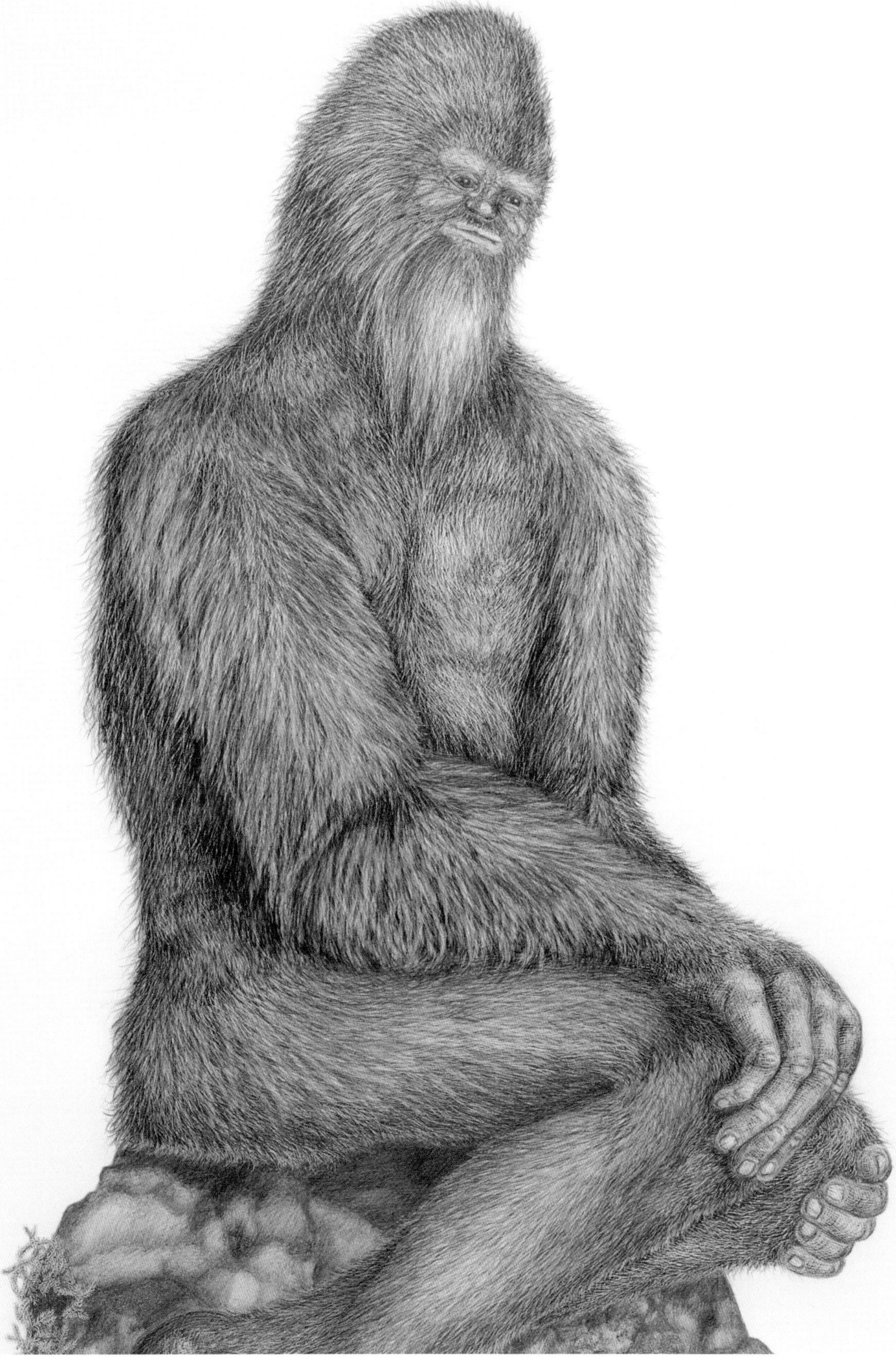

TARA TUCKER, *IMAGE IS EVERYTHING* (DETAIL), GRAPHITE ON PAPER

FOREWORD

"And the wild things roared their terrible roars and gnashed their terrible teeth and rolled their terrible eyes and showed their terrible claws."
—Maurice Sendak

Culture is the measure of our desire to understand things written in the terms of our limited capacity to understand anything. It's no wonder then that we consistently return to nature as metaphor and allegory for the human condition. As much a matter of narrative as it is a manner of narcissism, we anthropomorphize every aspect of our flora and fauna to see ourselves where we are not and to help us play out the little dramas that explain our lives. We make them terrifying or adorable, load them up with all sorts of associative attributes, and even give them the visage of our gods and demons, but as civilization gains ever greater disconnect from the animal kingdom, we come to consider the entirety of what we are not as an even more potent other—the wild.

Like most four-letter words that have come to be overused, it's pretty hard, at this point, to say what "wild" actually means anymore. The word probably lost all traction by the time Steve Martin entertained and endeared himself to Middle America as a "wild and crazy guy" in the late seventies, and just plain fell down altogether by the early nineties when Nickelodeon repurposed the phrase as the title for the kids game show *Wild and Crazy Kids*, but the essence of its meaning has always remained an expression of those reckless and dangerous energies we associate with youth. Forever the icon of youth culture is the leather-jacket-clad, motorcycle-riding Marlon Brando in *The Wild One*, the explosive first salvo in that generational war of teenage delinquency and rebellion that erupted in post-WWII America, a hardboiled archetype that, drunk on the proverbial fountain of youth, never gets old; coming back as the biker gang that terrorizes a small town in Corman's classic B movie *Wild Angels*, the brutally violent western outlaws of Peckinpah's *Wild Bunch*, and most hilariously as the messianic rock singer and revolutionary Max Frost, of *Wild in the Streets*, who rallies America's youth to change the voting age with the cry "14 or Fight" on the way to winning the presidency.

Rock music, never one to pass up any cliché, has continued that anthem, from the Troggs' "Wild Thing" to Steppenwolf's "Born to be Wild," and of course Lou Reed's "Take a Walk on the Wild Side." And perhaps this is fitting because we don't really start to imagine the wild until we can barely see it anymore. The myths of the Wild West only begin to register in our popular imagination long after it was well paved over, the great painters and poets of the wilderness coming about when the subject was far more fact than fiction. Our wildness is something like the pimply, thin social skin that fights to contain the greater body of uncontrolled emotions. Most celebrated was the case of Victor of Aveyron, the kid found totally feral in the forests of France in 1800, the original wild child, or *l'enfant sauvage*, a lesson of what happens when the cultivated and civilized go to seed, told not so very differently a hundred years later in the immensely popular Jack London novel *Call of the Wild*, where it is a dog that must abandon his domesticated ways to prevail. Perhaps that's the same zone of survival and discovery we'll always need, to find ourselves as Cheryl Strayed did in *Wild*, or truly and completely lose oneself as did that hapless lad of *Into the Wild*, but it's a journey we all know can only be undertaken in our youth.

When, in the 1920s, kids for the first time could take their cues on passion and sexuality from movies, and prohibition unleashed its legion of flappers, society wrung its hands and proclaimed it "wildness." In this way we must wonder what makes us wild, some bit of untouched nature in our heart of darkness or a lesson on transgression we teach ourselves like the inverse to our rules of politesse. The first recognized art movement of the twentieth century was called Fauvism, the fauves being French for the wild beasts. And though it's pretty hard now to think of Matisse as some wild beast, or how putting one of his paintings over your couch could be all that wild, maybe hanging a painting is not so different in that way than mounting some elk's head. Perhaps we can imagine that art is not so much wild as of the wild, a picture window onto a nature we do not see but feel, a place where Thoreau told us "All good things are wild and free," and Emerson exhorted us to "Drink the wild air."

—Carlo McCormick
Author and Critic
August, 2015

TIFFANY BOZIC

MARIN COUNTY, CALIFORNIA

Understanding Climate Change
I'm lucky because my husband is a biologist, and a lot of people in my community are working on this issue, so I am exposed to a lot of information without having to work at it.

Animals Emerge
When I first began showing my work in my early twenties, they were mostly self-portraits and paintings of my friends, but then the people nearly disappeared and were replaced by animals. I never consciously gave up painting people, I was just *more* interested in painting new and interesting things. I like to discover unexplored territory, and push myself to take on new challenges with every painting I make. So, for a while, I've been curious about what it feels like to inhabit a human mammal body with animal urges and instincts, and I find it more accessible to depict animals, like fables, to act out these dramas. If you paint a human, you have to deal with race, age, sex, etc. I found that all those things distracted from the universal qualities. I wanted to get away from that and try to discover other examples in nature to create my own language. Then, after becoming a mother, I grew more aware of my bones and flesh, and the polarities of the limitations and miracles my body could produce. So, in light of this, I recently made a portrait of my daughter, Tesia, growing out of fungus. I am working on a portrait right now where my face is breaking apart into a misty cloud of lichen and bubbles. So we'll see where it goes from here.

Knowing Your Influences
My good friend Isabella Kirkland is an artist who has been dedicated to contributing to conservation and education through her work. I have never met anyone before or since who has put so much thought and effort into her work. She is a true inspiration to me. And, of course, some of my earlier influences have included John James Audubon and Ernst Haeckel, who are environmentalists of a different sort and era.

Awareness and Impact
It is difficult to gauge the impact my paintings have on viewers; everyone sees them so differently. I've always been aware of the amazing natural spaces around me, ever since I was a child. And now, in my mid-thirties, it is so deeply entwined in my mind that I'm not even necessarily conscious of it. Typically I do not begin a painting with a goal or agenda. Every painting is a documentation of time as I worked through an idea, and I learn to understand the world around me through this process of peeling back layers. After the work is published, I'm mindful of the important questions my work can raise, but I'm not trying to be political. I am trying to unify and celebrate the things that we share with so many other living creatures on this planet. For example, most creatures know fear, desire, shame and loss. By studying nature, I'm discovering that the experience of being alive in a human body is humbling and wonderful, and the more I learn, the more I feel a deeper connection to all the timeless life around me. I want to encourage people to get outside and open their hearts to discovery.

Right Outside Your Door
I am an explorer, and I crave discovering new places, but right now I feel very nourished and inspired by the forest near my home. We've been traveling so much that I'm actually happy to be back in Marin County. My daughter is just turning three, and we are fixing up an old cottage under a grove of redwood trees. Right outside my door, I see the trilliums blooming in the spring, I hear spotted owls calling, and I can go for daily walks in the vast open space preserves.

DIVIDE, 35" X 40", ACRYLIC ON MAPLE PANEL

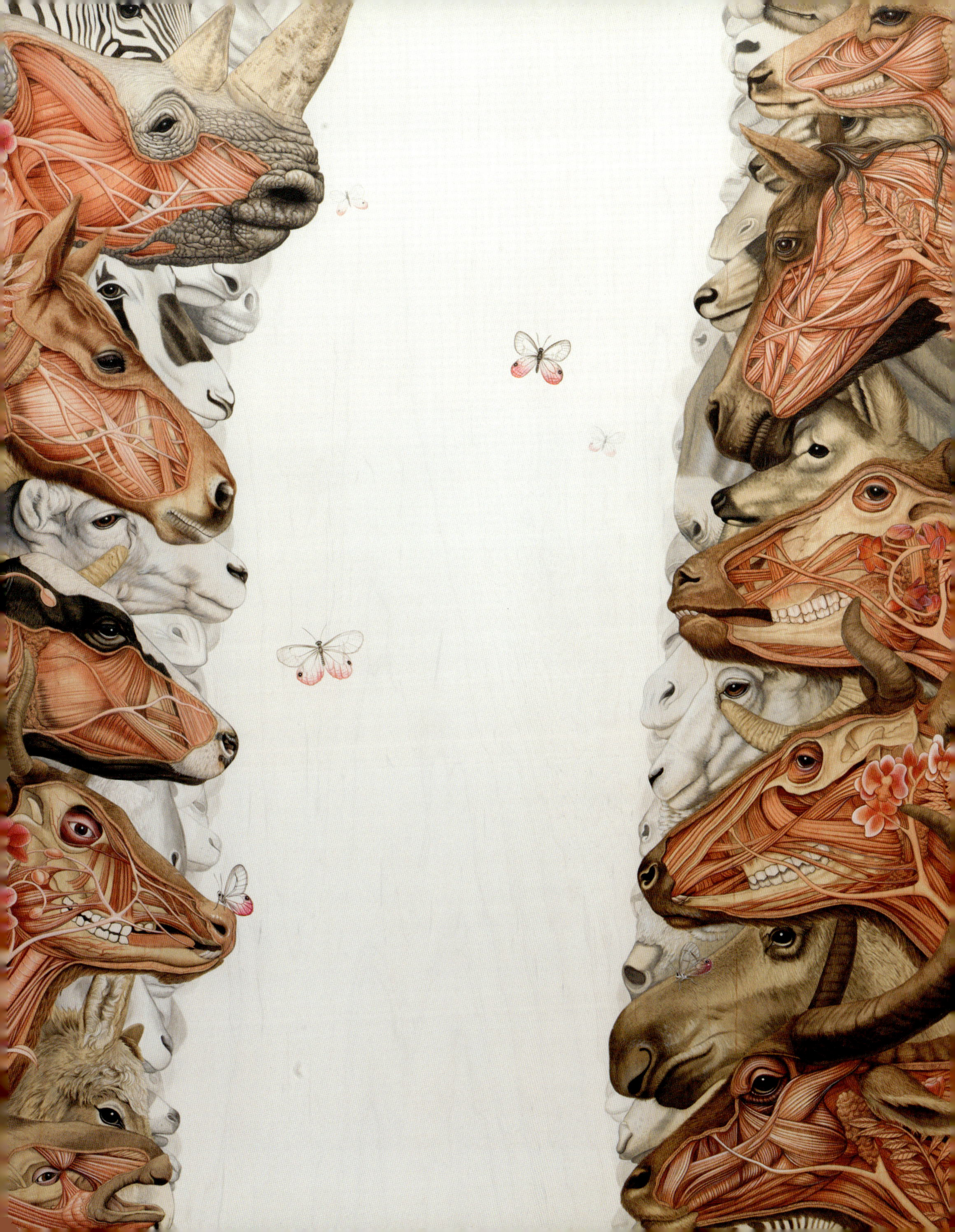

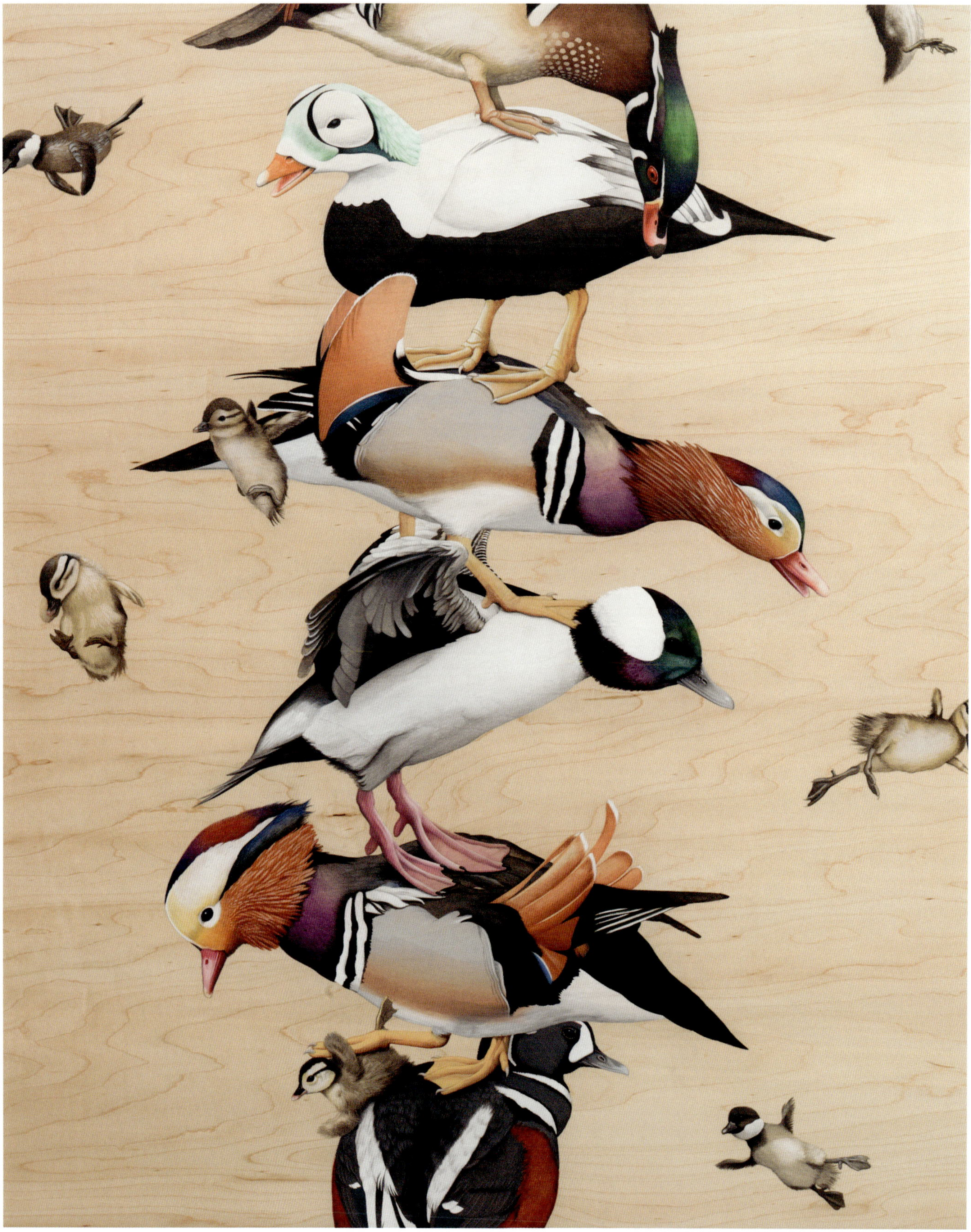

DUCKS IN A ROW, 36" X 42", ACRYLIC ON MAPLE PANEL

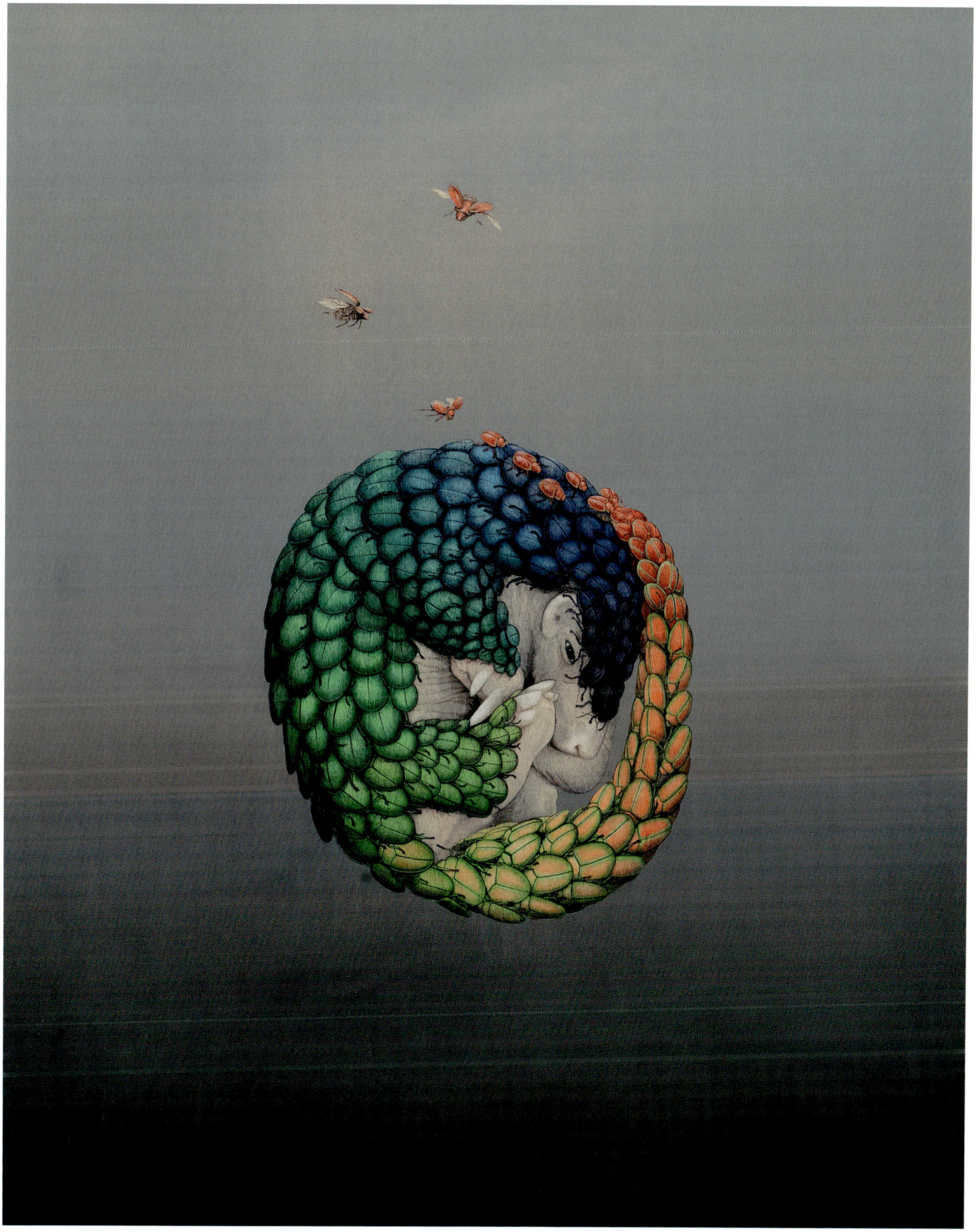

BEETLES FOR SCALES, 22" X 28", ACRYLIC ON MAPLE PANEL

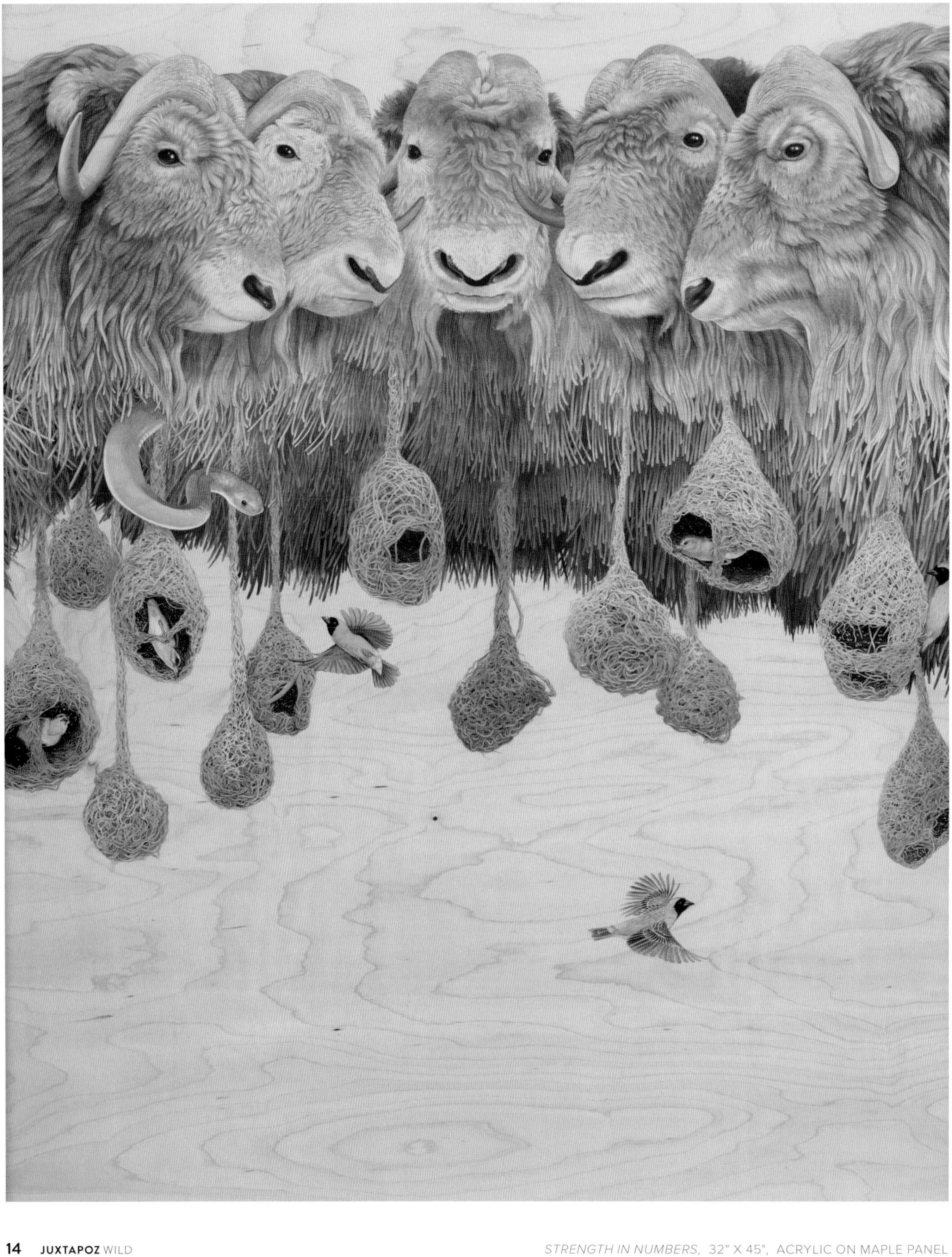

STRENGTH IN NUMBERS, 32" X 45", ACRYLIC ON MAPLE PANEL

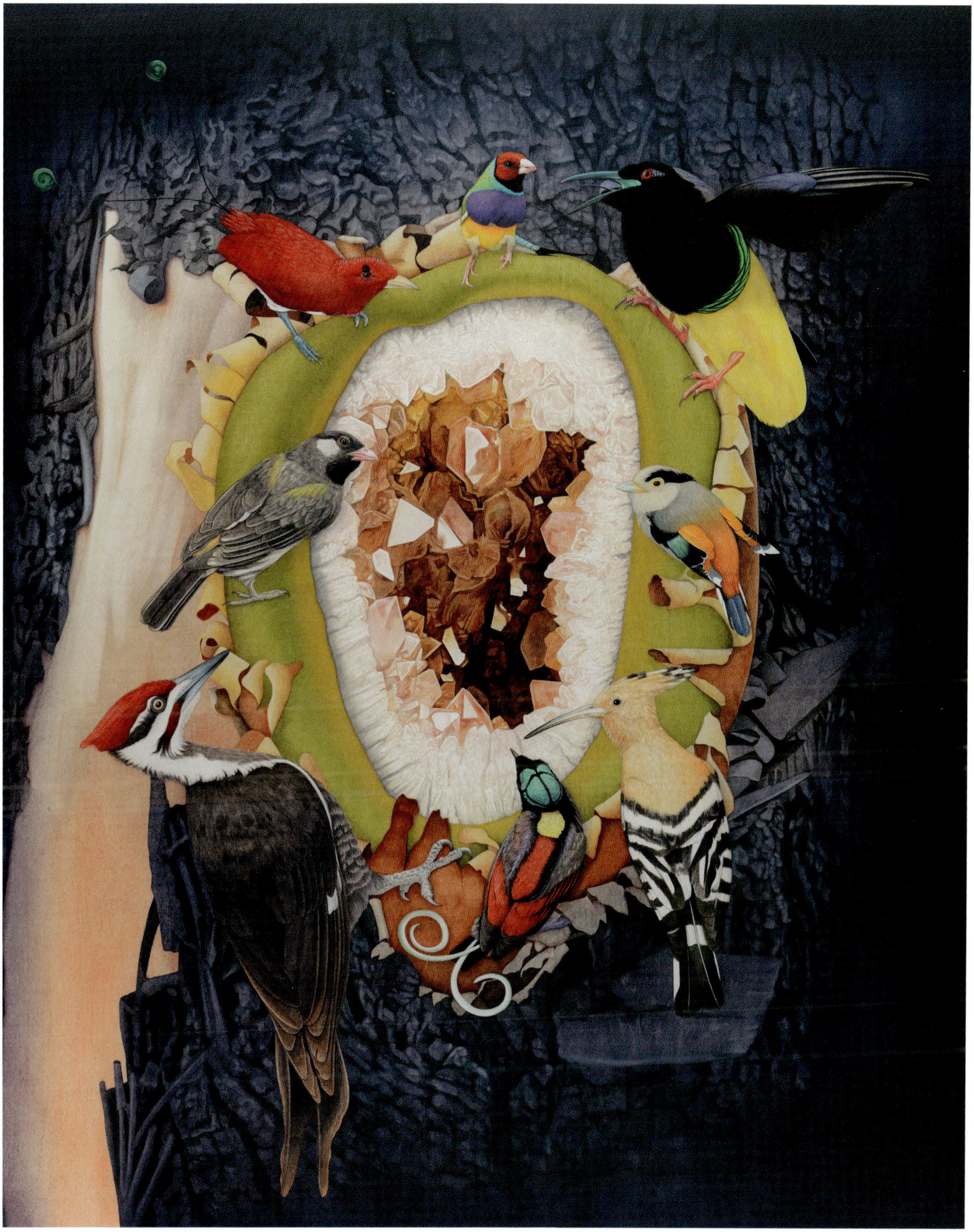

MUTUAL CORE, 36" X 48", ACRYLIC ON MAPLE PANEL

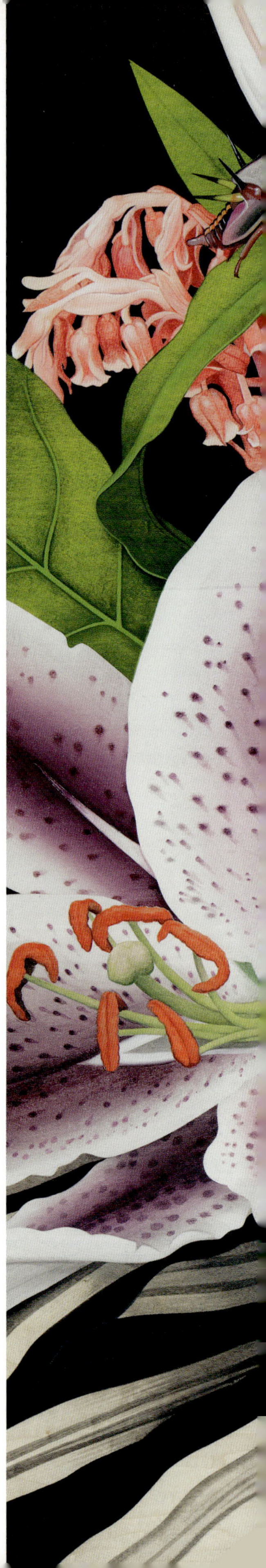

AGAPE
36" X 48"
ACRYLIC ON CANVAS

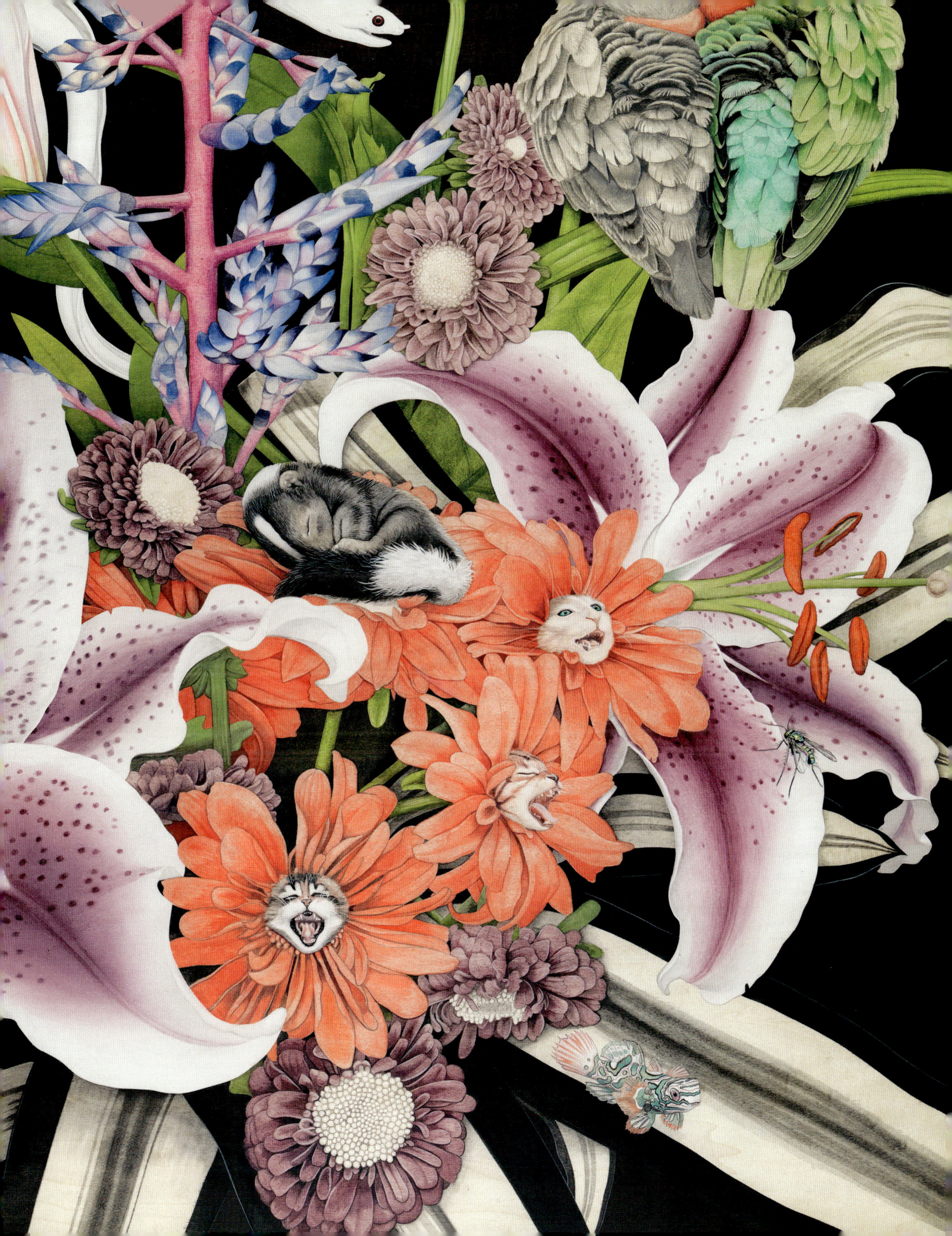

MARTIN WITTFOOTH

BROOKLYN, NEW YORK

Battle Tested
I like to be aware of what's going on in the world, though I don't specifically go out to look for this information. Rather, I regularly listen to podcasts and lectures and audio books that cover a broad range of subjects, and pretty often, environmental topics come up, considering it's one of the great battles of our time.

Post-Apocalypse Now
At some point in my search for something personal to explore in my paintings, I stopped painting the human figure and instead focused on landscapes that retained some man-made element in them, but otherwise the main players were animals and inanimate objects. Some people have called my works post-apocalyptic, but I rather see them as allegories of the contemporary human condition and our confusion and clash with the natural world that we've steadily departed from. I've just removed the human stand-in to portray a narrative and instead focused on letting the scenes I create resonate with collective symbolism.

Smoking Barrels
That painting materialized as a simple reaction of horror to the poaching industry. The strange coincidence that occurred while I was painting this piece was that a week into working on it, I came across news articles that announced that the black rhino, the same kind depicted in the painting, had officially been declared extinct in the wild.

Power Play
I think that a sense of power can be projected on a variety of animal forms, it's just dependent on how they're composed. I sometimes try and portray animals generally thought of as meek and fragile—foxes, birds, and so on—with a sense of majesty or high-tension, powerful energy, whereas at other times, I've depicted large animals with a subdued, calm atmosphere and softer poses, which greatly influences the presence that these figures project to the viewer.

The Allure of the Hudson Valley
Perhaps I'm a bit biased, but my favorite nature spot is my property in the Hudson Valley region in Upstate New York. I have six acres of land and I love every square inch of it—a nice mix of open field, a stream, and a forest. My second favorite place is Big Sur in California. The meeting between the ocean and dense, dark redwood forests is incredible.

ATMAN, 25" X 24", OIL AND GOLD LEAF ON LINEN

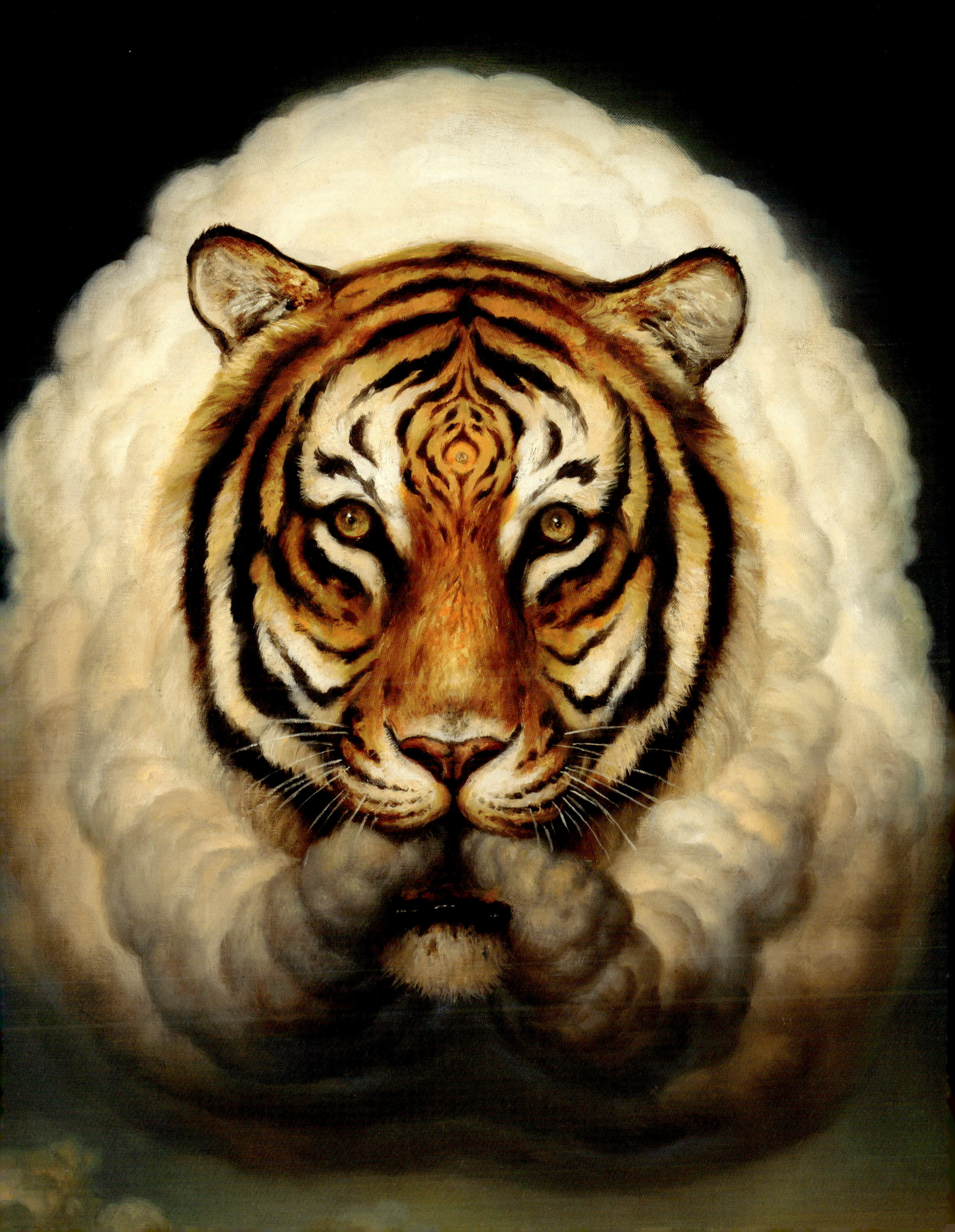

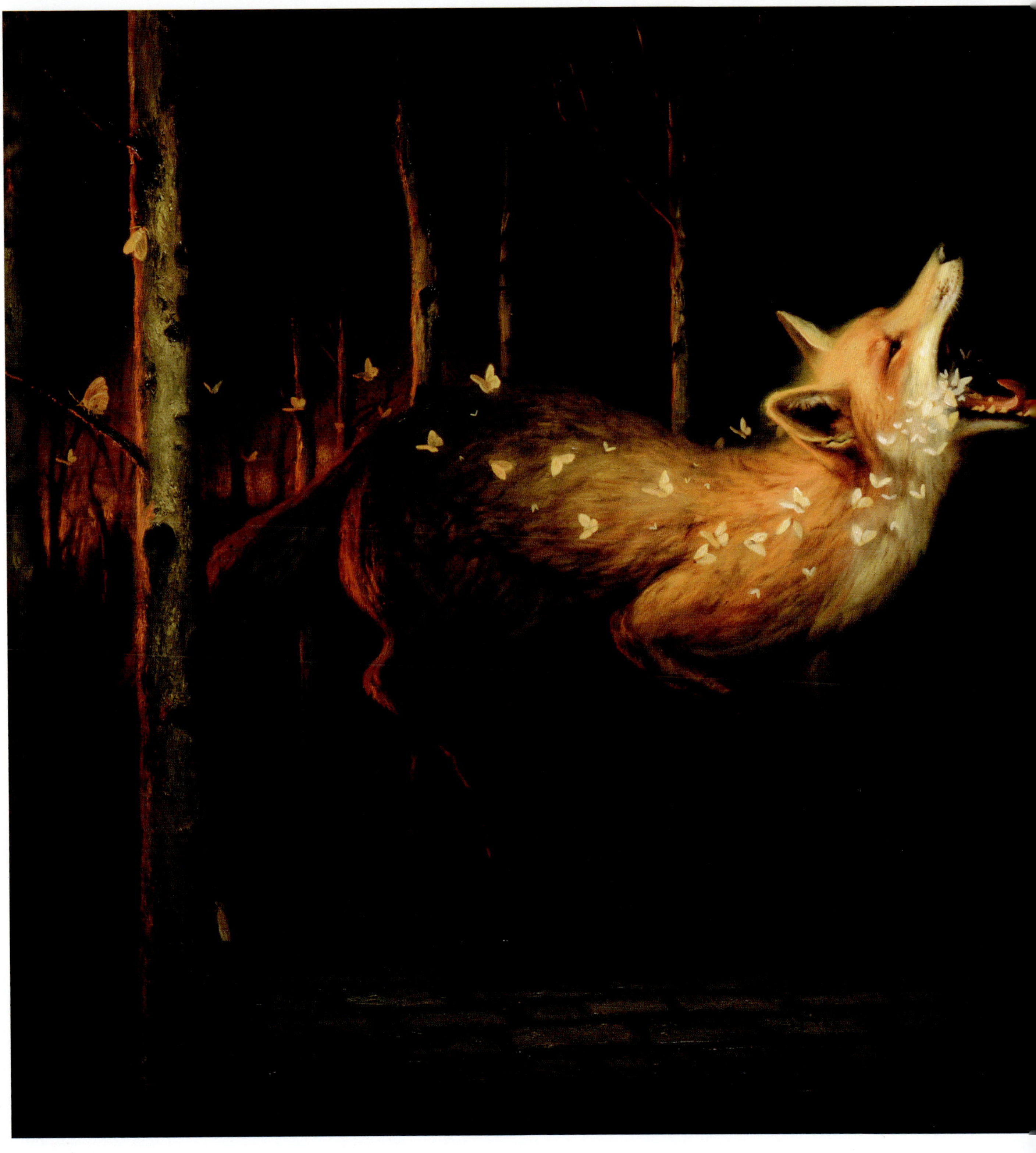

NOCTURNE II, 46" X 57", OIL ON CANVAS

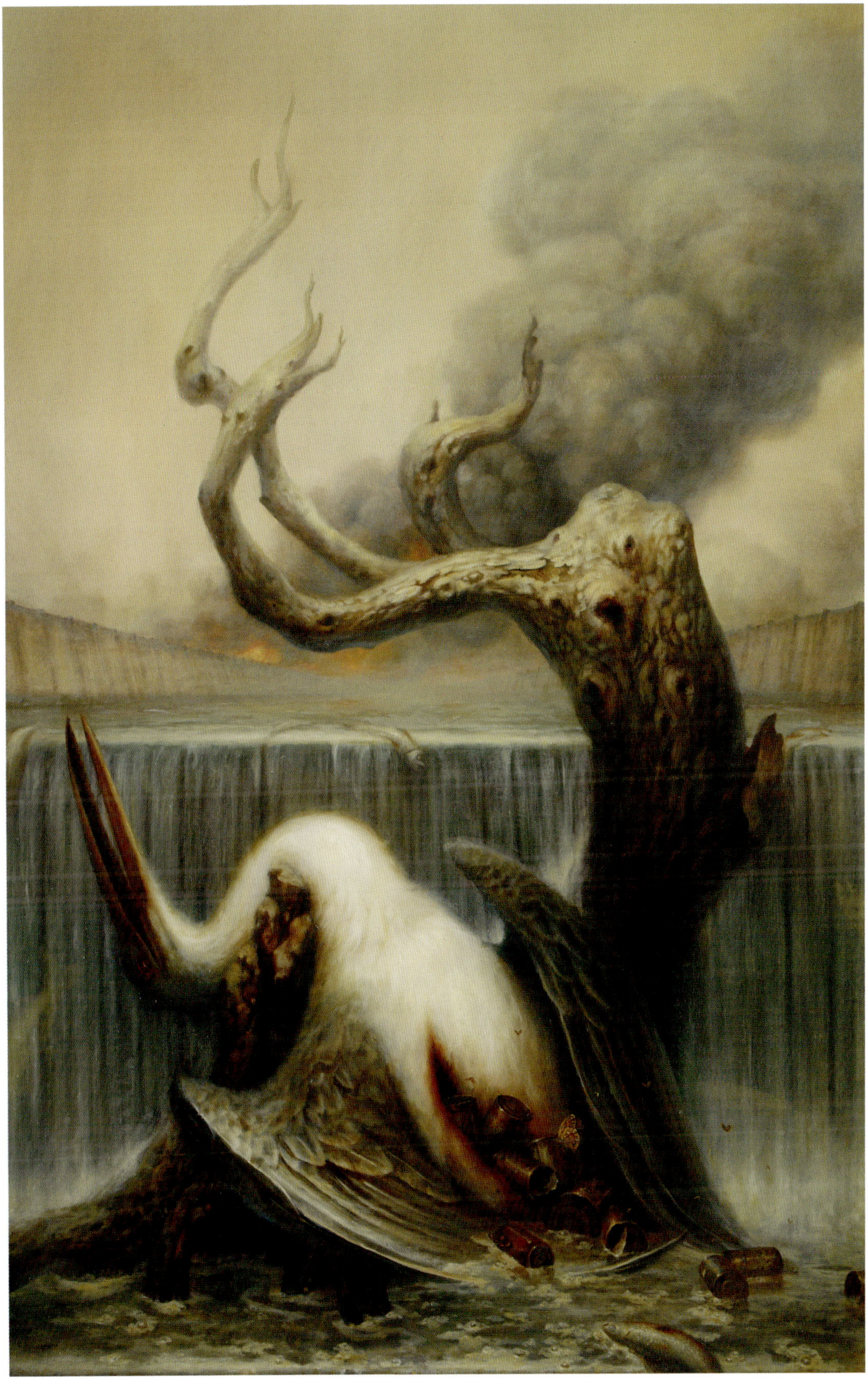

PIETA
50" X 30"
OIL ON CANVAS

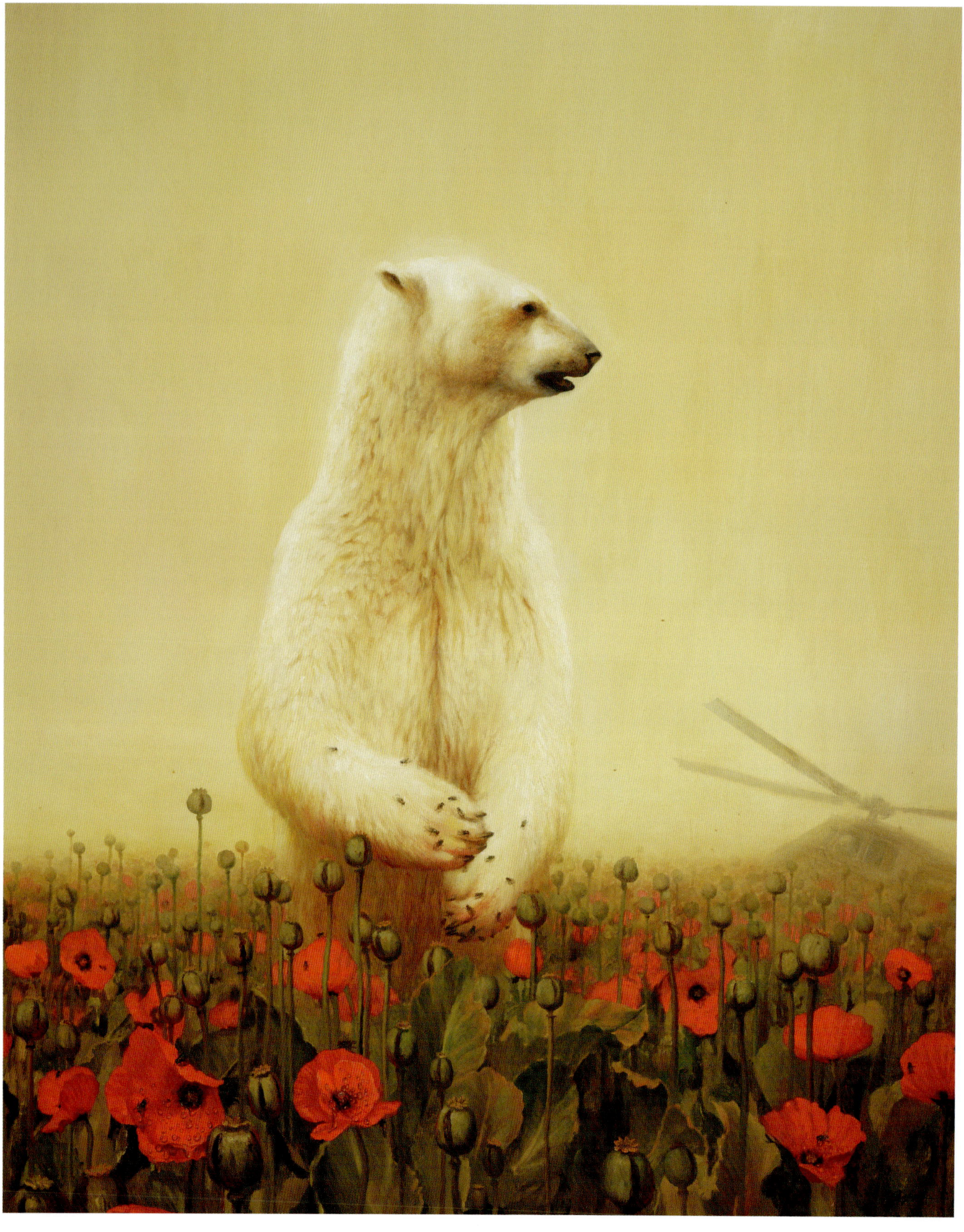

HARVEST, 68" X 54", OIL ON CANVAS

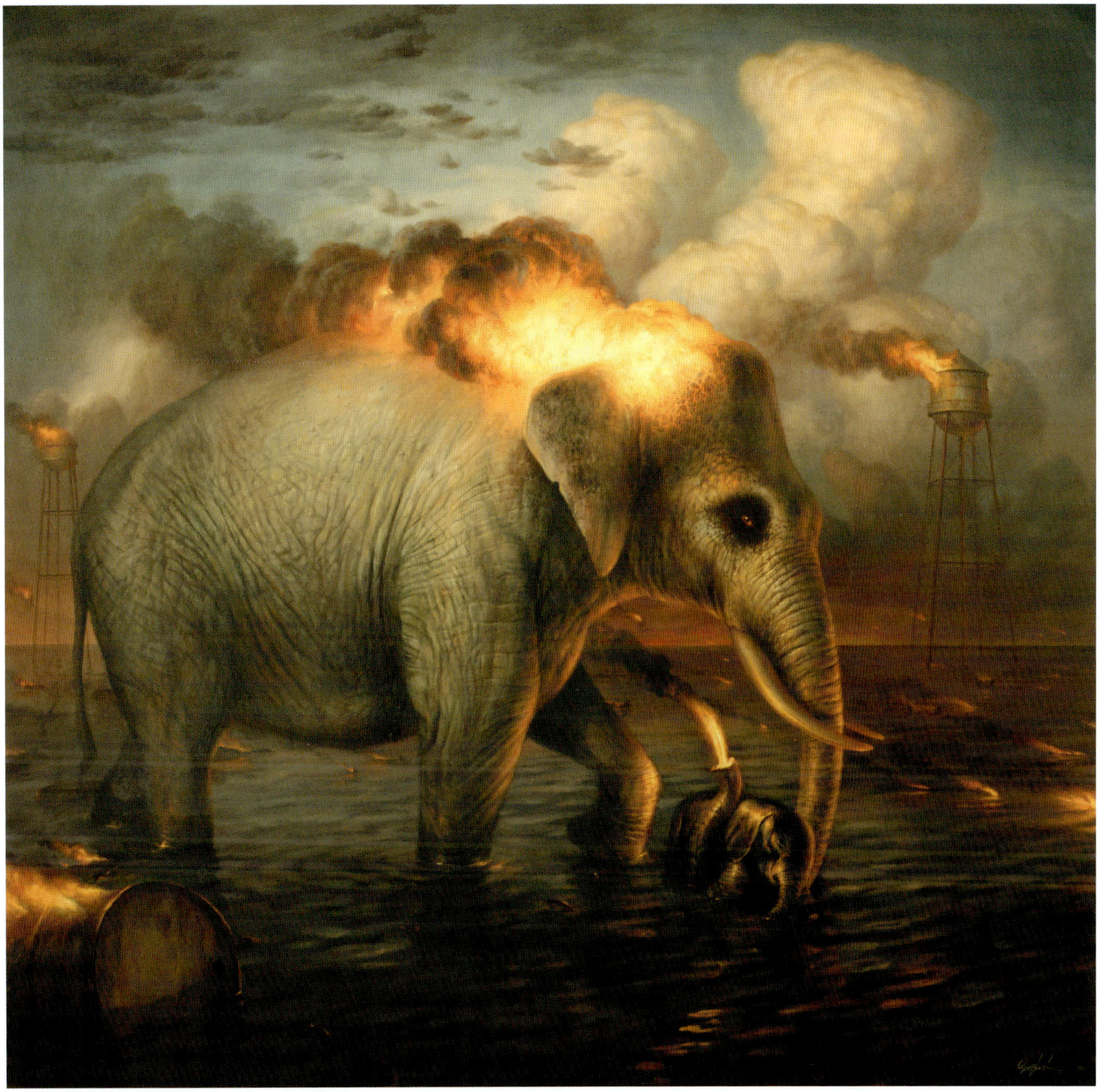

THE BAPTISM, 56" X 56", OIL ON CANVAS

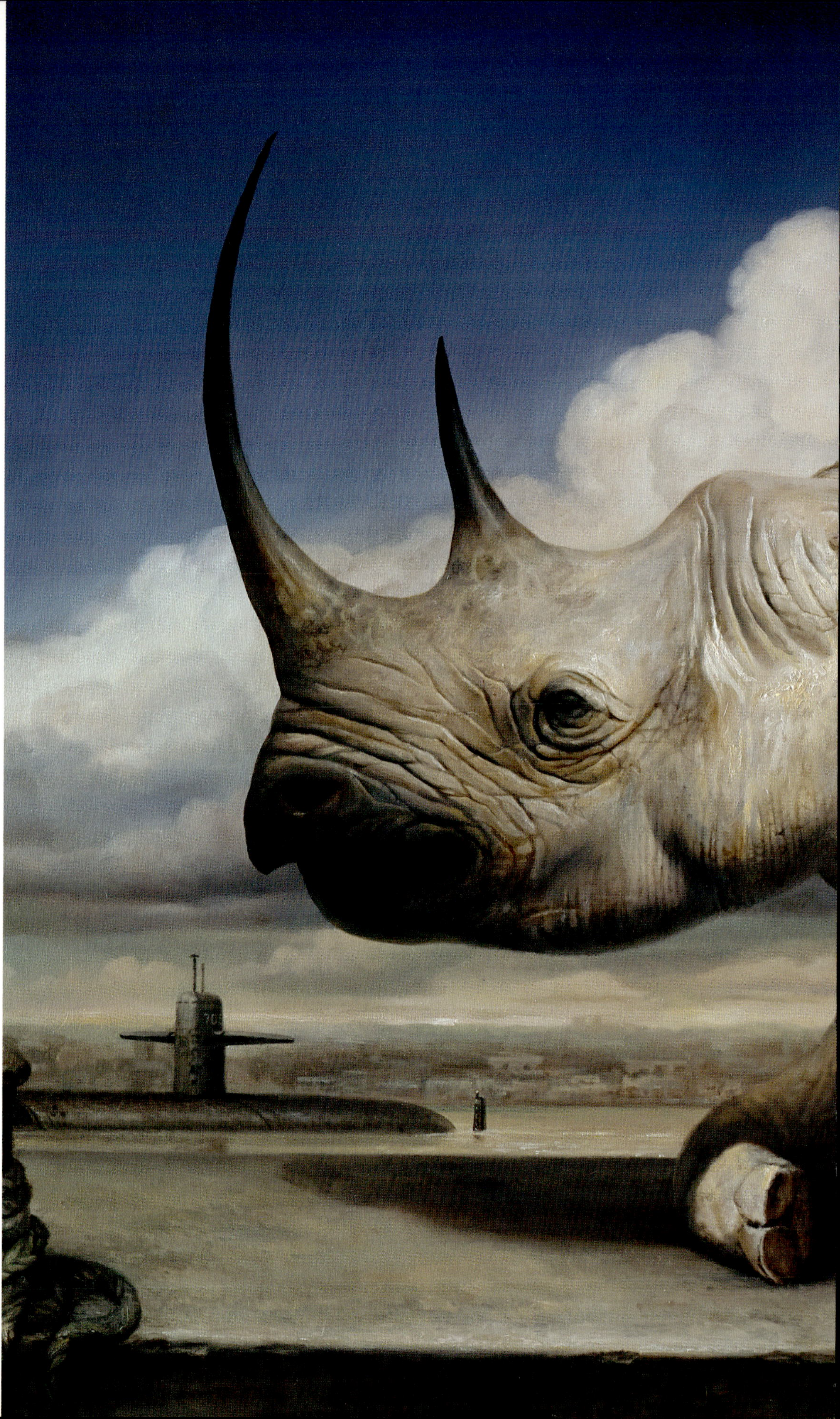

UNTITLED
68" X 96"
OIL ON CANVAS

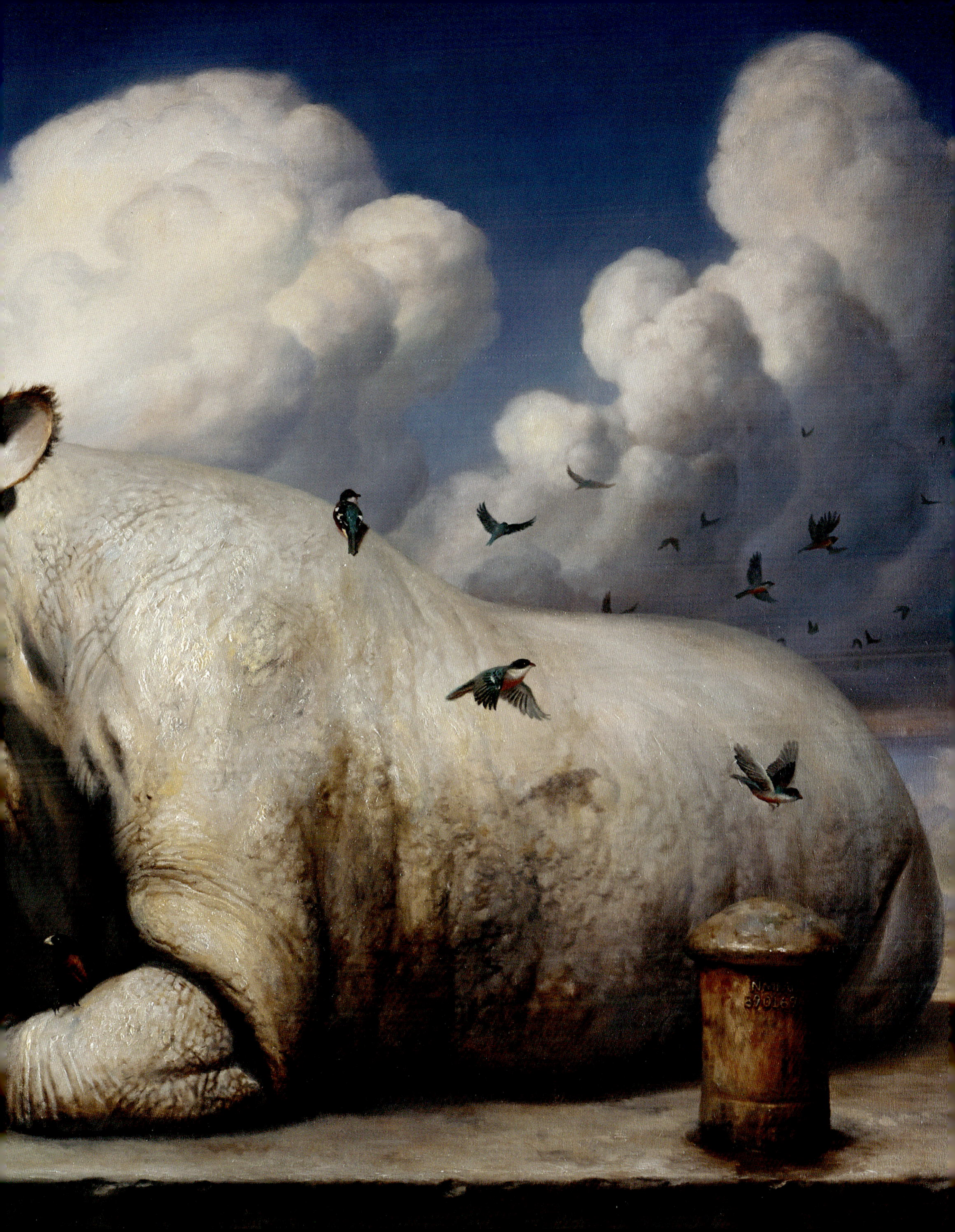

ADONNA KHARE

BURBANK, CALIFORNIA

Environmental Tragedies
The environment is always on my mind as I create the compositions and the narrative of my work. The issues are really concerning, not only for the animals, but for my daughter and our future. I'm worried we're going to destroy so much that can never be recovered. I'm fearful that we're leaving the world worse off than it was when we arrived. Mass extinction of plants and animals is real tragedy.

A lot of my work focuses on the animals that are near or heading towards extinction. For me, the animals I use are allegorical, so I can't say that a particular animal means one thing or another. But the overall theme of the piece is attempting to draw an emotion or connection with the viewer.

Animal Matters
I've always drawn animals. Even as a child, I felt I had a connection to them, almost like we had developed our own language. As I grew as an artist, the animals took on different meanings to symbolize stories and events. I often use the animals to draw correlations paralleling our worlds. We all suffer sadness and joy, gains and losses, so I'm using the animals to chronicle the ones in my life. I've always loved drawing. Carbon pencil gave me the boldness of charcoal and allowed me to have the line quality of graphite. It allows me the immediacy of the ebb and flow of my work, almost a stream of consciousness. There is no drying time and it erases and blends easily.

The Purpose of Art
My hope is that someone is affected by it and makes a change, even a small one.

Human Nature
The animals themselves represent people and situations in my life—my mother, father, daughter and so on. I've never wanted to tell people what to think about my work but rather elicit a response. Drawing animals allows me to tell a personal story almost anonymously, while allowing the viewer to draw on their own experiences. What I find most interesting is when two people looking at the same drawing see different things. I've laughed with some and cried with others.

Screaming Bear
For me, the Screaming Bear painting has had the most profound impact. It's a life-size bear with stitches on its head, screaming out butterflies and bees at the edge of a waterfall. It was started shortly before my father was diagnosed with a brain tumor, and finished just after he passed from it.

Legends
The most influential for me was Audubon. Seeing so many varieties of species, it felt like the possibilities were endless.

Favorite Outdoor Space
I've spent so much time backpacking in the high Sierras or living amongst the rocks in Lake Powell that it's hard to choose a favorite place. Being outside, away from distractions, wherever that may be, is where I'm happiest.

RHINOS, 8' X 6', CARBON PENCIL ON PAPER

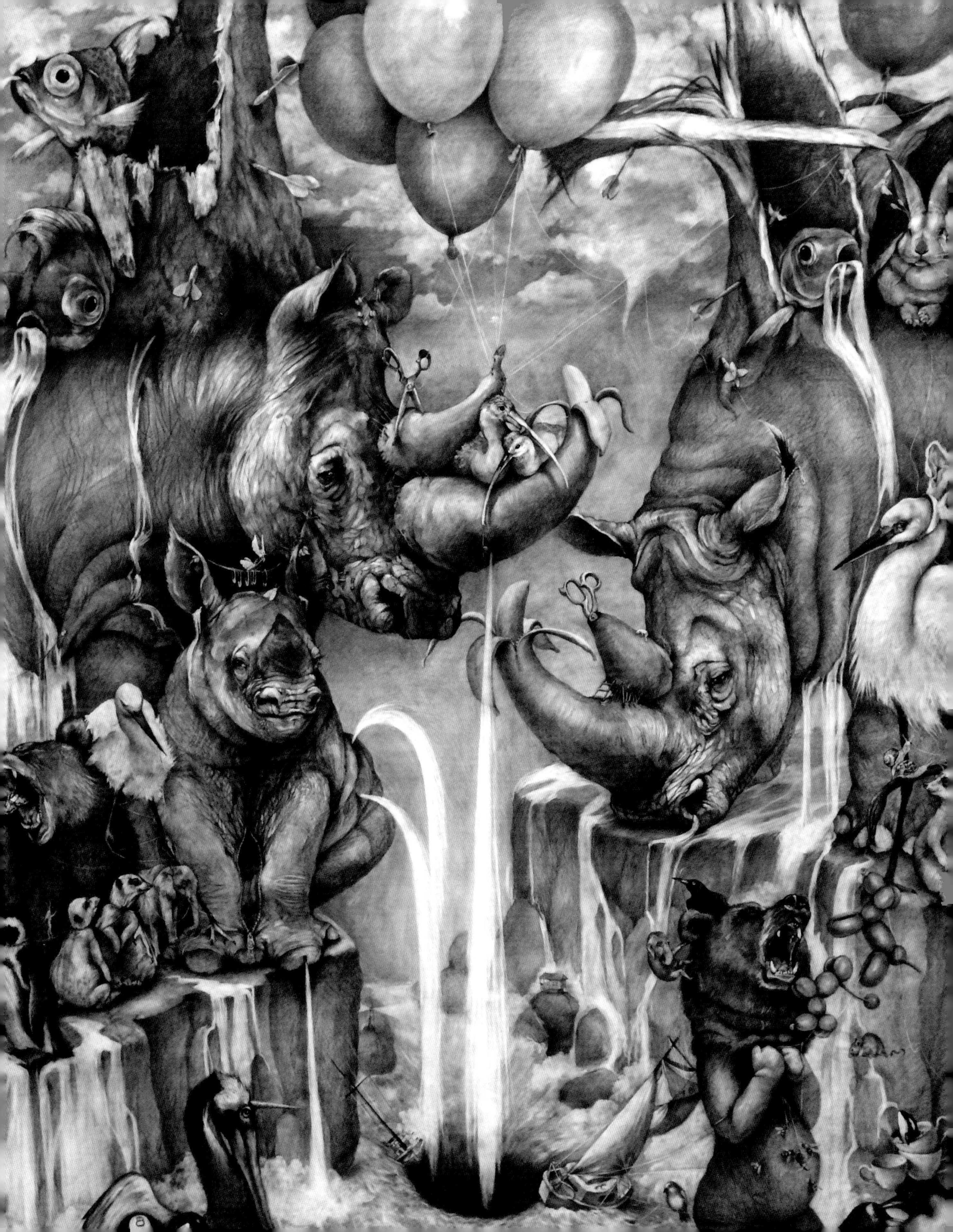

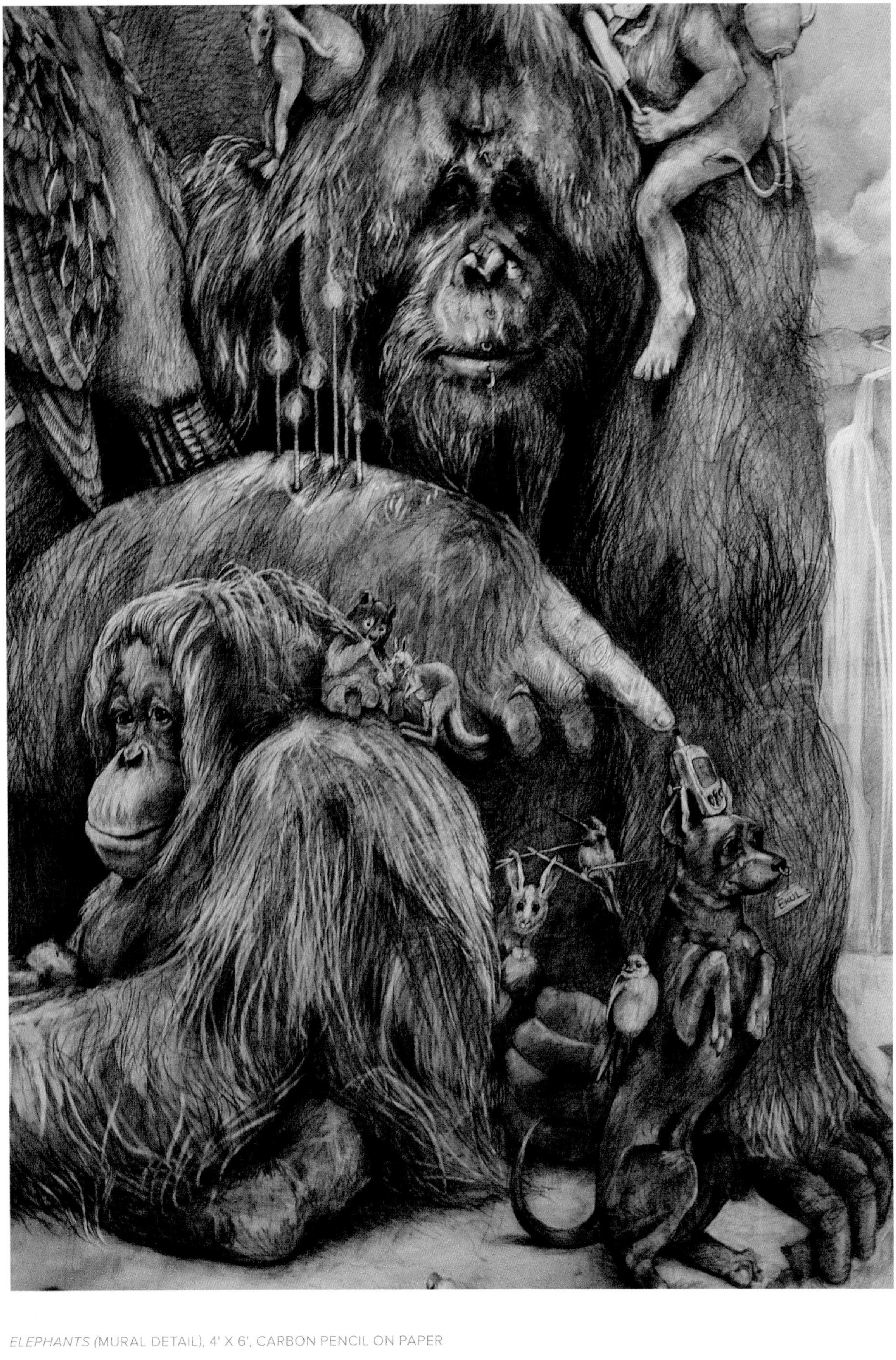

ELEPHANTS (MURAL DETAIL), 4' X 6', CARBON PENCIL ON PAPER

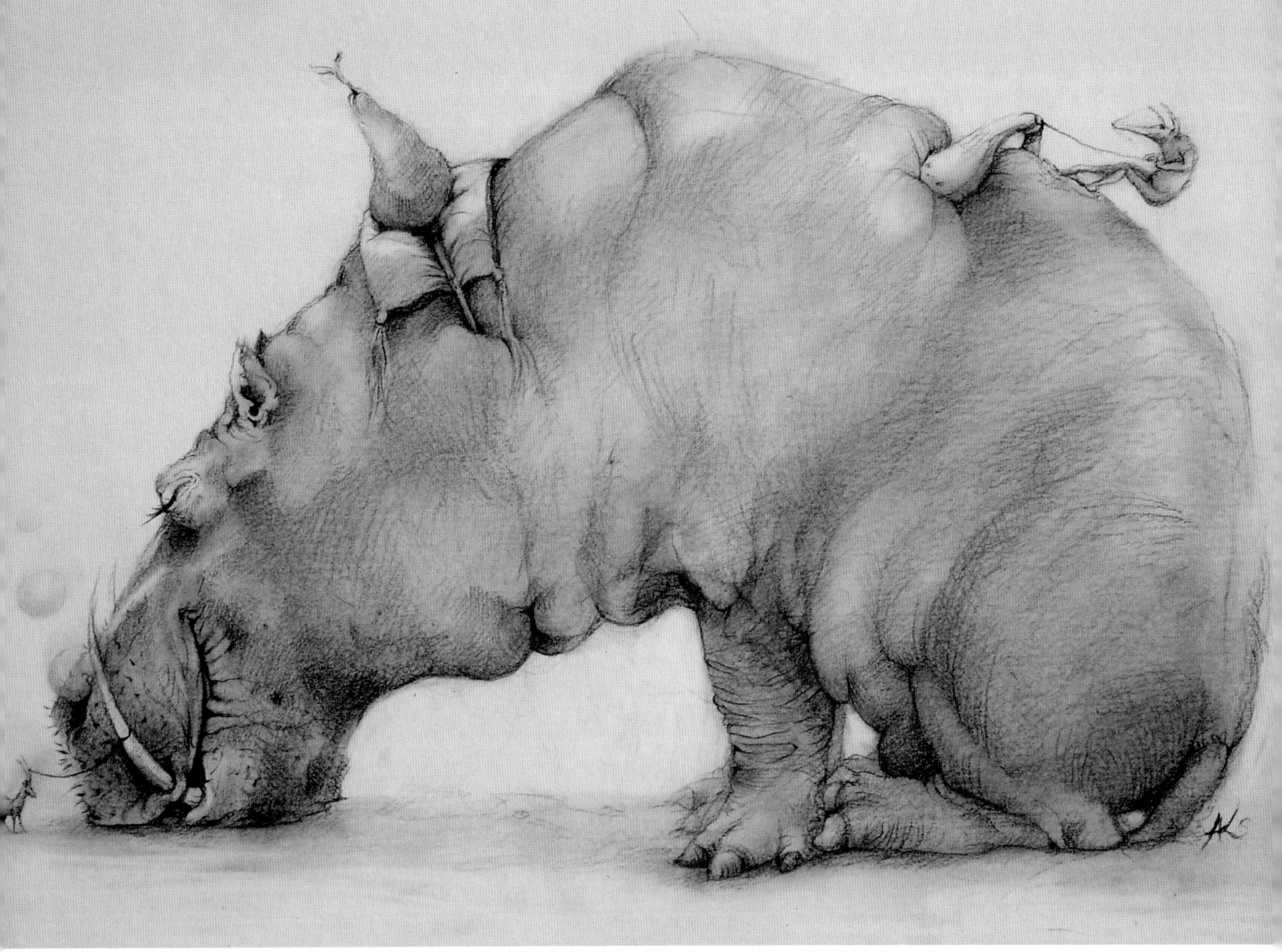

HIPPO WITH BUBBLES, 10" X 14", CARBON PENCIL ON PAPER

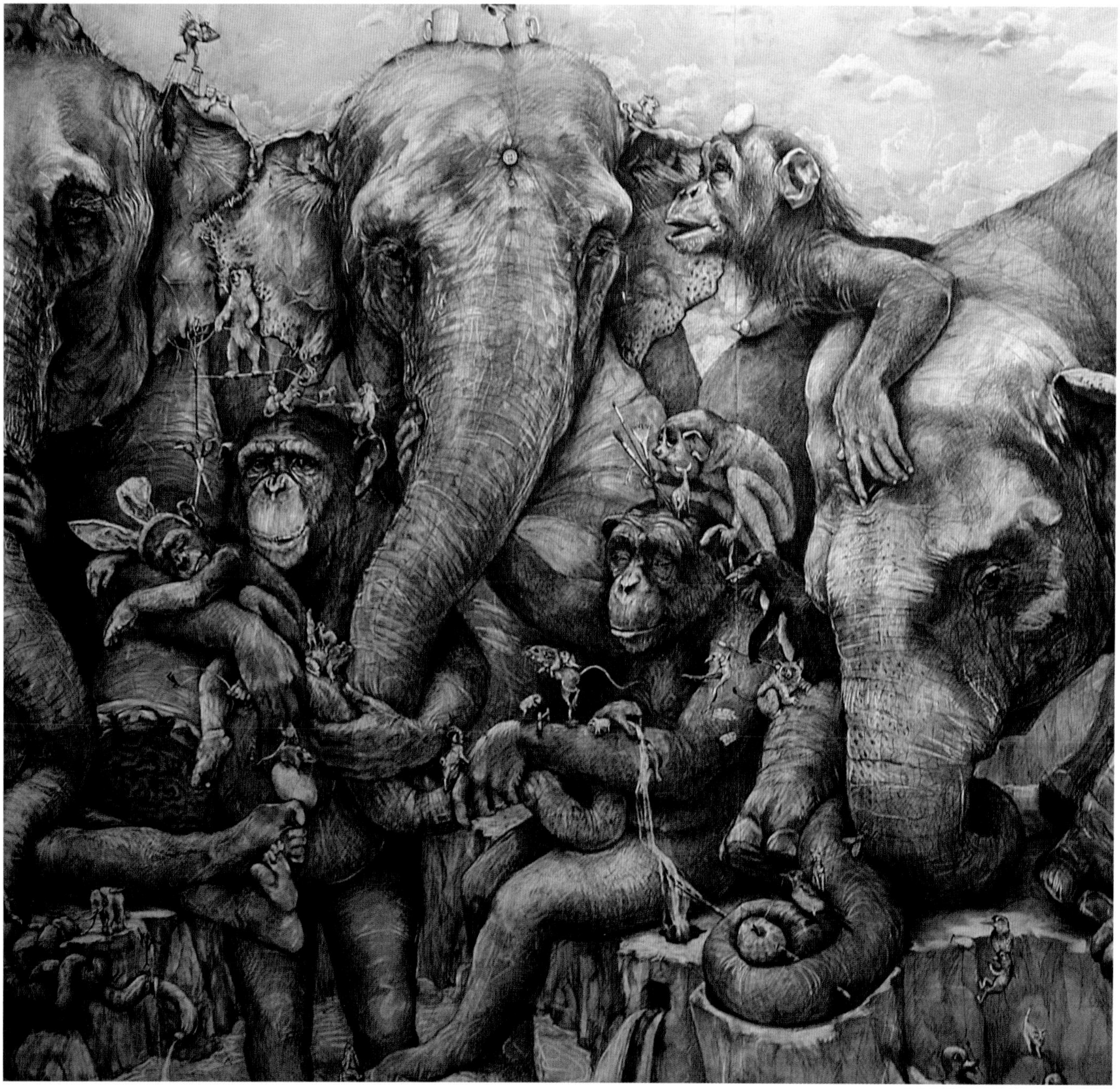

ELEPHANTS (MURAL DETAIL), 8' X 8', CARBON PENCIL ON PAPER

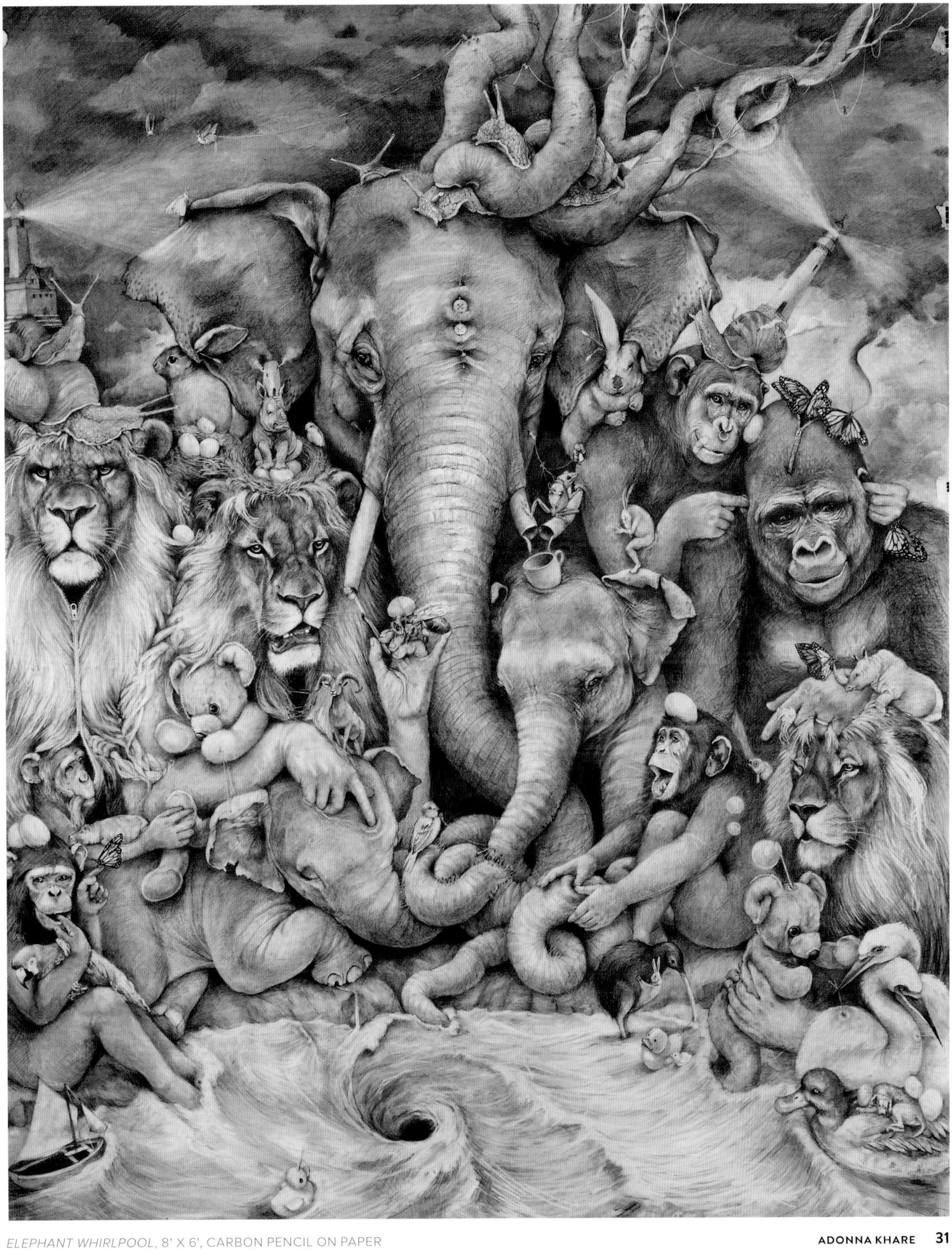

ELEPHANT WHIRLPOOL, 8' X 6', CARBON PENCIL ON PAPER

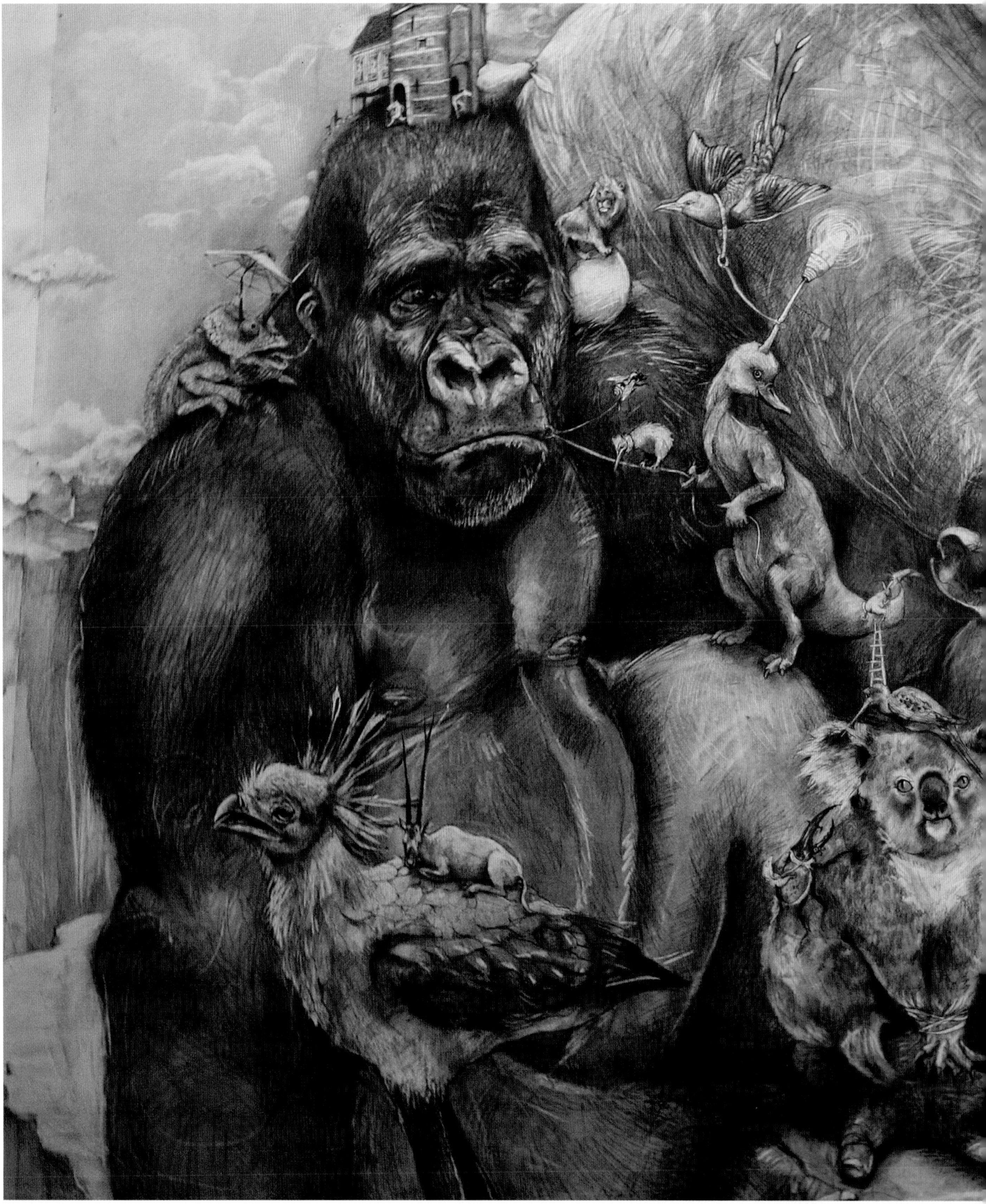

ELEPHANTS (MURAL DETAIL), 5' X 7', CARBON PENCIL ON PAPER

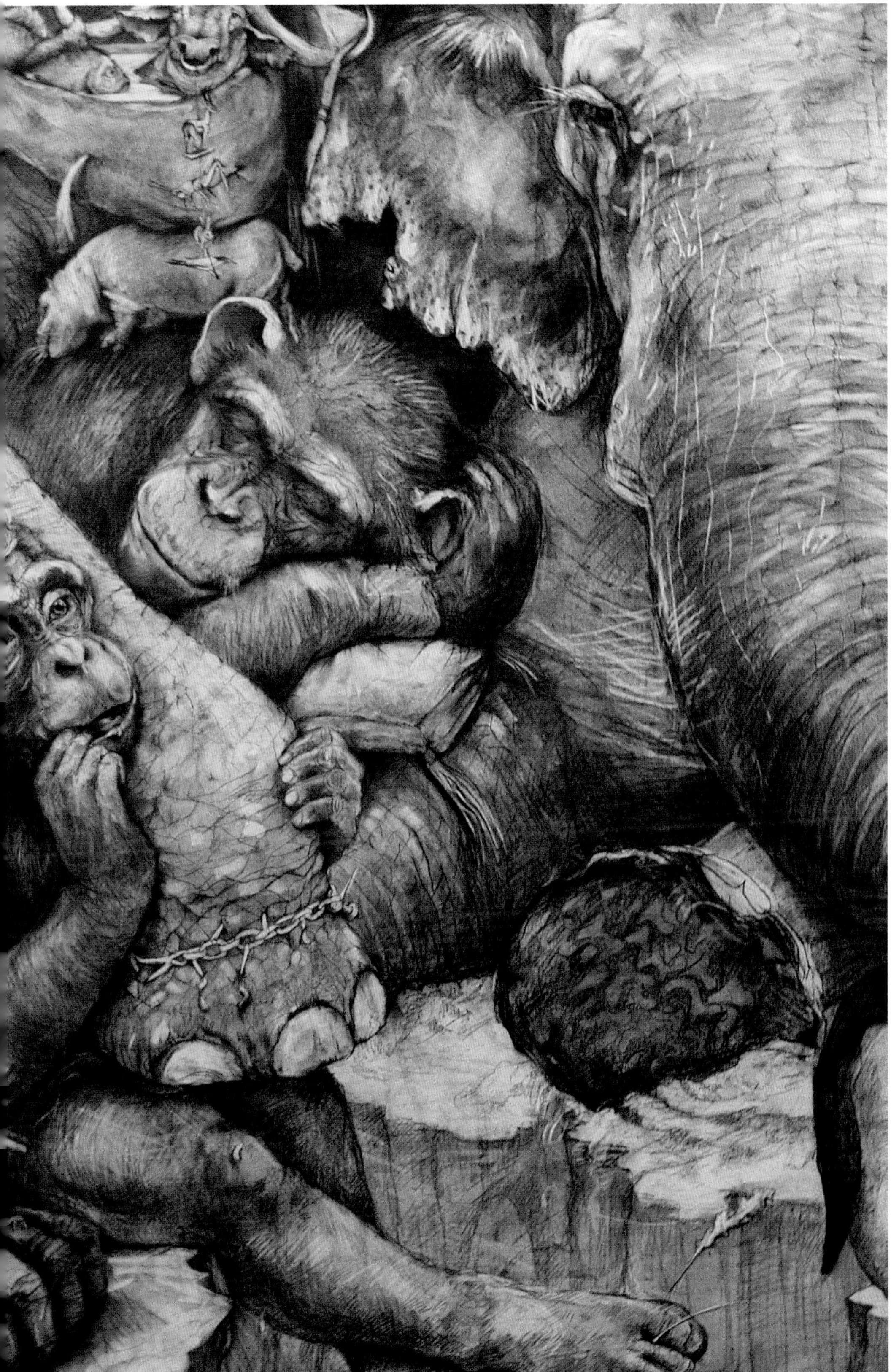

JOSH KEYES

PORTLAND, OREGON

Cinematic Spark
A couple films I saw as a kid really inspired my love of animals and animal imagery. *Watership Down, The Plague Dogs, Empire of the Ants* and the original *King Kong*. These movies tapped into imagination and inspired me to create my own narratives and stories. In school, I was really interested in biology and the structure of ecosystems. I made a few drawings and paintings illustrating the carbon cycle and food chain of the forest. I suppose that is also where my interest in diagrammatic and science textbook imagery began. The animal imagery that appears in the work now is rooted in both biology and metaphor, and personal symbolism.

Experimenting with Blobs
I had experimented with morphing humans into big Philip Guston blobs, overweight and surrounded by text balloons of gibberish, or just plain empty. It didn't feel right to me, so I scrapped the idea and decided to create diagrammatic platforms or still lifes with just animals and elements of city streets. I like to include statues when possible, they are kind of surrogates for human presence or a human ideology or attitude. I really like keeping the work open and, just like a diorama in a natural history museum, the viewer becomes the participant in the painting.

Grizzly Man
I used to think it was the shark or killer whale that was most powerful, but I have been leaning towards the grizzly bear or bull elk. Many of the animals I use correspond to a personal totemic hierarchy. It may sound silly, but each has a kind of emotional and psychological symbolism for me. In that way, it's like the early tribal cultures and their relationship with the animals. For me, painting a scene is like doing a math problem, balancing powers, like alchemy. Add this animal, pair it with another, add an overgrown signpost or car, raise the water level, etc. until the image arrives at a climax or dynamic tension, visually and psychologically.

Following an Unpaved Path
I think of the early Impressionists, breaking the rules and sharing their beautiful experience of nature and color. I think a number of artists in the sixties and seventies paved the way for others to follow with an emphasis on environmental issues. Though not created in an environmentally conscious way, Robert Smithson's *Earthworks* were and still are groundbreaking, as are Robert Morris's earthworks and observatories. Andy Goldsworthy may be the most recognizable and accessible artist to the mainstream community. His creations with found materials are poetry. In the contemporary world, I think Gregory Euclide's work and process are at the forefront. It is not just the making but the lifestyle that becomes the message.

The Gorgeous Gorge
Since moving to Portland Oregon, the woods and waterfalls along the Columbia Gorge are breathtaking. It feels so ancient here, moss, streams, and the smell of earth and old trees. It brings out the Tolkien nerd in me. The beaches along the coast are also spectacular, especially Haystack rock at Cannon Beach. It is a romantic landscape and most folks here have a strong relationship with it.

TURBULENCE, 11" X 14", ACRYLIC ON BIRCH PANEL

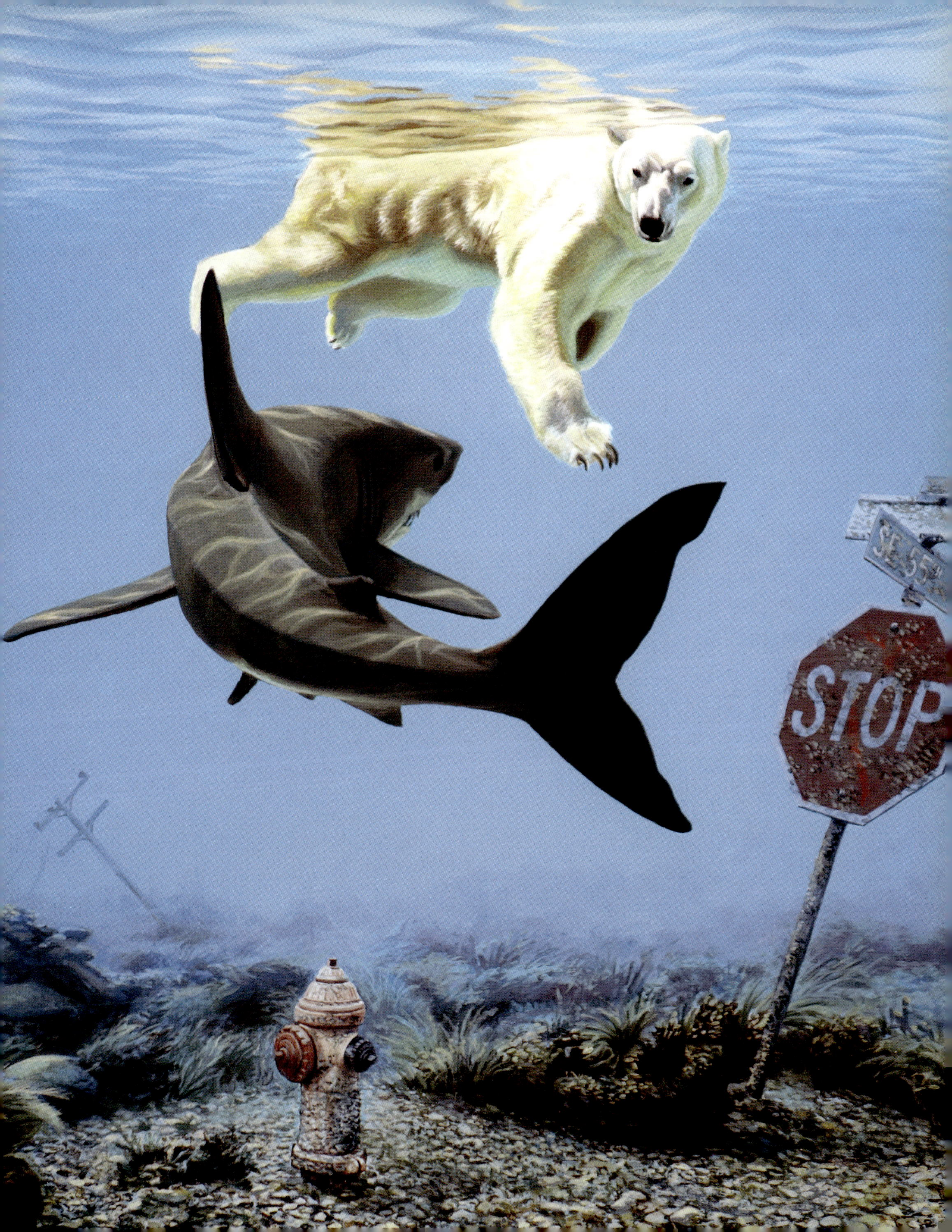
SE 55
STOP

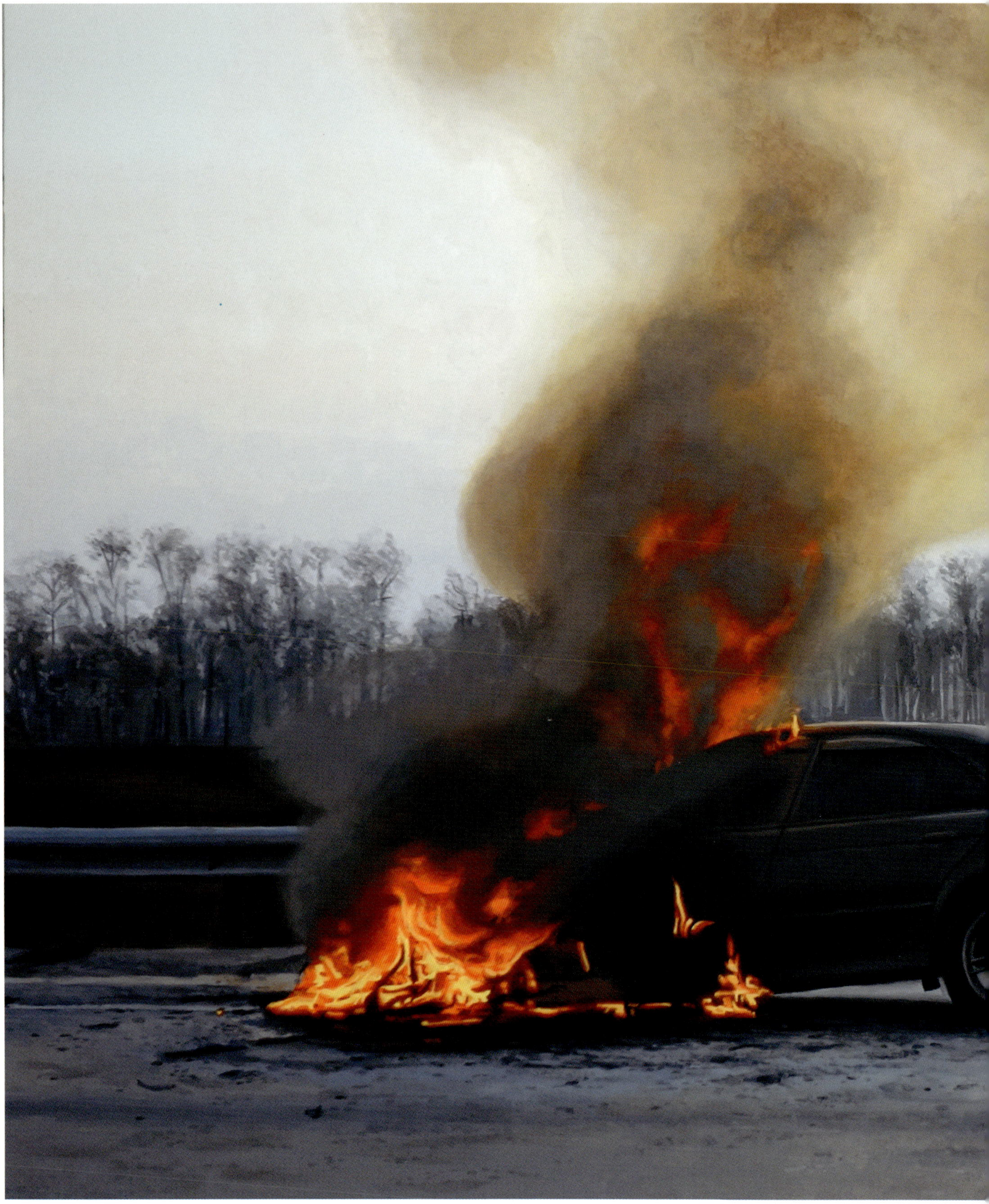

THE ROAD I, 12" X 20", ACRYLIC ON BIRCH PANEL

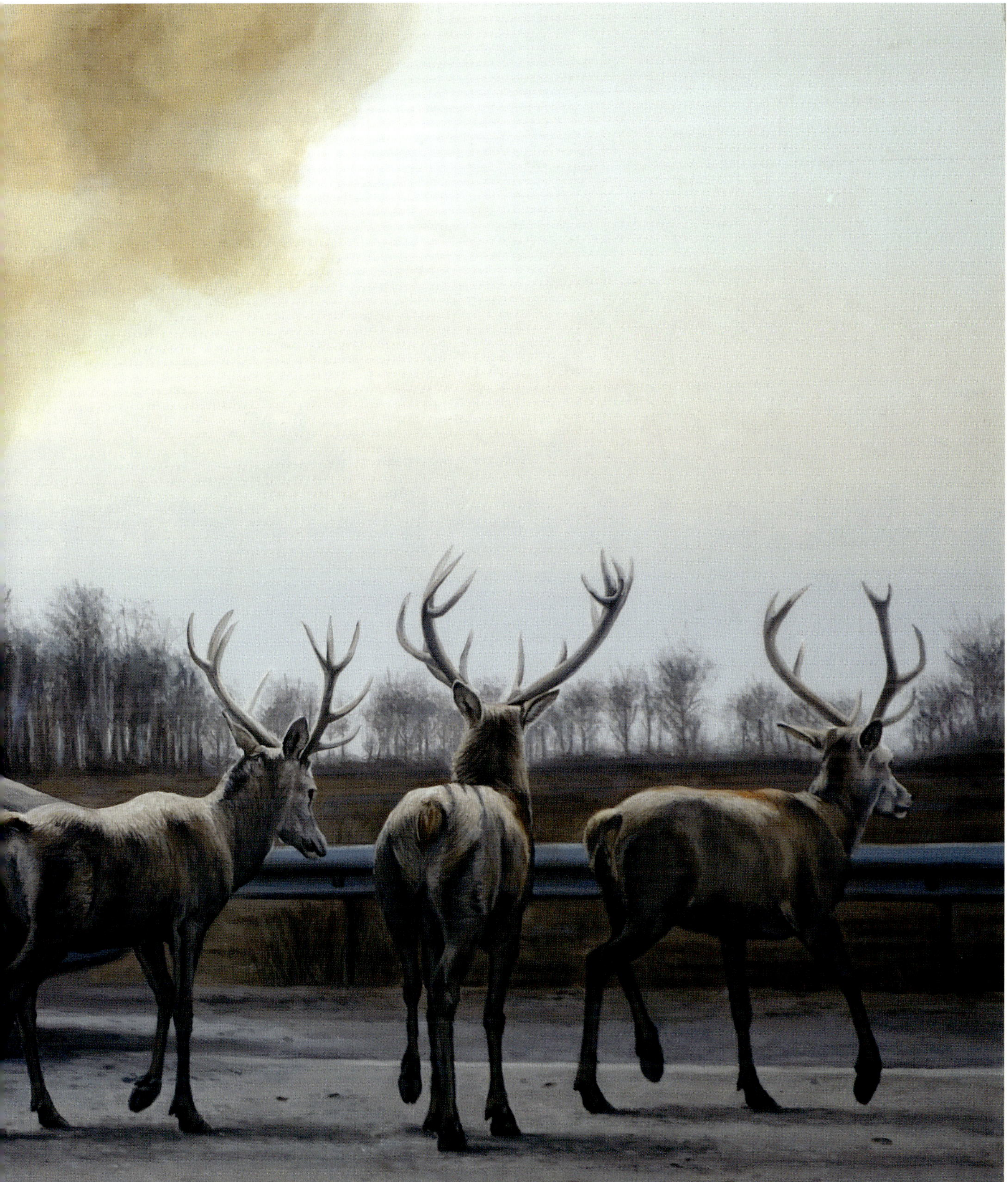

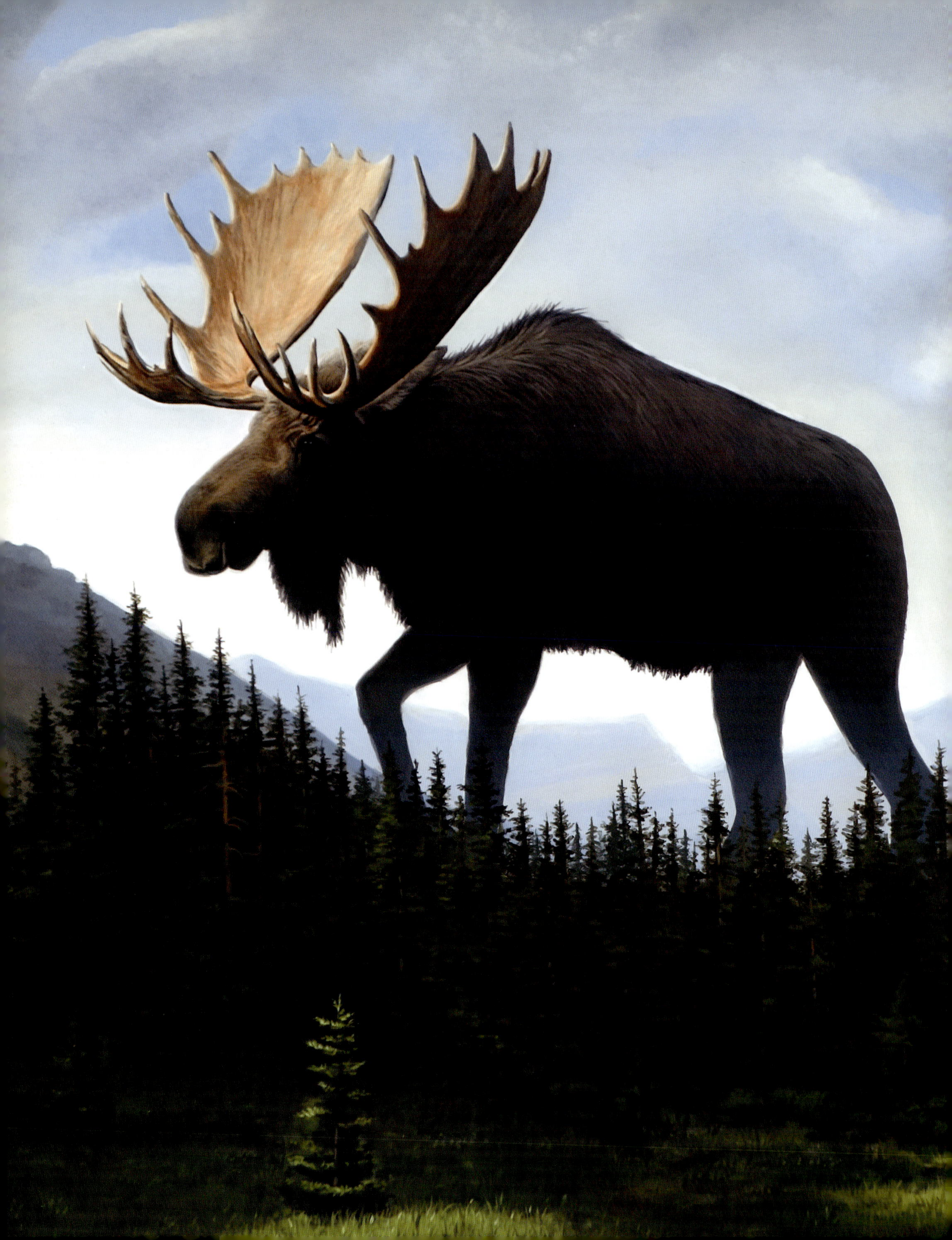

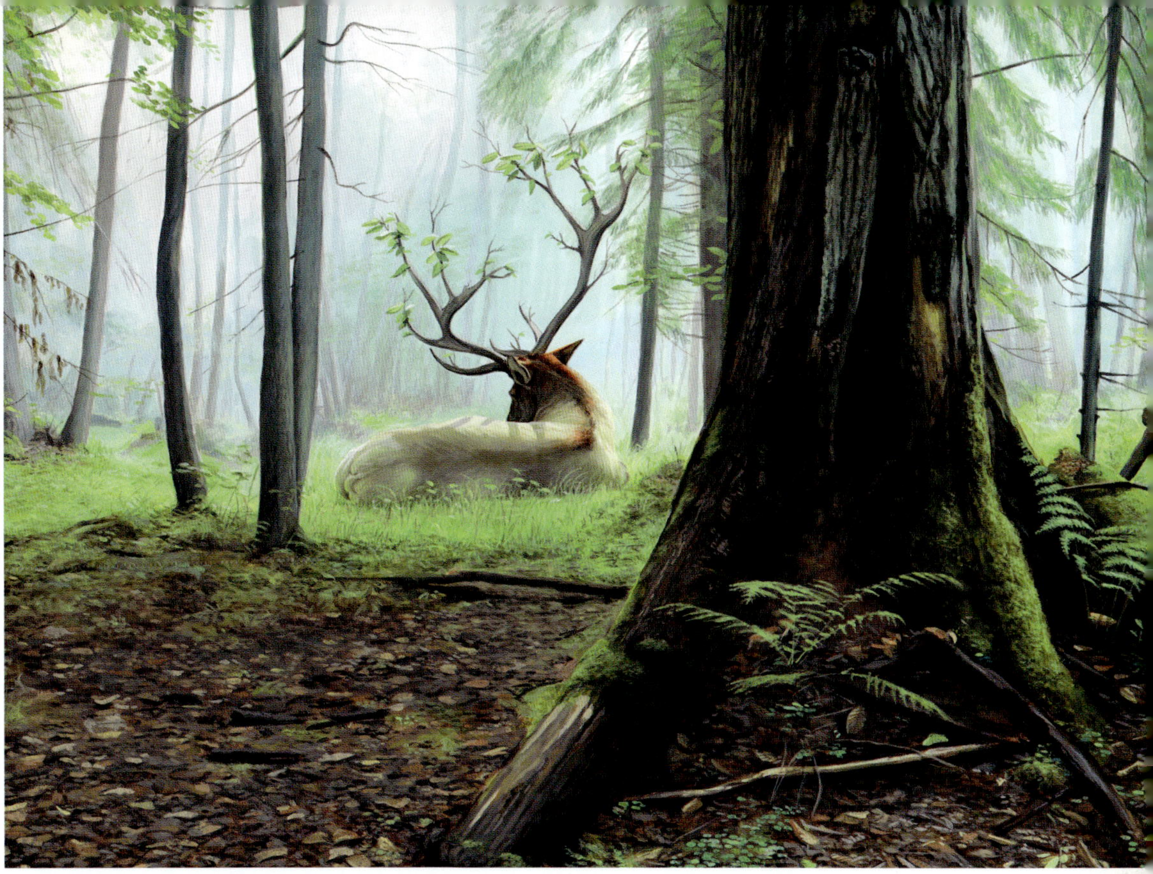

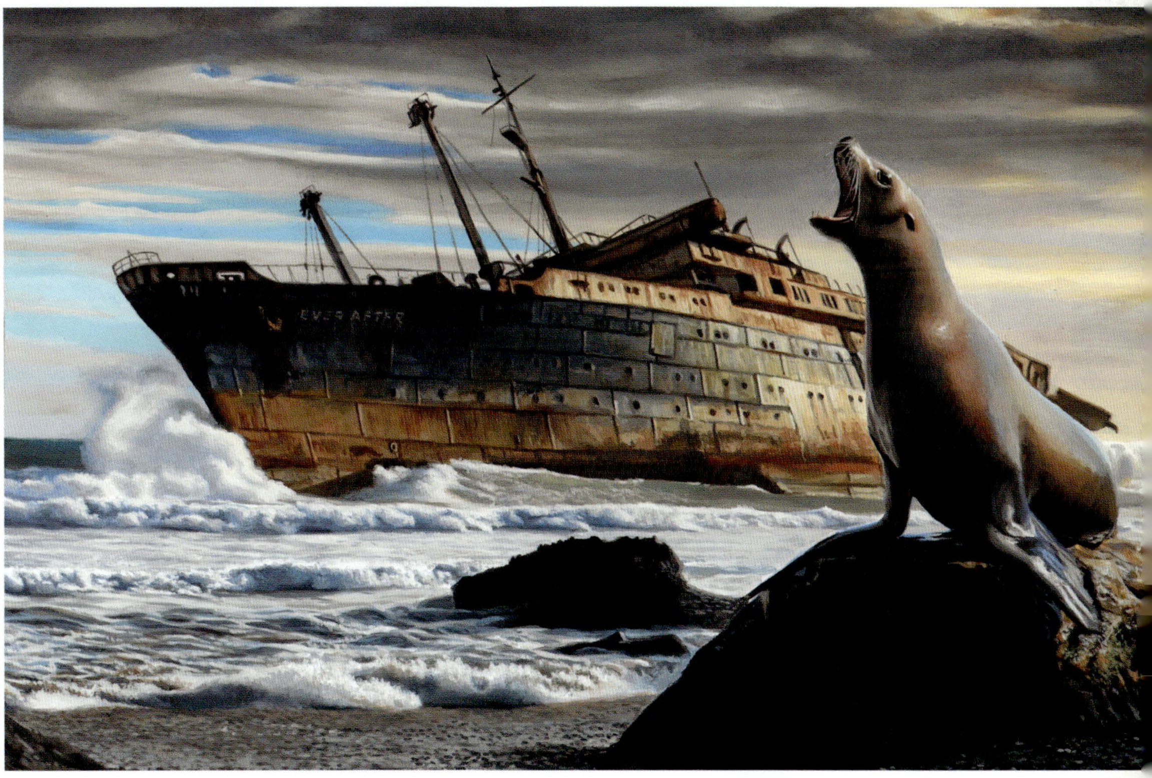

CLOCKWISE FROM LEFT:

RAINMAKER (DETAIL)
12" X 16"
ACRYLIC ON BIRCH PANEL

DREAMING
14" X 18"
ACRYLIC ON BIRCH PANEL

EVER AFTER
8" X 12"
ACRYLIC ON BIRCH PANEL

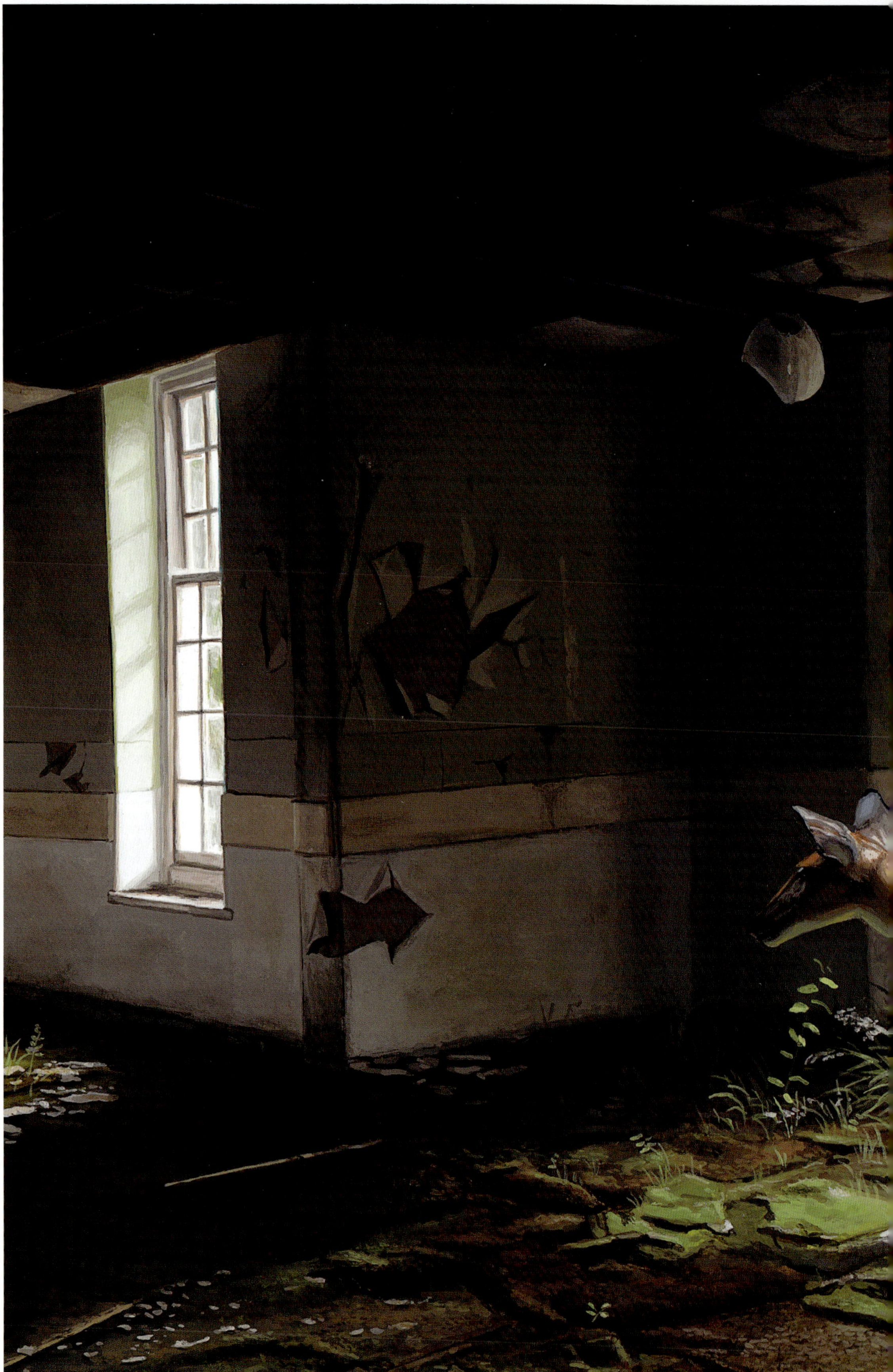

AFTERNOON OF A FAUN
16" X 10"
ACRYLIC ON
BIRCH PANEL

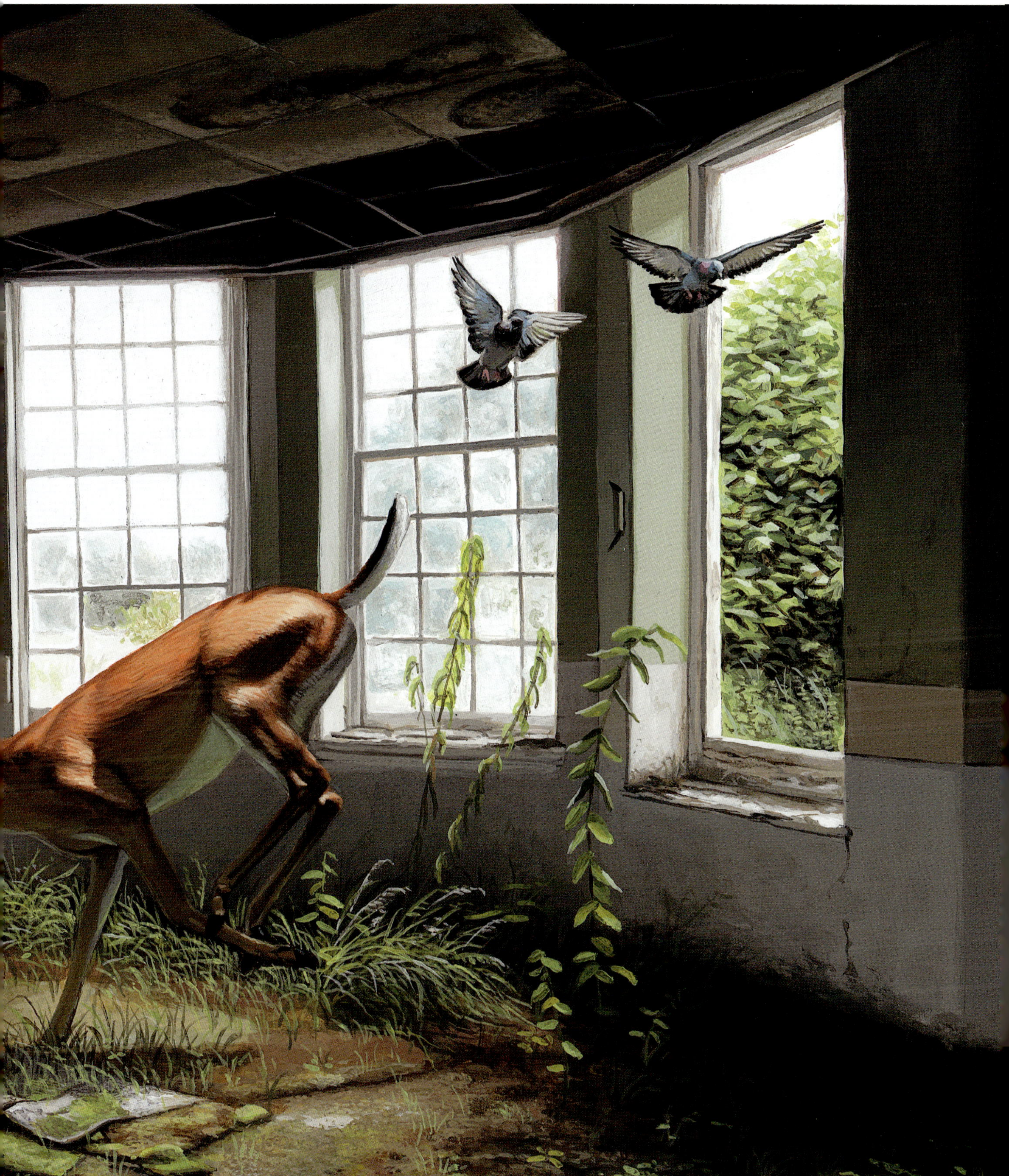

RYAN McLENNAN

NORFOLK, VIRGINIA

Animals Emerging
Political and environmental issues played a small role in my art initially, maybe to develop a landscape, but I never really considered them as motivation to create the work. I pay little attention to that sort of thing, though I enjoy and appreciate nature. I took trips to national parks for direct observation and to photograph. Animals made their way into the work as an escape from Abstract Expressionist-type painting and a shift into drawing.

Metaphorical Questions
Literature and film had the greatest impact on me and still do. I wanted to explore narrative. Cultural history and existentialism were also driving factors, the animals being a surrogate. Questioning of morality, spirituality, class, education and so on, were considered to build the fictional scenarios in the paintings.

New Faces
Humans appear in my current work, as I have abandoned the animals and illustrative quality, though I still explore these similar themes.

ABOMINATION, 59" X 52", ACRYLIC AND GRAPHITE ON PAPER

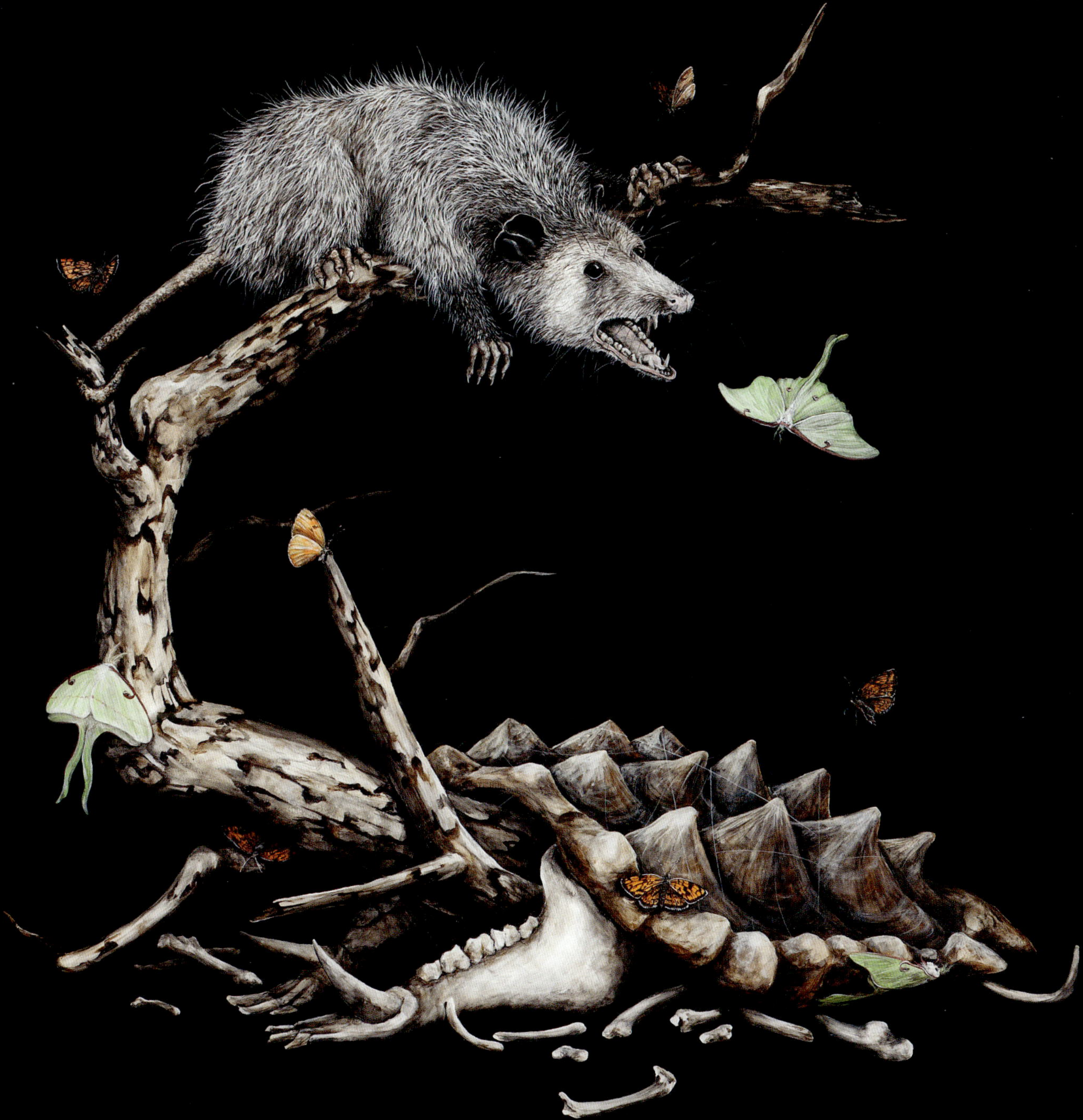

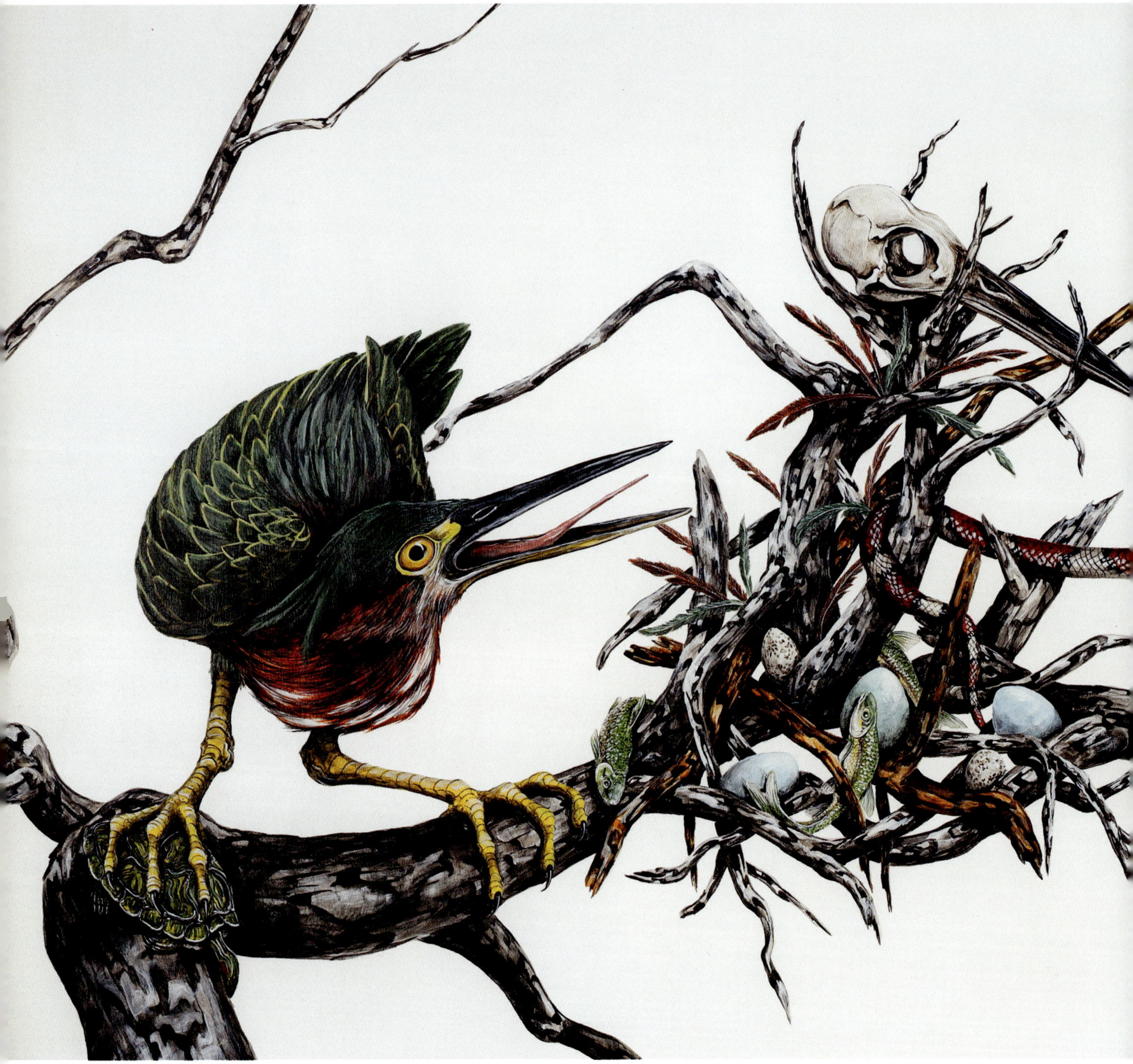

HEATHEN, 22" X 46", ACRYLIC AND GRAPHITE ON PAPER

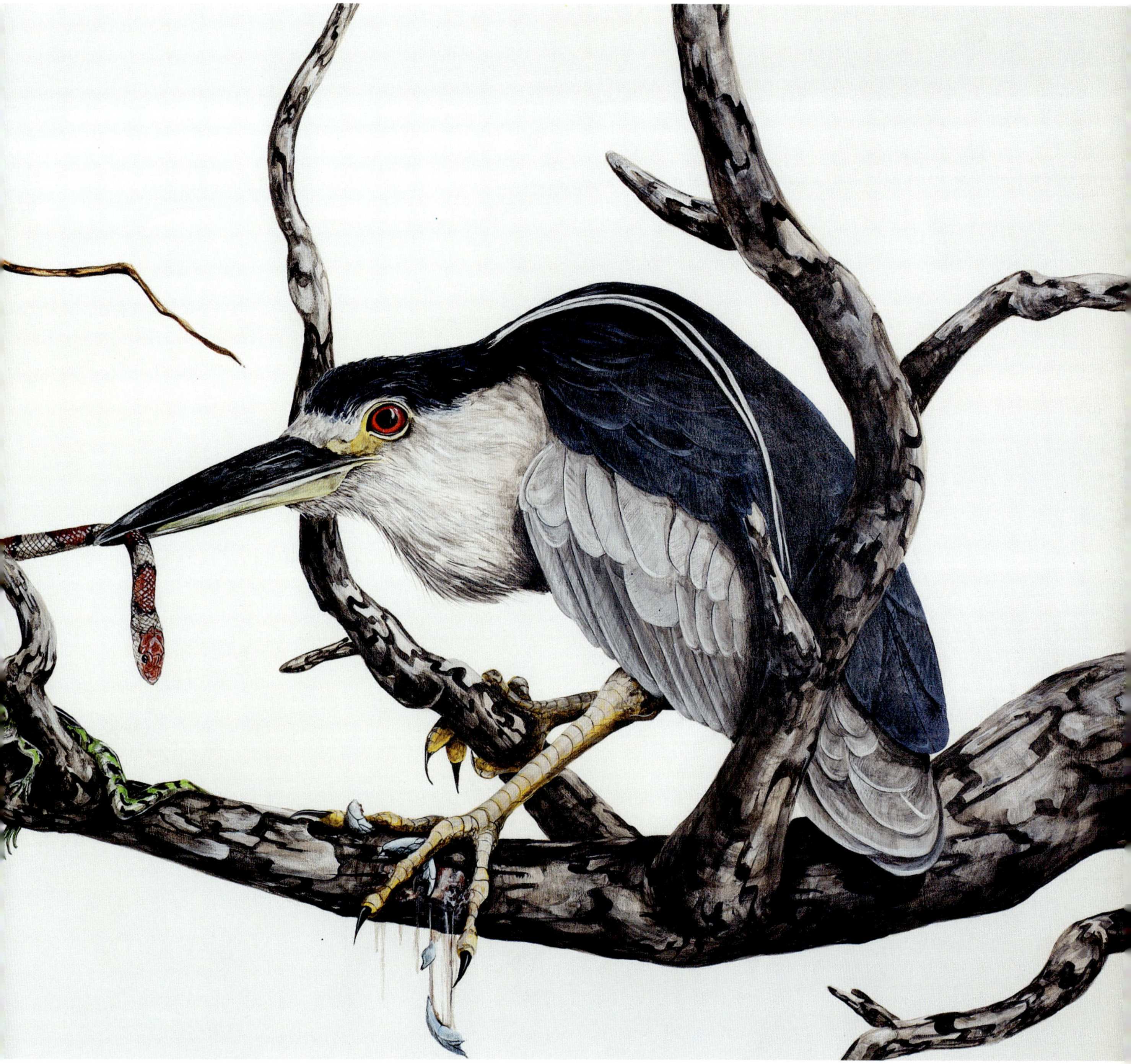

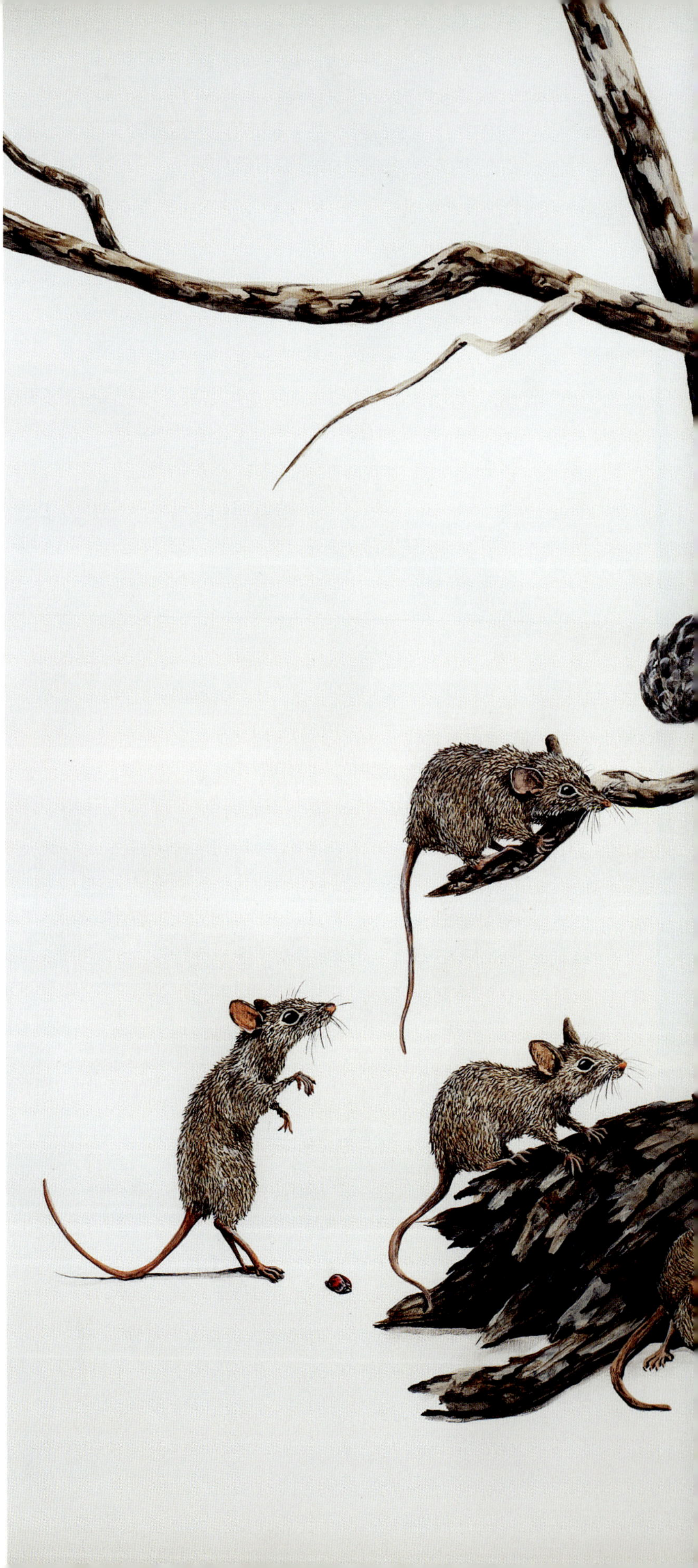

CURING
29" X 36"
ACRYLIC AND GRAPHITE ON PAPER

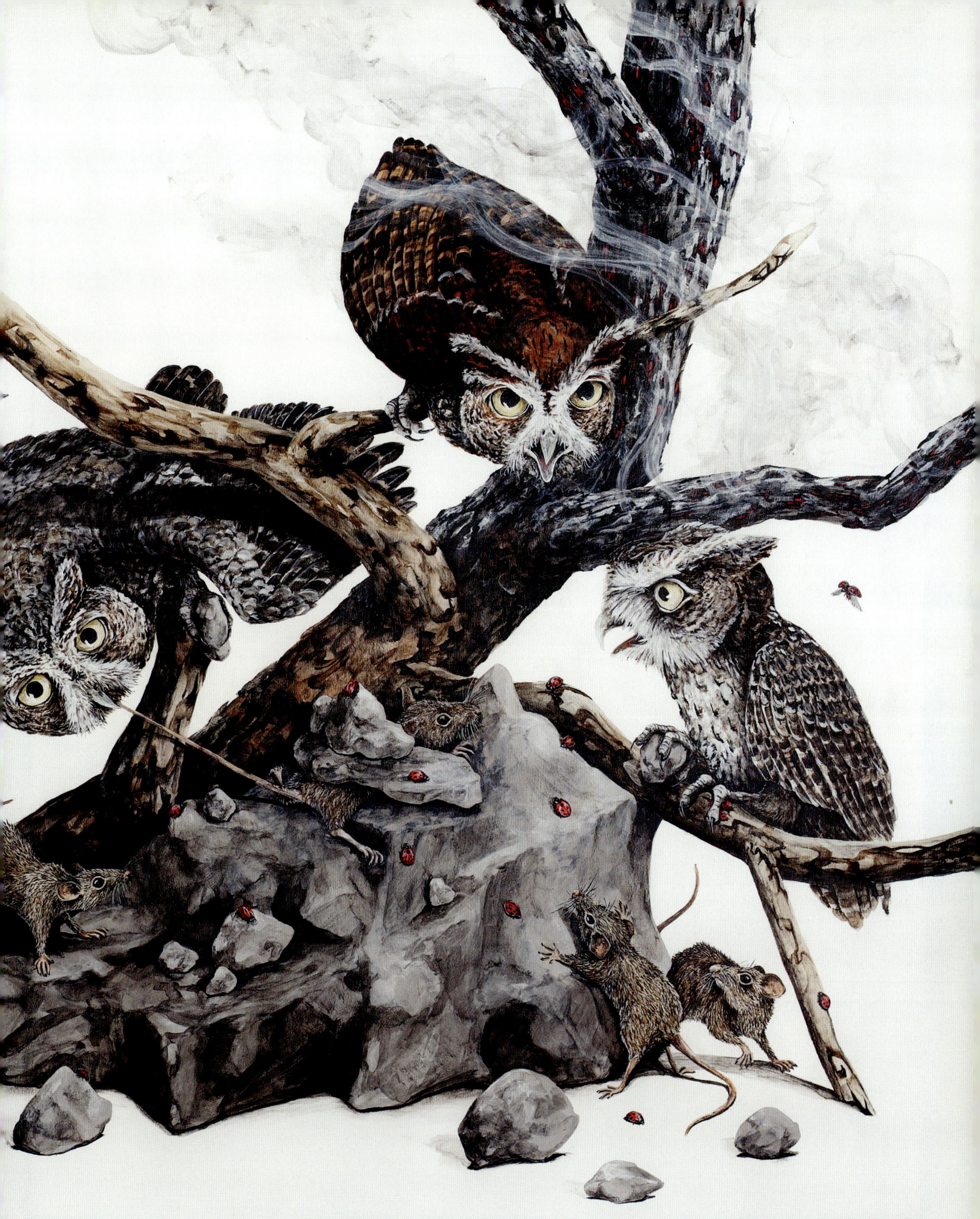

JOHN PUSATERI

AUCKLAND, NEW ZEALAND

A Southern (Hemisphere) Perspective

I try to keep up to date on environmental news and issues relating mostly to New Zealand. There are various endemic land and marine animals currently at risk, such as the Hector's dolphin, the smallest and rarest dolphin, and the kakapo, a large, flightless parrot. New Zealand has 2,788 endangered species, and a further 3,000 are believed to be endangered but cannot be classified as such due to the lack of information about them.

The Birds

Animals, birds in particular, started appearing in my work in 1999 when I was living in Syracuse, New York. The West Nile virus had recently broken out and dead crows were everywhere. I would find them, and other birds, every day on my walk to the printmaking studios at Syracuse University. They were laying on the ground, freshly dead and looked like they were just sleeping. I began to document this and make work about these birds.

On the Precipice

My biggest fear about the changing world around us is that inequality will continue to increase and society will suffer the consequences of this. I generally dislike bureaucracy, middle-management and corporate doublespeak, and these all seem to be increasing. I often wonder when the ball will drop.

Skin and Bones

I have incorporated humans into my work in a variety of ways. My *Skin and Bone* series of stone lithographs incorporates a human skull along with a bird, which was initially done as a scale reference, and in many ways, I'm thinking about and working within systems such as museum collections and specimens, scientific research, councils and the bureaucracy surrounding them. I have also made a series of large charcoal drawings entitled *Wrest* that depicted a male and female fighting.

The Owl Spirit

Owls are probably the most powerful birds that I work with for a few reasons. Their forward-facing eyes give them a presence and gaze that is unmistakable and, at times, unnerving. They are almost completely silent while flying and can seem to appear out of nowhere. Culturally, they are often messengers of death or bad luck, and this also adds to their power.

I have learned that owls have asymmetrically-positioned ear canals, one being higher up on the skull, and are able to perceive a prey's location with much more accuracy. I've also learned that birds with camouflage are difficult to draw as the pattern breaks up their form and disrupts how we perceive them. In New Zealand, they've been able to find out when certain invasive mammalian species arrived by dating the hundreds of years worth of owl pellets surrounding historic nesting sites.

New Zealand's West Coast

One of my favorite places is Karekare Beach on the West Coast of Auckland, New Zealand, where the rugged cliffs and dunes surround the wild and dangerous beach. This place is truly a wilderness. The water is crystal clear and the sand is a mix of blond and black with a fresh river cutting through and entering the sea.

NIGHT, NIGHT, 52 3/8" X 38 1/2", PASTEL AND COLORED PENCIL, ARCHIVAL DIGITAL PRINT ON RAG PAPER

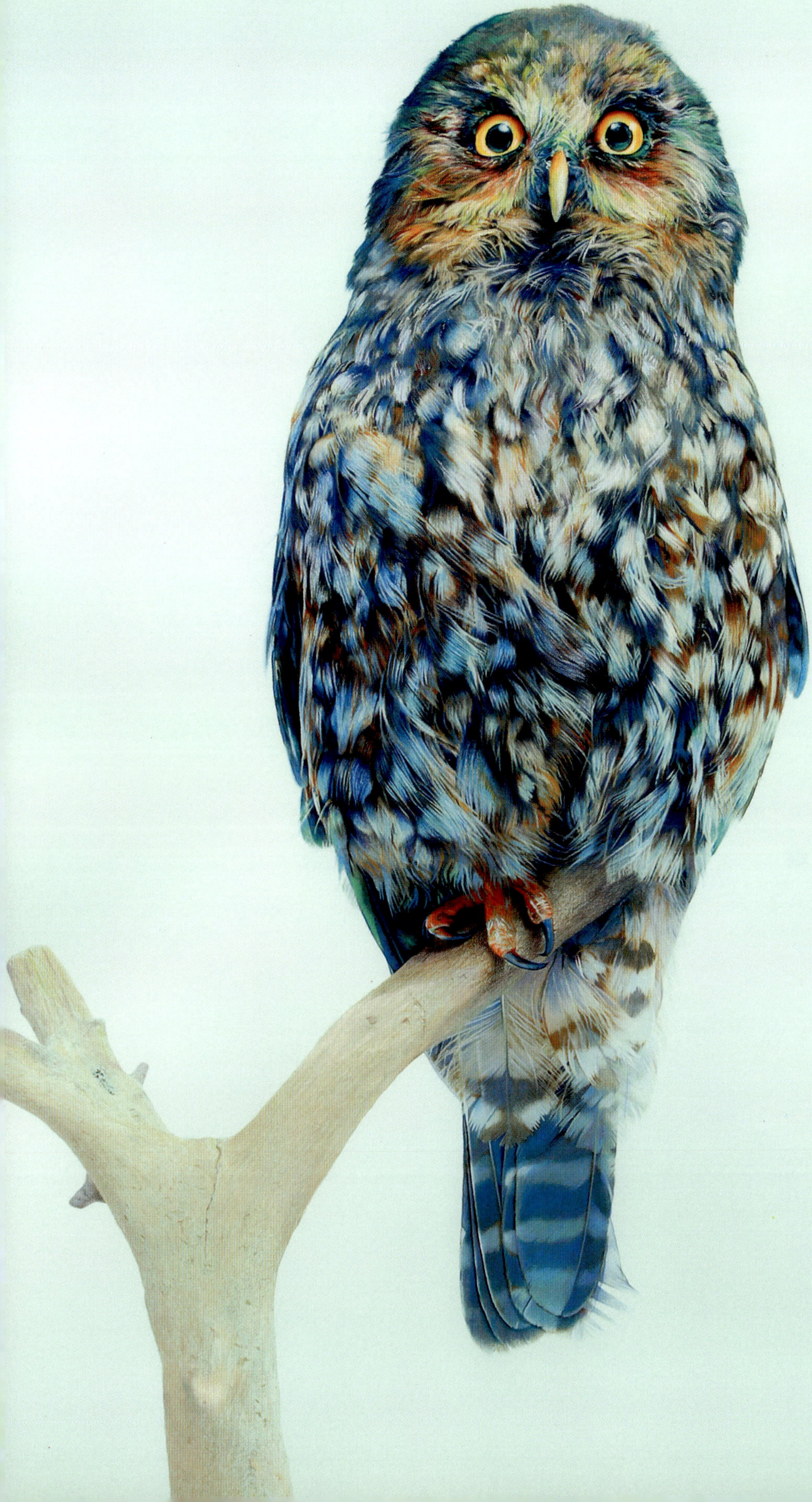

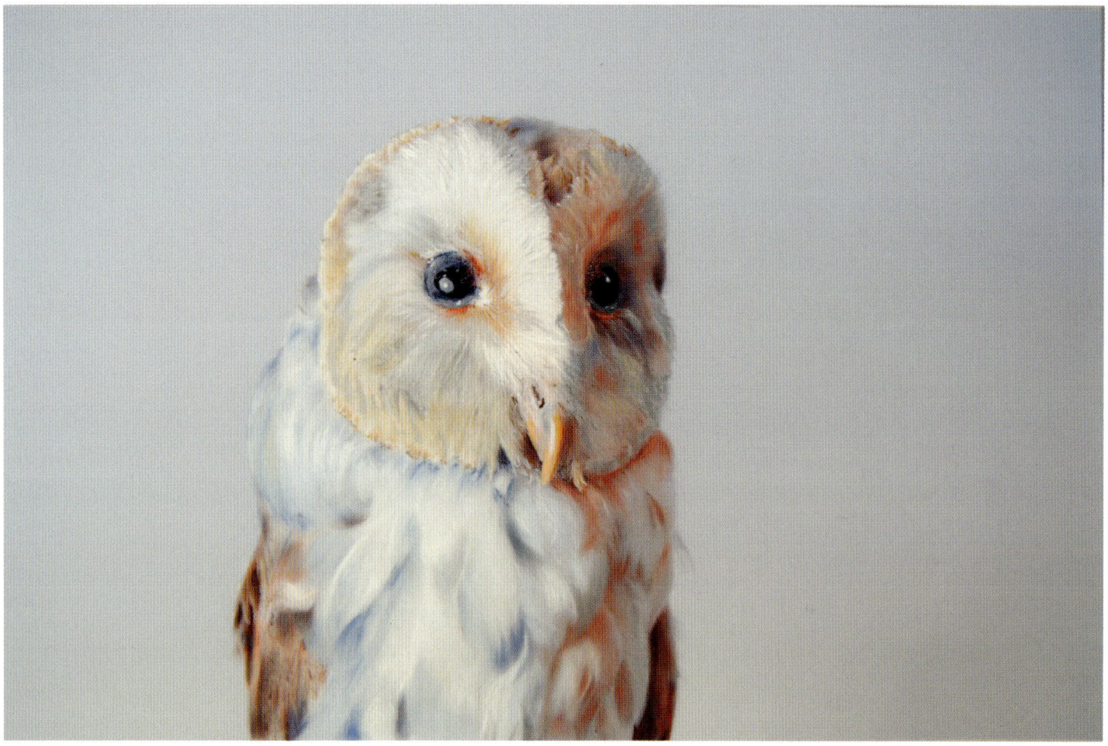

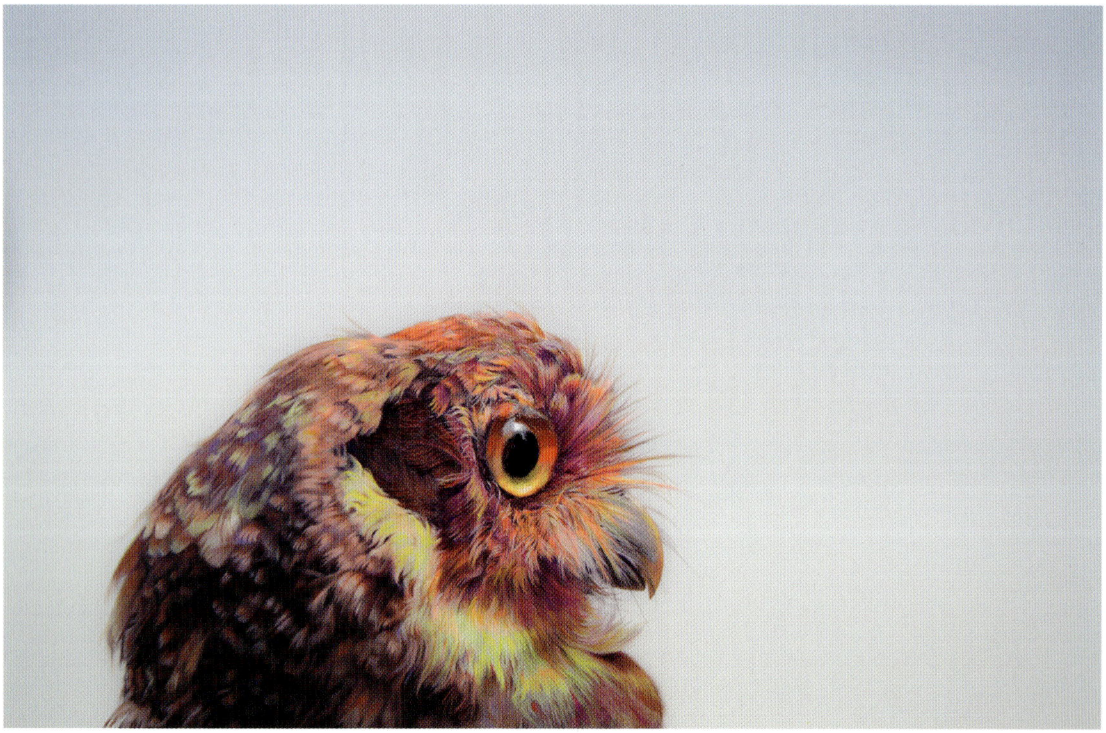

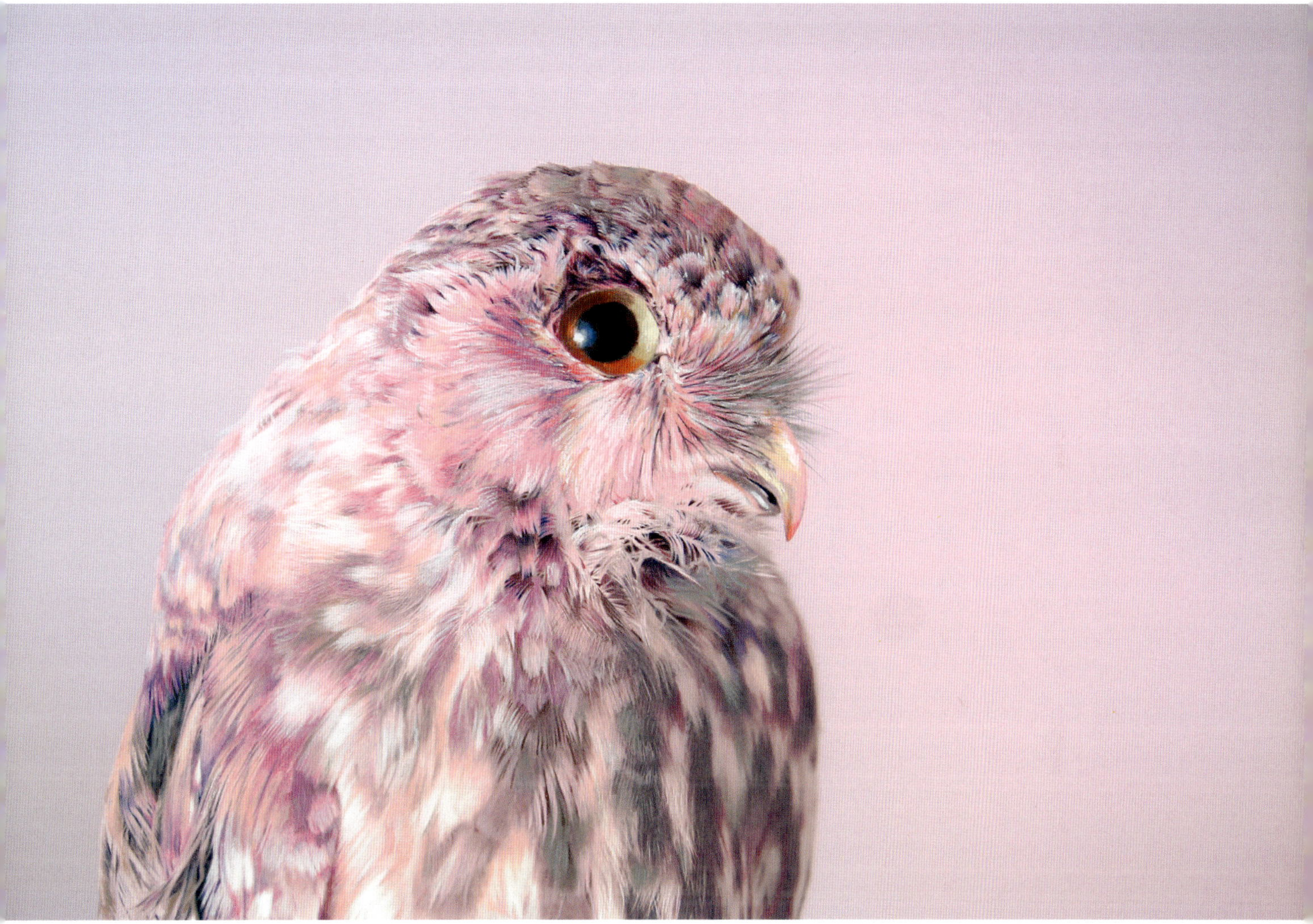

CLOCKWISE FROM TOP LEFT:

COUNCILLOR VI
13 3/8" X 20"
COLORED PENCIL, ACRYLIC INK, PASTEL, CHARCOAL, ARCHIVAL DIGITAL PRINT ON RAG PAPER

JUROR NUMBER 4
15" X 22"
COLORED PENCIL, PASTEL, ARCHIVAL DIGITAL PRINT ON RAG PAPER

JUROR NUMBER 10
15" X 22"
COLORED PENCIL, PASTEL, ARCHIVAL DIGITAL PRINT ON RAG PAPER

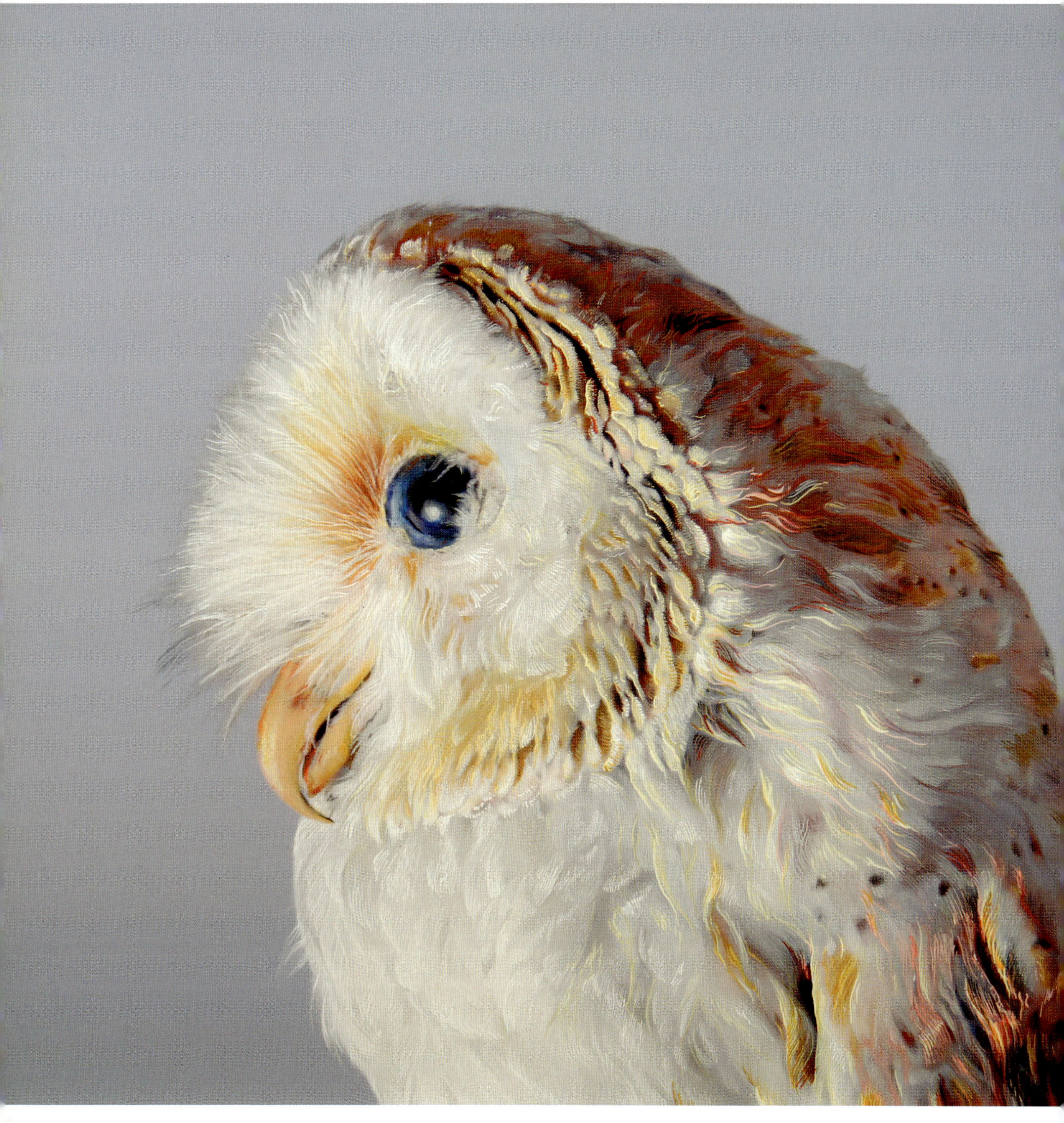

FOWL VIII, COLORED PENCIL, ACRYLIC INK, PASTEL, CHARCOAL ON ARCHIVAL PAPER

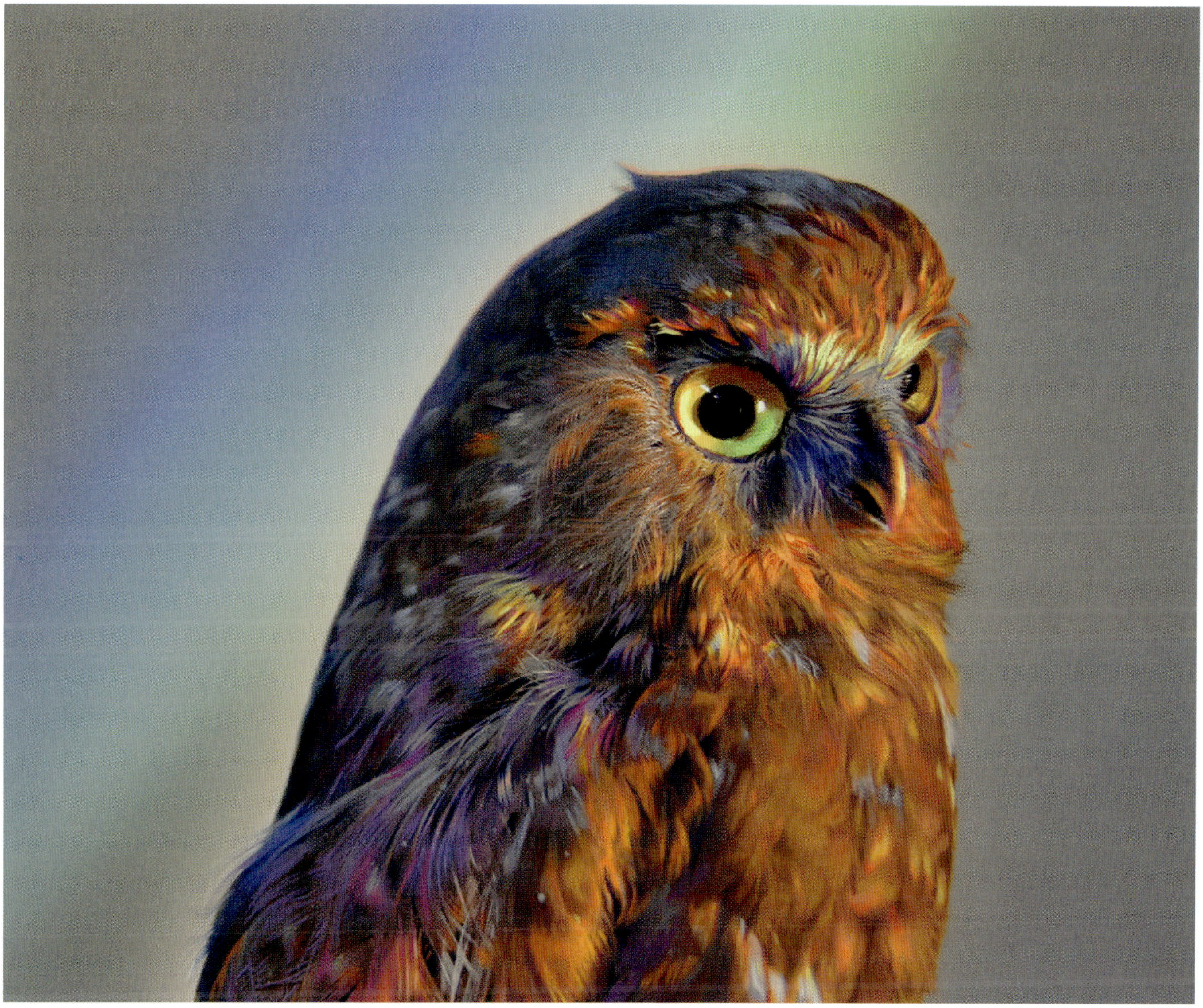

JUROR NUMBER 6, 15" X 22", COLORED PENCIL, PASTEL, ARCHIVAL DIGITAL PRINT ON RAG PAPER

SAGE VAUGHN

LOS ANGELES, CALIFORNIA

Free Fallin'
The world is broken. We did it, it's done. Now it's time to enjoy the free fall.

Teen Wolf
I have a lot of dreams about werewolves. And I love coyotes. They're like a reminder that the wild is very close and, while you're sleeping, it will come and eat your cats.

Bird's Eye View
Since I make work for humans, the notion of human beings is naturally implied in the work. I use a particularly illustrative style when depicting the birds, butterflies and flowers in order to focus the viewer's attention on the idea that these creatures bring to the piece, rather than an actual bird pictured in the image. It's the idea of a bird, or the wild things above our heads, or the idea of flight or rest.

The Reluctant Candidate
For a very long time, I felt it was beneath art to respond to politics. But then I read about poets being jailed and executed during the Pinochet era in Chile, and I realized how anemic our art is with regards to social change. After seeing how impactful Shepard Fairey's portrait of Obama was, I feel like I would be proud to have a political stance with some of my work. I just don't think the coyotes are running for congress anytime soon.

Favorite Place in Nature
The LA River.

LA BIRD, 15" X 10", ACRYLIC, INK AND VELLUM ON CANVAS MOUNTED ON PANEL

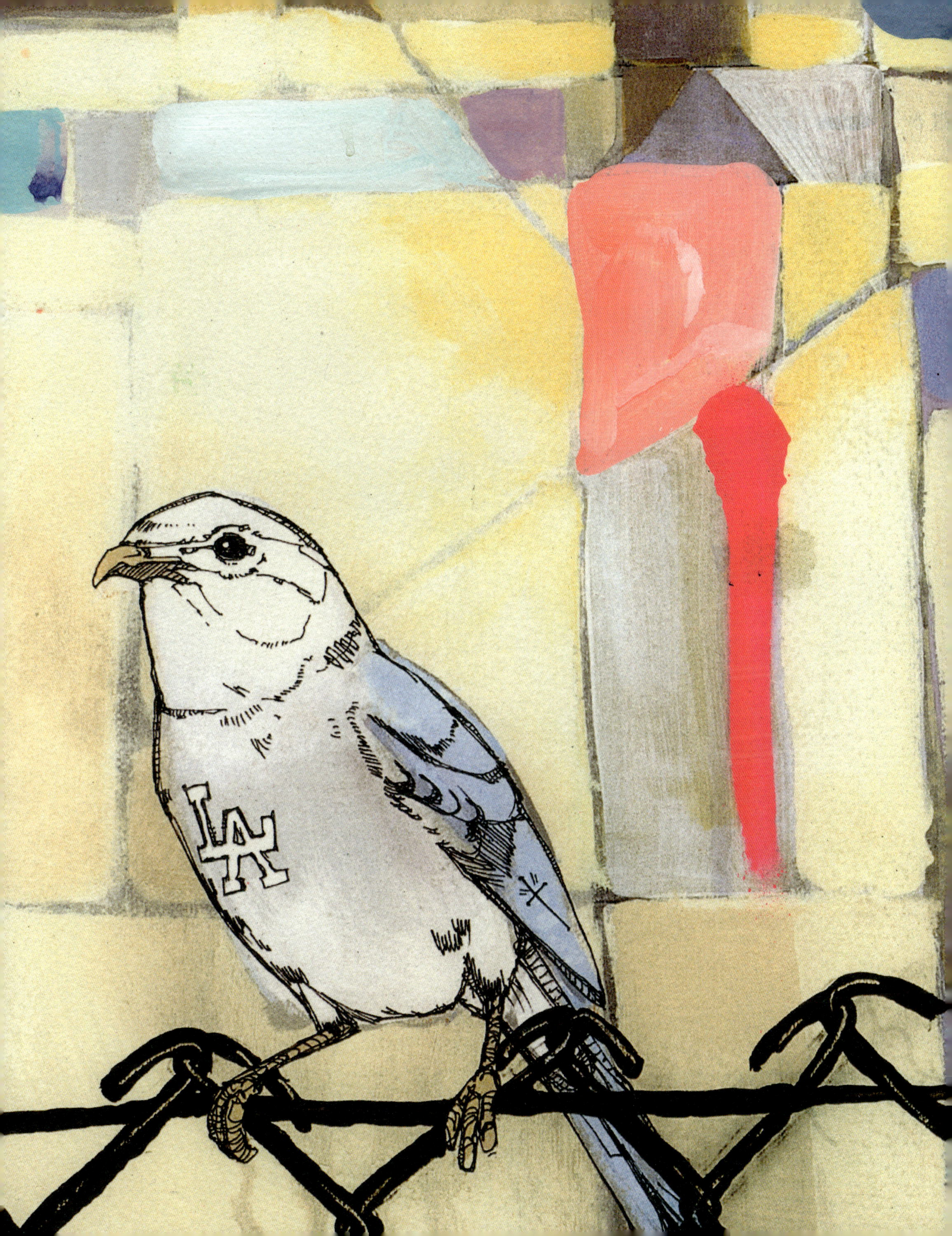
LA

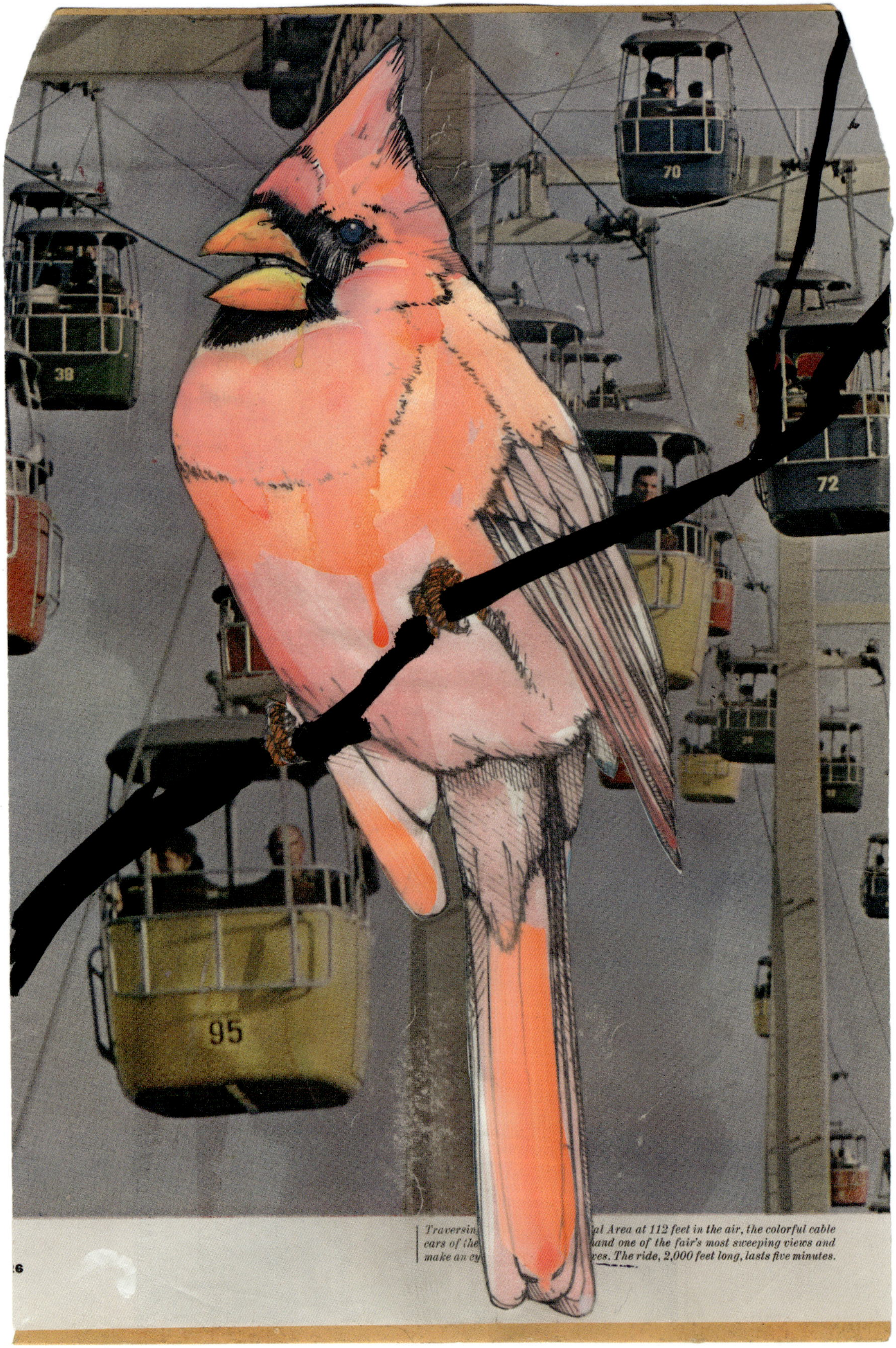

TOO HIGH, 10" X 13", ACRYLIC, INK AND VELLUM ON ENVELOPE

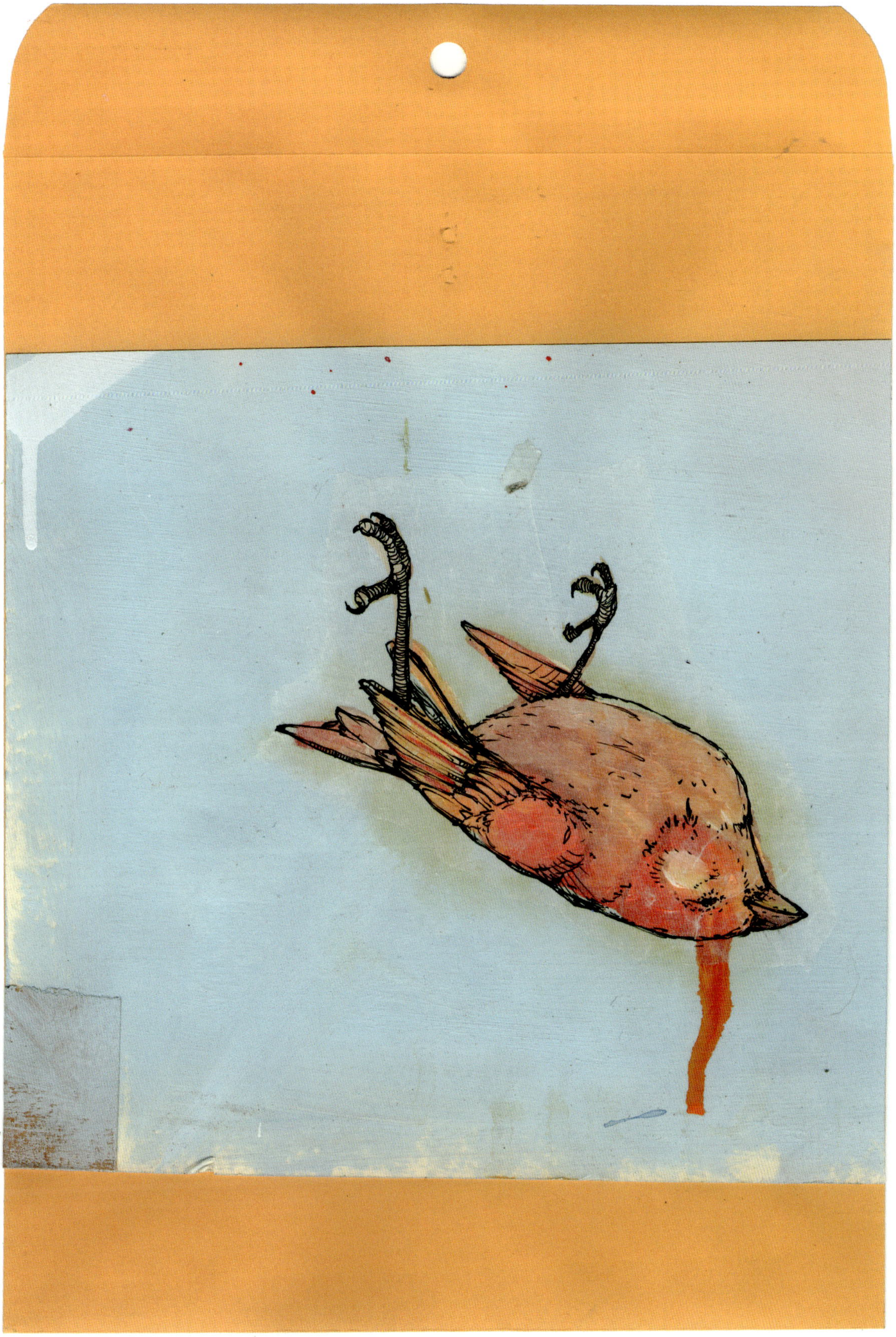

DEAD BIRD, 10"X 13", ACRYLIC, INK AND VELLUM ON ENVELOPE

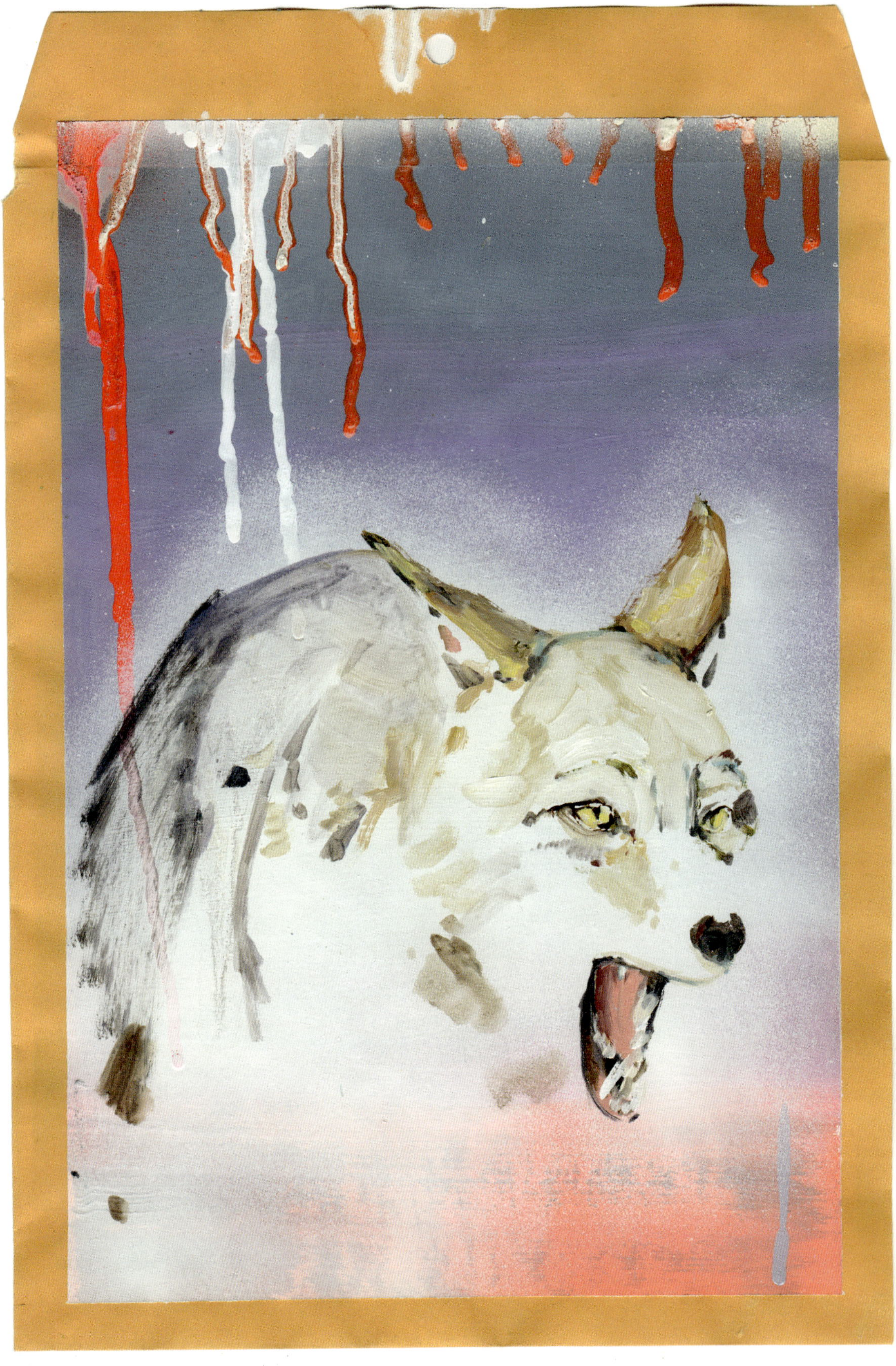

COYOTE BREATH, 10" X 13", ACRYLIC, INK AND VELLUM ON ENVELOPE

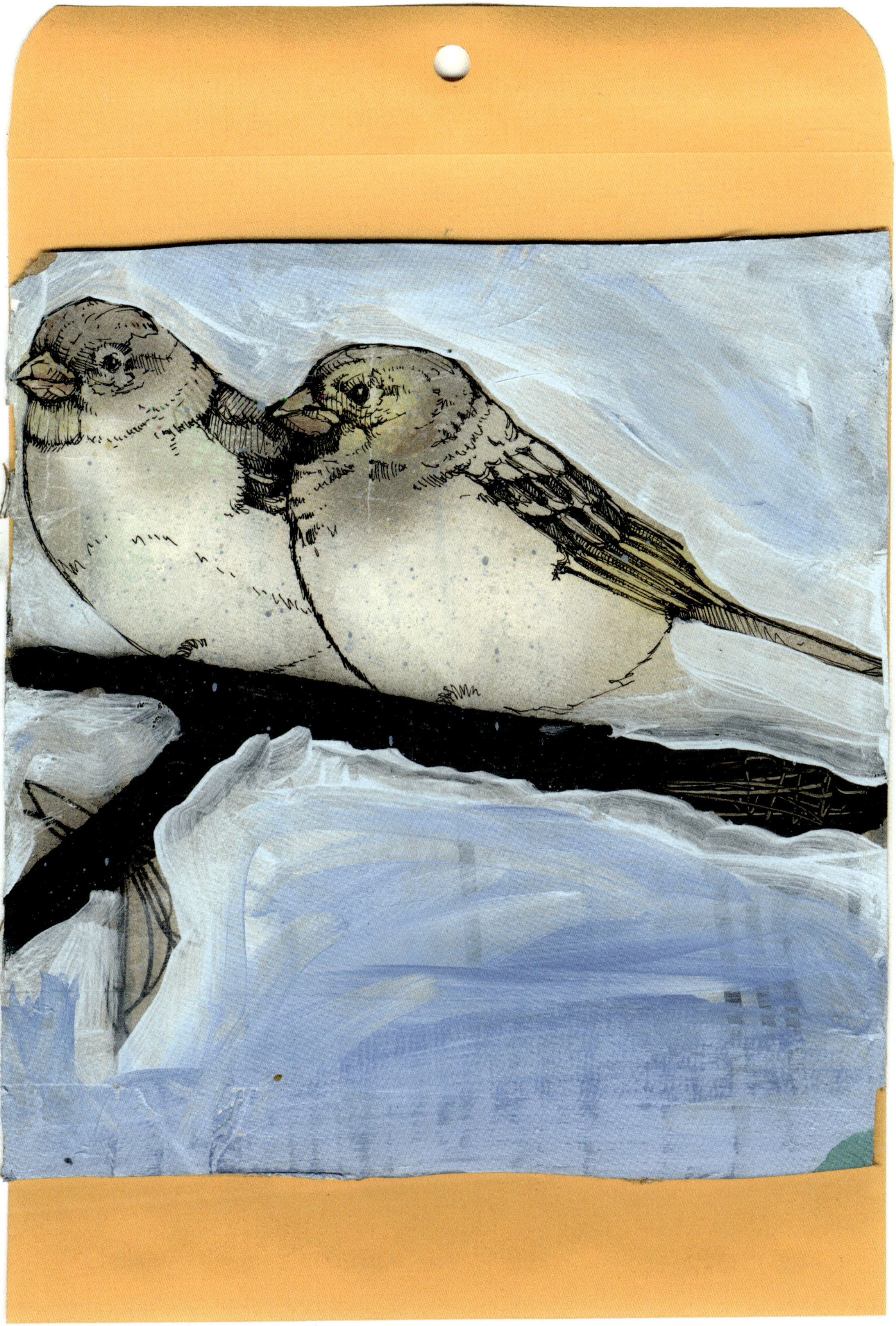

SHITTY BIRDS, 10" X 13", ACRYLIC, INK AND VELLUM ON ENVELOPE

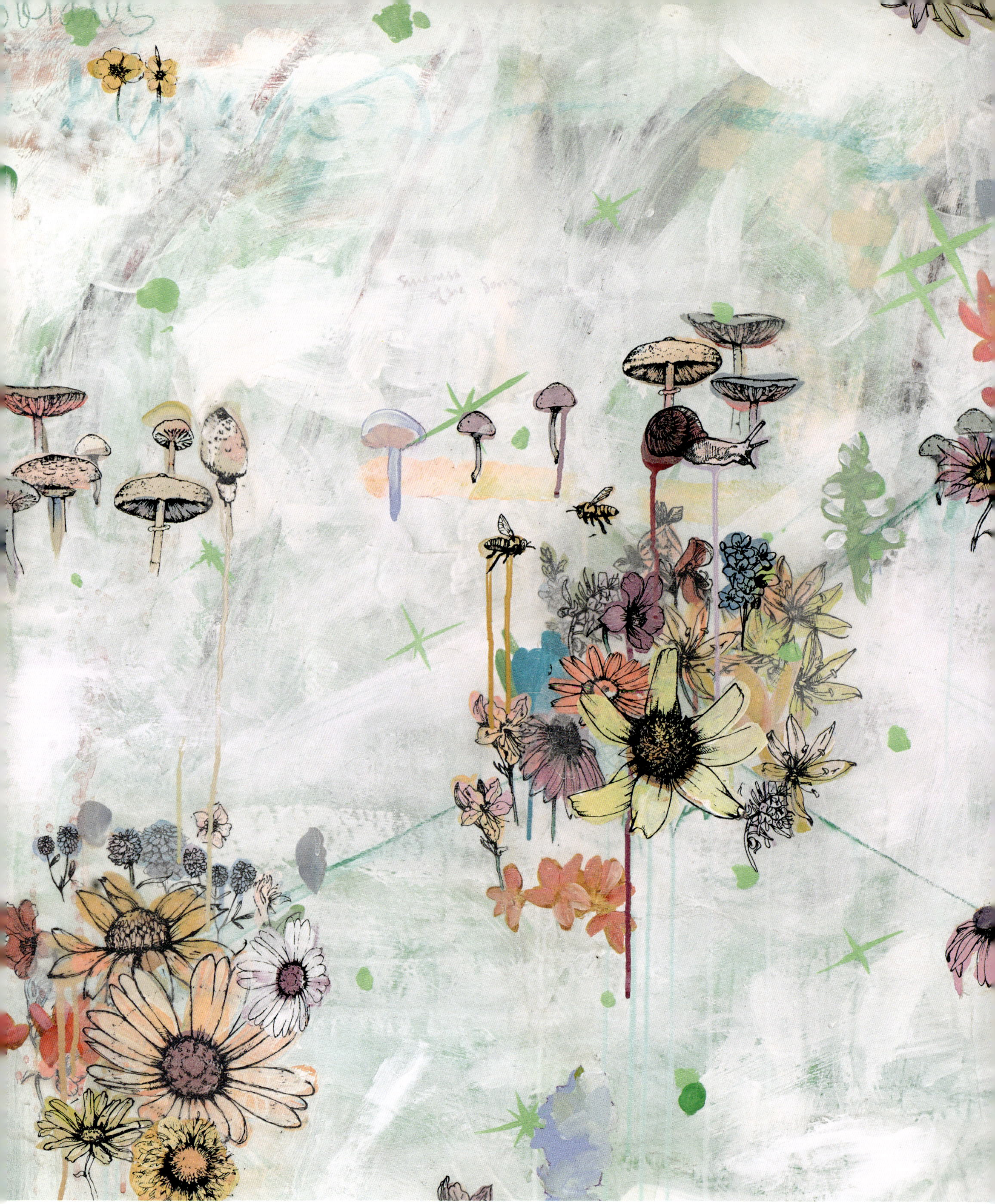

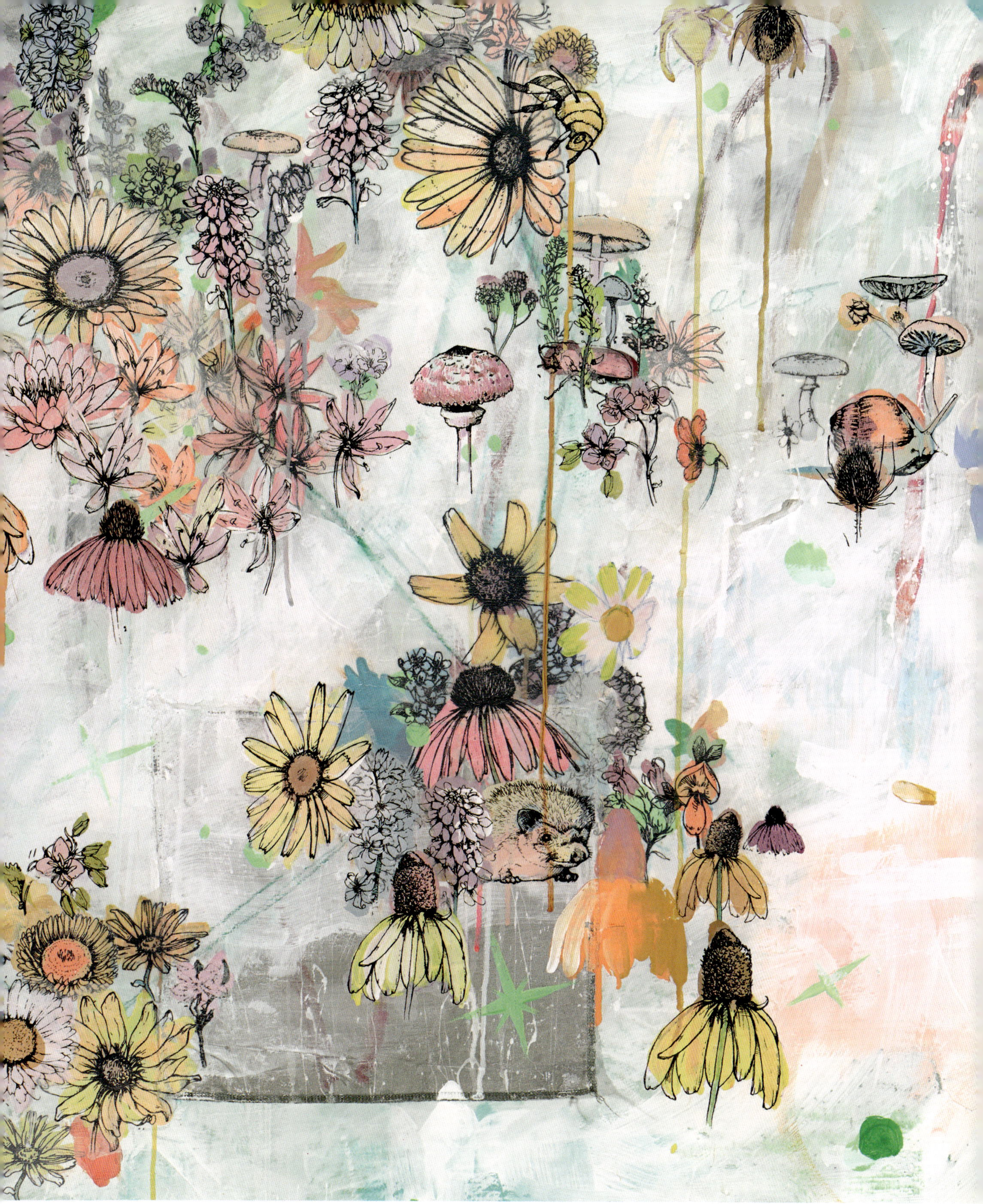

PLEIADES (DETAIL), 38" X 60", ACRYLIC, INK AND VELLUM ON PAPER

LAUREL ROTH HOPE

SAN FRANCISCO, CALIFORNIA

Shrinking Species
Loss of biodiversity—whether it's the extinction of the golden toad or the Yangtze River dolphin, the dwindling diversity of our food-crop varieties, or our own intestinal flora, we're losing biodiversity at a rapid rate.

Animal Angles
I think that viewers tend to project themselves and their social reactions into work that includes humans more than they do with animals. I have done some work with humans in it, but I like to approach things from multiple angles. Often, I've found the most interesting way to do that is by looking at systems and then finding animals that represent the idea I want to work on. The world is a great big interesting place, and we're just one part of it.

High and Mighty
The mountain gorilla is the most powerful animal I've sculpted in many ways, yet it is critically endangered. There are fewer than a thousand left. I'm currently working on a new series about European starlings. While they are not individually powerful, they are amazingly successful as an invasive species. The 60 originally released in Central Park in 1890 have multiplied into over 200 million in North America alone. They are arguably more successful and therefore, more powerful, despite the size, muscle, intelligence, and charisma of the mountain gorilla.

Hard to be a Hero
I recently had the privilege of showing with Walton Ford, whose work I've admired for some time. It's gorgeous, disturbing and heartbreaking. Though it is narrative art rather than visual, Margaret Atwood's *MaddAddam* series fits the bill for me, although her total career is definitely more diverse than primarily environmental. John James Audubon combined beauty and science in ways that influenced history and gave us reasonably accurate records of several species that were soon-to-be extinct. I could almost call him one of my heroes except for his involvement with and attitudes about slavery.

Pigeons as a Barometer
Despite the strong feelings I have for finding sustainability with the environment, I don't think of my work as overtly political, and I don't think most people respond to it as though it is. Sometimes people like to tell me how much they hate pigeons, though.

Bit by the Bug
I grew up in Northern California, so I find home in rocky beaches, redwood groves, oak woodlands, and ferny creek beds. For most of my twenties, I either worked for the Conservation Corps or as a park ranger in Marin County, so the land there, besides being famous for its natural beauty, holds a lot of personal history for me. The first "environmental" job I did was helping to rebuild the Cataract Trail on Mount Tamalpais. We carried railroad ties (which are *really* heavy and smell of creosote) up the mountain on our shoulders to replace old steps originally built by the Civilian Conservation Corps in the 1920s. Mosquitoes bit us when it was cold, deer flies bit us when it was hot, my shoulder was black and blue for months from carrying those railroad ties, and it was altogether wonderful.

Photos are by Andy Diaz Hope and are courtesy of Gallery Wendi Norris and the artist.

BIODIVERSITY RECLAMATION SUITS FOR URBAN PIGEONS: PASSENGER PIGEON II,
CROCHETED YARN, HANDMADE PIGEON MANNEQUIN, WALNUT STAND
11"H X 10"D X 4" W

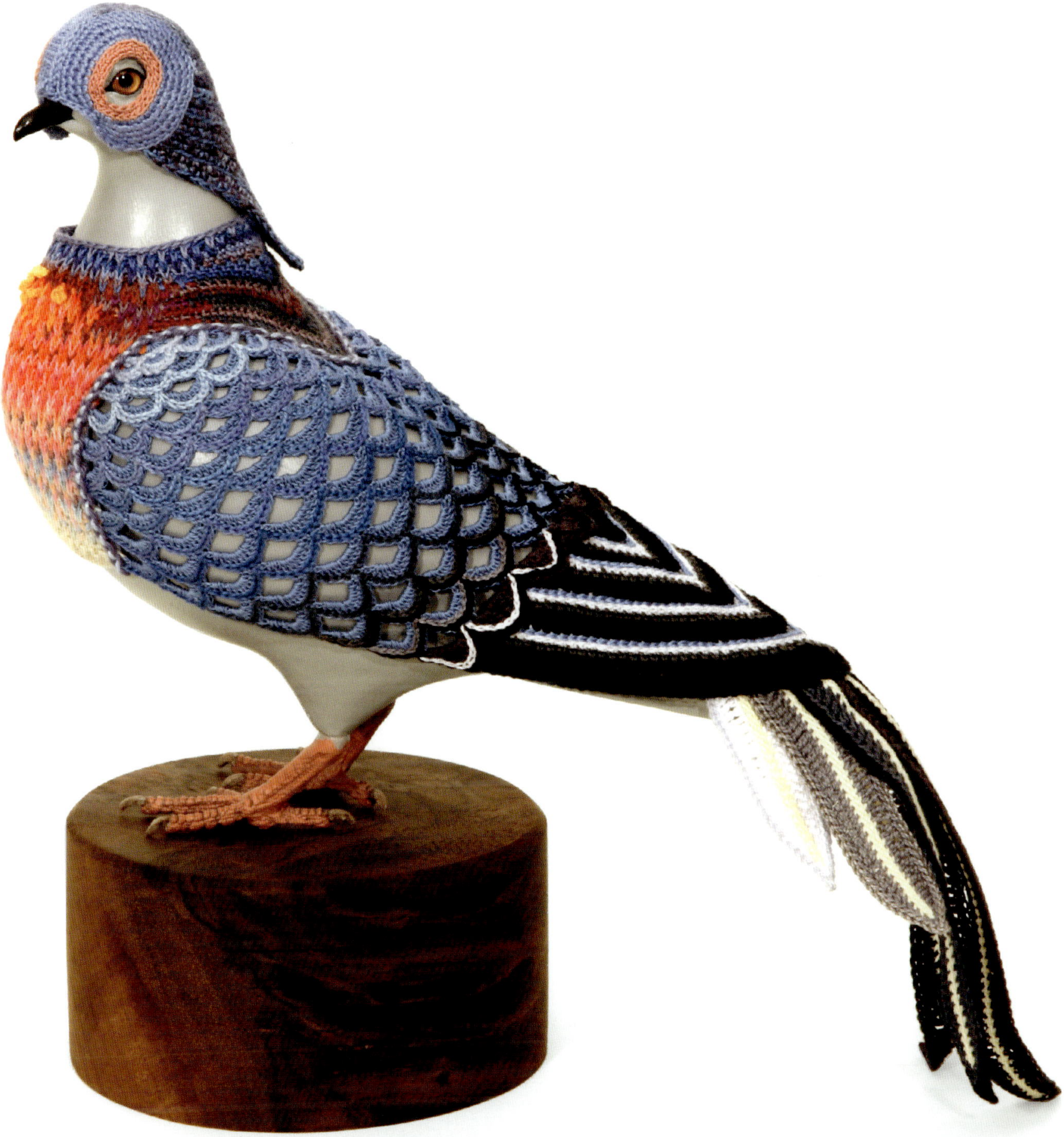

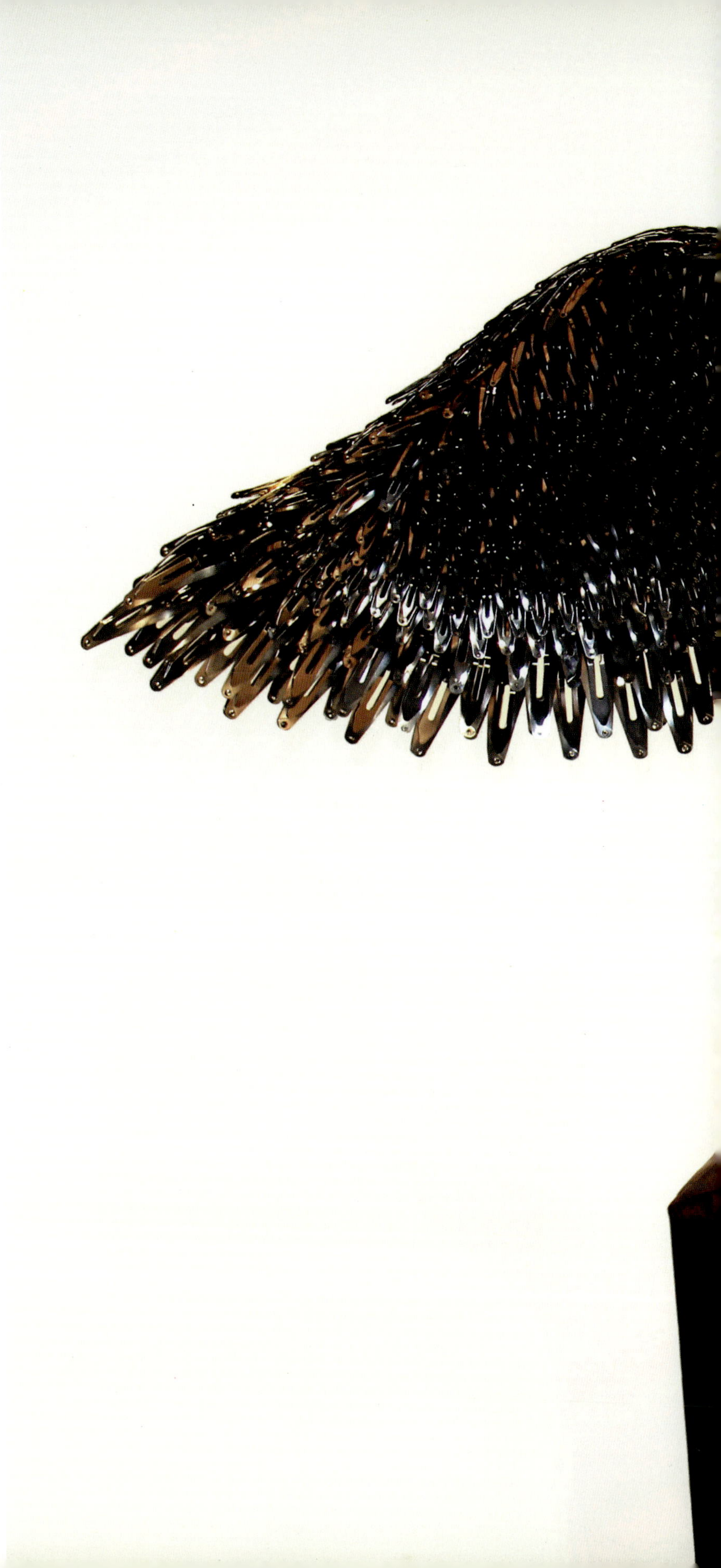

REGALIA
MIXED MEDIA INCLUDING FAKE FINGERNAILS, NAIL POLISH, BARRETTES, FALSE EYELASHES, COSTUME JEWELRY, WALNUT, SWAROVSKI CRYSTAL

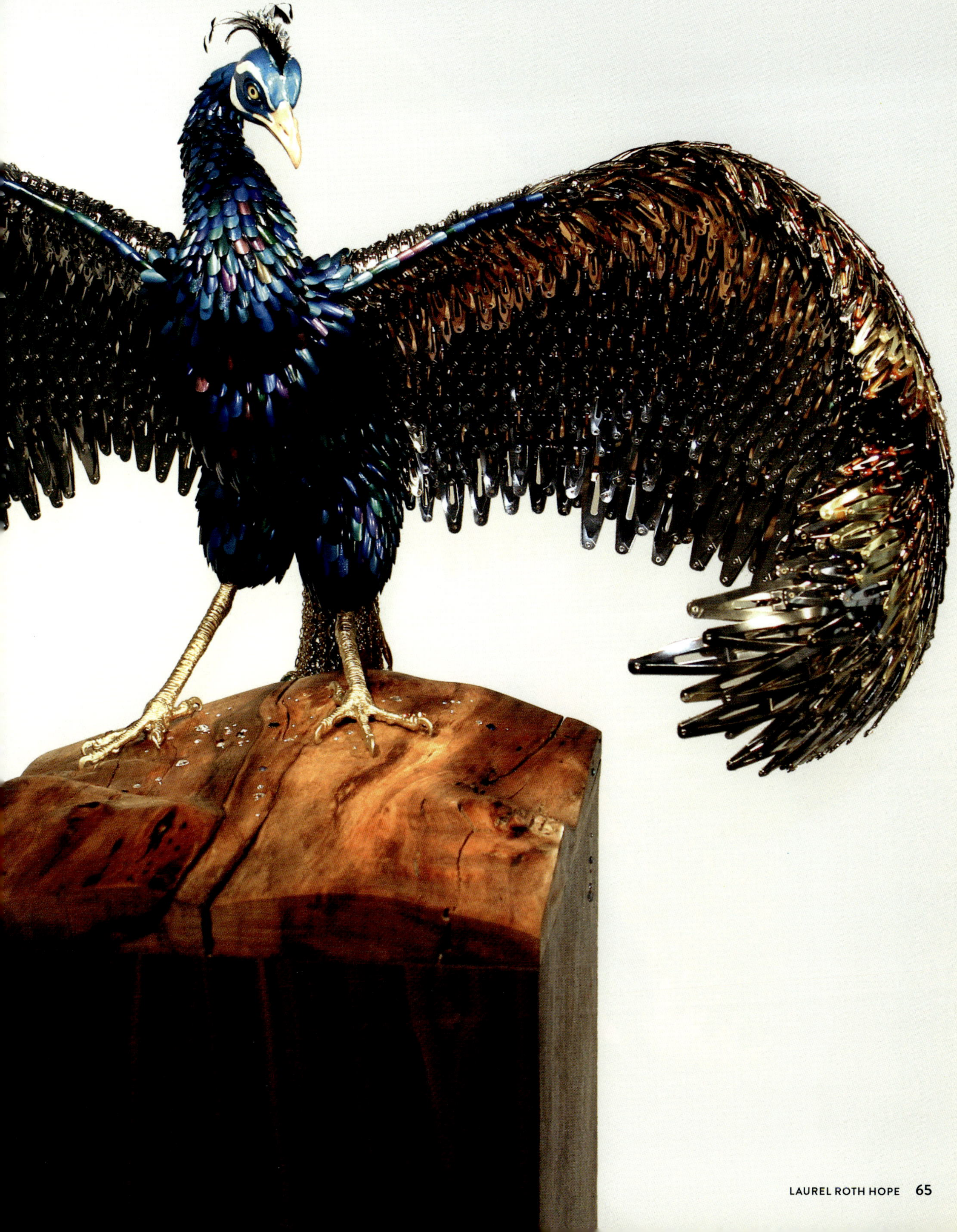

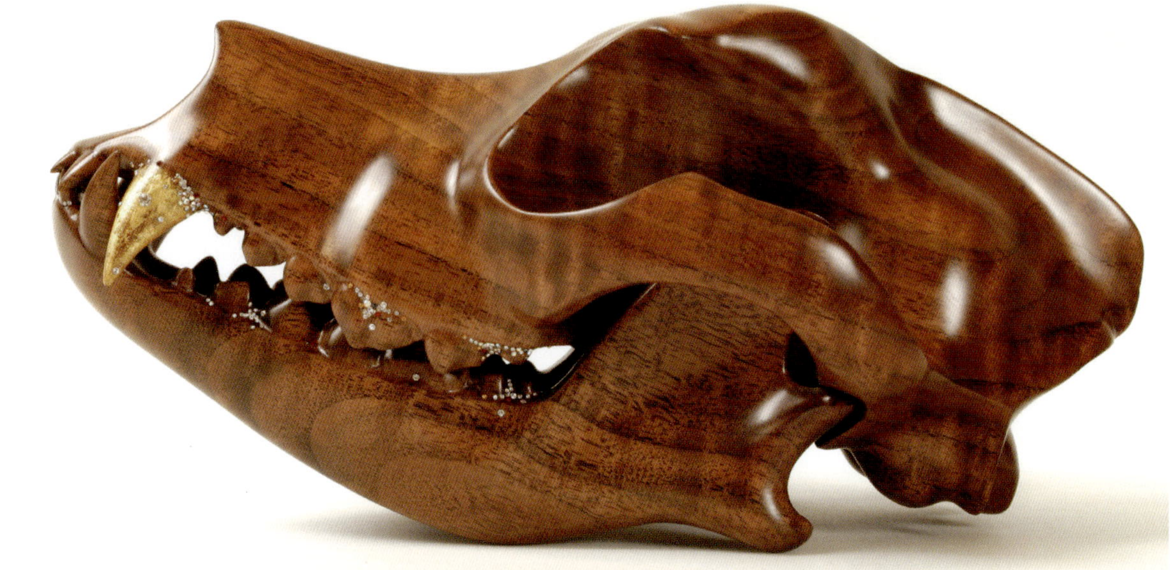

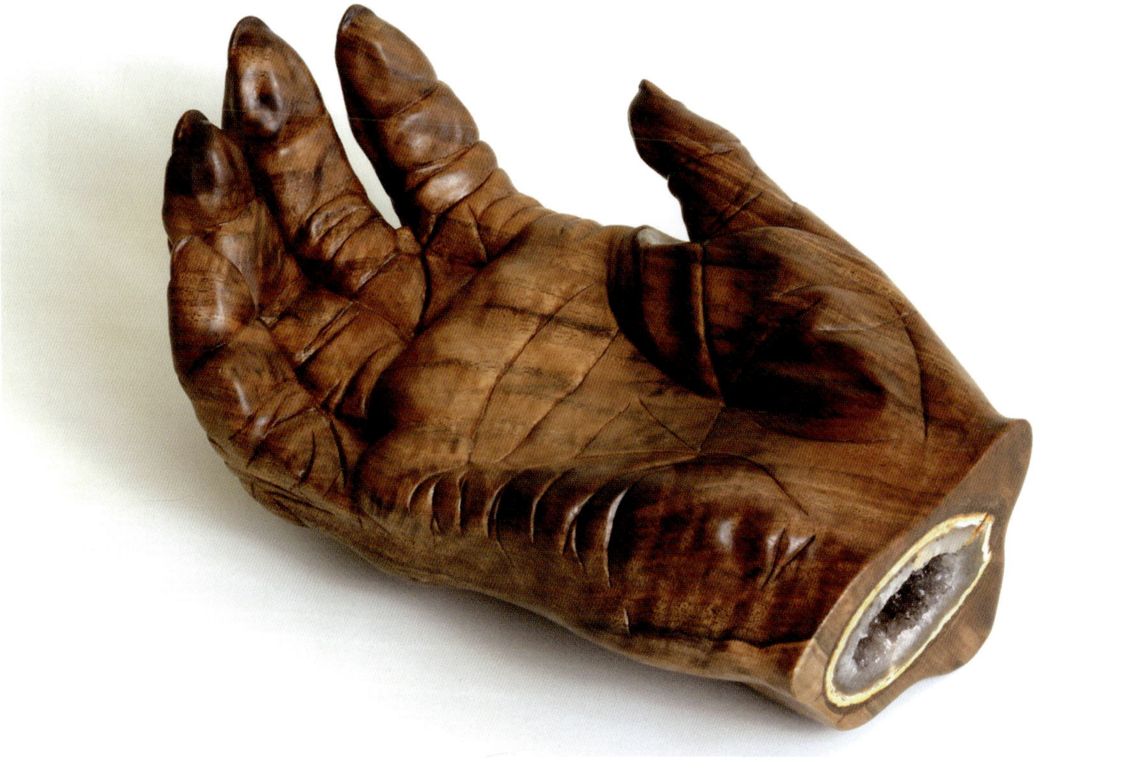

FROM TOP:

MAN'S BEST FRIEND: GREAT DANE
9" X 7" X 6"
WALNUT, GOLD LEAF, SWAROVSKI CRYSTAL

RELIQUARY: GORILLA HAND I
4" X 11" X 7"
WALNUT, EPOXY, QUARTZ GEODE

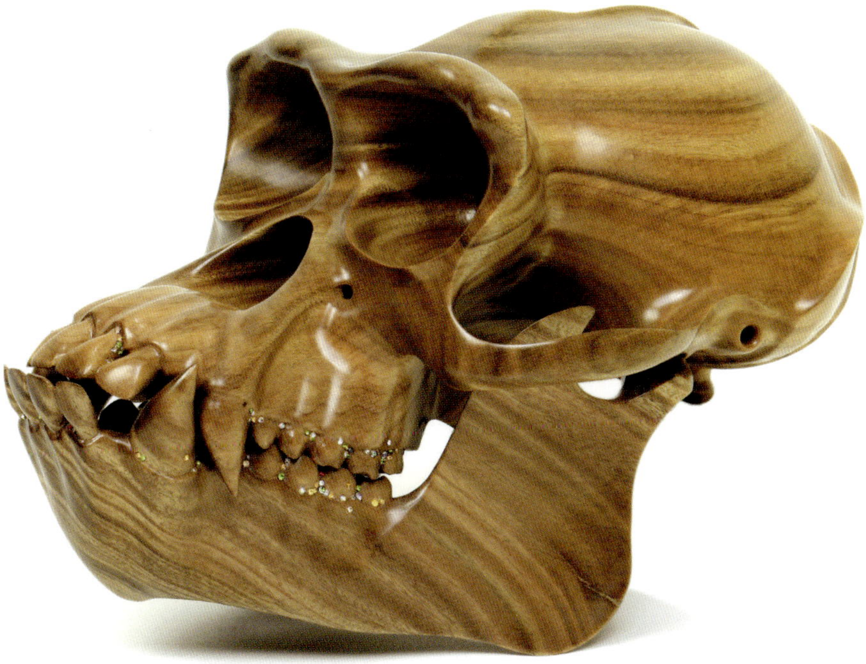

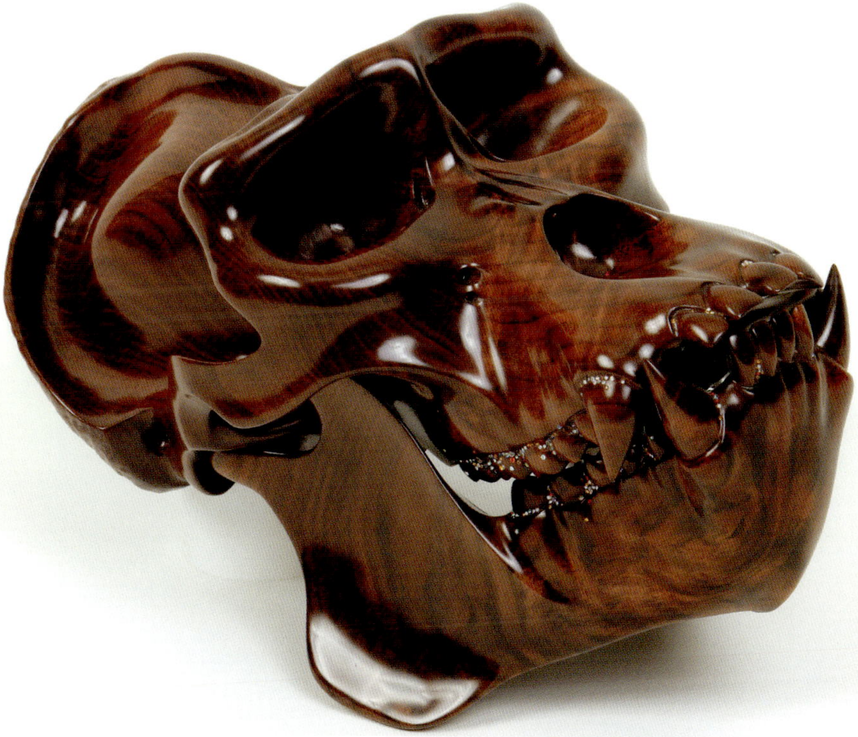

FROM TOP:

HOMINID: CHIMPANZEE
10" X 6" X 7.5"
VERA WOOD, SWAROVSKI CRYSTAL

HOMINID: MOUNTAIN GORILLA
13" X 9" X 8"
WALNUT, SWAROVSKI CRYSTAL

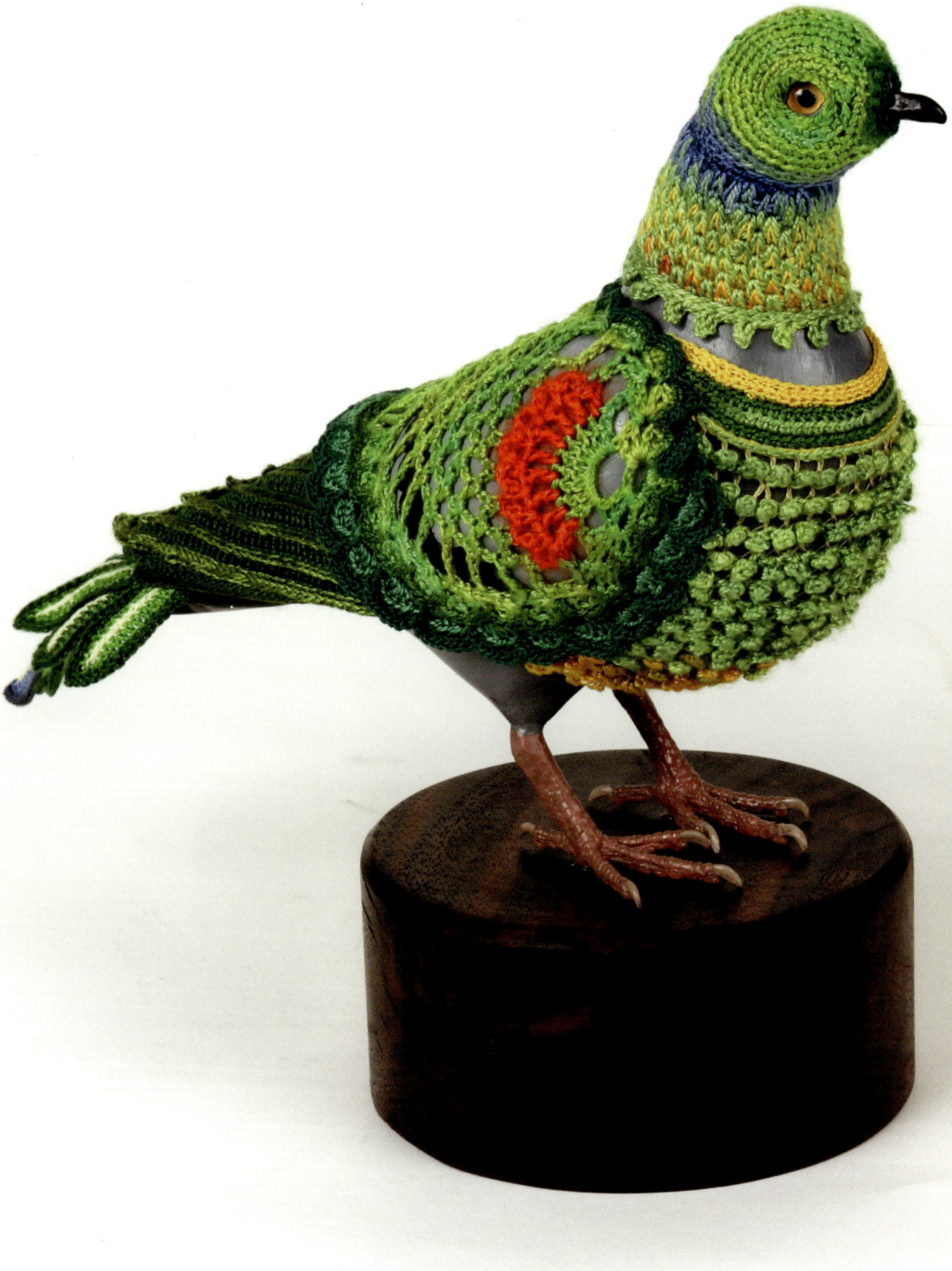

BIODIVERSITY RECLAMATION SUITS FOR URBAN PIGEONS: SEYCHELLES PARAKEET
8" X 9" X 13", CROCHETED YARN, HANDMADE PIGEON MANNEQUIN, WALNUT STAND

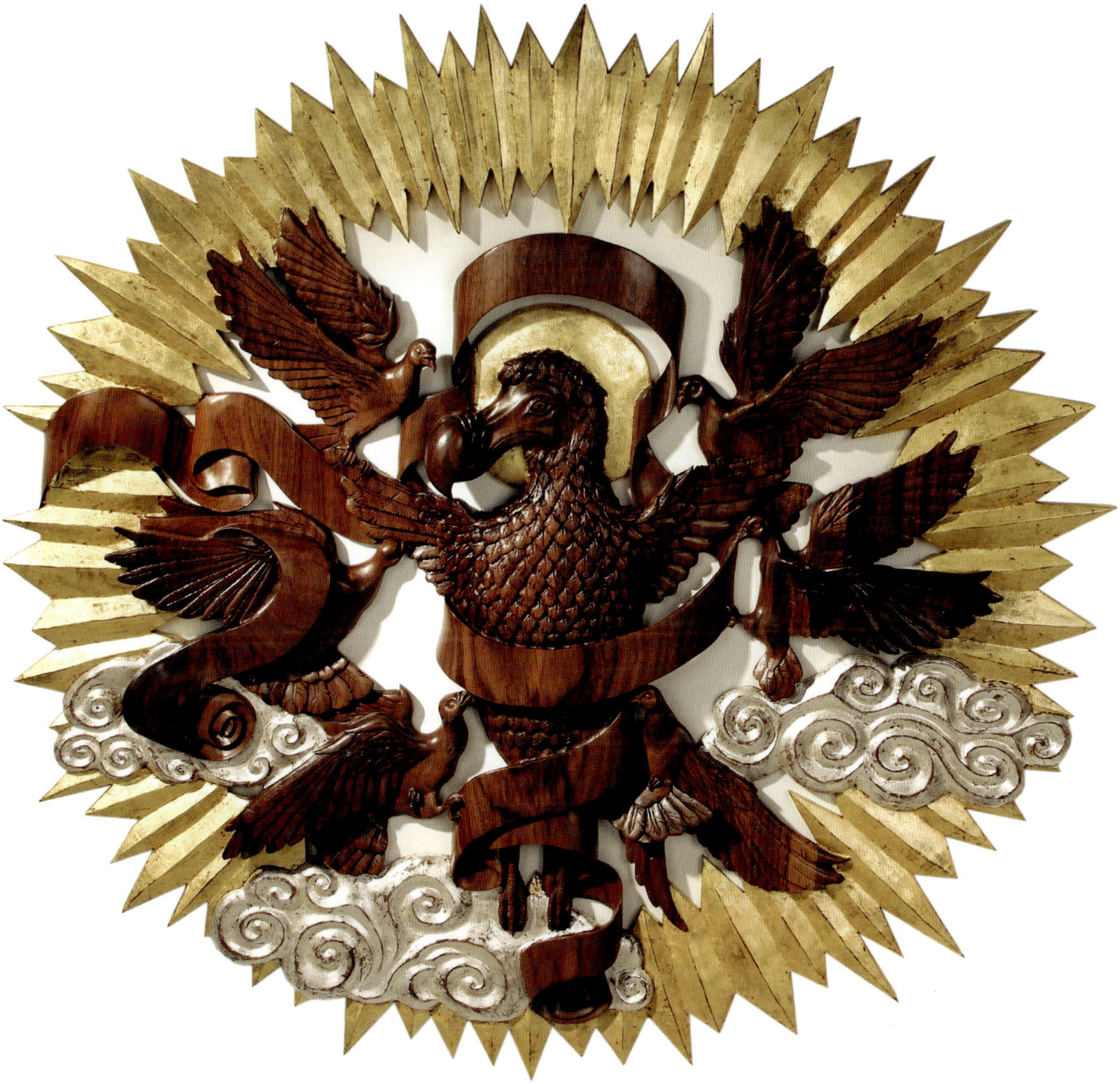

FLIGHT OF THE DODO, 40" D, WALNUT, GOLD LEAF AND SILVER LEAF

LAURA BALL

SAN DIEGO, CALIFORNIA

Irrational Consumption
Shifts in animal populations and environmental changes that reshape natural habitats are the kinds of things that I pay attention to. For example, in 2014, over twelve hundred rhinos were poached in South Africa, which was a large increase from the previous year. The northern white rhino population decreased from seven in 2014 to five in 2015, with only one male. But there are a few more Amur Leopards than there were last year, due largely to captive breeding programs. Also, the loss or gain of large sections of land can affect the migration or breeding territories of local species groups, cutting off food supplies or passages between hunting grounds, resulting in big reductions in species populations.

I am more concerned about the irrational, depraved desire to consume these rare and increasingly endangered animals—the ones that are endangered due to direct human causes, such as poaching, clearcutting, overfishing, pesticide use and interruptions in the food chain, which affect many species along the way.

I pretty much ignore politics completely—environmental promises are often empty, and abandoned when the winds of favor shift. That said, I am absolutely one of those softies who will care about the polar ice cap melting because they show a polar bear looking glum.

Changing Places
Animals started off as human companions in my work, or as an internal viewer—maybe a moralizing viewer? They were infrequent at first. When I started working with mythology, creating heroic journeys, the animals played more integral roles, acting as guides, guardians or threats to be conquered, like a dragon, each one helping the heroine along her path. They have slowly taken over the work, replacing the human figure completely and, instead, representing the human subconscious. The animals populate the landscape of the human psyche, acting out our less than moral urges.

Strong and Subtle
Two artists I appreciate are Walton Ford and Félix González-Torres. Walton Ford makes work that is so shockingly beautiful that you love it before you get the message, and he wraps stories of colonization into the work—one group dominating another group. That isn't directly environmental, but it plays out on a political and economic platform that would directly affect the environment and policies. González-Torres weaves amazing images of relationships out of simple but beautiful, often conservative, materials. If you read his work and carry that viewpoint into the world, it could definitely affect the way you interact with and consider nature, animals, the world and everyone in it.

A Safe Refuge
I do create internal narratives for myself that are political in nature, but I doubt that those stories come through to a viewer. I use these rare and special animals, and I give them a world to move into once they are killed off in this one. By combining them with mythic creatures, I am giving them a place to find refuge, and to live on. It is hopeful, but it should also show how devastating it is that these animals will only live on in the subconscious once we kill them all off.

Going Out to See Within
I love to go anywhere I have a chance of seeing animals in their natural habitat. Even the trails I run on, in a nature preserve outside of San Diego, offer opportunities to see them. I see road runners, rattle and king snakes, coyotes, and other critters running around. Seeing dolphins or sea lions at the beach always makes me happy. There aren't many places where we cross out of our cemented areas into the wilder ones on a daily basis, unless we go out of our way to do so.

NOLA (DETAIL), 42" X 52", WATERCOLOR AND GRAPHITE ON PAPER

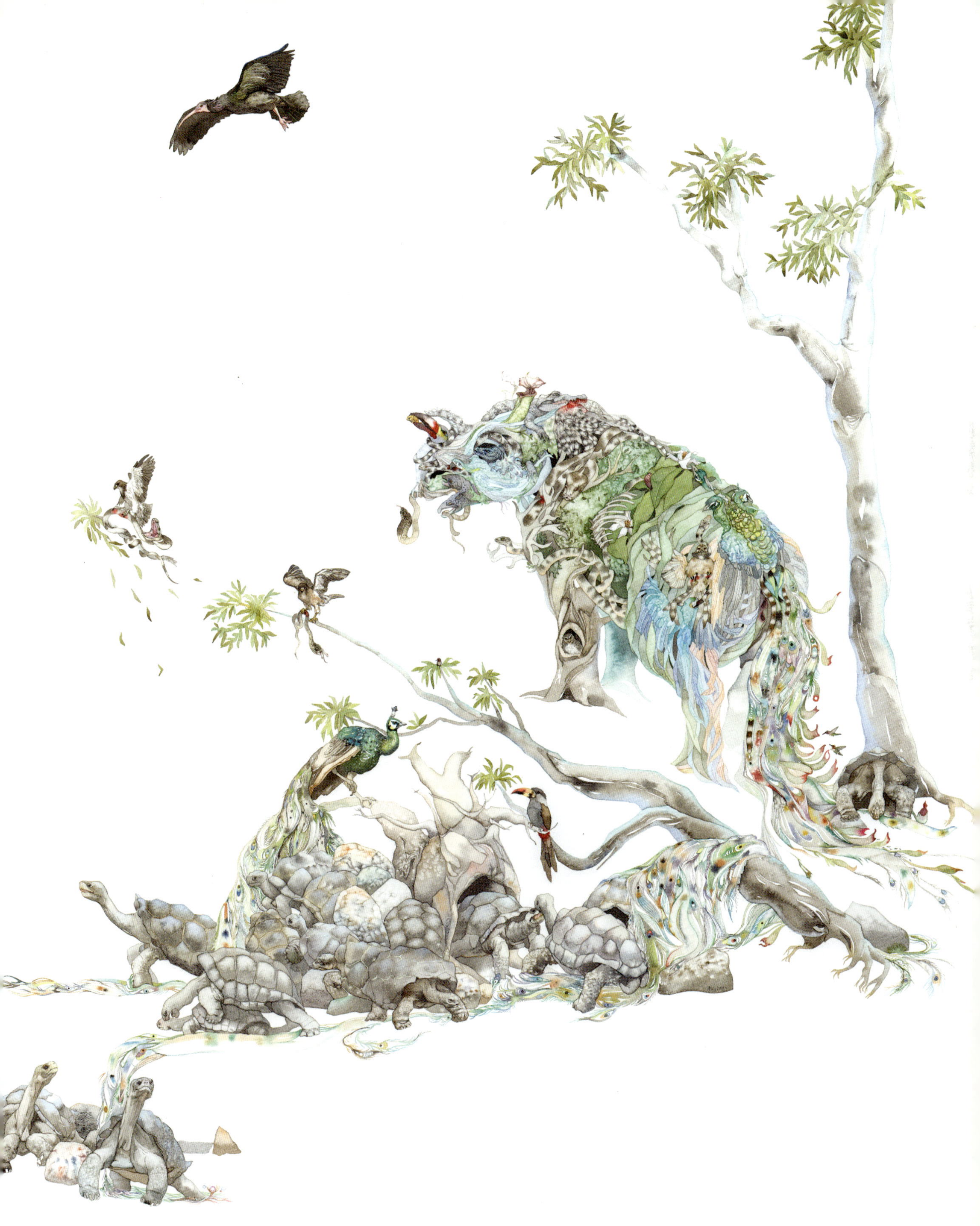

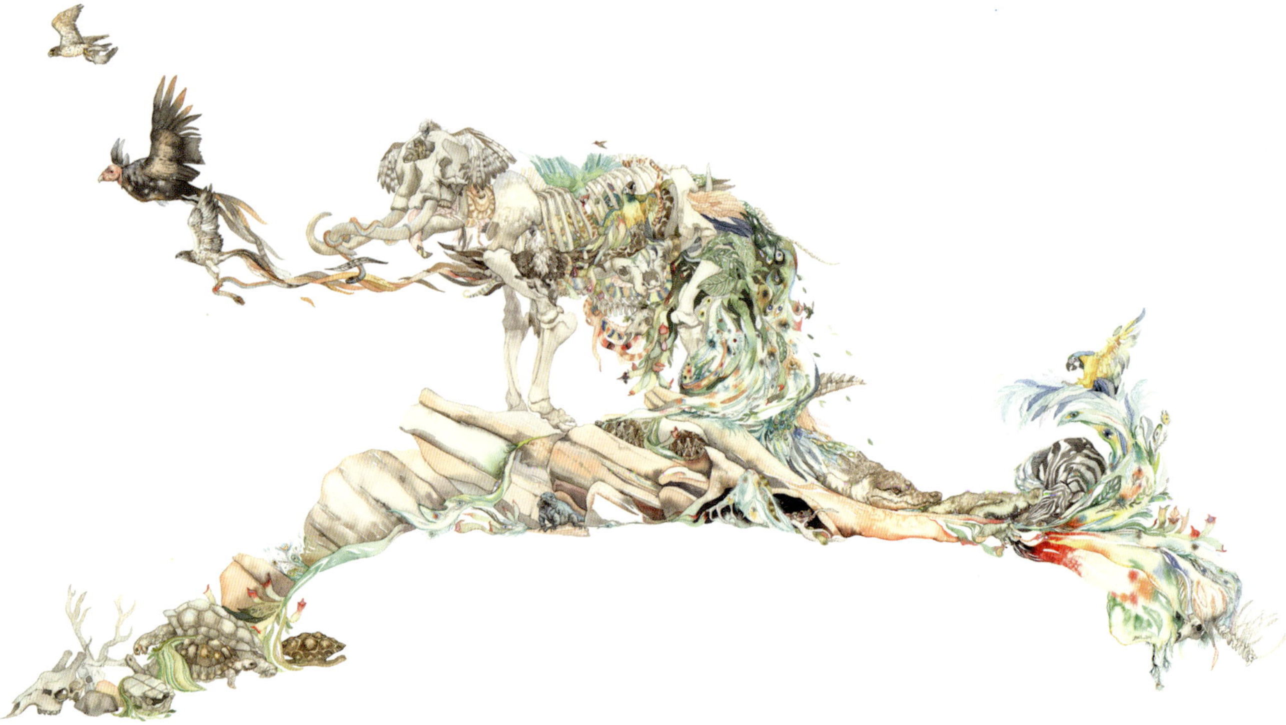

OUTPOURING, 52" X 33", WATERCOLOR AND GRAPHITE ON PAPER

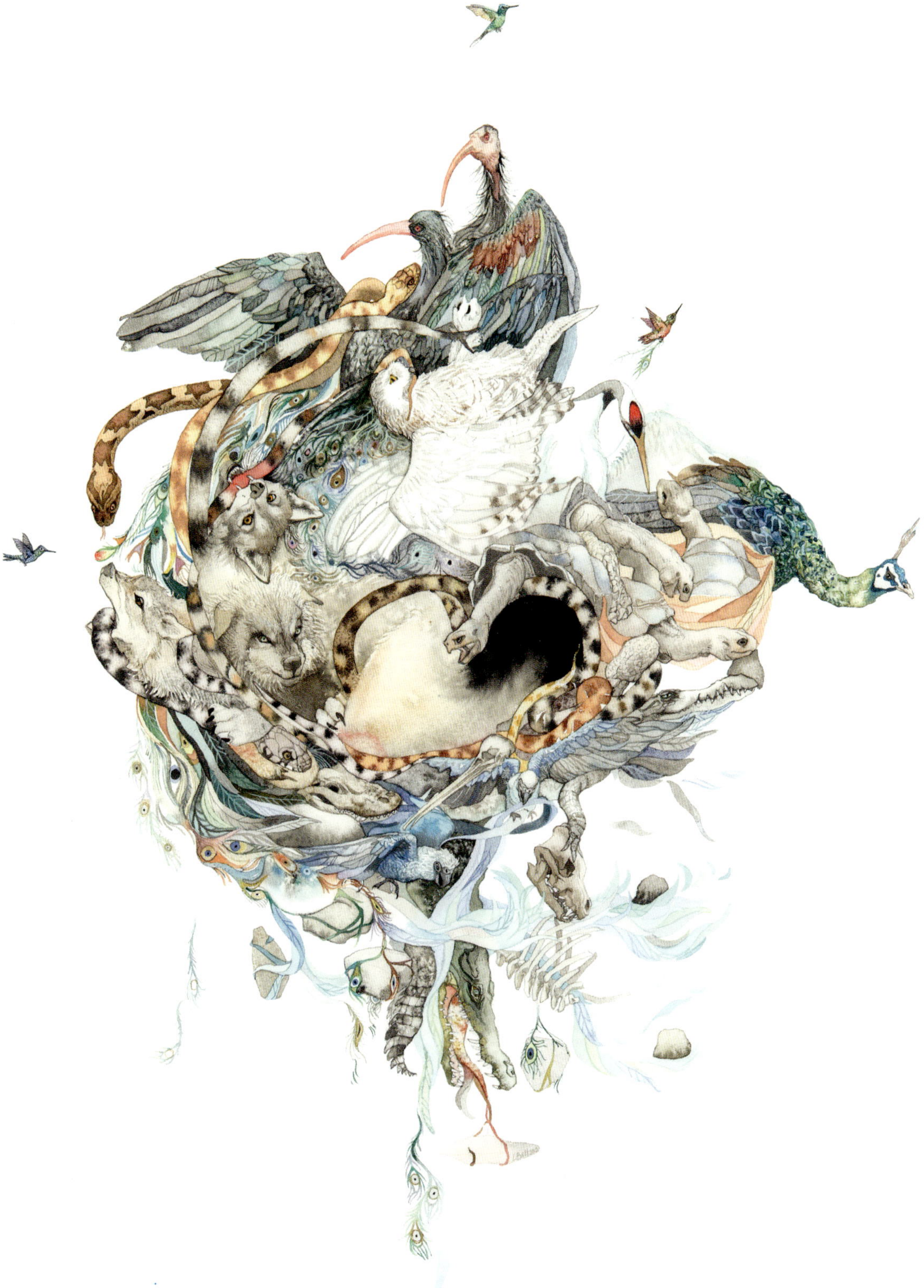

CERBERUS MANDALA, 22" X 30", WATERCOLOR AND GRAPHITE ON PAPER

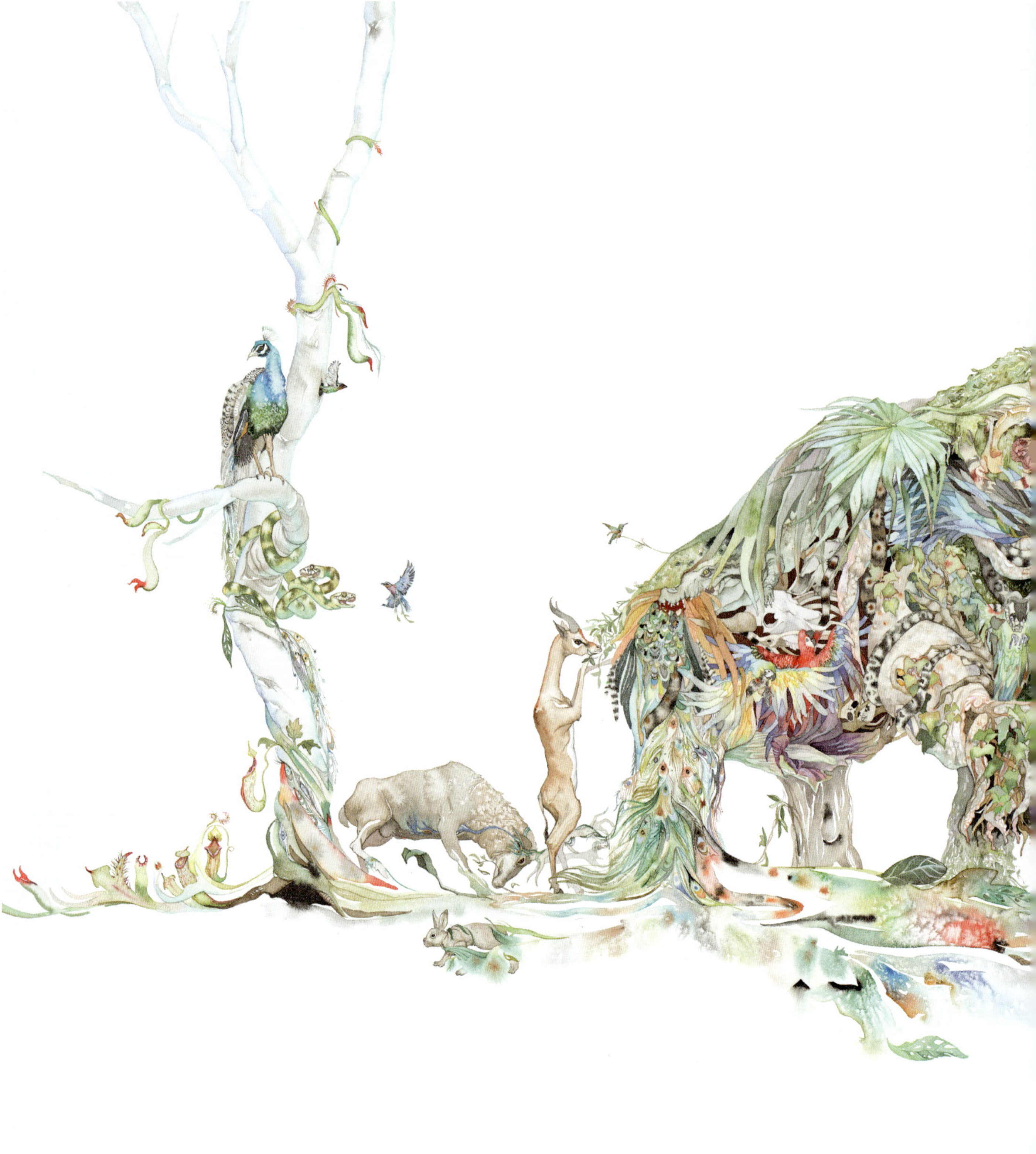

SYMBIOSIS (DETAIL), 52" X 32", WATERCOLOR AND GRAPHITE ON PAPER

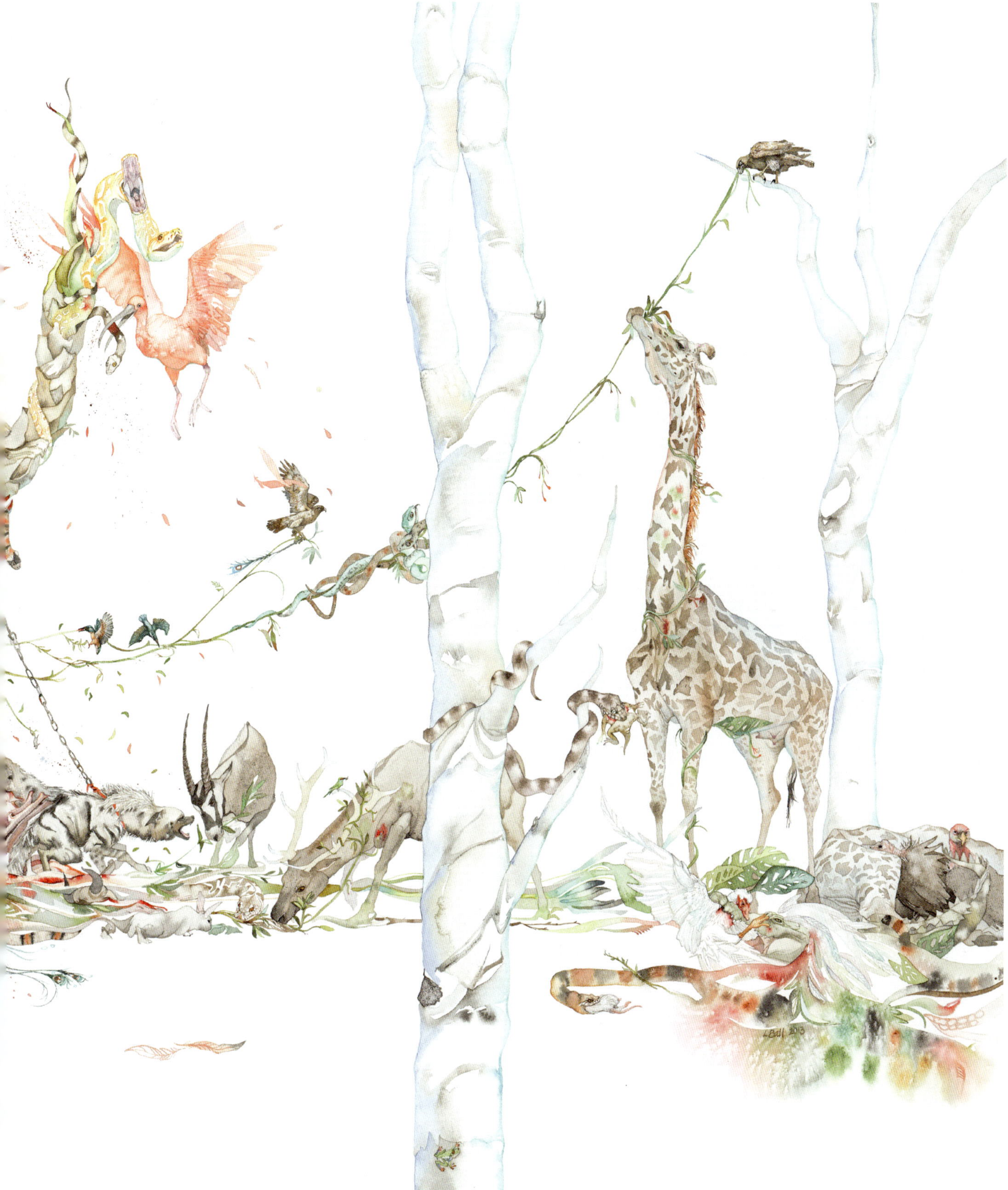

KEVIN EARL TAYLOR

SAN FRANCISCO, CALIFORNIA

Subconscious Activism

There are so many issues that deserve attention. I try to stay educated about as many as I can. Overfishing and harvesting, declining populations, and climate change are a few that remain suspended in a state of emergency. In spite of all the damage we've done in a short period of time, I do my best to stay positive and direct my energy toward being productive and insightful. Subconsciously, I'm sure that I embed my concerns within my work by making paintings that prompt interest in the natural world. I can only hope that my contribution might support, influence, and inspire efforts towards preservation and change.

Get Real

I grew up interacting with all sorts of animals. Most days of the week, I'd go fishing with my grandparents out on a lake. I'd look at the seagulls and wonder about the dead fish floating upside down in the water. I loved the rare sight of a snake crossing the road. I tried to catch birds, raccoons, turtles, and insects with homemade traps my uncle and I would make. I remember being careful not to harm my prisoners and would let them go right away, though occasionally, I kept a few as pets. I have so many memories of running around with dirty hands, actually taking part in nature. I was a wild child in a more literal way and it must have had an affect on me.

I can't remember my reasoning at the time, but when I was in high school, I became a pescetarian—a choice I haven't strayed from in twenty-nine years. I probably would have gone complete vegetarian, but I think I felt OK eating fish since I had caught and prepared so many to be eaten with my own hands. Once I started making art, I think I just drew from subjects that I'd had the most experience with. My early work had plenty of animals, but there were humans, text and inorganic objects all the same. That stuff was based much more on free association and improvisation. I called them "abstract narratives." As my work developed, I simplified things more and more, and moved further away from stylization. Using realism and human-less imagery became a way to provide solitude to the viewer, invoke mystery and present beauty, all of which remain important aspects of my approach.

The Tree Whisperer

There was this guy named Rudy Mancke who I think had a profound affect on me as a kid. He had a TV show on South Carolina public television called *Nature Scene*. Each week, he'd have a new guest join him and they would just walk around the woods in different areas of the state. He would talk about plants, animals, and whatever else they came across that he found interesting. To me, he seemed to know so much about everything. He was an artist for sure. Someone of the same spirit as Jacques Cousteau or John Muir, who were also driven visionaries, emphasizing the importance of preserving natural resources long before it became a mainstream topic.

Southern Solitude

I've always felt at ease on the edge of the ocean. I love the sights and smells of the California coastline, but the beaches of South Carolina, where I grew up, are just as amazing. There are a few island preserves, so no one can live on them, and you have to visit them in a little boat. You can take a friend or two, your dog, and find yourself all alone there. There are twisted driftwood branches, white sand, inland creeks, and even alligators. It's hot, but the water is perfect, and you just jump in to cool off a bit and let the sun dry you off. I love the woods and finding a lake with a mound of perfect skipping rocks. The mountains, waterfalls and hot springs—it's really all one big thing.

THE GHOSTS OF THE FOREST SHARE OUR BERRIES, 13" X 10", GOUACHE ON BLOTTER PAPER

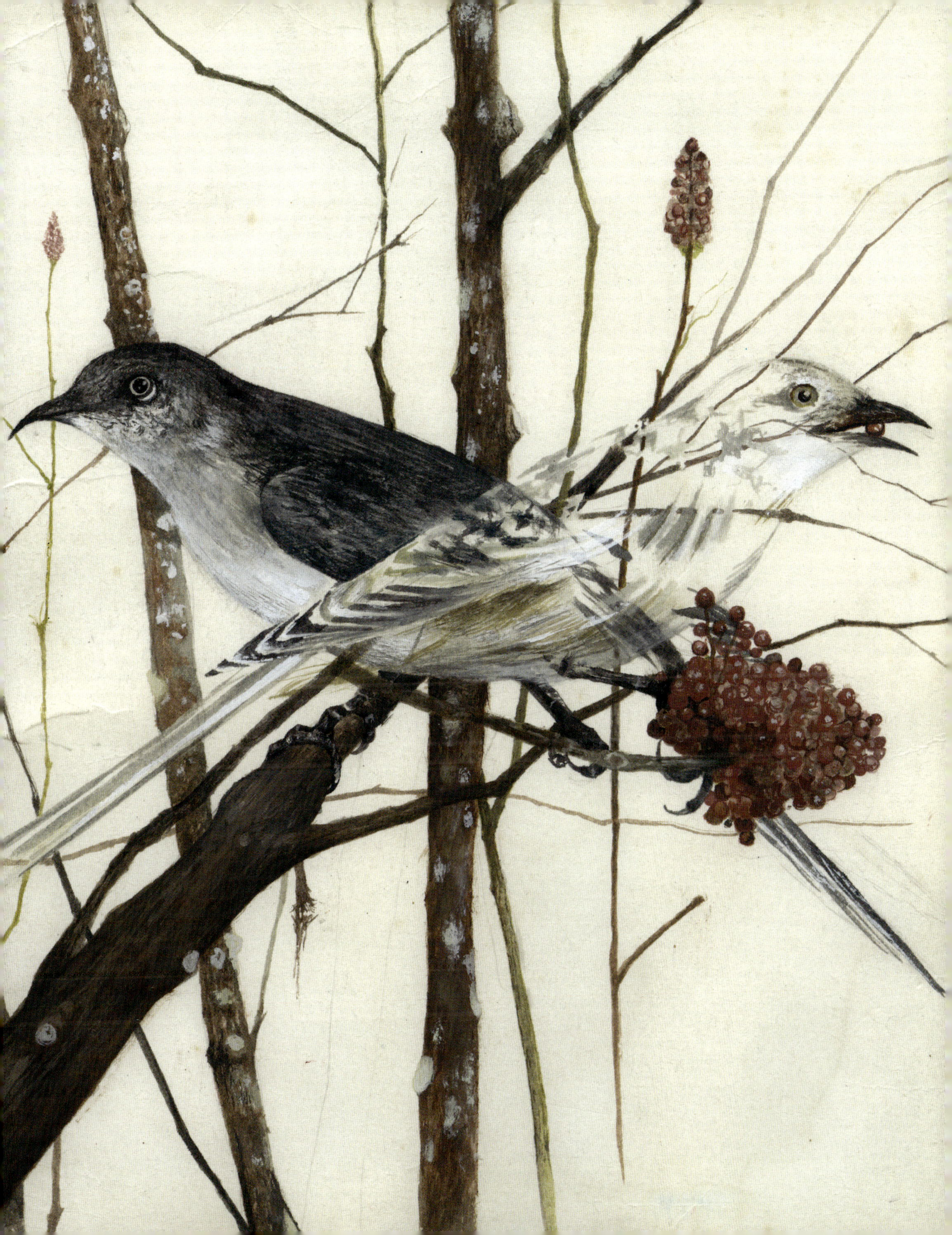

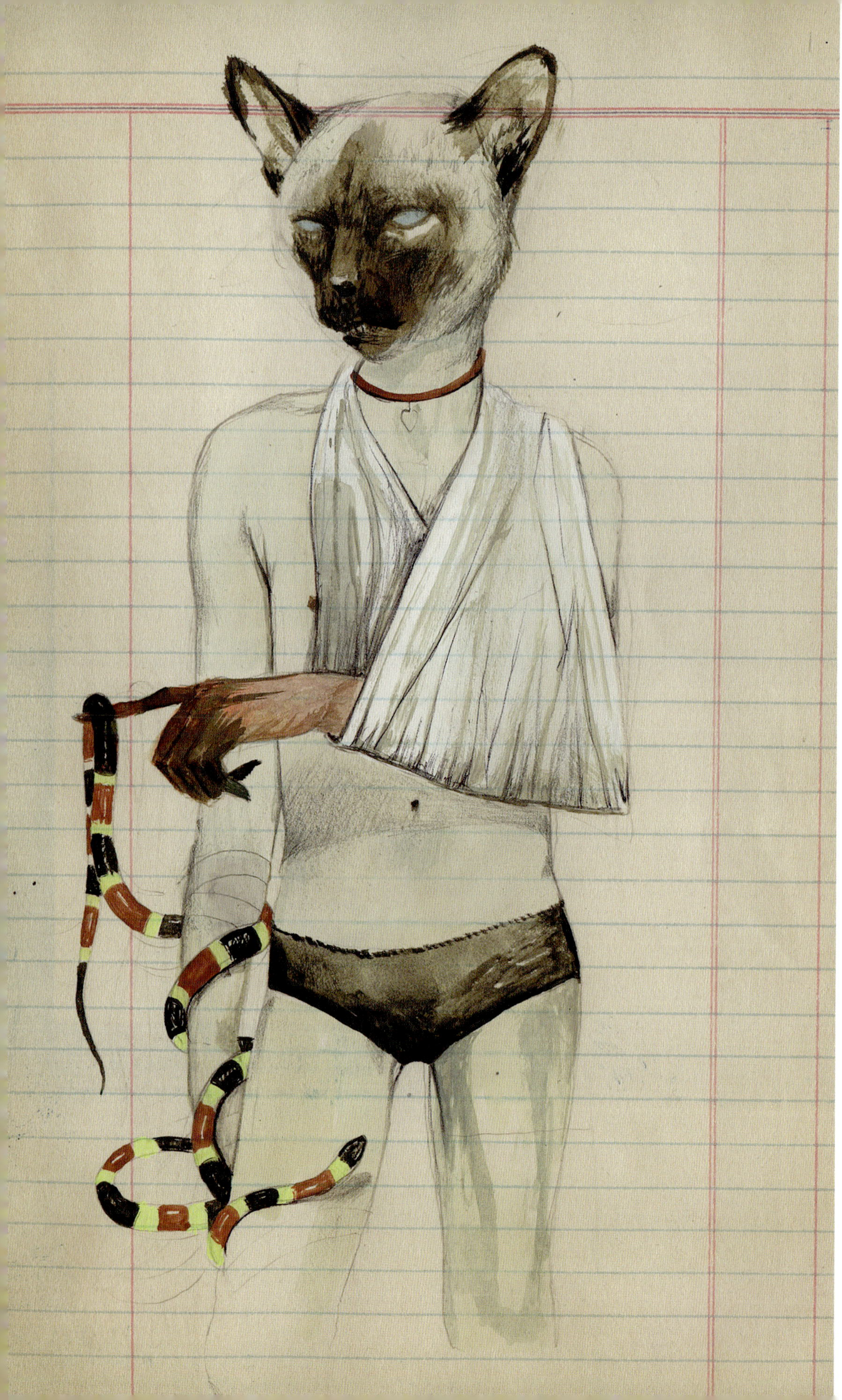

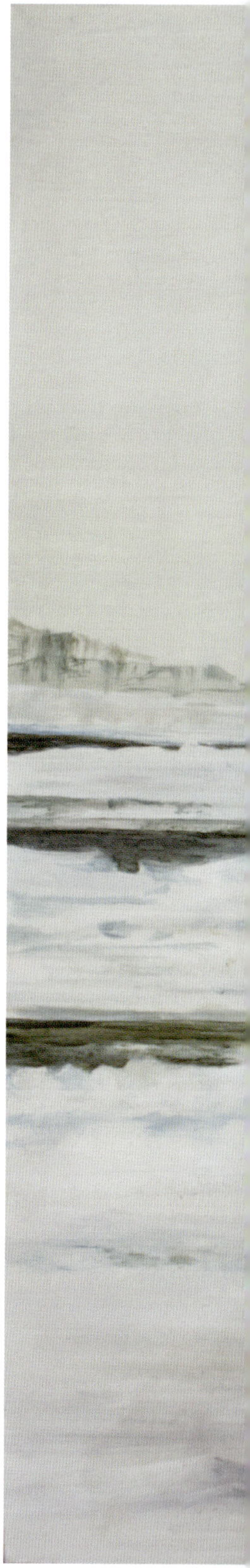

TOURNIQUET,
8" X 6",
OIL ON PANEL

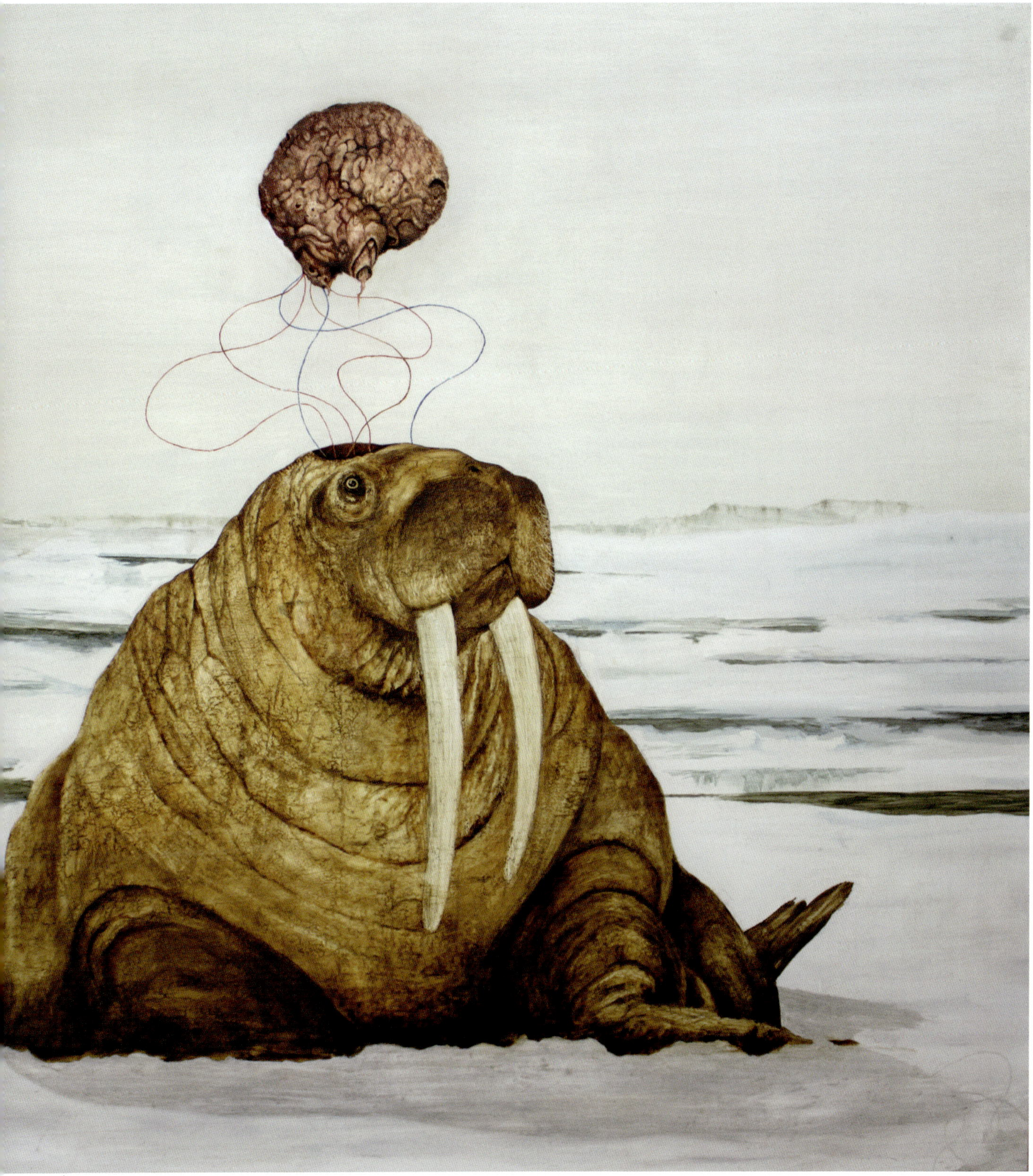

FRIGID INTELLECT, 48" X 48", OIL ON PANEL

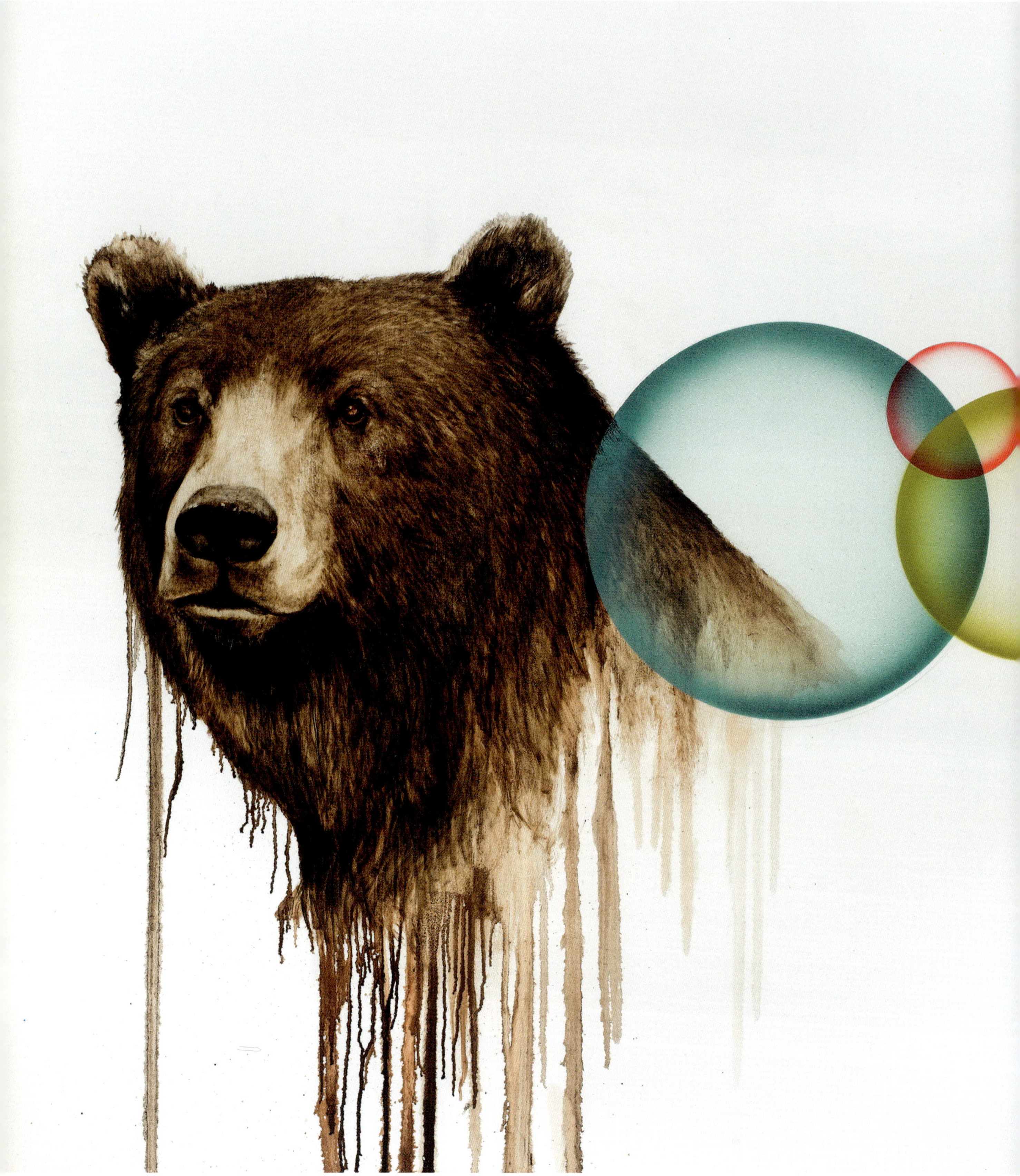

GENETIC ENERGY, 36" X 48", OIL AND ACRYLIC ON PANEL

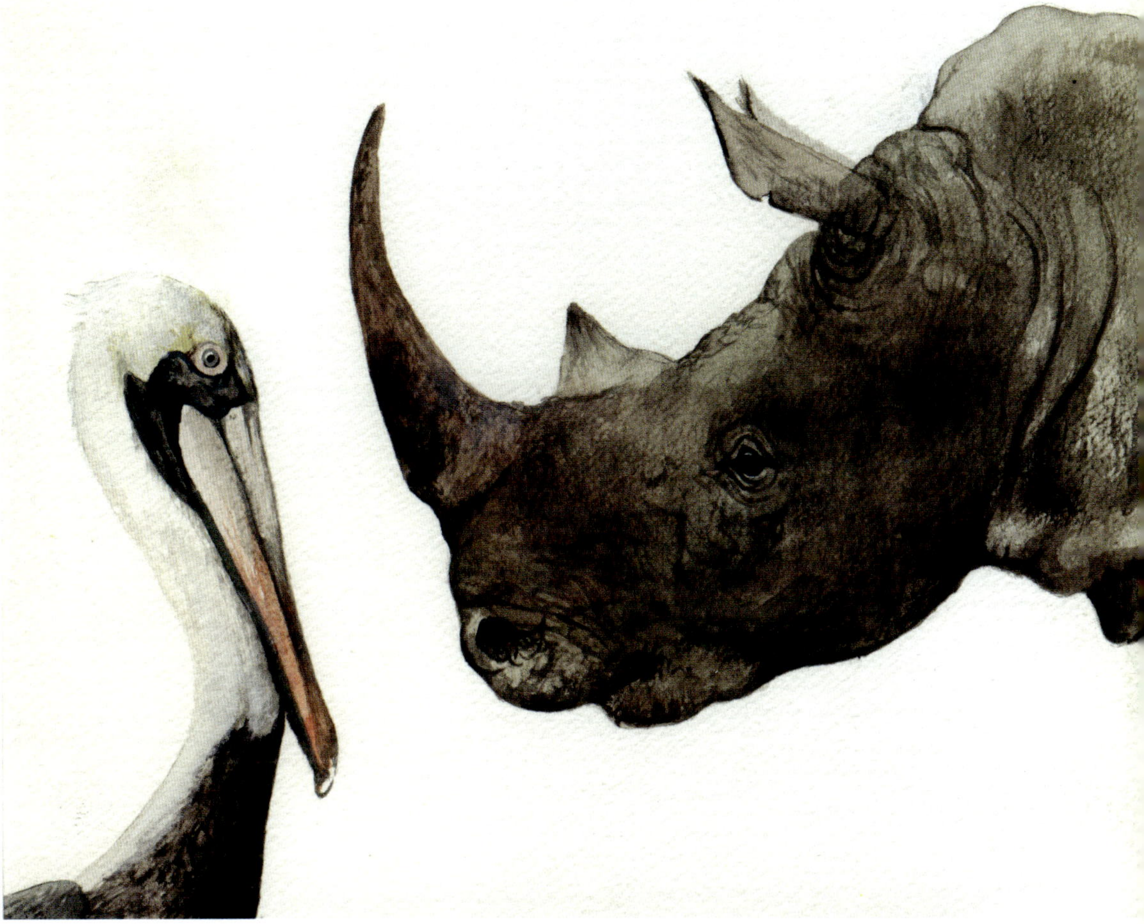

NEGOTIATION, 8" X 8", GOUACHE ON PAPER

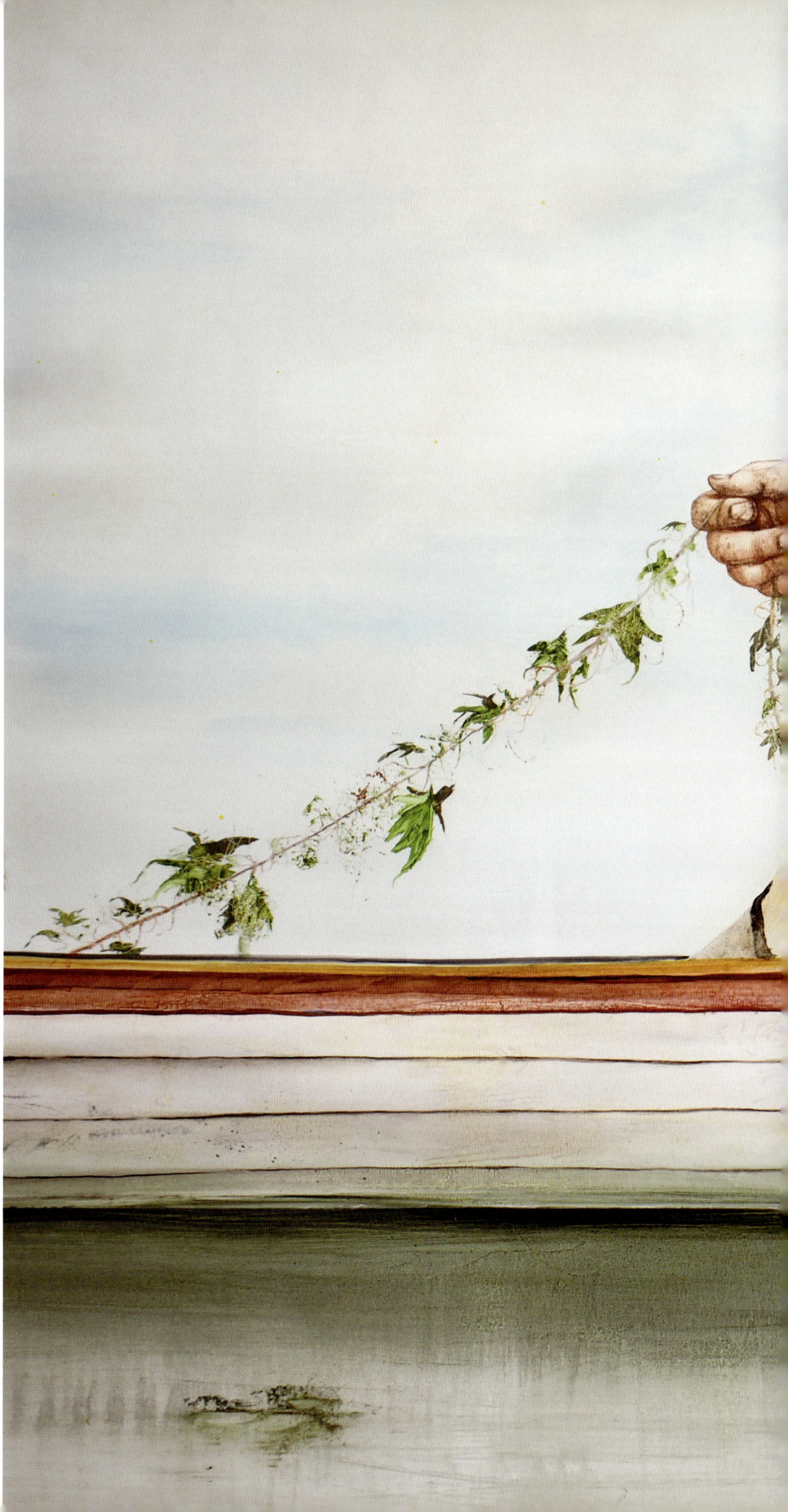

APPROACH
84" X 132"
OIL ON CANVAS

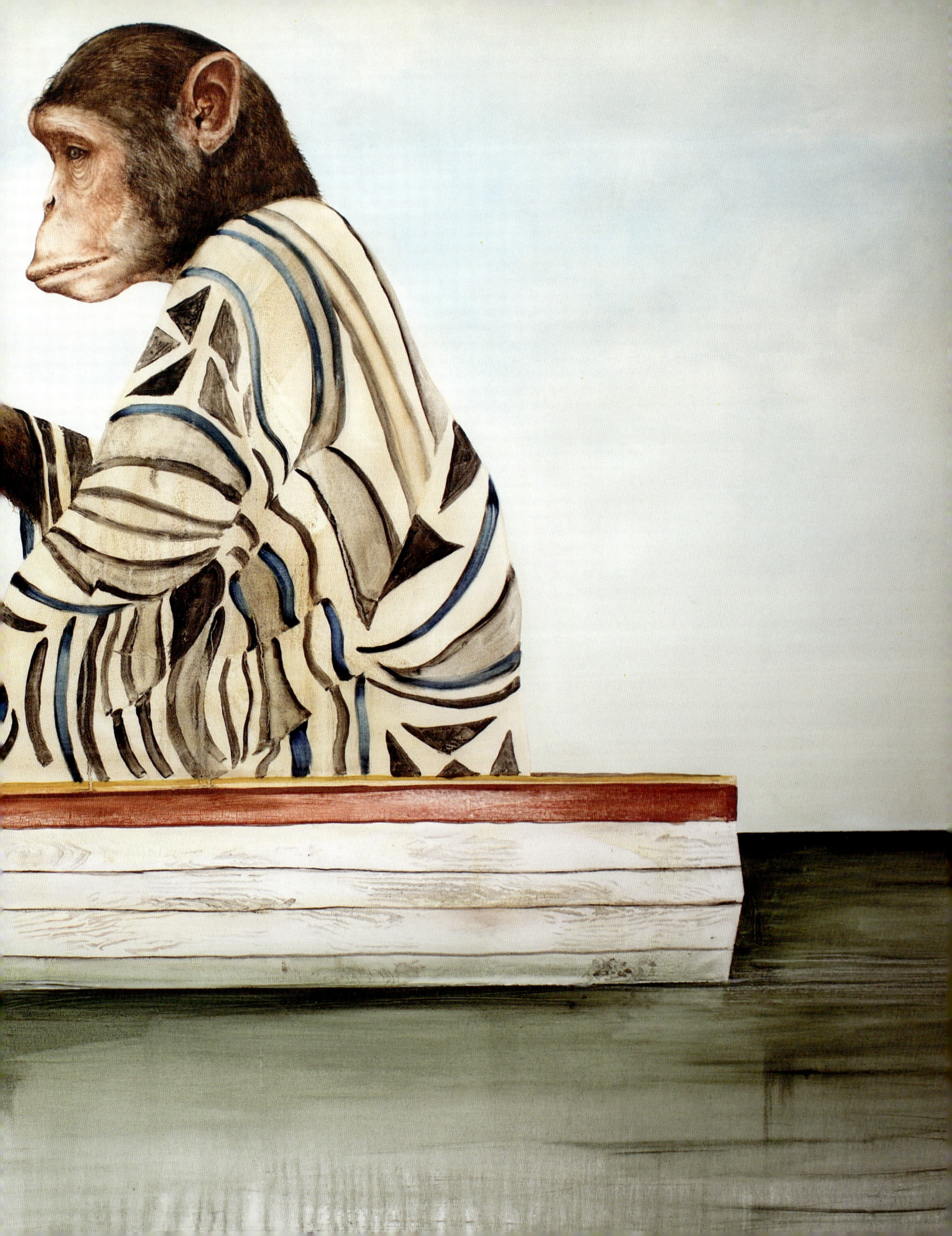

ROA

GHENT, BELGIUM

No Time To Waste

In this global society, in my opinion, it's impossible not to have heard or experienced any environmental concerns unless you are ignorant to them. When I was a teenager, we would wear Greenpeace T-shirts with big letters, "No Time To Waste," and I feel there's been lots of precious time wasted the past years—politics about depleting oil sources intertwining with war and environmental disasters. The way humanity threatens the planet, led by corporate politics, is too surreal for my understanding. Most of my attention on these topics goes to the effects on the animal species; how animals lost territory, which sometimes leads to extinction. When I arrive on the location where I will paint, I mostly do some research about the local fauna and also about the way local society or politics are engaging with their surrounding nature.

Wall of Wonders

I've been drawn to animals since I was a kid; animals have always been an inspiration for my drawings. Of course, the way I portray them became different as I grew up. In murals and artwork, they represent the whole transition from birth to carrion, from asleep to alive, from static to dynamic, in close relation to humanity. Painting large murals in an urban landscape is a bit like repopulating the city, almost as a memorial wall for the native animals that lost their land to human settlement.

Pushing the Wrong Boundaries

Fear is a bad adviser, but I am personally very concerned about Africa and Asia; the rhino killings, industrial agriculture and more exploitations. But my biggest fear is the outcome if people keep pushing the borders, pushing ourselves over the cliff, and further opening Pandora's box.

A Varied Influence

Aboriginal art, in general, is an influence, and also contemporary installation artists. Historically, I am interested in Animalier painters and still life painters such as Chardin, and Zurbarán's paintings of sheep. Many different times and styles are incidental but personally inspiring for my art.

The Best Compliment

I wouldn't necessarily describe my work as political. Probably every depiction and expression can be related somehow to our contemporary world. My works are reflections about life, and if that can lead to awareness of some kind, that's a big compliment.

Painting About Where You Are

The chosen animals are almost always native to the place I am painting; the animal will represent the location, but in close relation to the wall's shape and context. The context will determine my choice. Every place is different in many ways, and that is what contextual muralism is about; you take notice of the location and try to incorporate it into your mural, physically and mentally.

The Savanna

I like desolate beaches, but also savannas and forests—and in this perspective, Africa is amazing.

JOHANNESBURG STILL LIFE, LATEX PAINT AND SPRAY PAINT

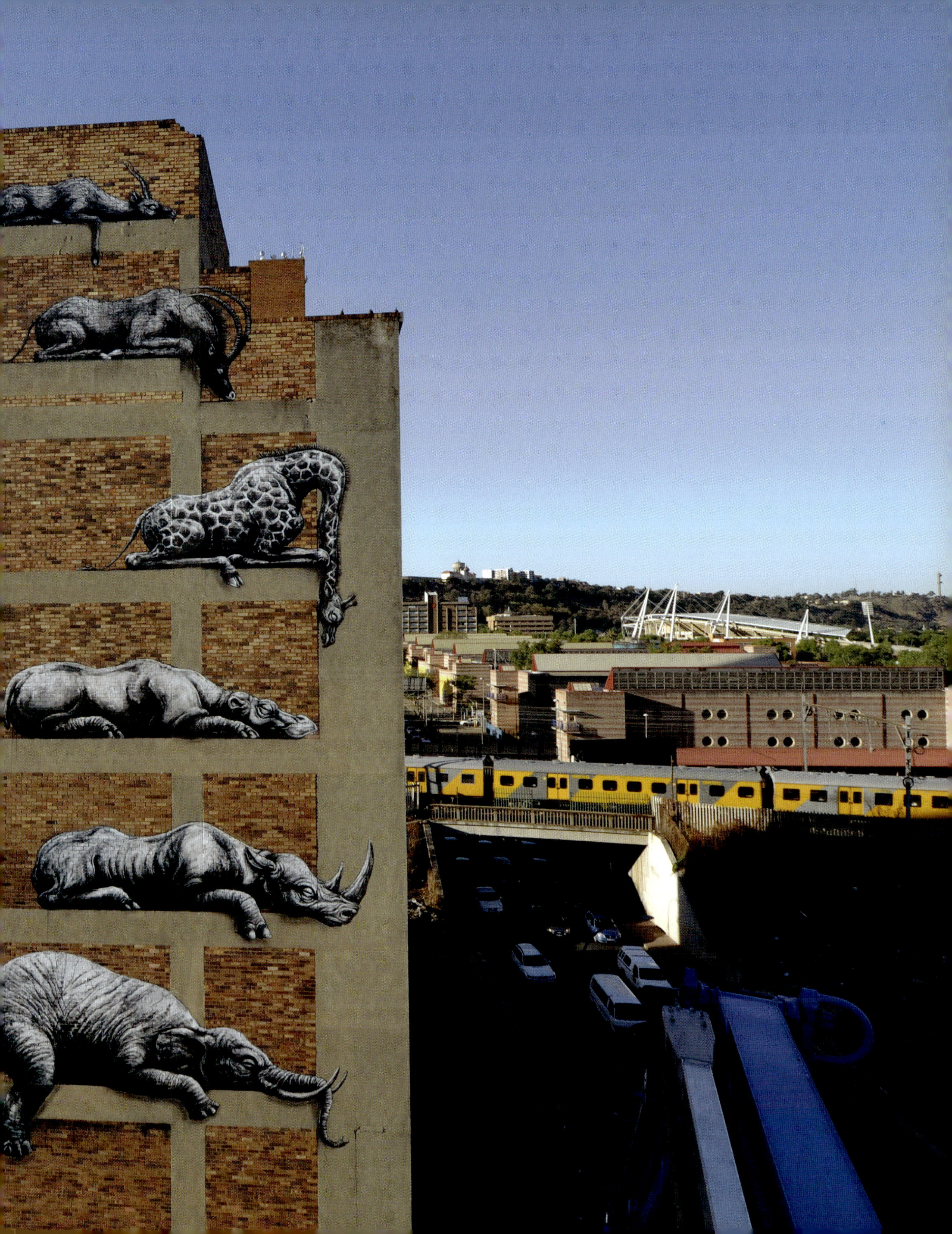

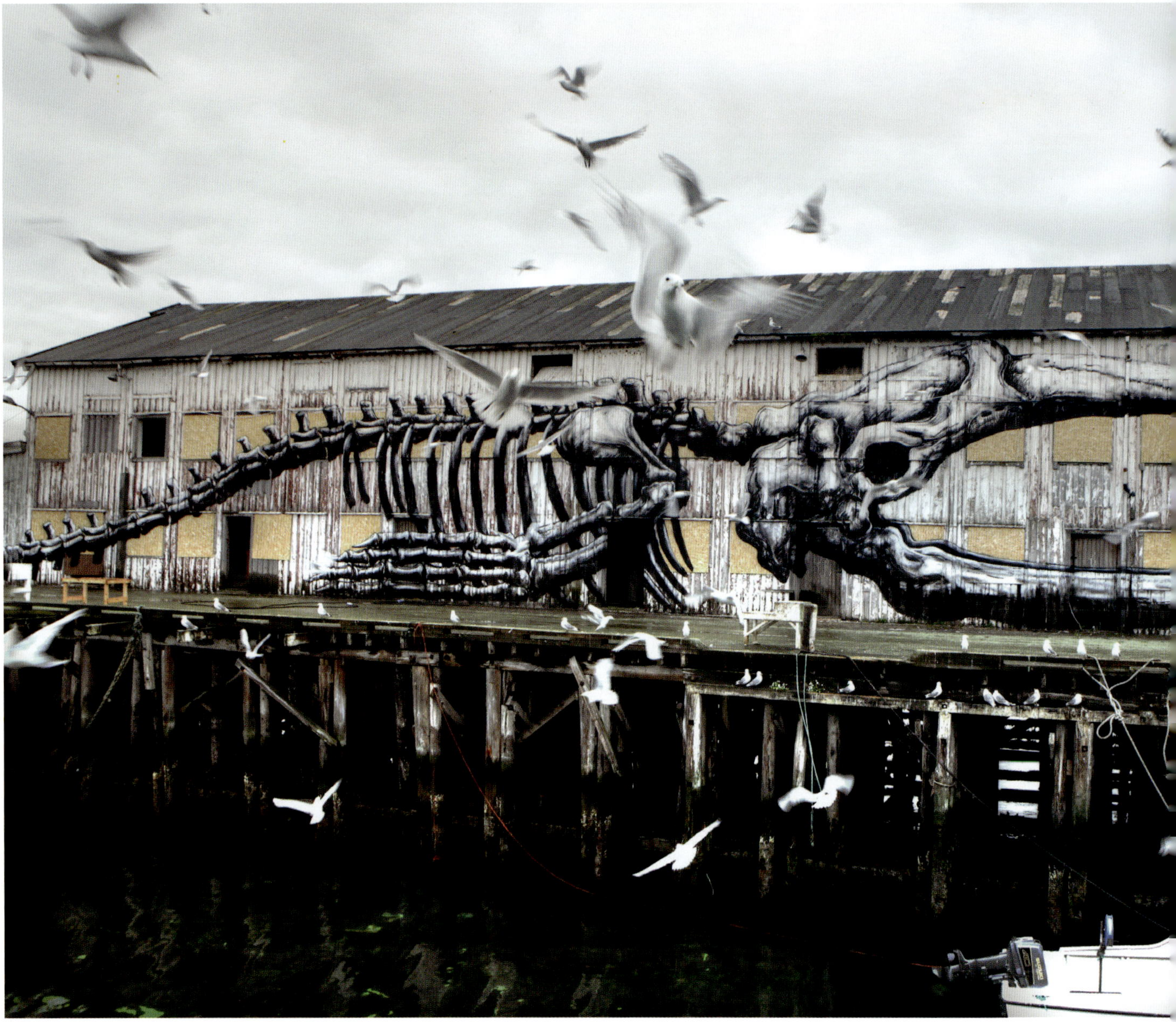

VARDØ WHALE SKELETON (NORWAY), LATEX PAINT AND SPRAY PAINT, PHOTO BY IAN COX

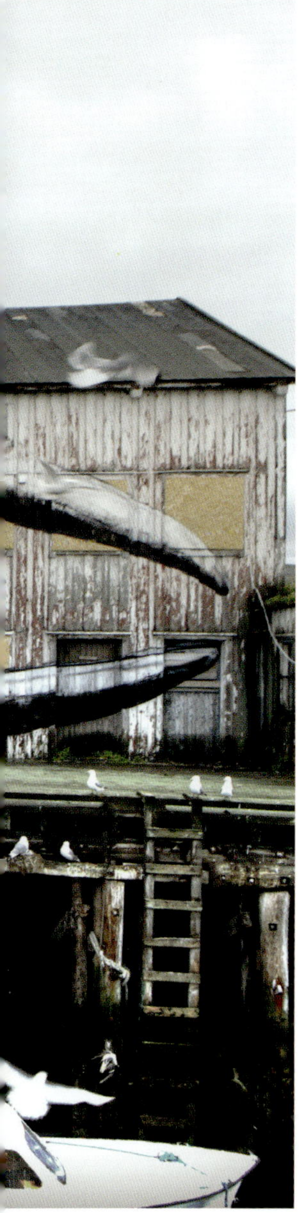

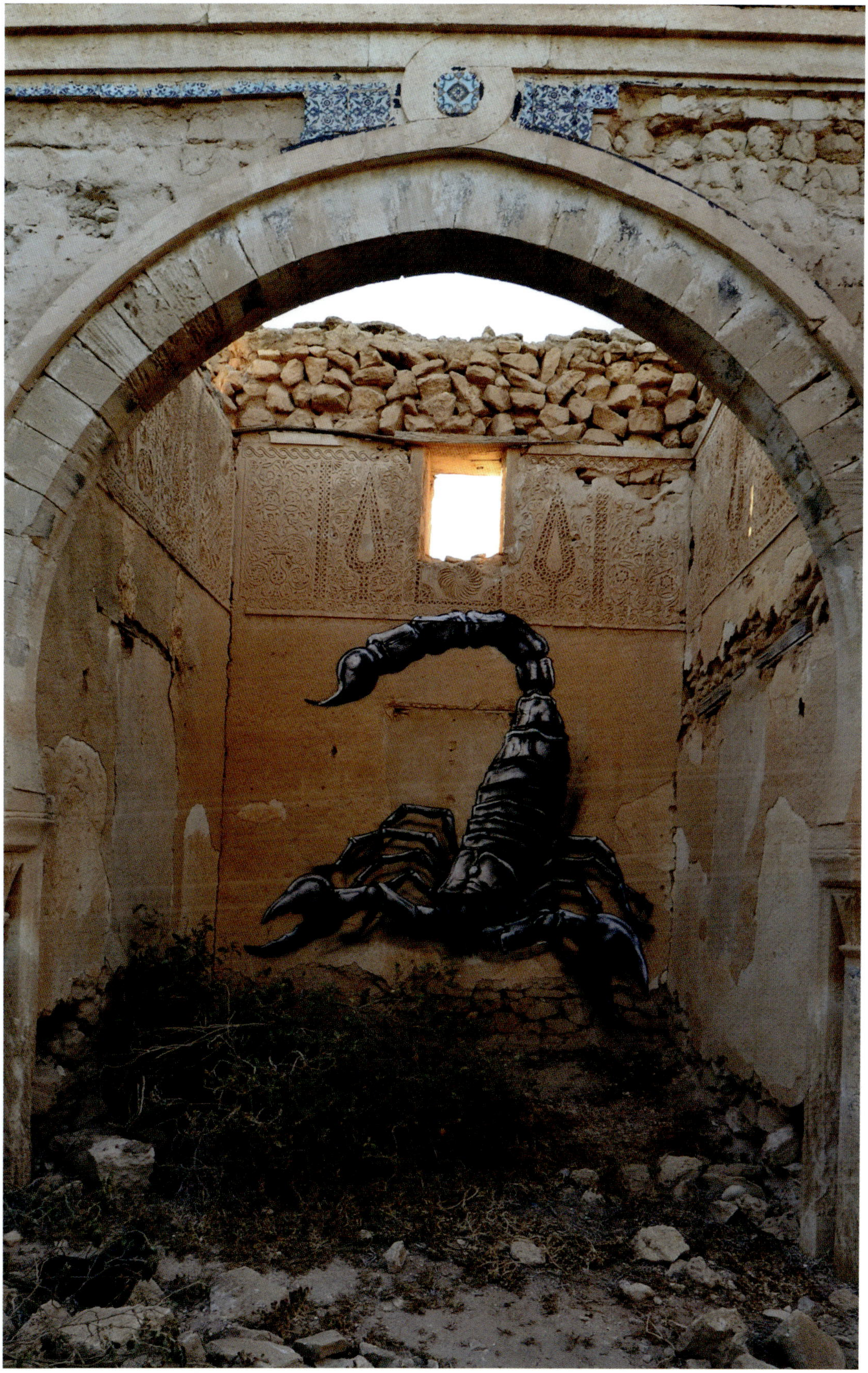

DJERBA SCORPION
LATEX PAINT AND
SPRAY PAINT

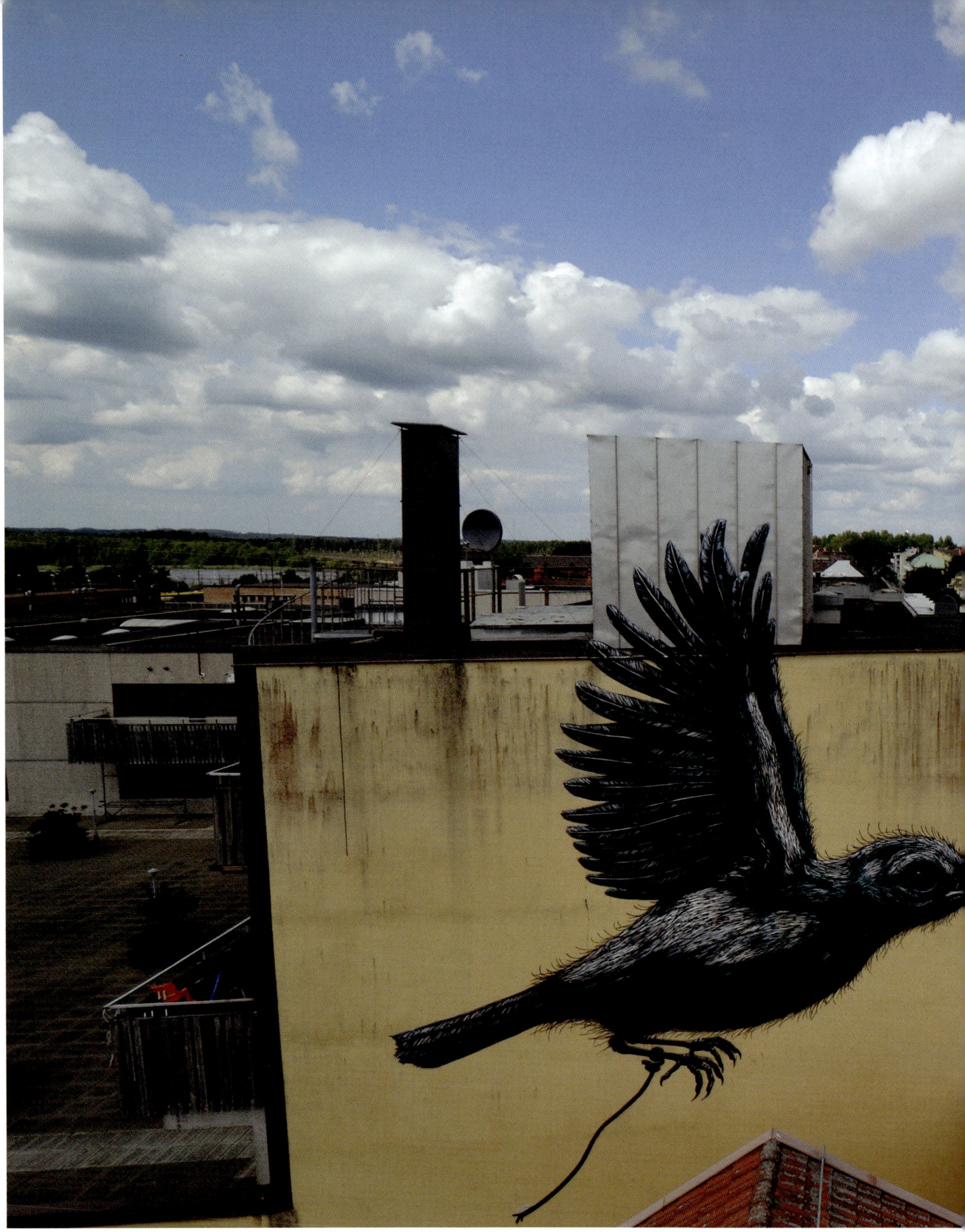

NÄSSJÖ BIRD, LATEX PAINT AND SPRAY PAINT

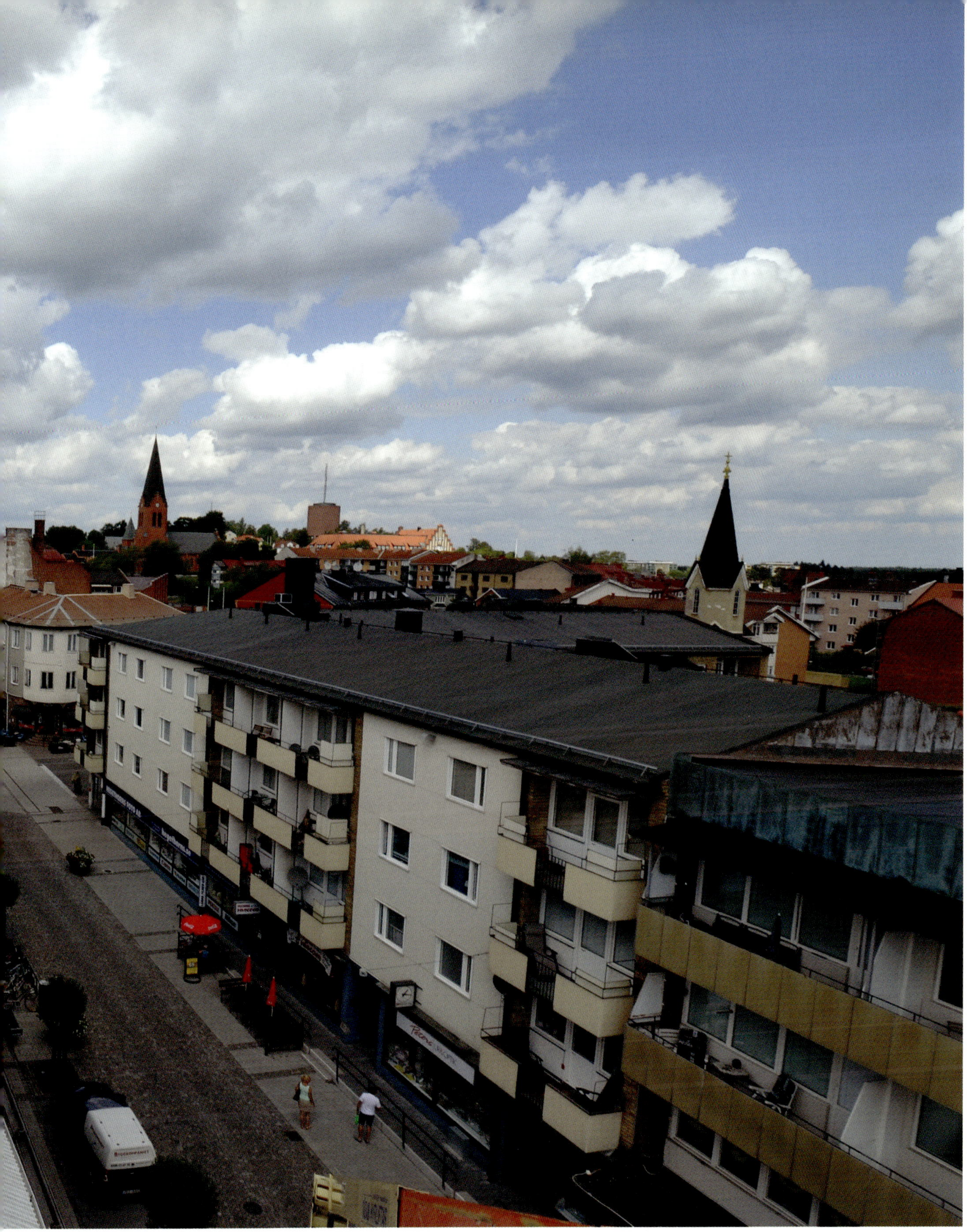

COREY ARNOLD

PORTLAND, OREGON AND THE NORTH PACIFIC OCEAN

The Double Life
I come from a unique perspective in that I live a double life as an artist and a commercial fisherman, and I grew up in a farming family. I'm personally responsible for the deaths of millions of crab and fish, all in the name of seafood. Our family farmed avocados, so I grew up shooting squirrels, gophers and rabbits as critter control. Meanwhile, my cat slept on my face at night, and I volunteered daily at a wildlife rescue center down the street. I suppose that I'm more of a realist when it comes to environmental issues, so I choose my battles carefully.

Embedded Activism
My work often explores the subject of human and animal relationships with a curiosity towards modern man's place in the natural world. I've started to use my photography as a voice to bring awareness to issues that concern me. When a large, open-pit copper mine named Pebble Mine was proposed upriver from the sockeye salmon grounds that gave me my start as a commercial fisherman in Alaska, I began documenting the fishermen and communities that survive off of the millions of salmon that fertilize the ecosystem of Bristol Bay. Separately, I've also been involved with Project Pressure, helping to bring awareness to climate change via glacier photography expeditions.

Facts of Life
I have gotten mostly positive feedback about the work I've done with commercial fisheries. I am pro fish and pro fisherman, but it can be a challenge to please everyone. Fishing is a gritty business and fish don't always look their best when photographed, just like a slaughterhouse photograph doesn't always hang well over the dinner table. That said, I prefer to include the blood and the grit, and show photos that tell the truth. Every fish dies a horrific death and becomes food for something else, whether in nature or by the hand of man. I want Americans to be more realistic about where their food comes from. Our greatest challenge is sustainably harvesting our food in a way is respectful to the future of the planet.

Positive Revolution
I think there will be a mass migration North beginning in my own lifetime. I fear for the future of Alaska and the Arctic, in general, as Earth's growing population takes its toll on some of the wildest land left on Earth. I hope to photograph this change as it happens so that we can all view ourselves from the outside and stay focused on positive changes for our future.

A Critical Eye
One of my influences was the photographer Joel Sternfeld, and particularly the book *American Prospects*. Sternfeld produced a body of work in the '70s and '80s that focused on the changing landscape of America and the challenges we face in pursuit of The American Dream. The images are massive in detail, often focused on the boundaries between human-occupied and wild space. The series lays bare a growing American identity crisis in a very introspective way.

Fjord Fantasy
If you ever see a picture of the Lofoten Islands in Norway, you will never forget it. Lofoten is dotted with small fishing villages docked in fjords, overshadowed by seemingly inverted mountains jutting up from the sea. The waters are swarming with cod, herring and whales. Winters are harsh, and spring brings a brilliance to the light that I've not see elsewhere on Earth. When I close my eyes, I dream of Lofoten.

FIGHT OR FLIGHT, 30" X 40", DIGITAL PIGMENT PRINT

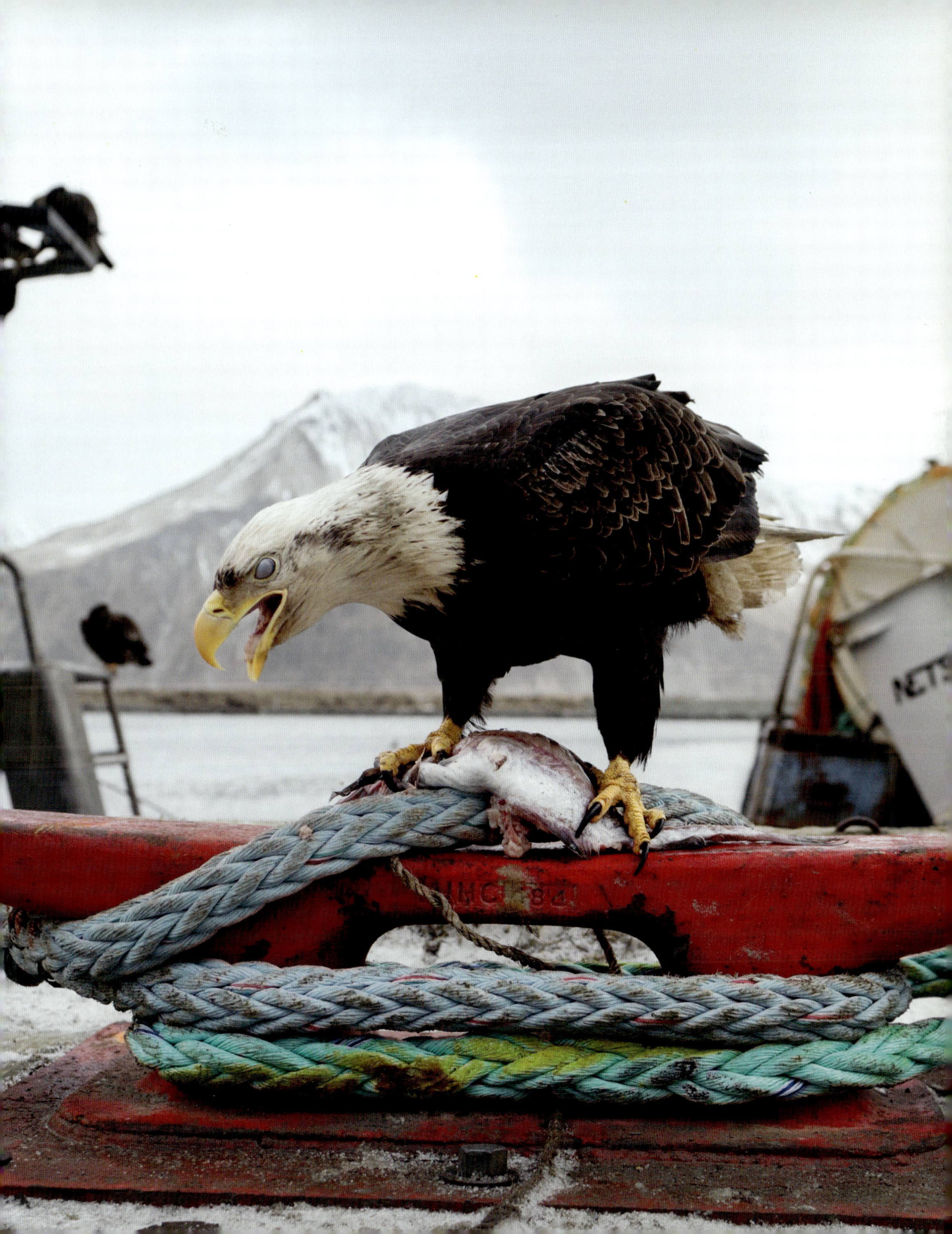

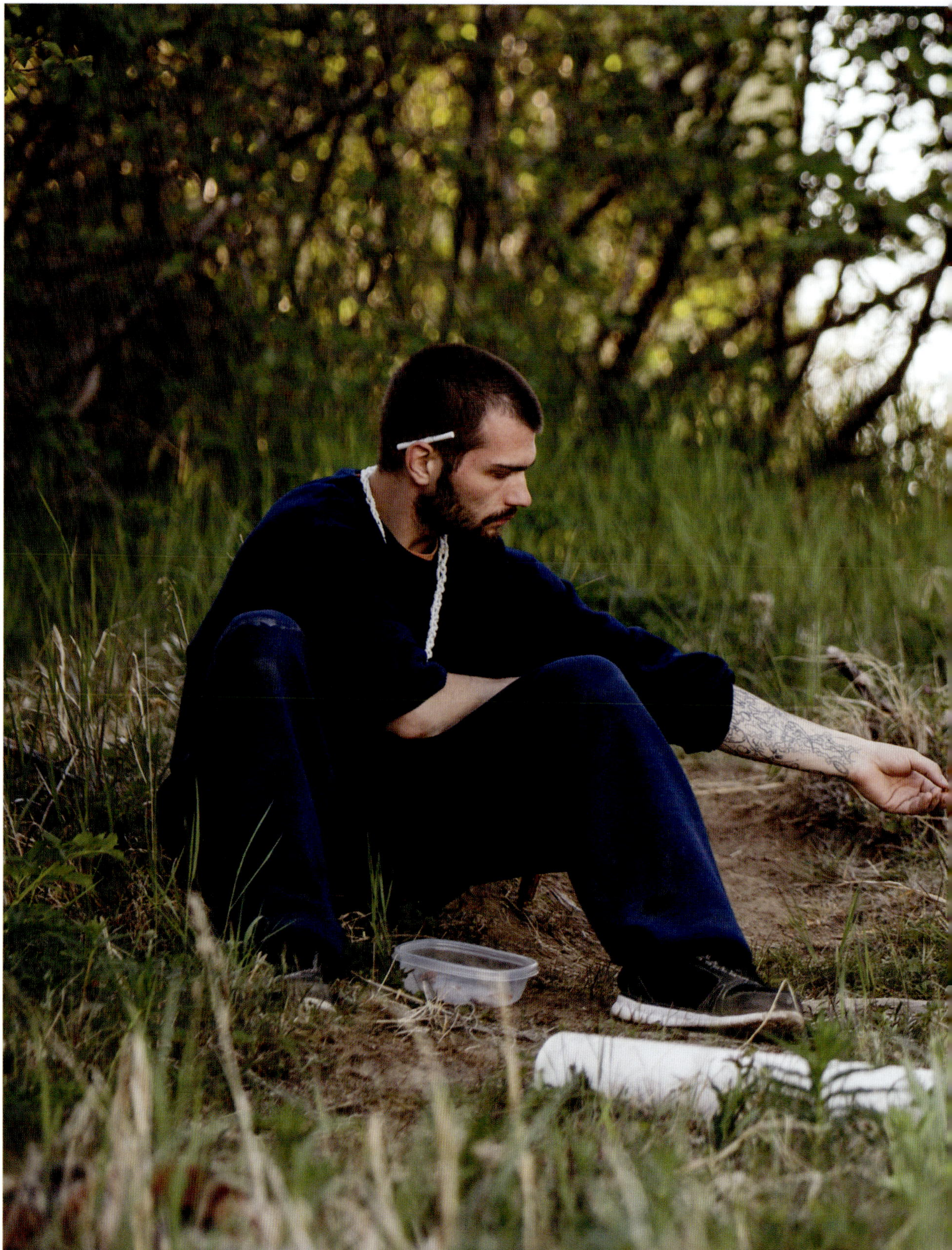

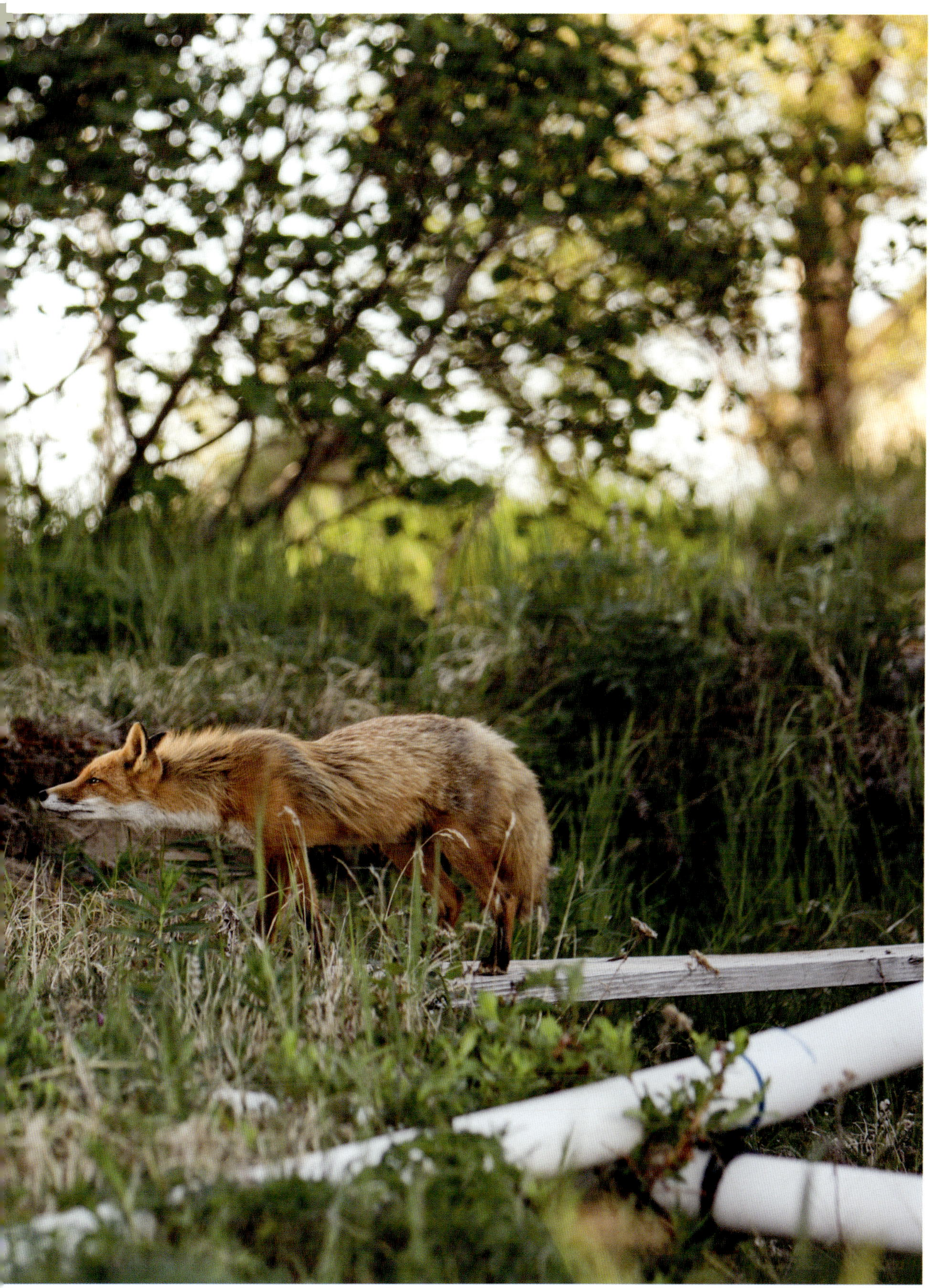

FRIENDS WITH BENEFITS, 20" X 29", DIGITAL PIGMENT PRINT

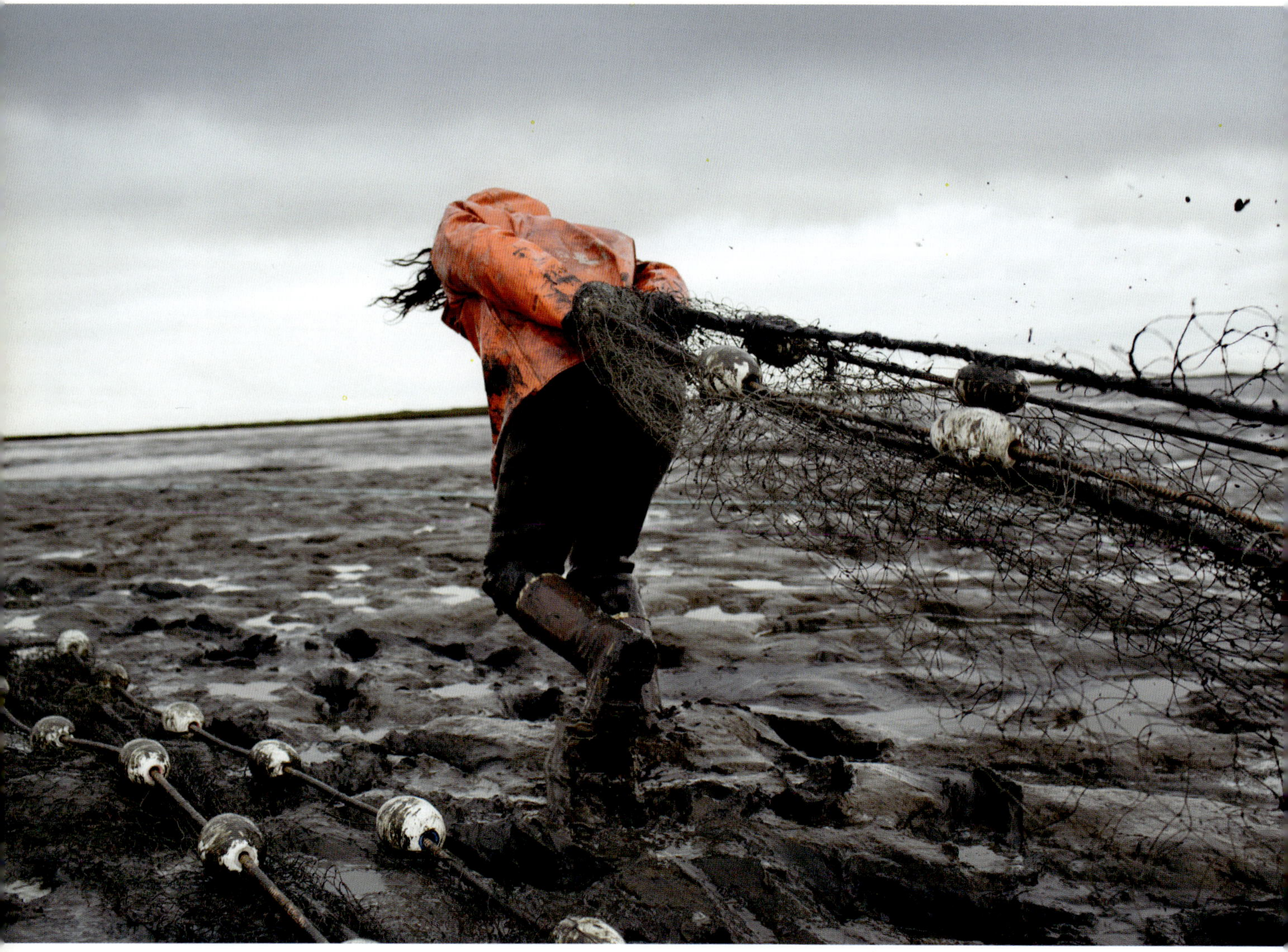

THE MUD SET, 30" X 44", DIGITAL PIGMENT PRINT

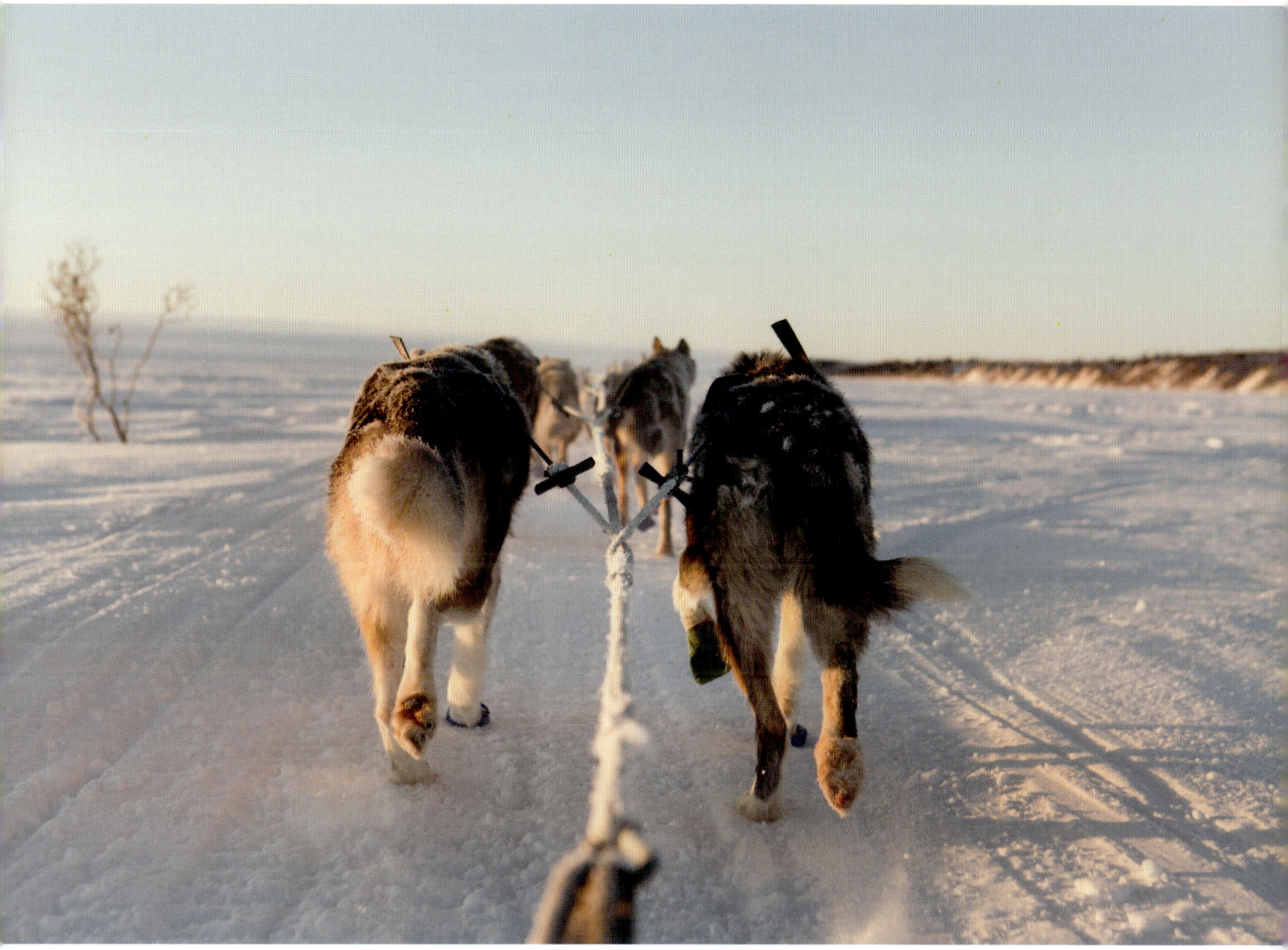

UNTITLED ALASKA, 30" X 40", DIGITAL PIGMENT PRINT

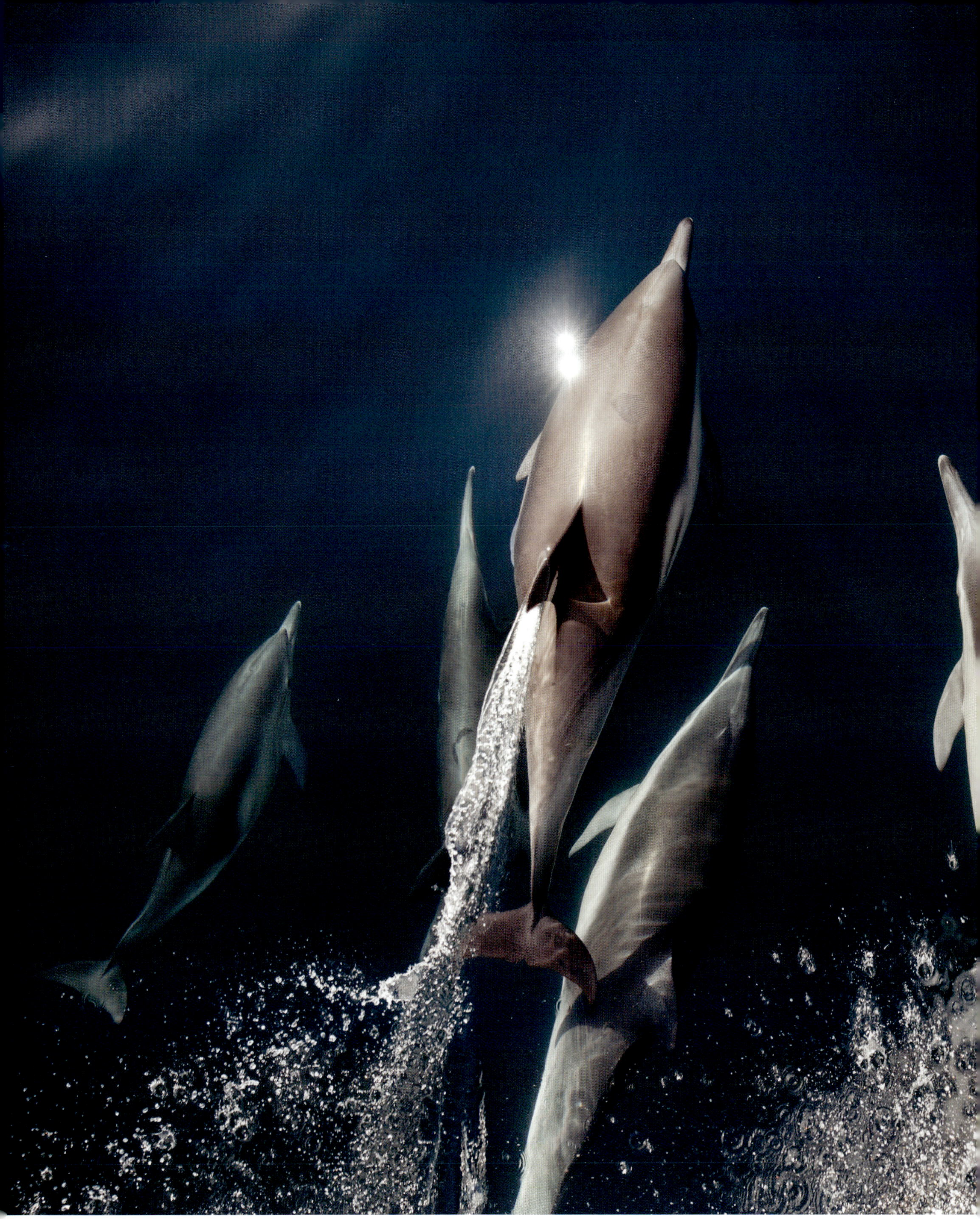

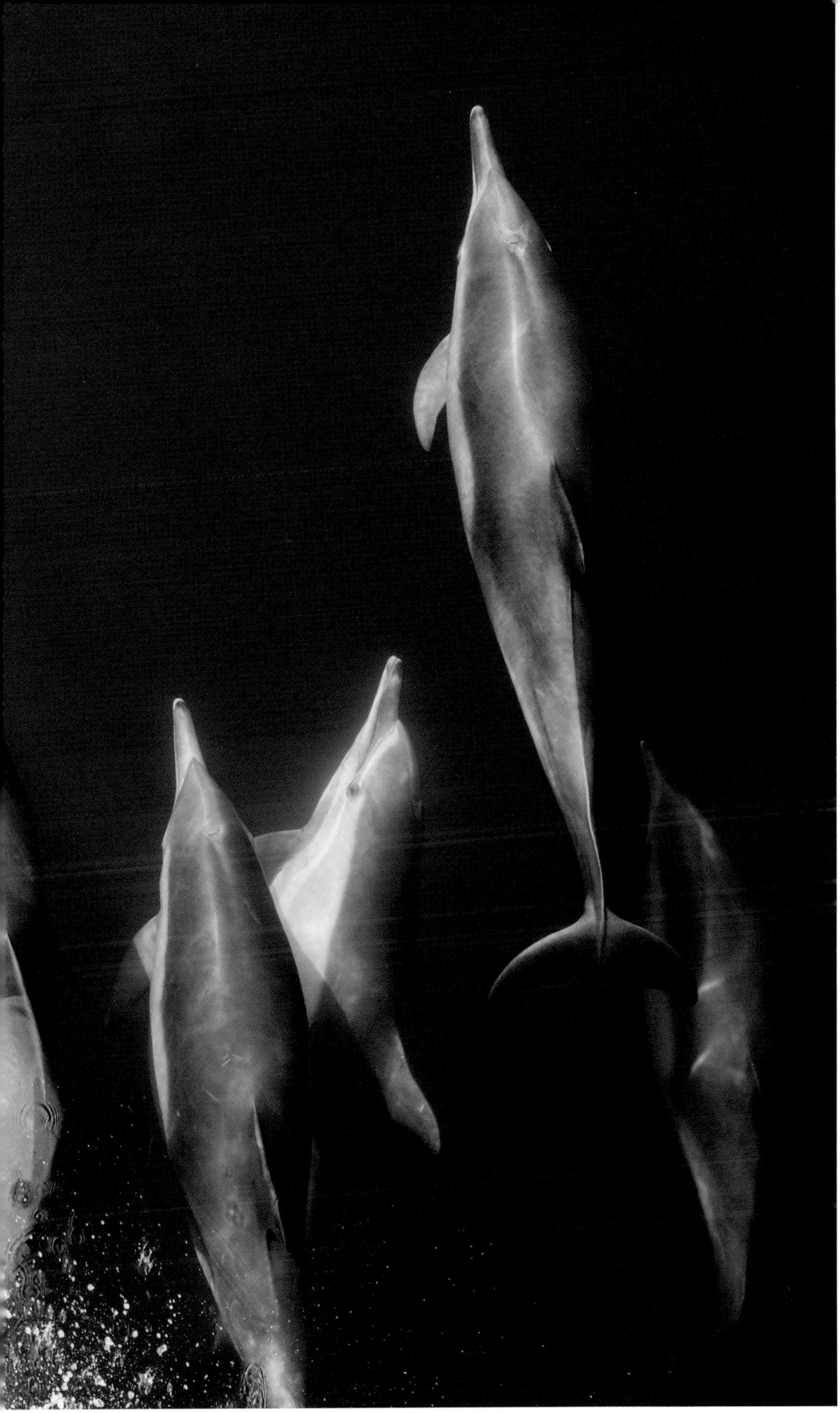

THE MAJESTIC DOLPHIN
30" X 44"
DIGITAL PIGMENT PRINT

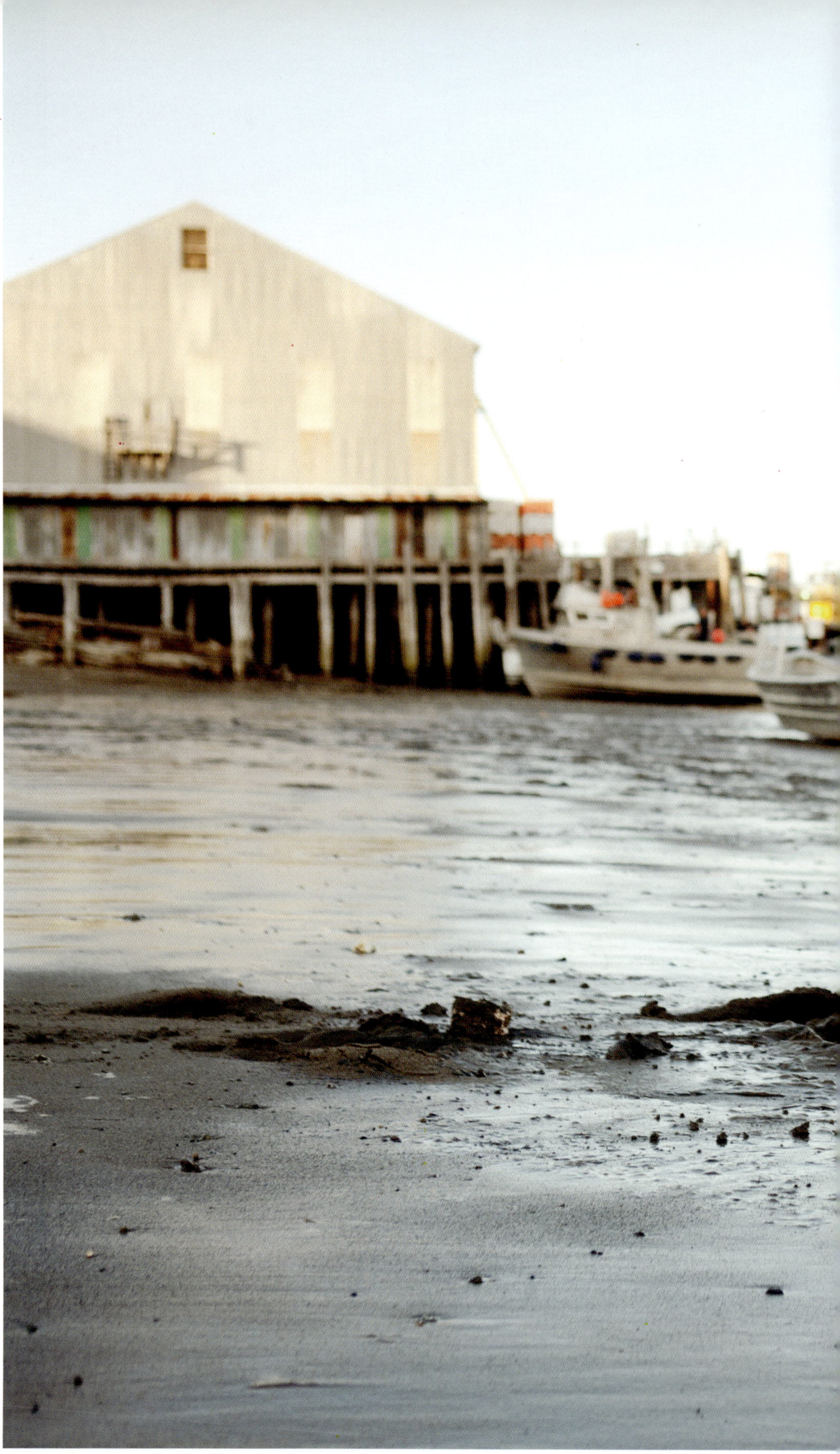

WOUNDED BEAR AT RED SALMON CANNERY (DETAIL)
30" X 44"
DIGITAL PIGMENT PRINT

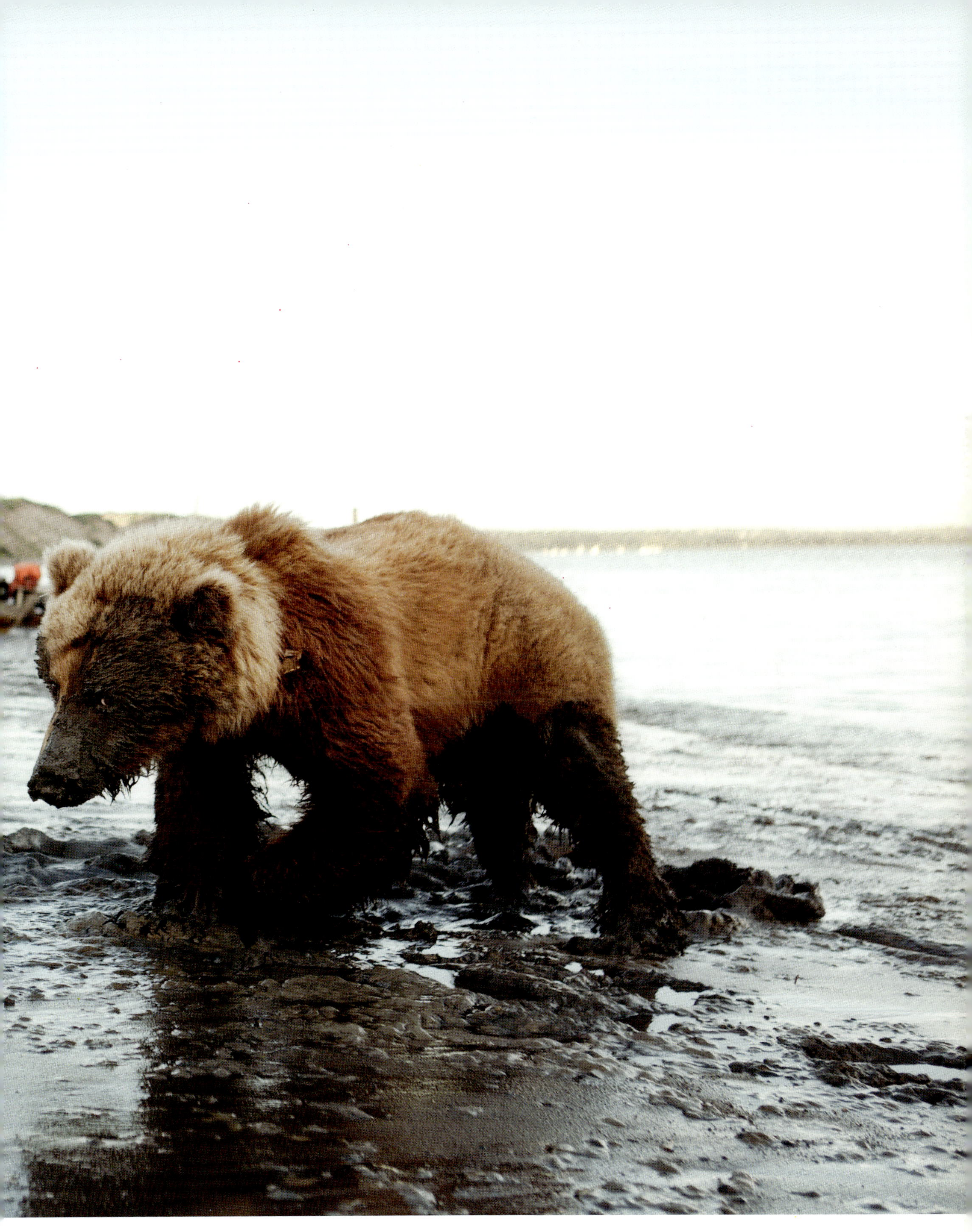

ANDREA MININI

MILAN, ITALY

Animal Instincts
The first animal I painted was the puma. I was just playing with the Adobe Illustrator blending tool, and I picked that animal because it's a worldwide familiar shape. That was the stepping stone to start the synthesis process. It's easier to get to the essential point using a shared symbol.

At Capacity
I'm afraid there are too many of us. The real challenge is finding a balance between considering everyone's needs and keeping planet resources safe.

Strength and Vulnerability
Whales are probably the most powerful animal I've painted. The whale is incredibly strong and weak at the same time, like nature. Whales are intelligent and have their own language to communicate. They build deep relationships and affinity with those similar to them, just like humans. But they are a species at risk.

Artists of Influence
The first one that comes to my mind is Antoni Gaudí. He didn't deal with the environment in terms of ecological concerns, but he found in nature his inspiration and still shows great respect for it. Actually, his creation, The Park Güell, was made with reused, broken ceramics as decorations, so he was eco-friendly!

Miles to Go
It's impossible to pick one favorite place. I can say that there are many places that I haven't seen and would like to.

POLAR BEARS, VECTOR ILLUSTRATION

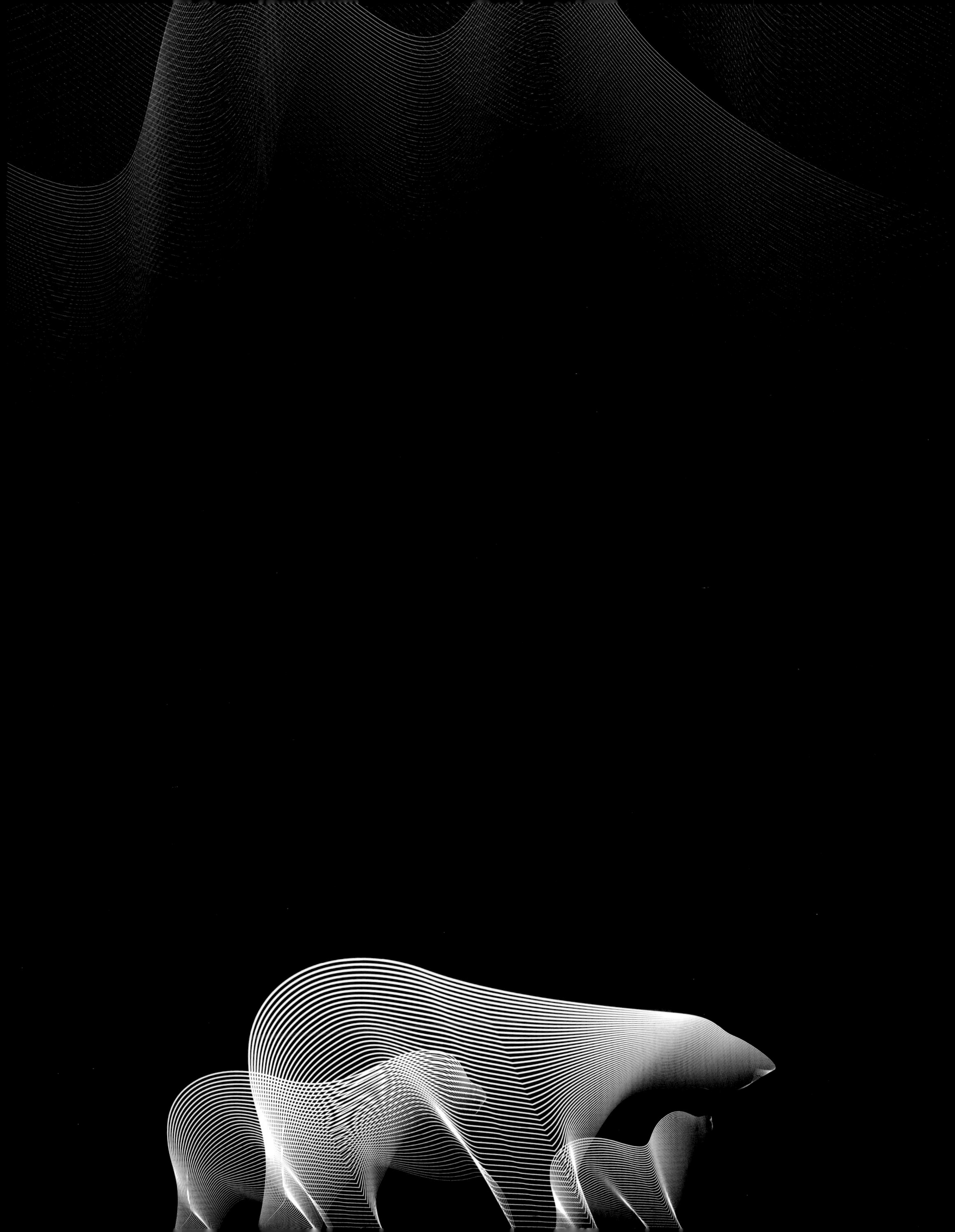

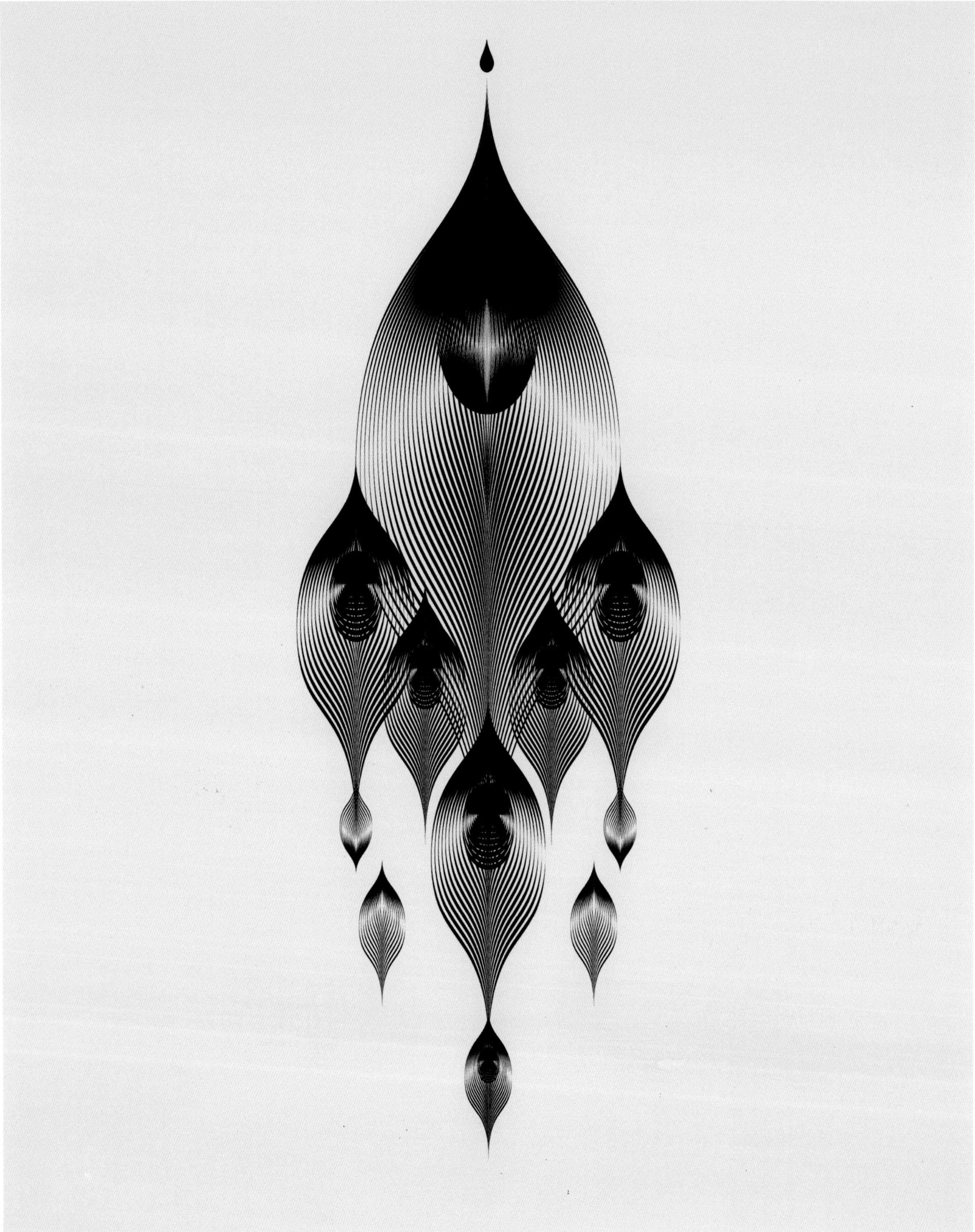

PEACOCK, VECTOR ILLUSTRATION

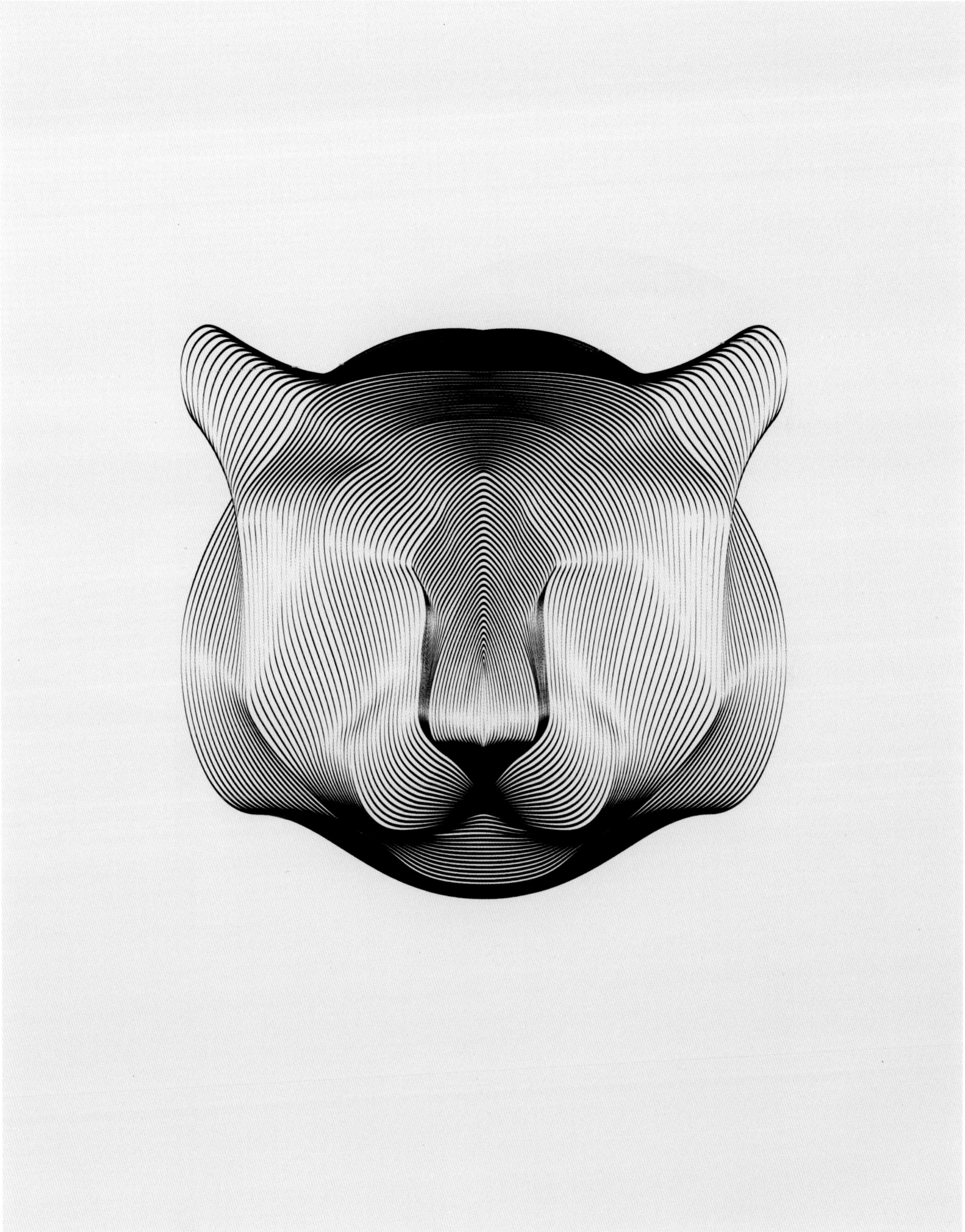

PUMA, VECTOR ILLUSTRATION

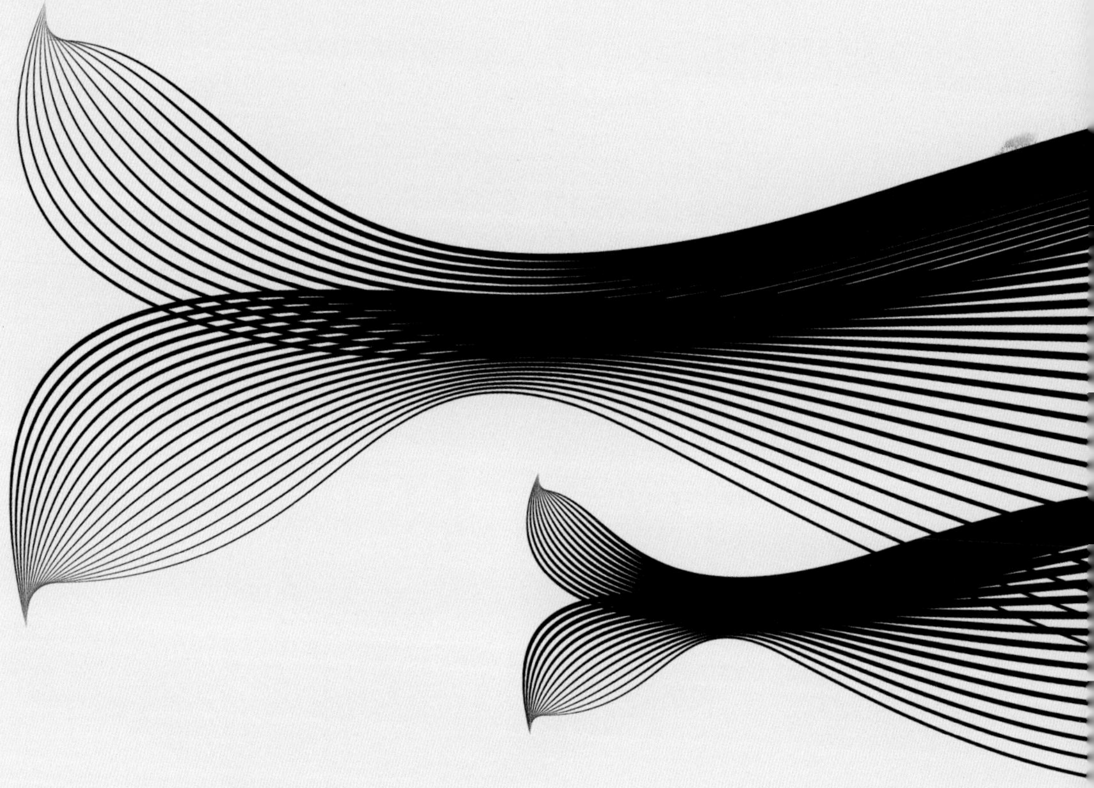

WHALES, VECTOR ILLUSTRATION

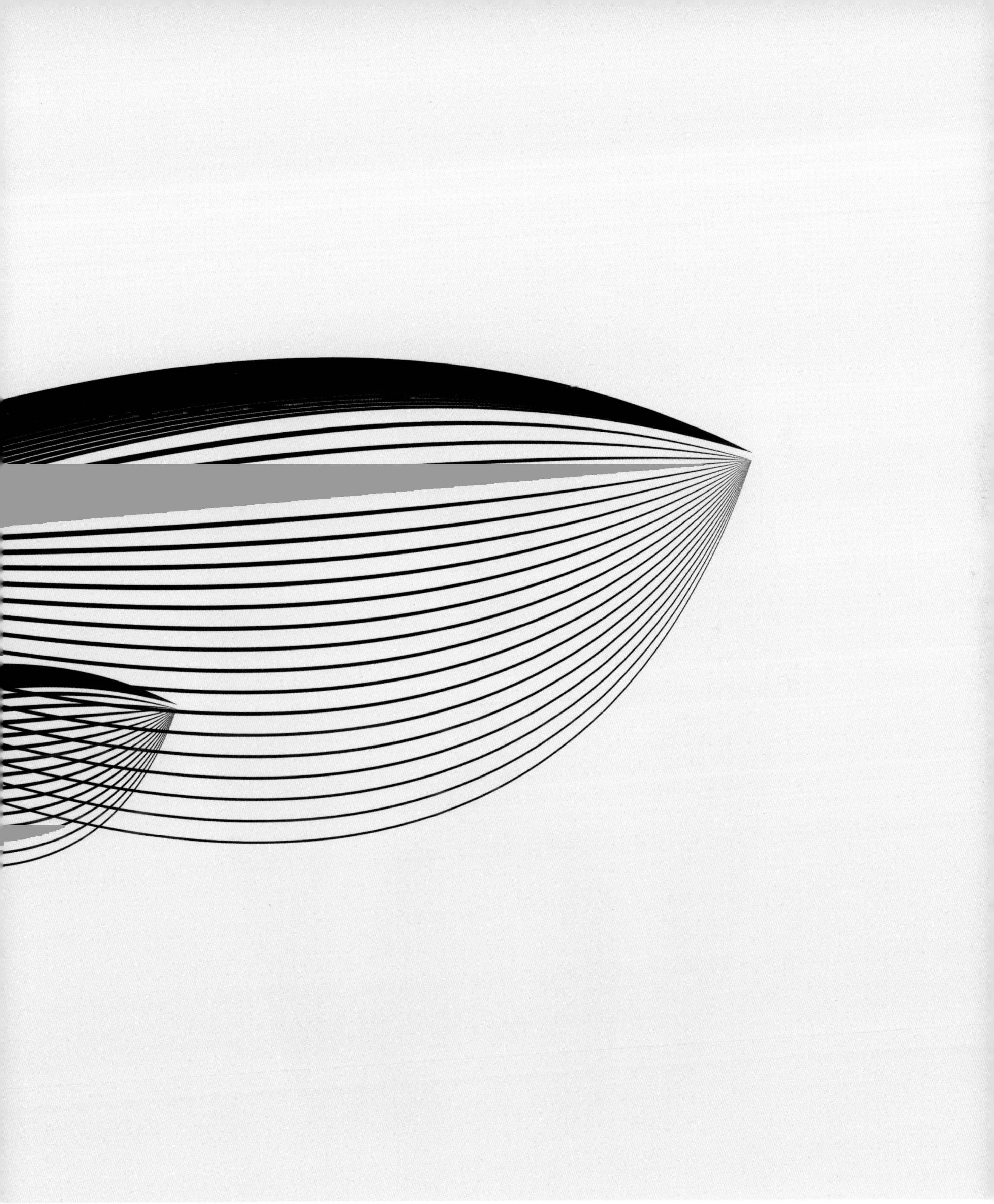

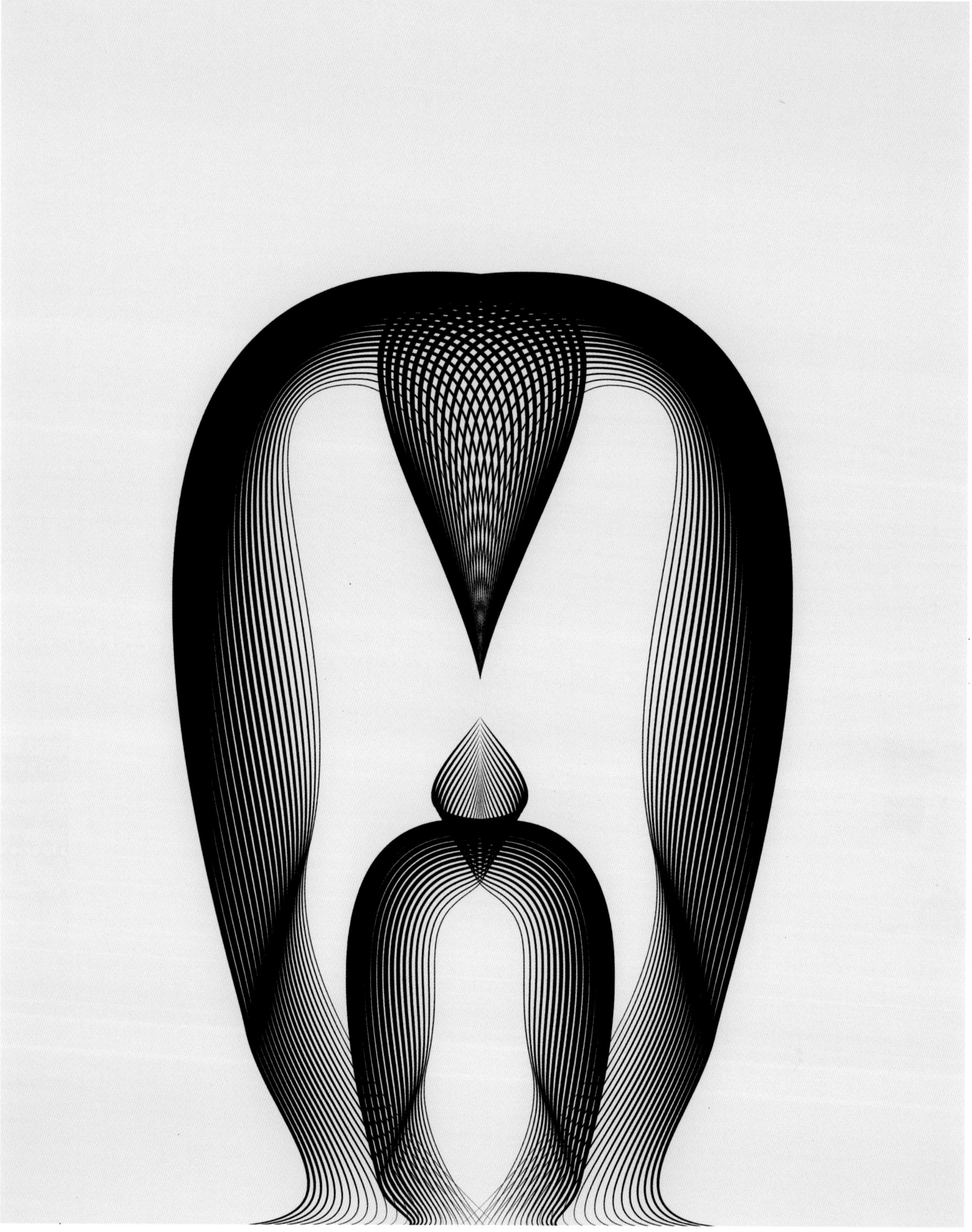

PENGUINS, VECTOR ILLUSTRATION

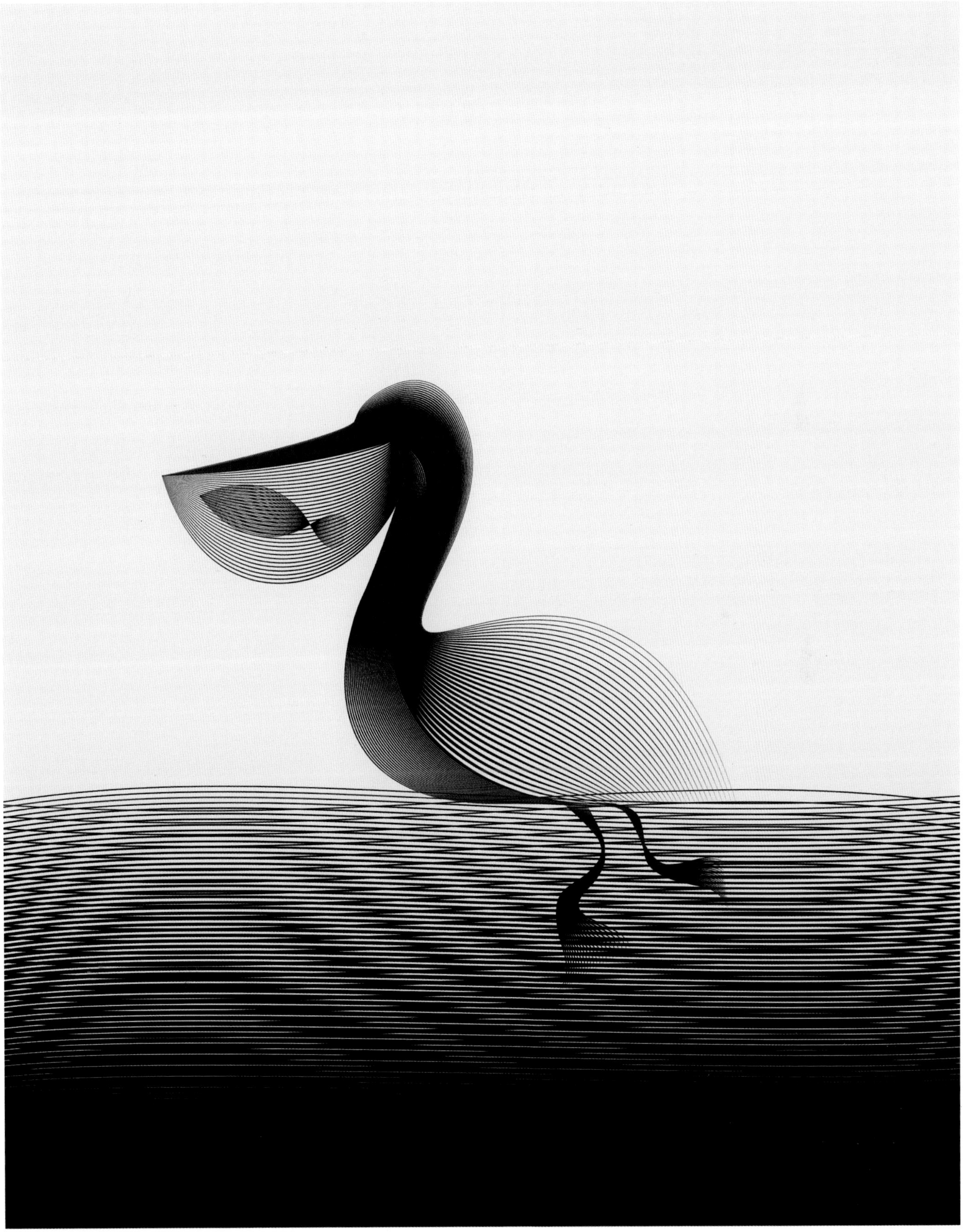

PELICAN, VECTOR ILLUSTRATION

AJ FOSIK

PORTLAND, OREGON

The Truth

Climate change is just a manufactured, fear-mongering tactic perpetuated by the left wing media to generate votes from Prius-driving, soft-headed, liberal, yuppie morons... is what I would say if I was a complete asshole.

The Caveman Condition

Animals in my work represent struggle, specifically the image of predators. The reason why we're all so drawn to that imagery is that the caveman buried something down deep in your brain, under that carefully constructed, deathproof box-store shopper, which gets a tiny existential titty twister. It punches you right in that nagging part of your brain that knows it's going to die.

The creatures in my work are metaphorical, and I don't spend a lot of time worrying about resemblance to any particular animal. The open maw of a predator is the inevitable end we all face.

Road to Nowhere

I fear that it's already too late, that the existing power structures and fearful minds are going to steer this whole stinking mess straight into oblivion for a few lousy shekels. And that I'm going to end up in some Cormac McCarthy dystopia searching for cans of peaches in a cannibal-filled basement.

Chronic Fatigue

My fatigue has increased dramatically, and my willingness to process the horrible state of the world has decreased significantly. It's hard to feel like there is any hope when every time I turn on my computer, it's just assholes wrecking the world for no good reason—rhinos being wiped out for boner pills that don't even work, giant Walmart-fueled floating garbage continents in the ocean; it's all so fucking depressing. I really have to resist the urge to bury my head in the sand and just hope it all goes away.

Drop in the Bucket

The ocean along the Oregon coast is always terrifying and awe-inspiring, and it forces you to acknowledge the tiny speck of nothing that you are, while simultaneously making you feel a part of everything. It's also nice to swim there in August sometimes.

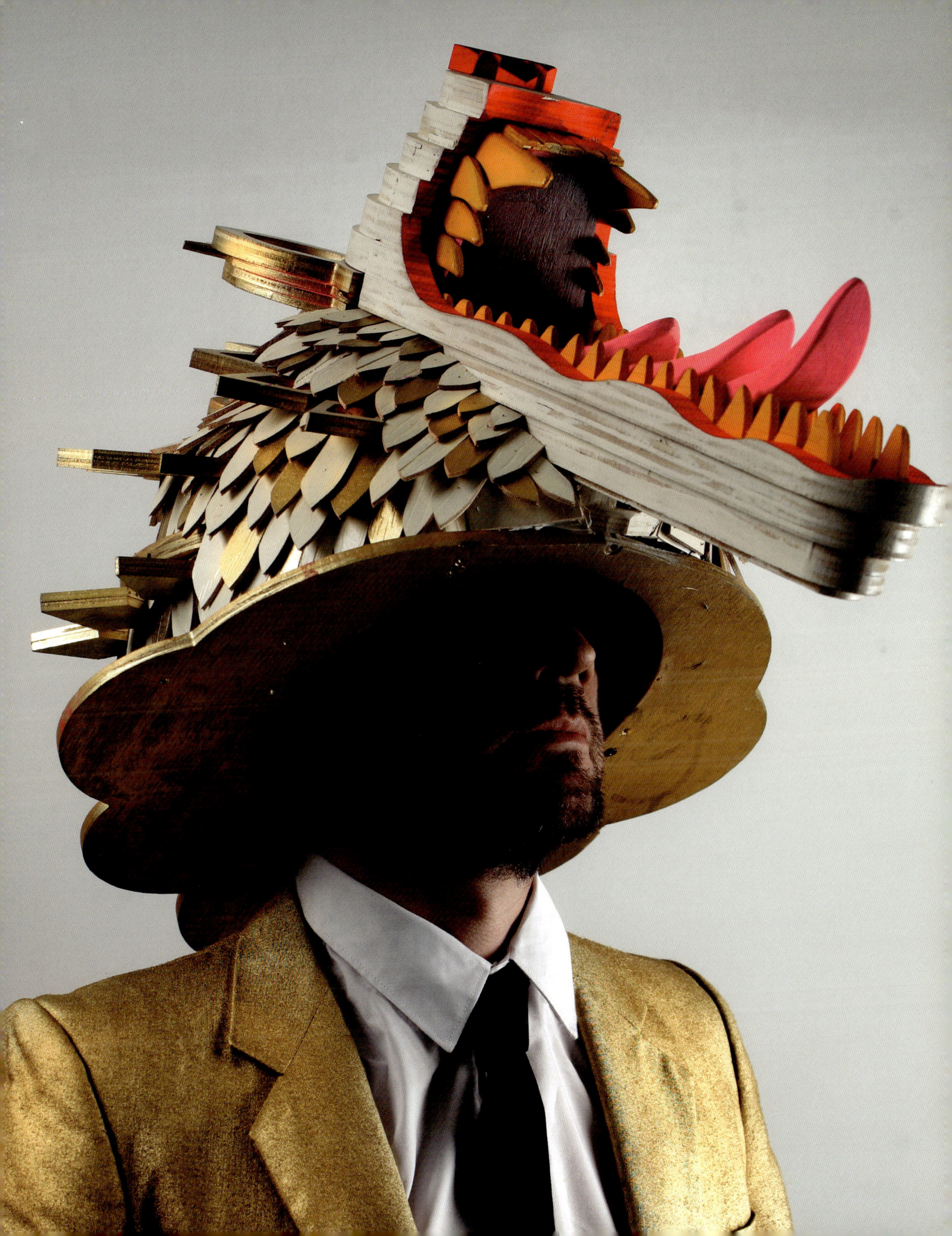

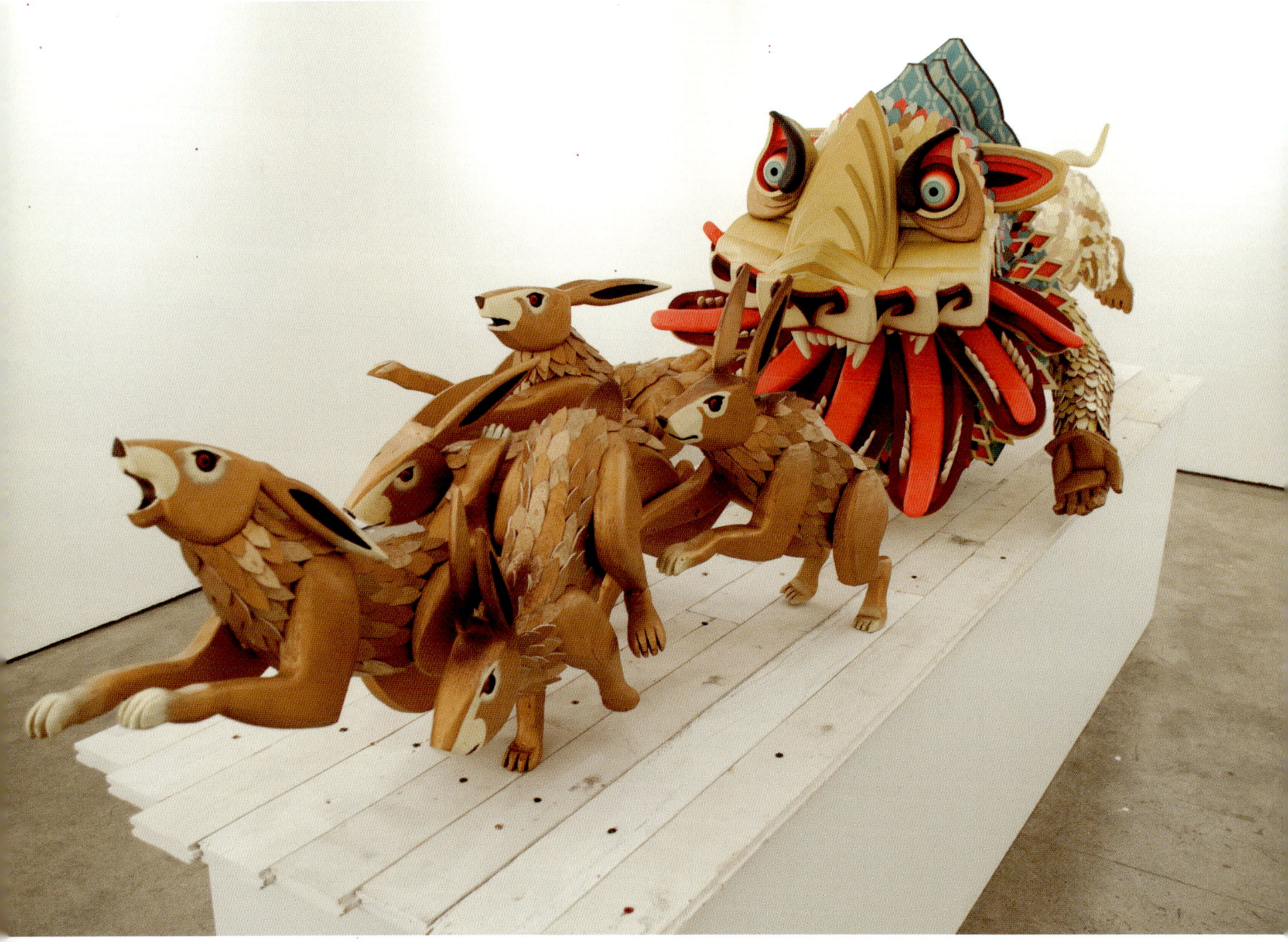

ABOVE:
THE SHEPHERD INEVITABLY CONSUMES THE FLOCK
WOOD, PAINT AND NAILS

RIGHT:
BLUE GREEN CHIMERA
WOOD, PAINT AND NAILS

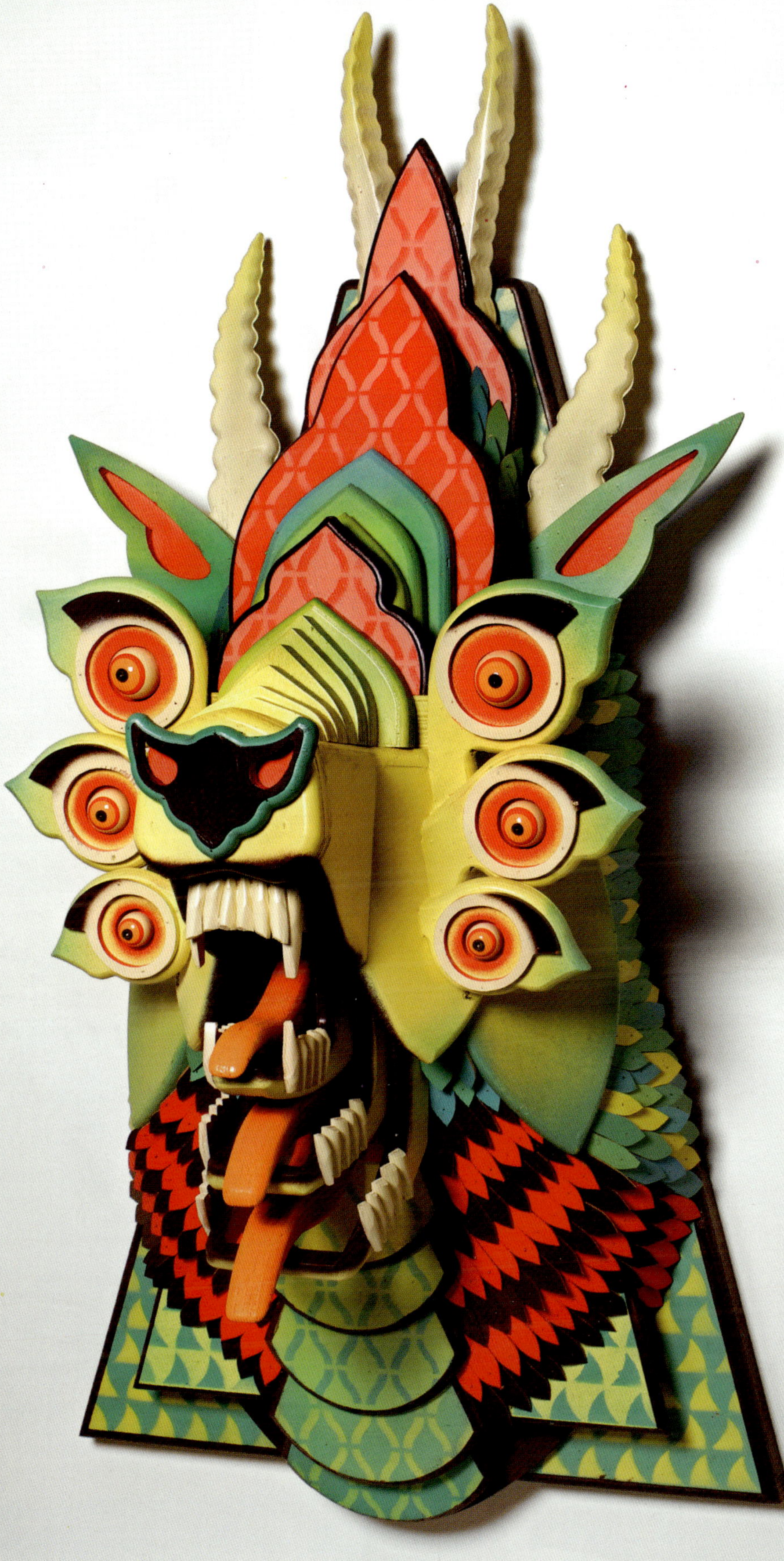

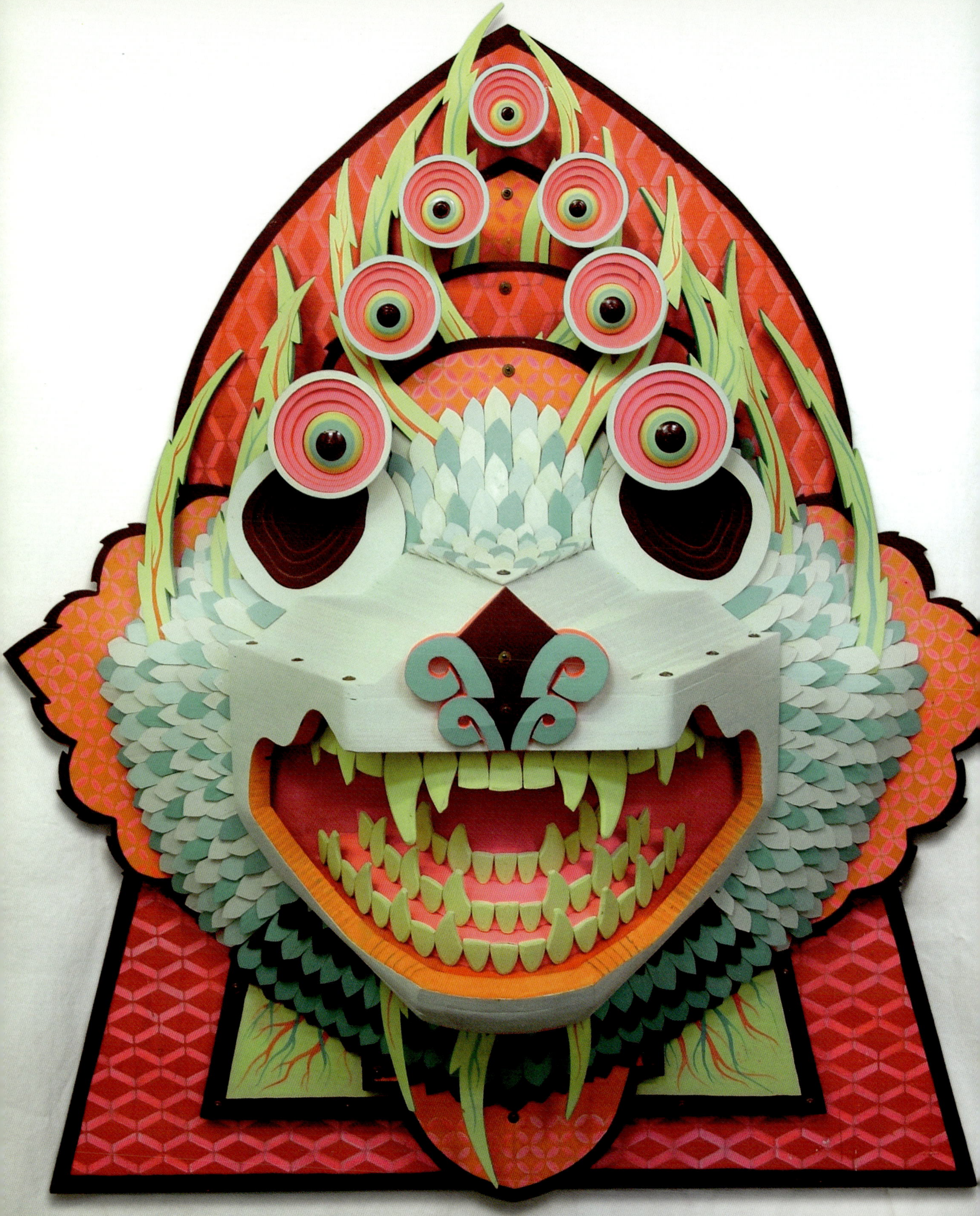

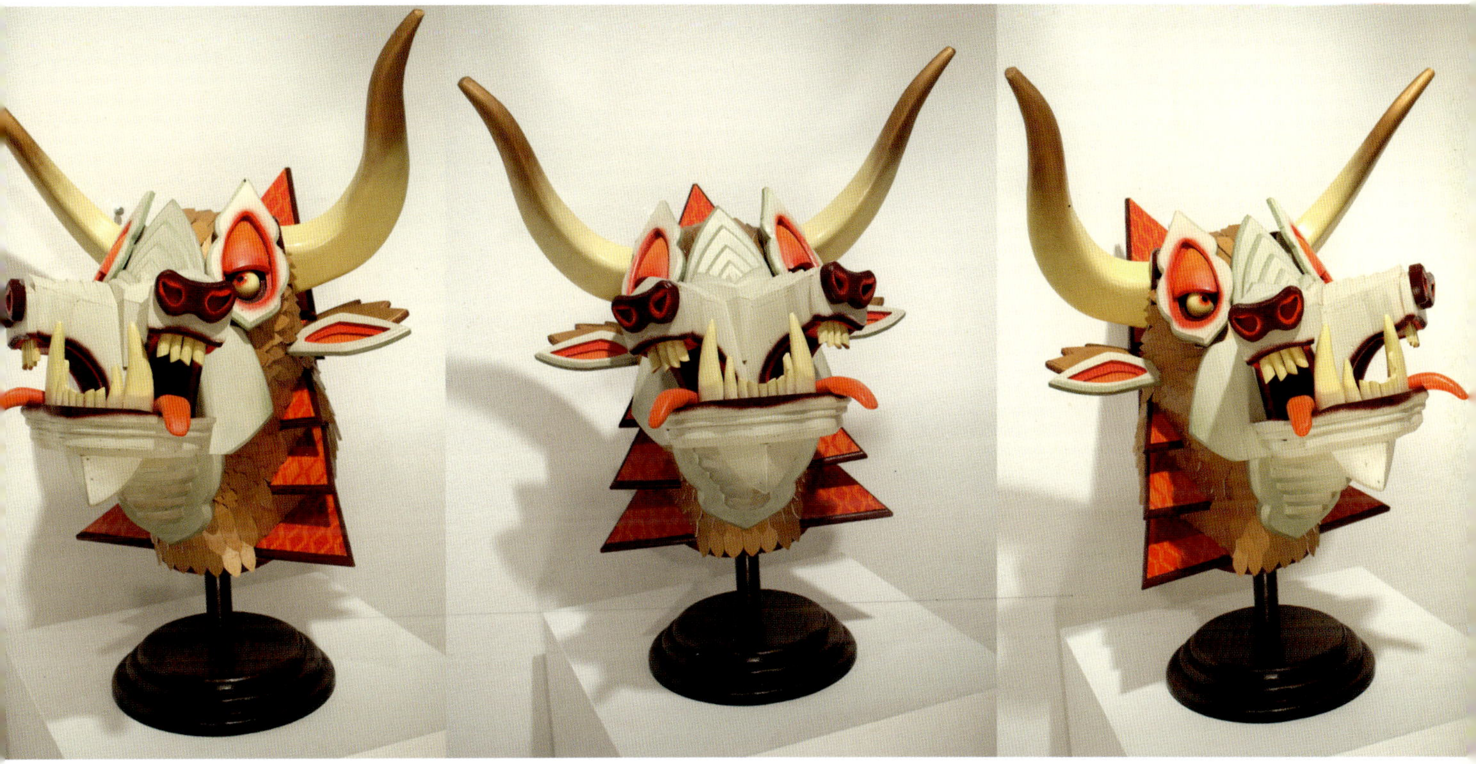

LEFT:
ATOM BRAIN
WOOD, PAINT AND NAILS

ABOVE:
BELIEVE IT OR ROT
WOOD, PAINT AND NAILS

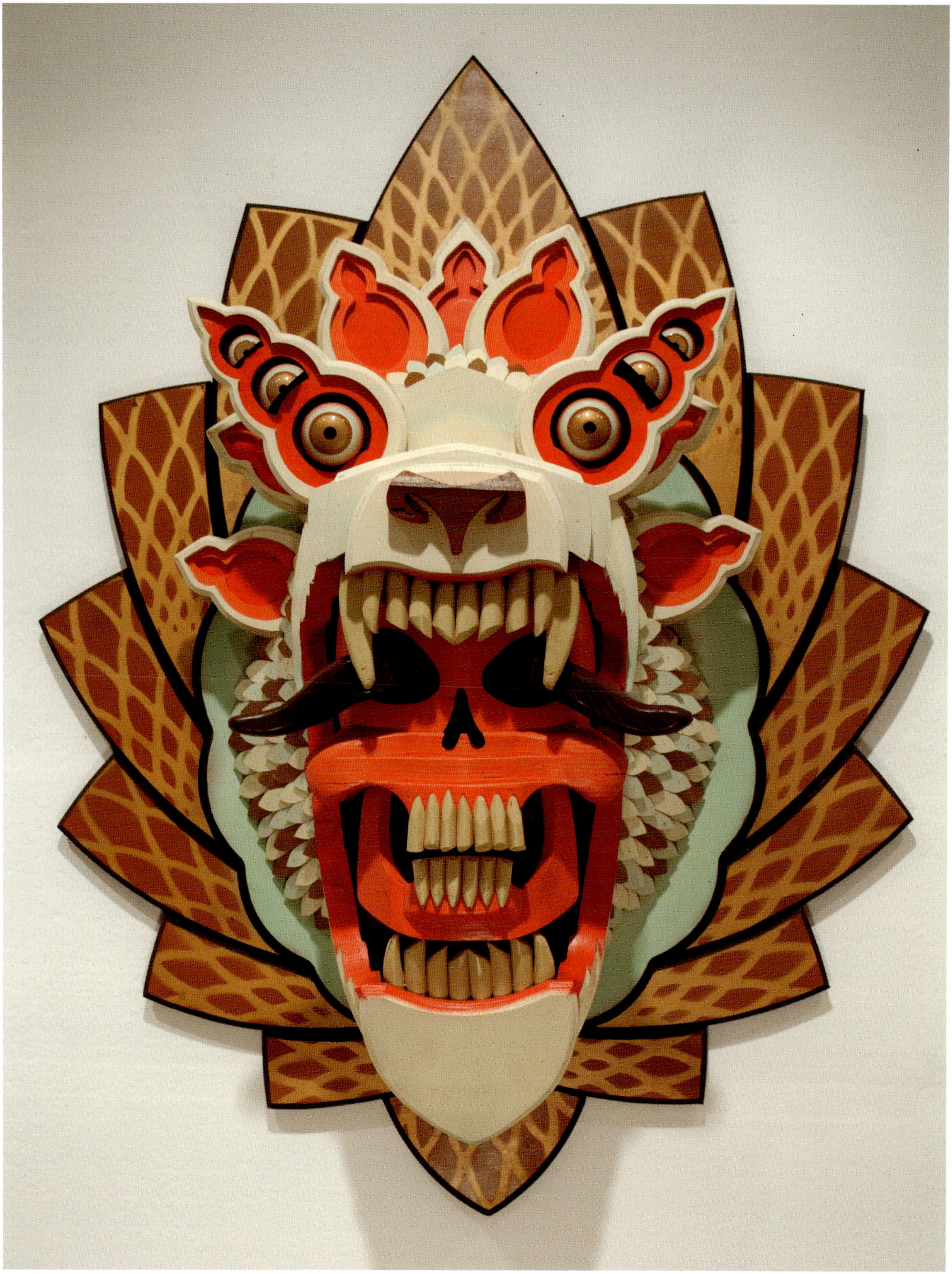

TONGUES BLACK AS STICKS, WOOD, PAINT AND NAILS

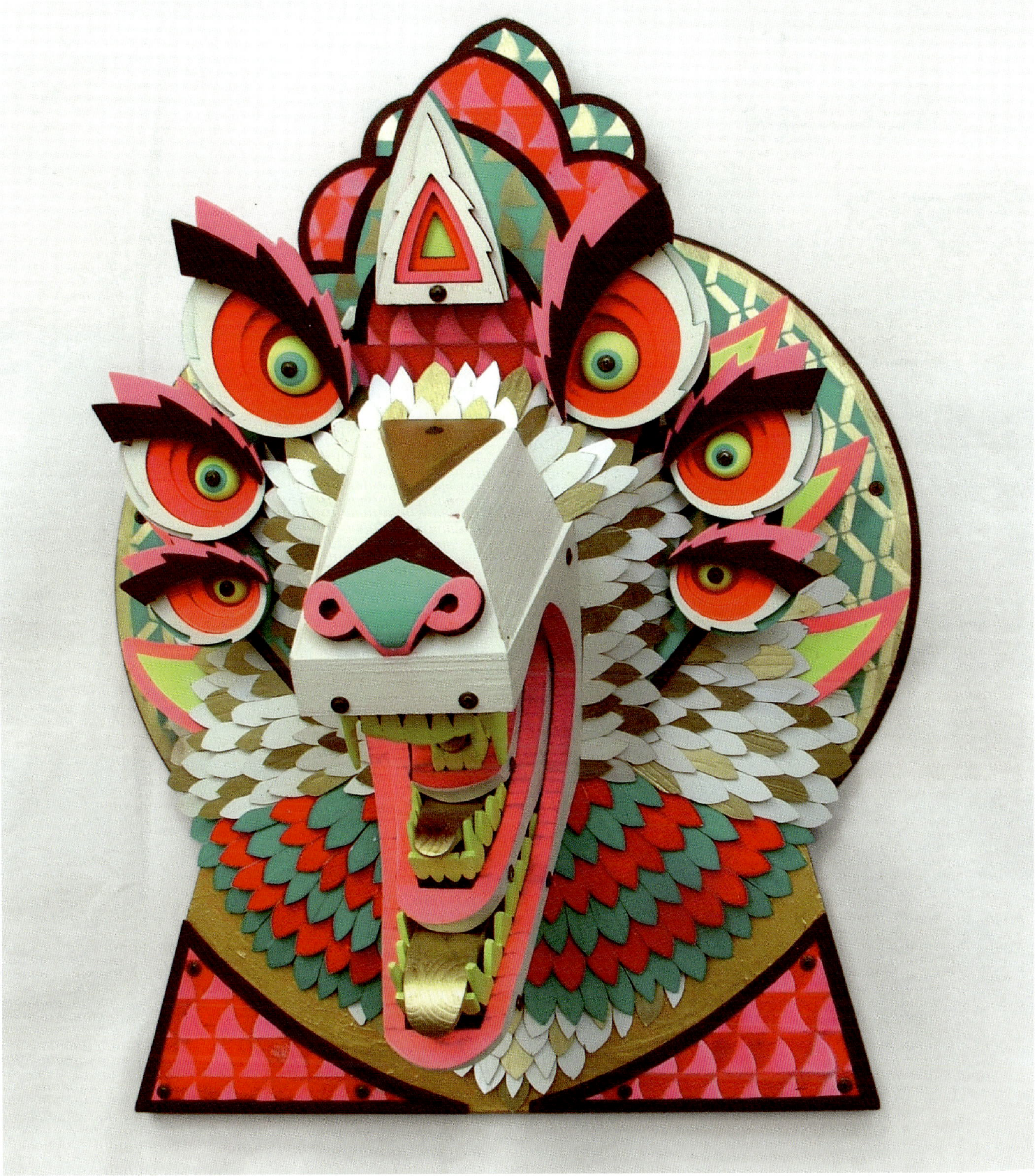

AS GOOD AS ANY GOD, WOOD, PAINT AND NAILS

ERICAILCANE

BOLOGNA, ITALY

Animal Allegories
When I began to paint and draw, I started drawing animals. I'm incorporating humans, but doing it with animal bodies. Every species has his own characteristics, and I like to change the story every time.

Gut Instincts
I'm putting together sensations and information. I'm not thinking a lot about what I'm doing and for which reason.

Ecological Concerns
This is a part of our everyday life. It's impossible not to pay attention to these things. I don't have any particular fear, just a bit of paranoia sometimes. I think that everything is changing every day, so it's normal and natural, but we'll never be ready for these changes we're facing now.

Favorite Location
Altopiano del Cansiglio is my favorite place because I spent a lot of my time there.

CONIGLIO, GOUACHE AND PENCIL ON PAPER

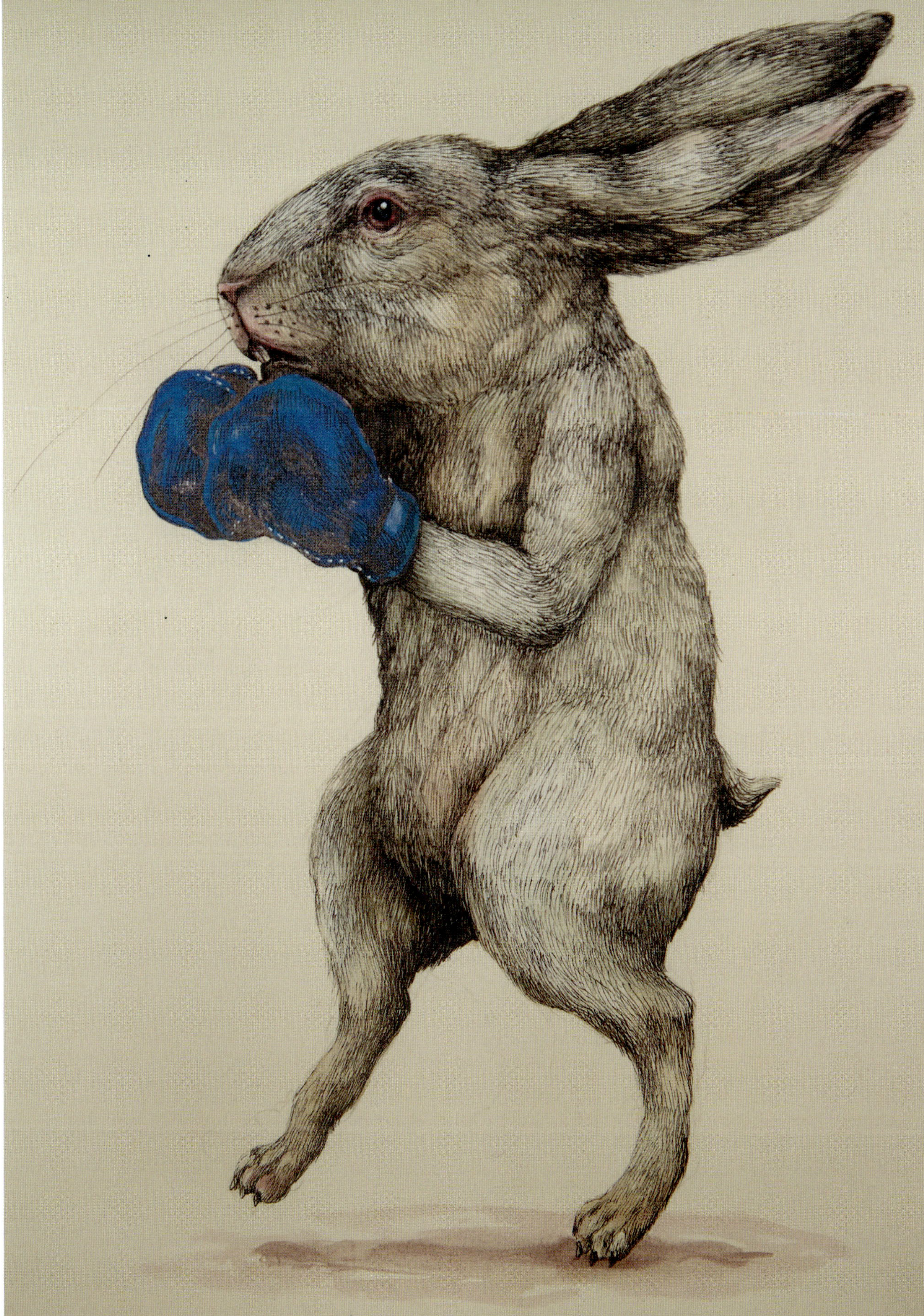

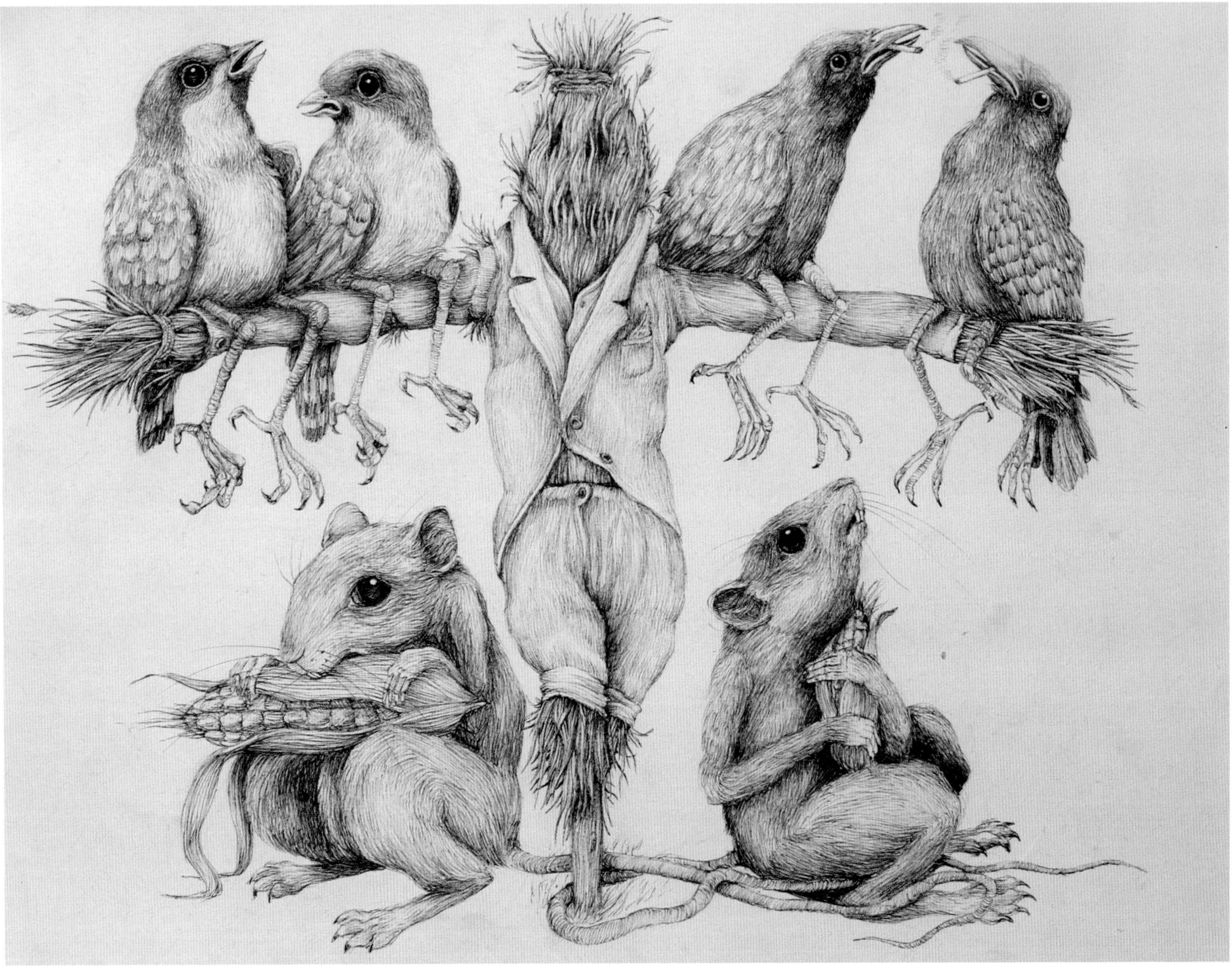

NON POTEVA ANDARE PEGGIO, INK ON PAPER

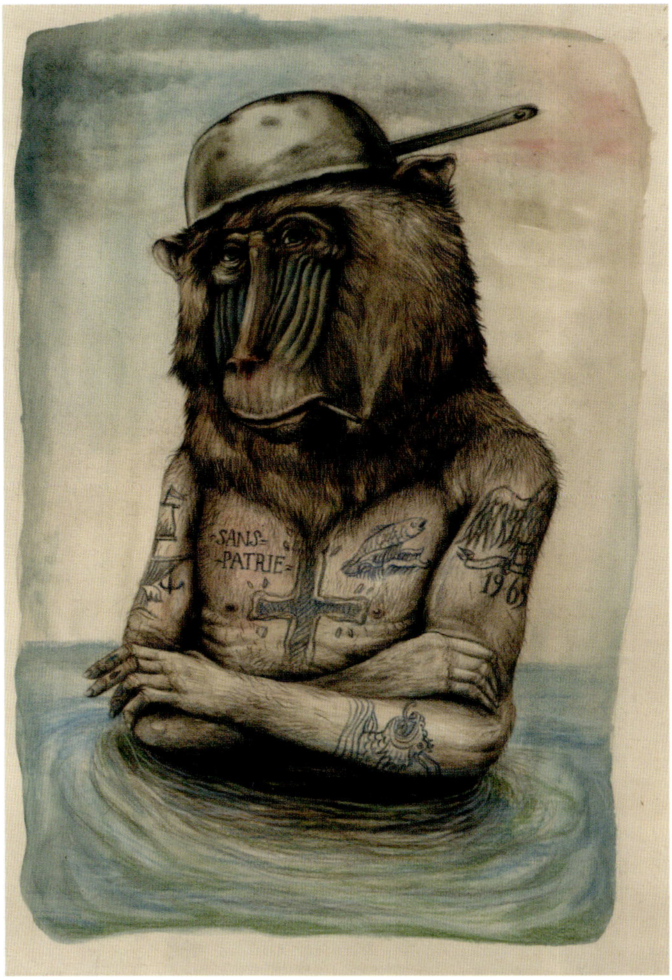

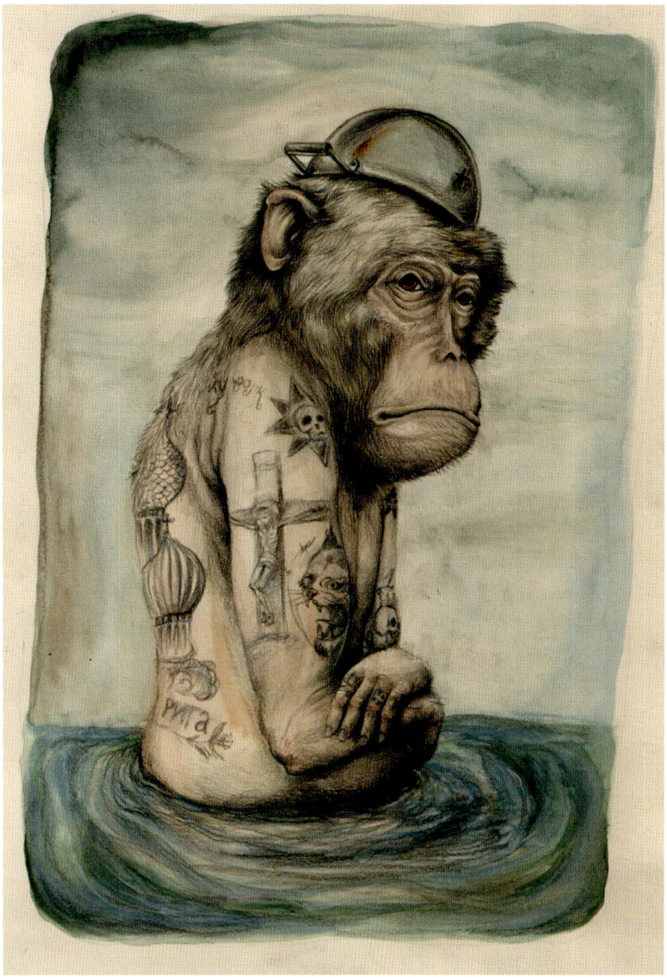

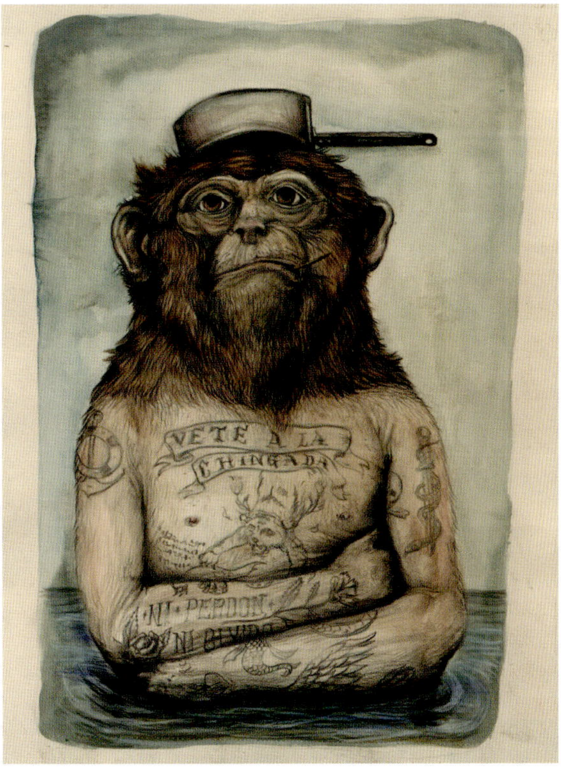

CLOCKWISE FROM TOP LEFT:
SANS PRAIRE
GOUACHE AND PENCIL ON PAPER

SATURNO
GOUACHE AND PENCIL ON PAPER

CARON DIMONIO
GOUACHE AND PENCIL ON PAPER

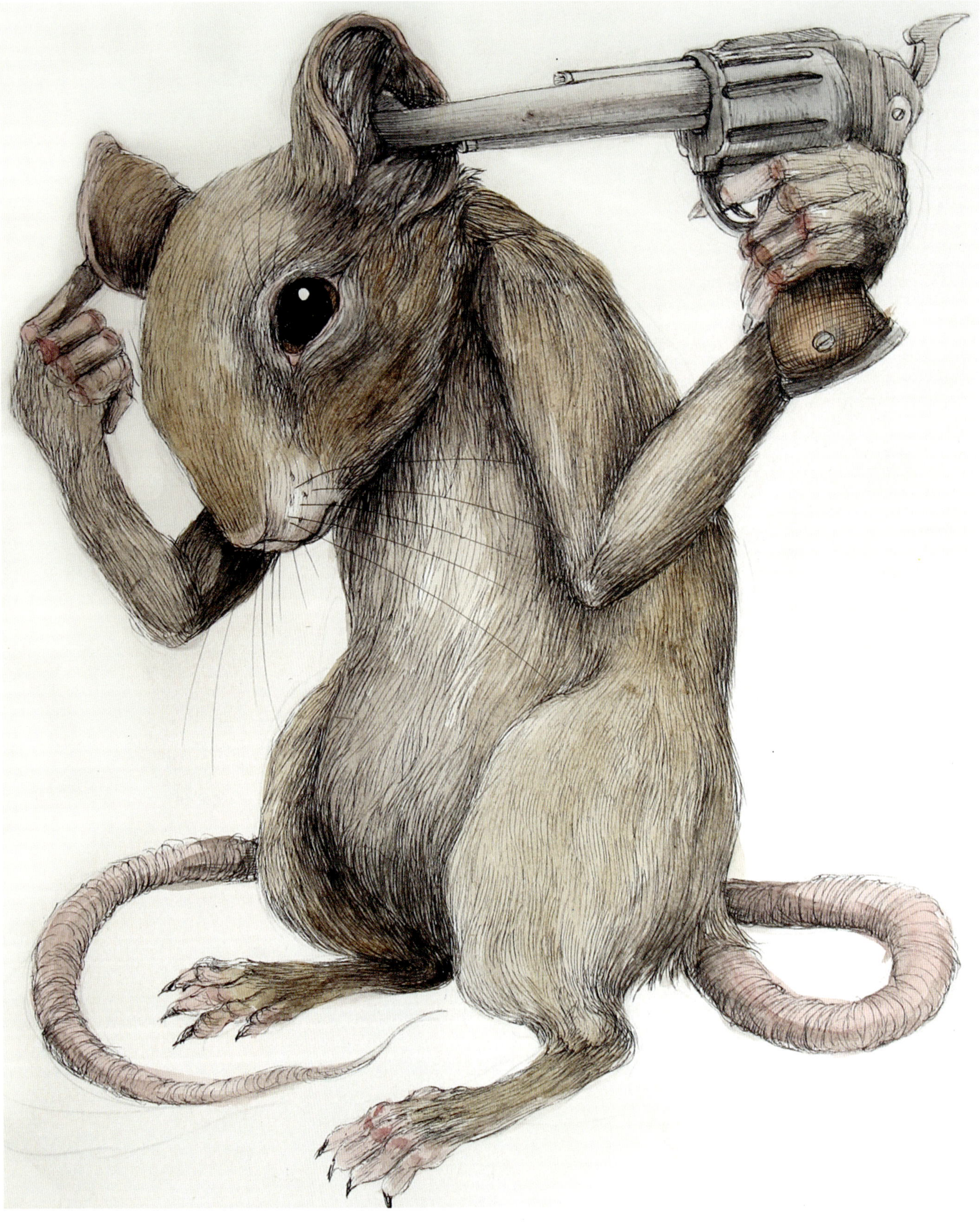

UNA VITA VIOLENTA, ACRYLIC ON PAPER

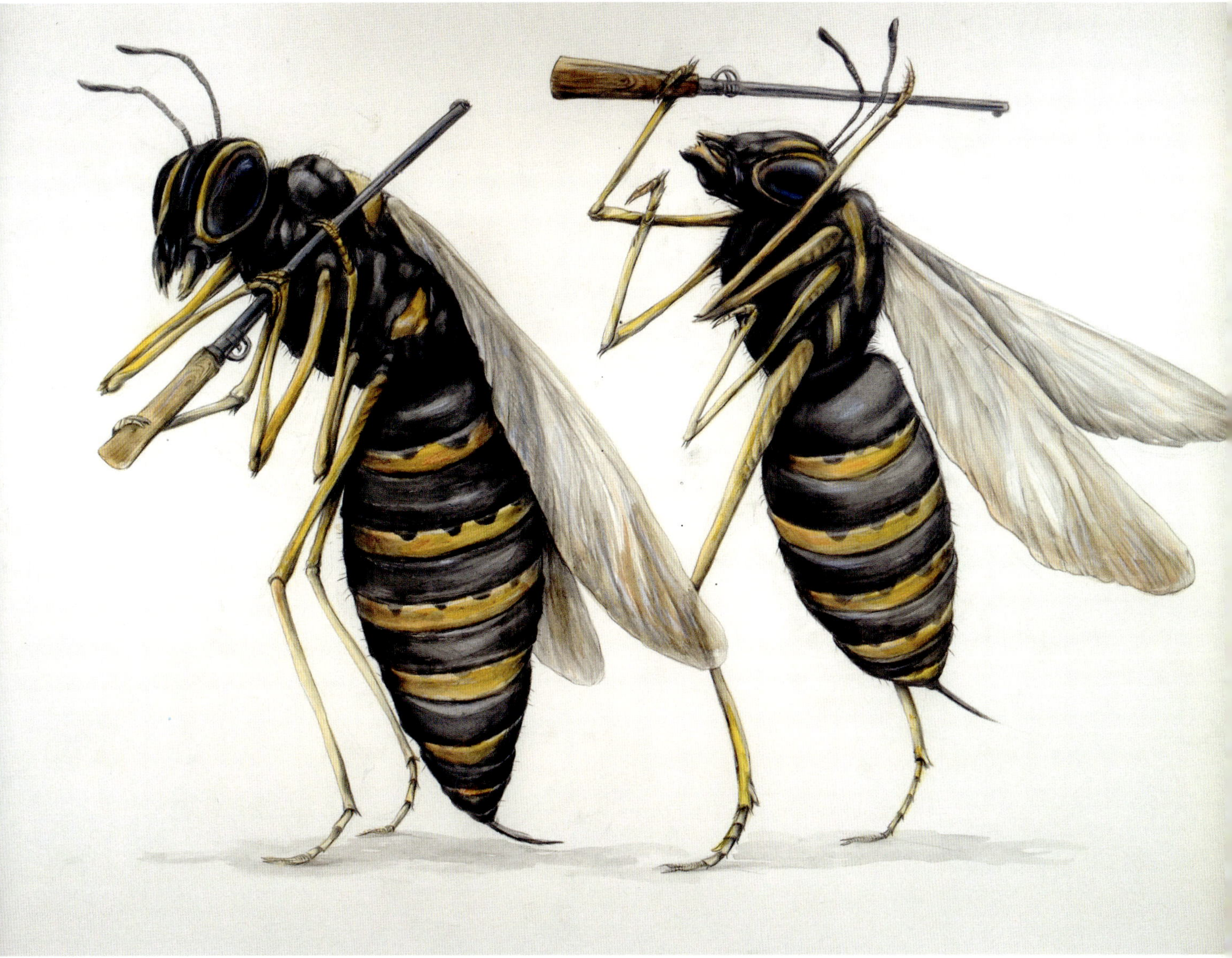

VESPE, GOUACHE AND PENCIL ON PAPER

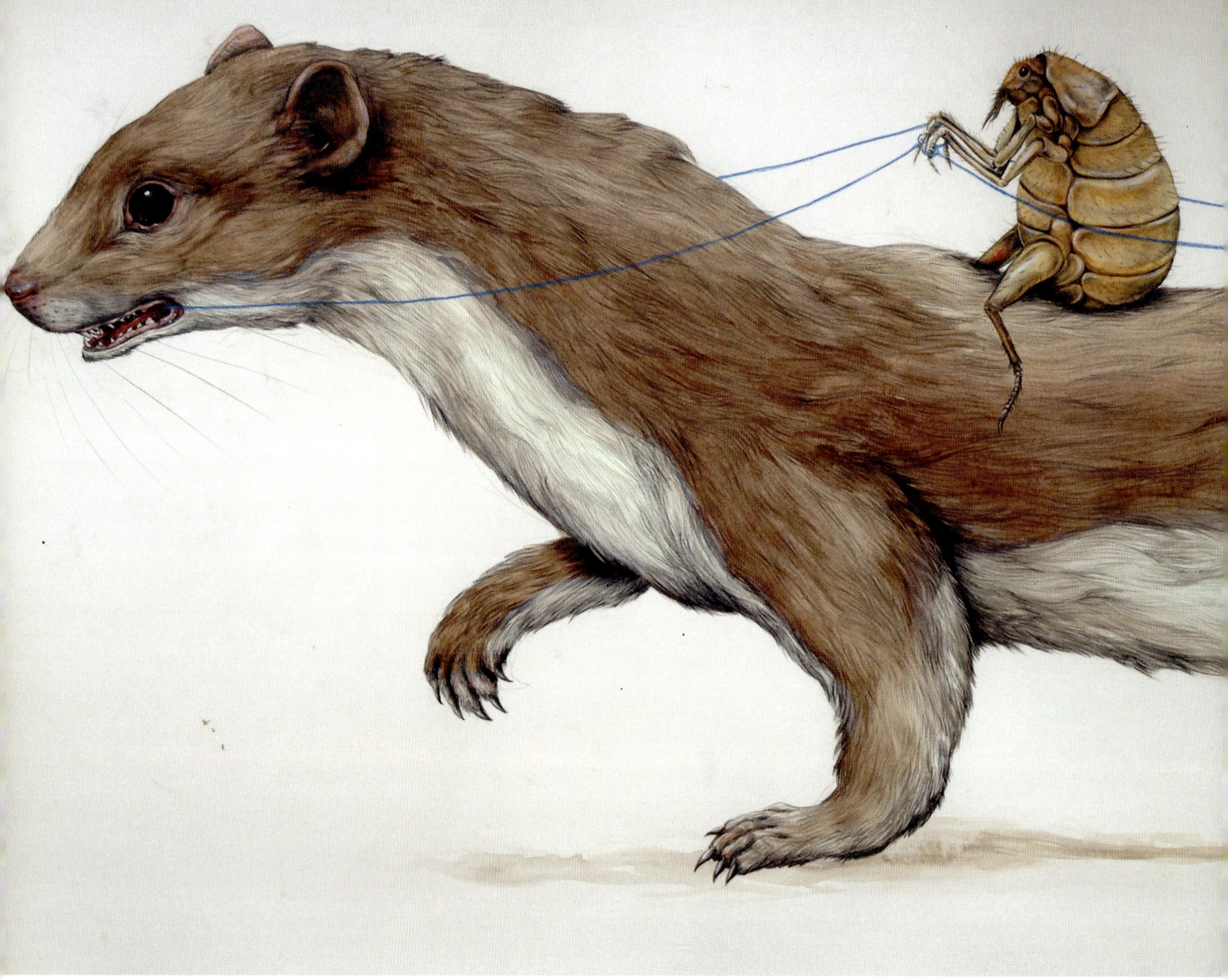

FAINA, GOUACHE AND PENCIL ON PAPER

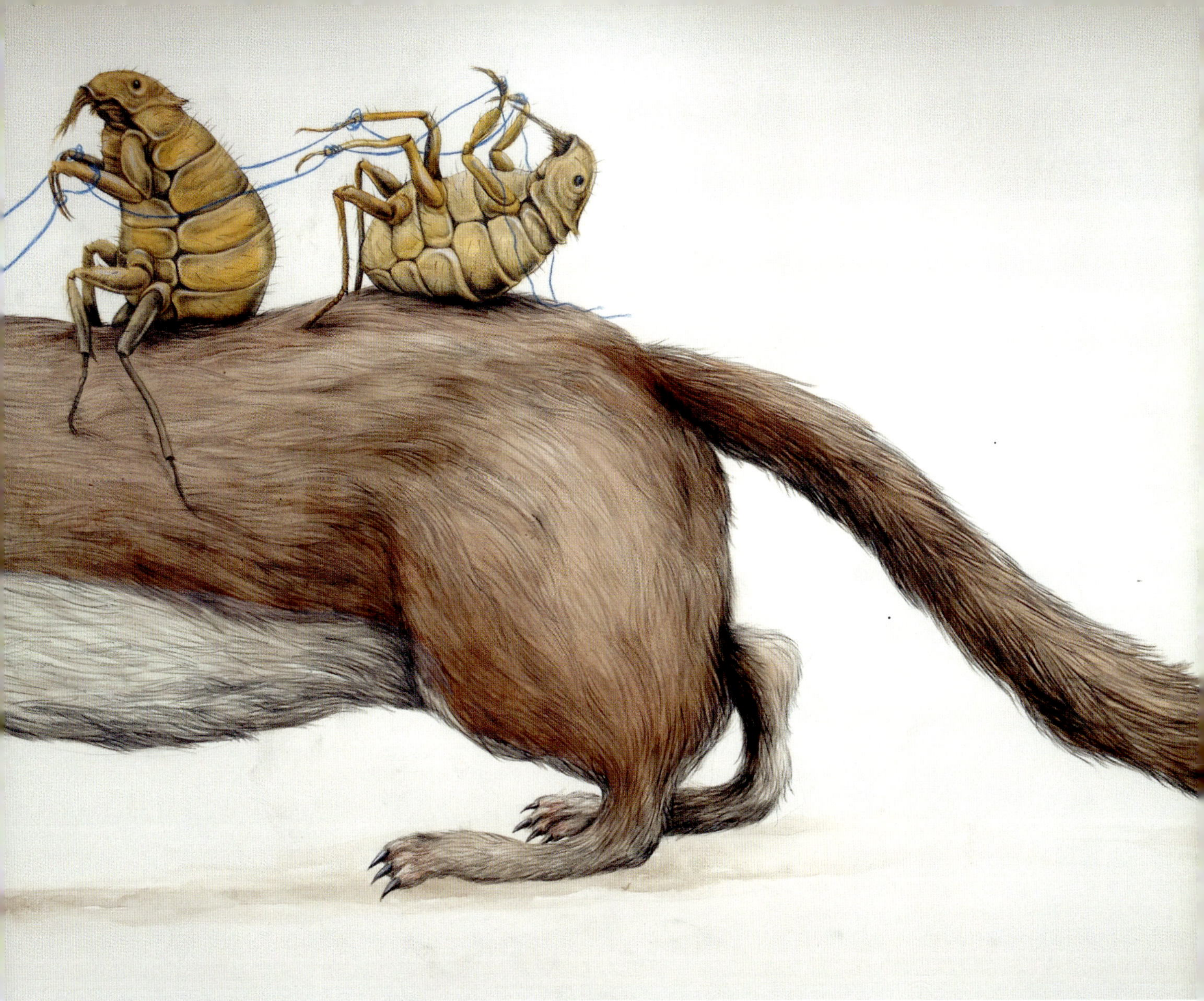

CATHIE BLECK

CLEVELAND HEIGHTS, OHIO

The Elephant in the Room
I wasn't one of those girls who drew horse heads in class, but I am in awe of those who can identify every muscle. My pictures were primarily images of families and creatures, or characters living in exotic places in the sky. As a child, my favorite animal to draw was elephants.

Animals have a way of appearing magically and unintentionally, and I find myself working rather intuitively lately. Animals keep returning in an uncontrollably, subtler way. When I paint or draw, the objects or species become obscured and transformed into some swirling motions of interconnectedness with our shared environment. I usually portray animals in an adaption of their natural habitat. Depending on the narrative, I might integrate them into plant matter or melting ice.

Wings of Wisdom
Humans are mixed with animals, whose role becomes a symbol of force and influence. In my series, *Inheritance*, the owl holds its head very directly, its imposing eye expressing calm poise, stillness and perceptive vision, while perched on a waterfall. The woman, the protagonist, receives the owl's strength and courage to move forward through the force of water that appears to be clouded by chaos, and of course, haunting animals!

I have created a cast of characters that reappear in my work, reflecting on the inner human condition through different animal characteristics. Birds convey freedom of light, moving from place to place like the passages of a human on a spirit journey, the egg and nest associated with the cocoon, nurturing and hope. Through its metamorphosis, the moth symbolizes elegance and truth, and also serves as a metaphor for those who make personal sacrifices, never asking anything in return.

When artists use people in a narrative, the viewer brings their own personal experience to the painting, and that can be far riskier.

Brotherly Love
How we relate to our environment reflects how each of us honors and experiences it. I want to believe that, at our core, we are all altruistic beings. That attribute only seems to be apparent when disaster strikes, or through an exchange with nature in its most glorious state, when we fall in love through this immersion. But droughts and floods definitely make us pay closer attention to the direction we are heading.

I have my own garden in the summer and have planted a large flower garden that attracts a lot of bees, and we're preparing to start our own beehives. Beekeeping originated here in Ohio, so there are a lot of resources available and free to the public. I feel fortunate that I can use my art talents as a vehicle to engage people to get involved in securing a better future for our animals, especially those that are endangered. I am working on a commission for the World Wildlife Fund, and in the past, have created images for the U.S. Department's Earth and World Ocean Days. We are capable of being united on this front and, as artists, we have the responsibility to inform and inspire as we move forward.

The more I study forms from the natural world and get close to animals (including kayaking with orca whales up close, which was amazing), the clearer it becomes that we are all very integrated, like brother and sister, on this planet. Whatever our talent, we can have an impact on the future. Beauty can be a very powerful catalyst for change. If we can overcome our own egos, then compassion and love for all living things will flourish.

Fuzzy (Furry) Math
I'm currently fascinated by Pandemelons, which are small marsupials found in the forests of Tasmania and New Guinea. I was introduced to them in Australia, and watched them perform this crazy patterning dance, always remaining the exact geometric distance from one another, switching rapidly from one place to another within a very unusual social relationship. They're small and they look like a cross between a wallaby and a large squirrel.

A CHOICE, 48" X 60", INKS, LAQUER, GOLD LEAF AND CLAY PIGMENTS ON PANEL

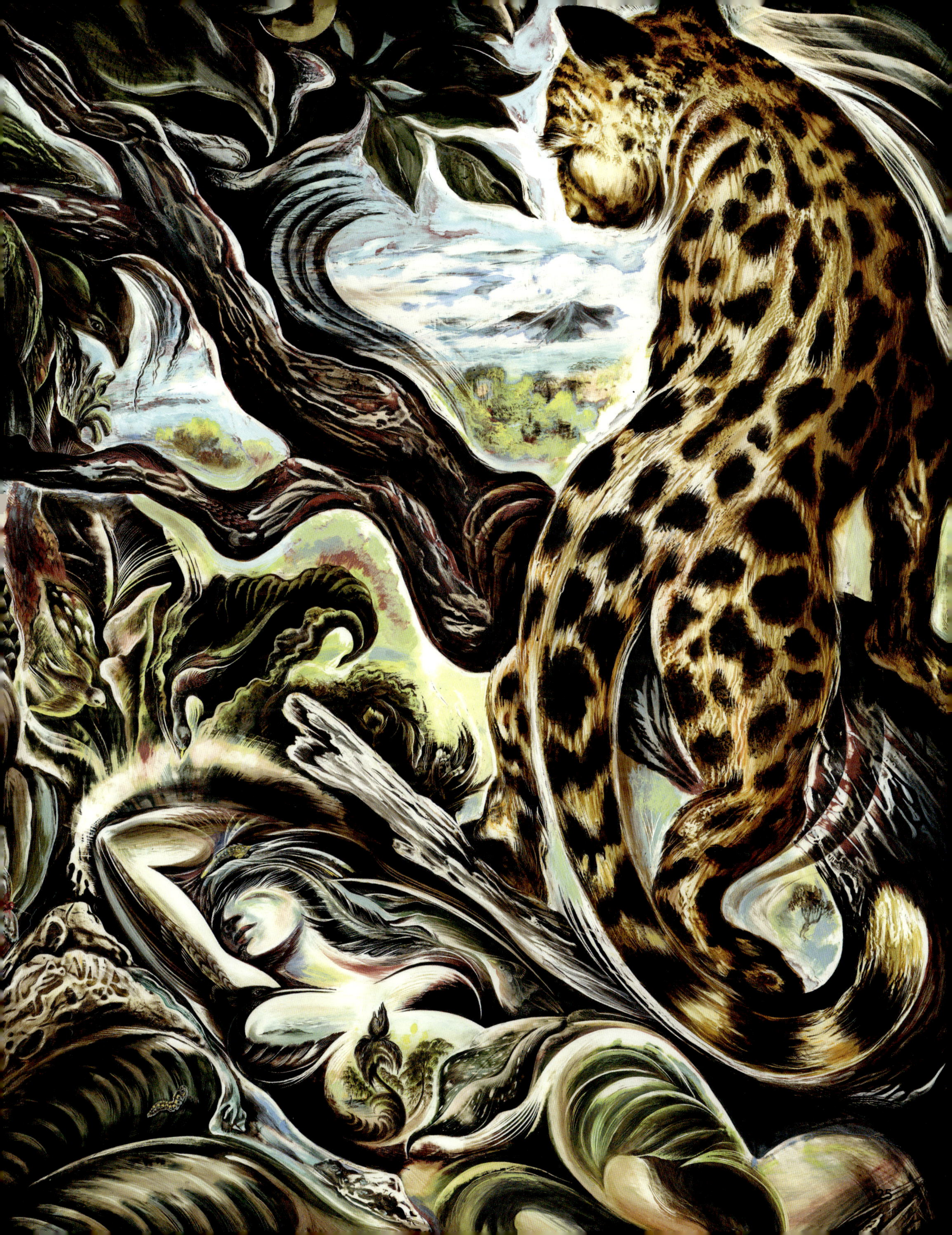

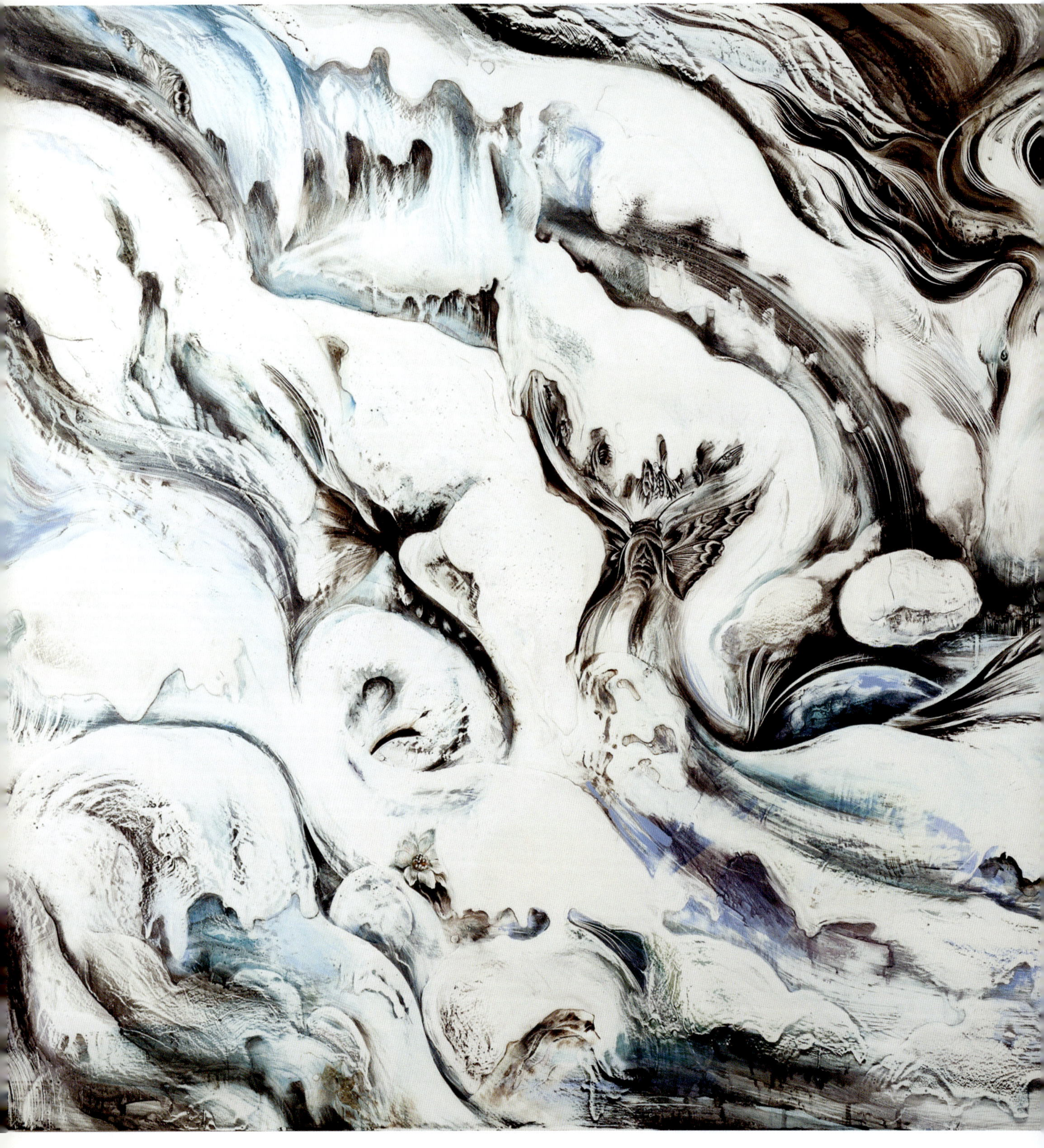

SACRIFICE I, 90" X 46", INKS, LAQUER AND CLAY PIGMENTS ON PANEL

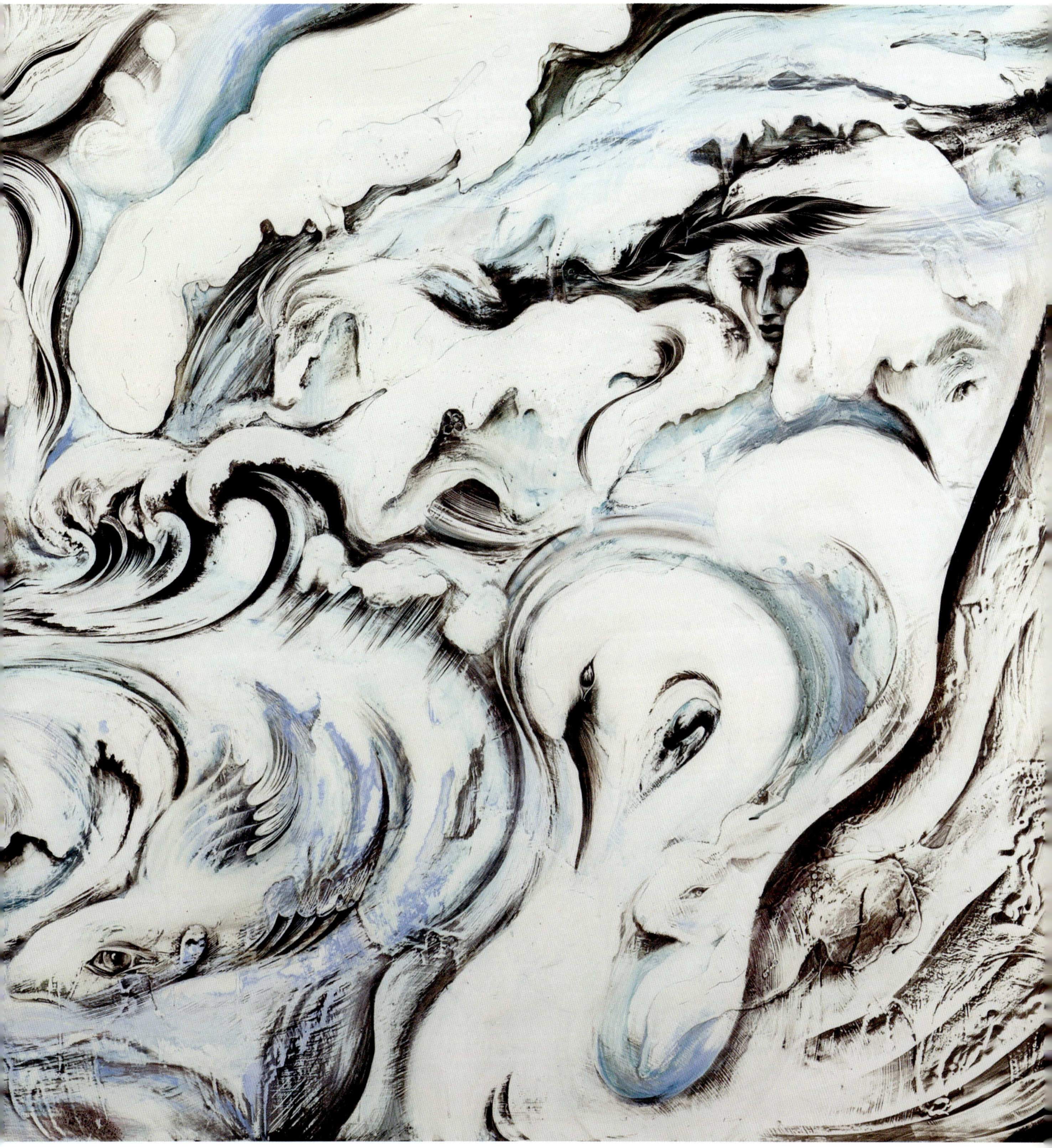

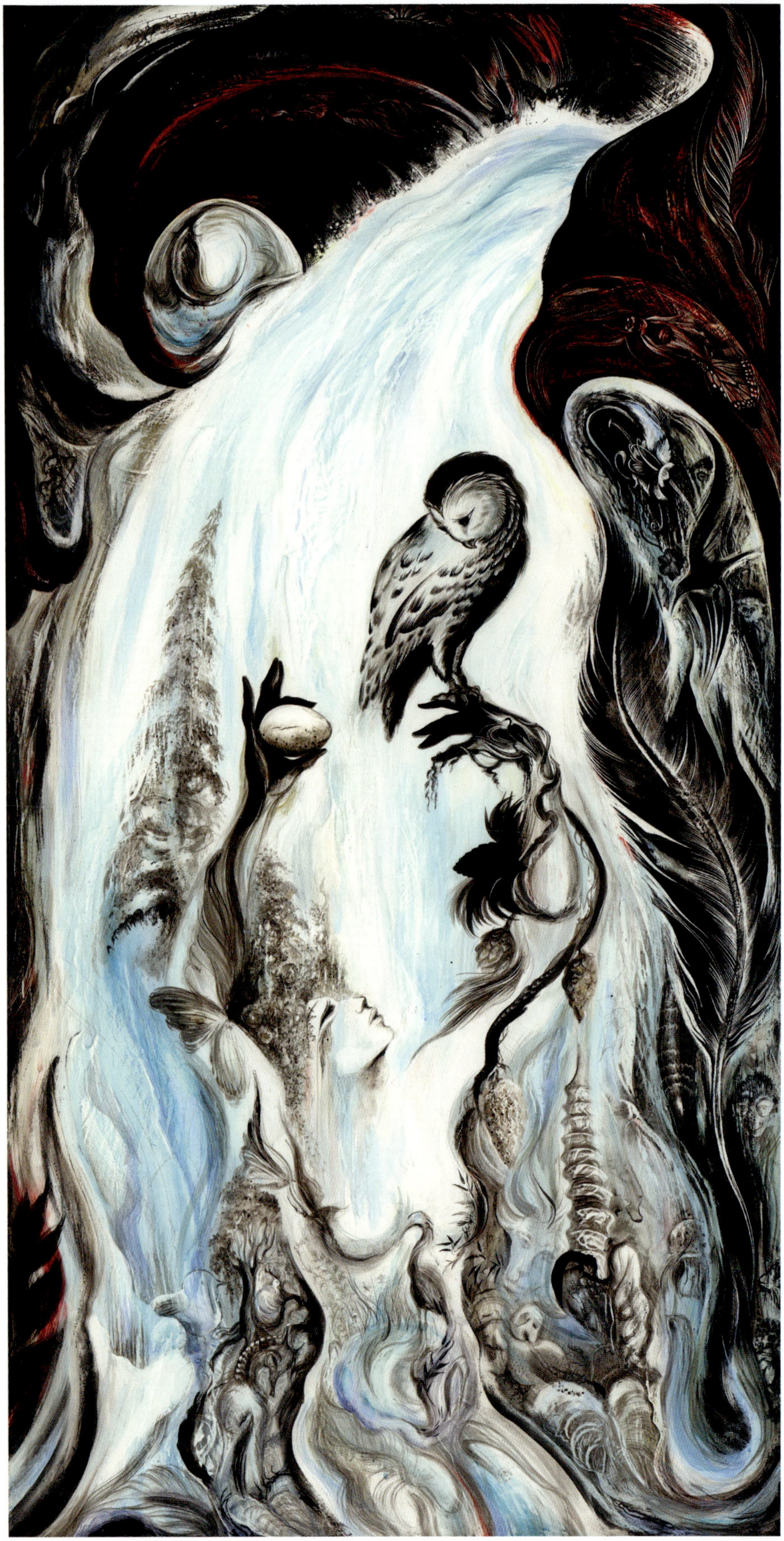

INHERITANCE II
30" X 60"
INKS, LAQUER, GOLD LEAF AND CLAY
PIGMENTS ON PANEL

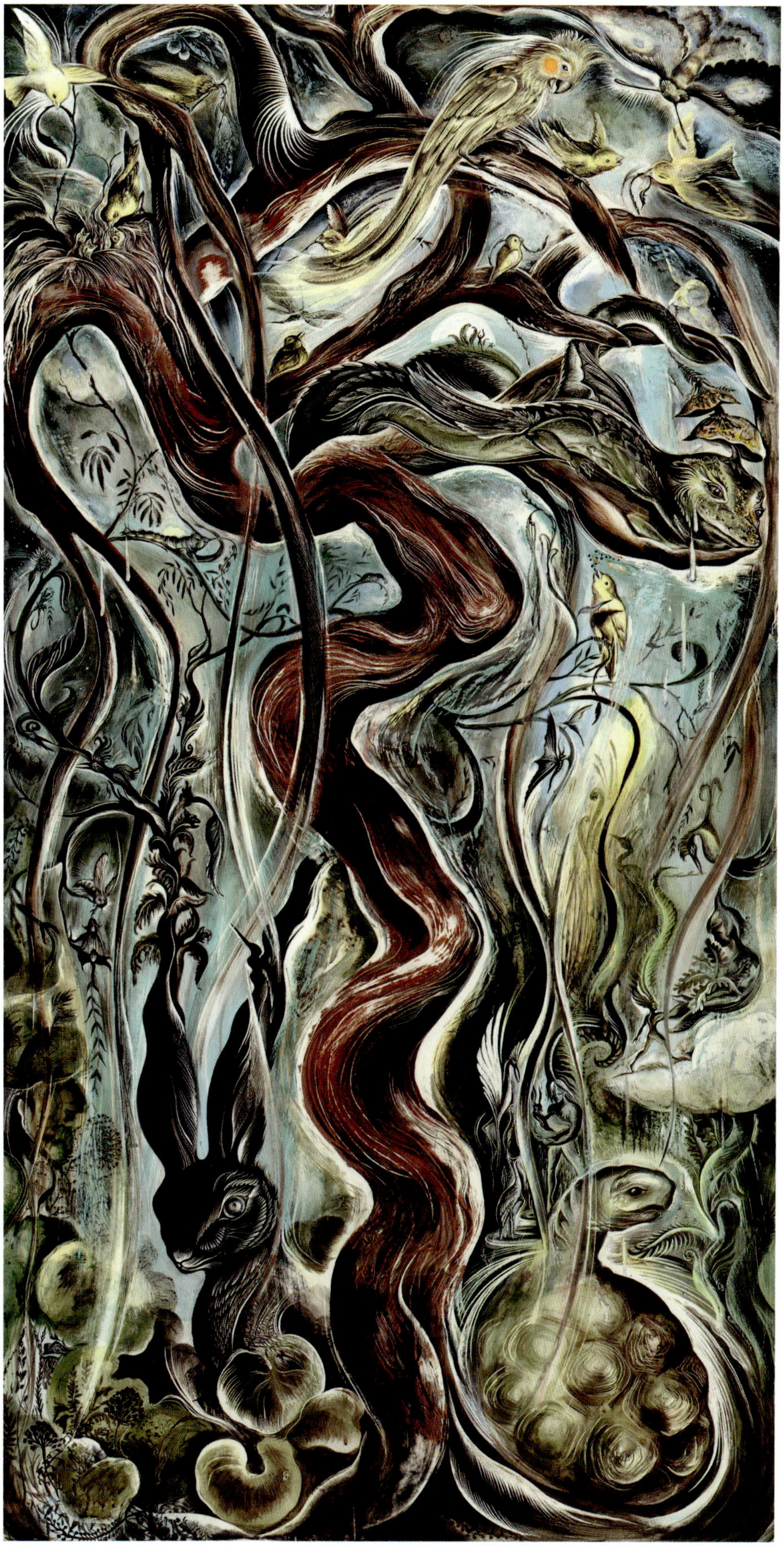

RENAISSANCE II
30" X 60"
INKS, LAQUER, GOLD LEAF AND CLAY
PIGMENTS ON PANEL

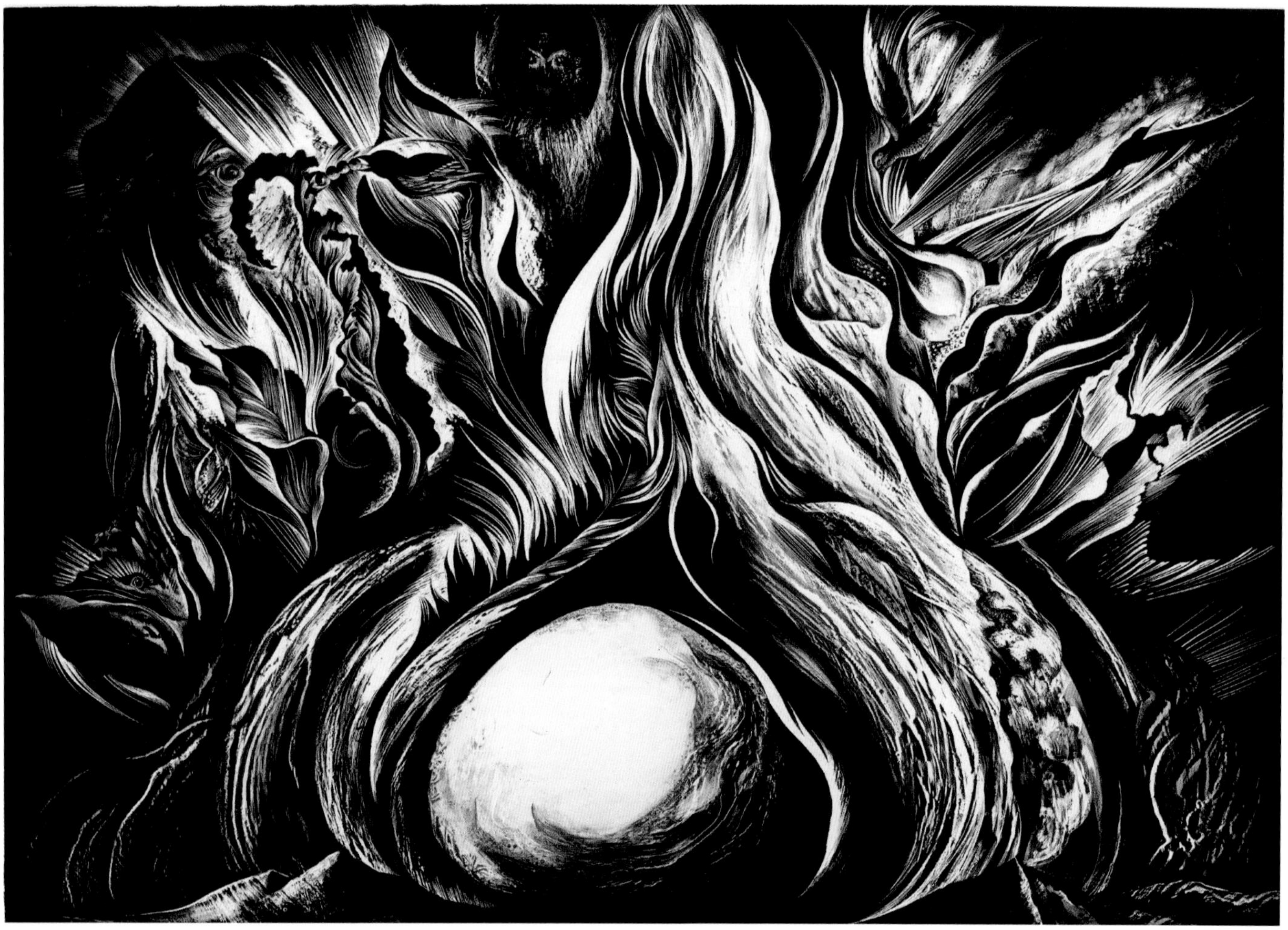

FIRE, 36" X 50", INKS, LAQUER AND CLAY ON PANEL

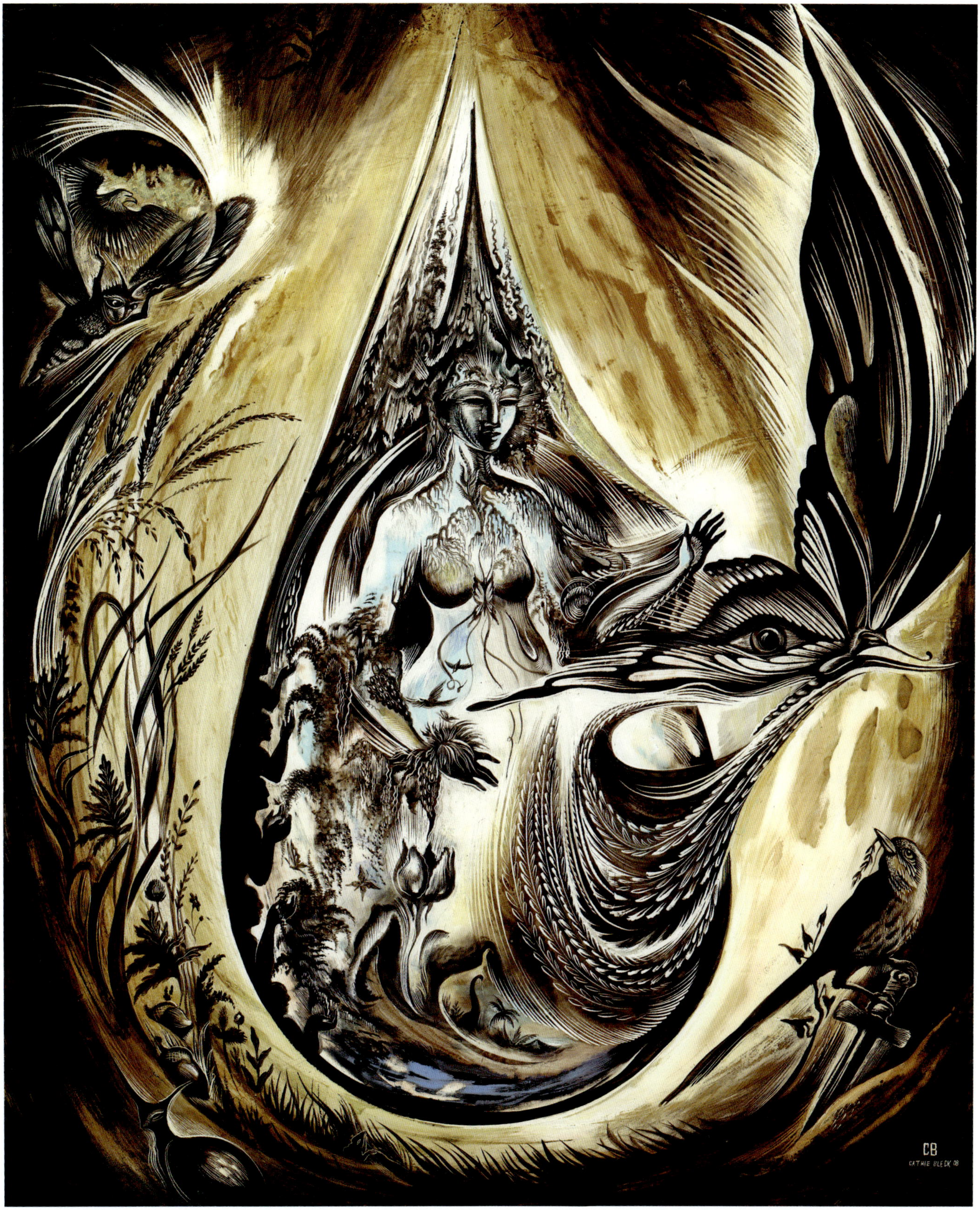

AQUA REGIA II, 16" X 20", INKS, LAQUER AND CLAY ON PANEL

DALEAST

WUHAN, CHINA AND CAPE TOWN, SOUTH AFRICA

Taking Care of Business
I don't pay much attention to environmental news or politics, actually, though I wish I could pay closer attention to those topics. I found I hardly have any interest in that. I mean, I do care about those things, but I don't know if I should really trust the news and politics out there nowadays. They are also constantly changing based on certain unnatural purposes. I would rather make sure that I have done the recycling and taken care of my own waste.

The Self-Imposed Perception
I believe we are all experiencing a different world-projection according to our individual perceptions. As we're constantly experiencing the changes in our world, fear is reacting on different manners and scales, as well as the hope, which comes with the fear as a package. No matter how big the future's changes will be, I guess my biggest fear is that I am not prepared enough, and that I will still hold the fear with me, so I hope that... well, maybe it's better not to have the hope, either.

Force of Nature
Cape Town, South Africa has this energy force that drags me into nature. I guess it's one of the crucial places for me to get wild.

NEVER LANDING, COPENHAGEN, DENMARK
PHOTO BY IAN COX

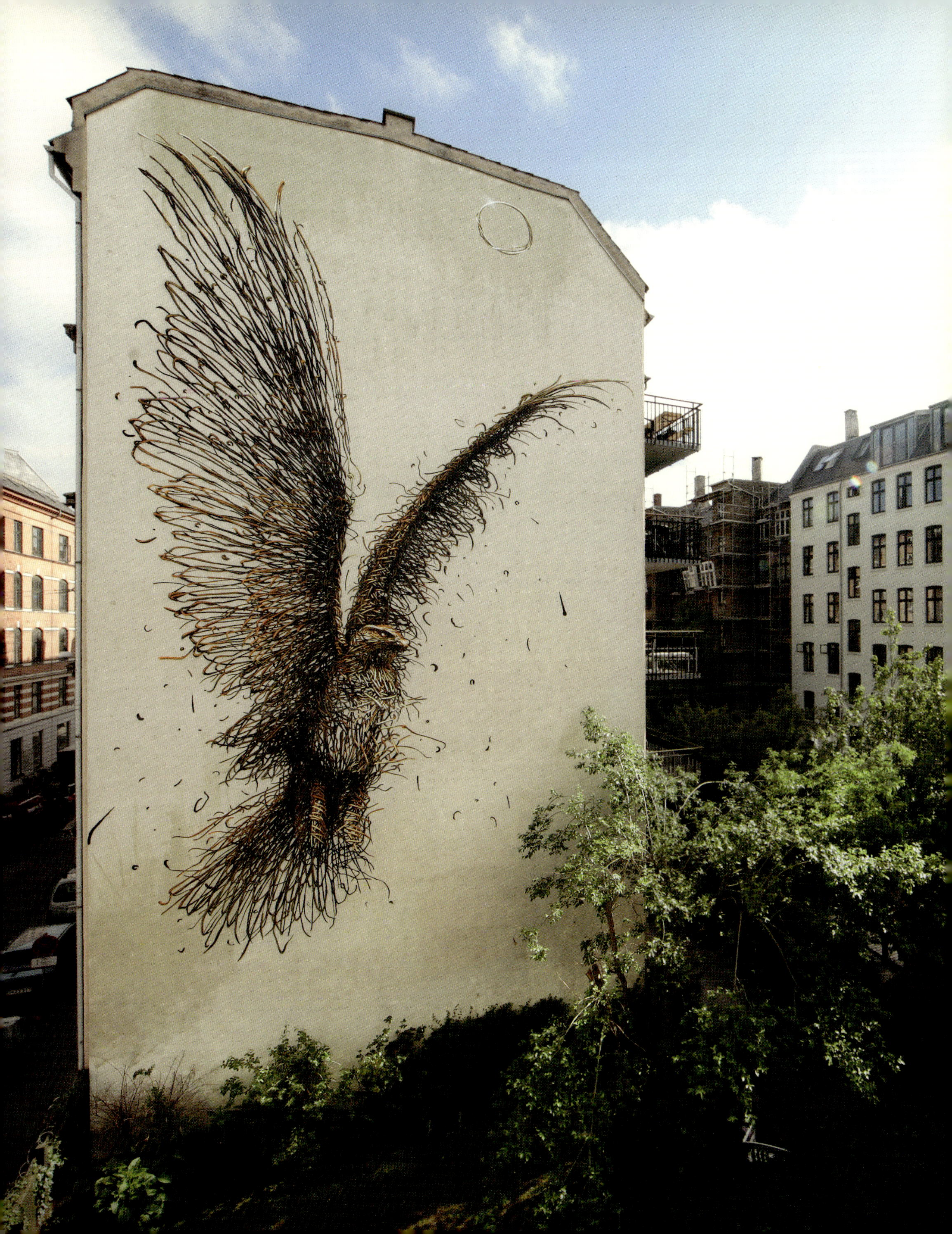

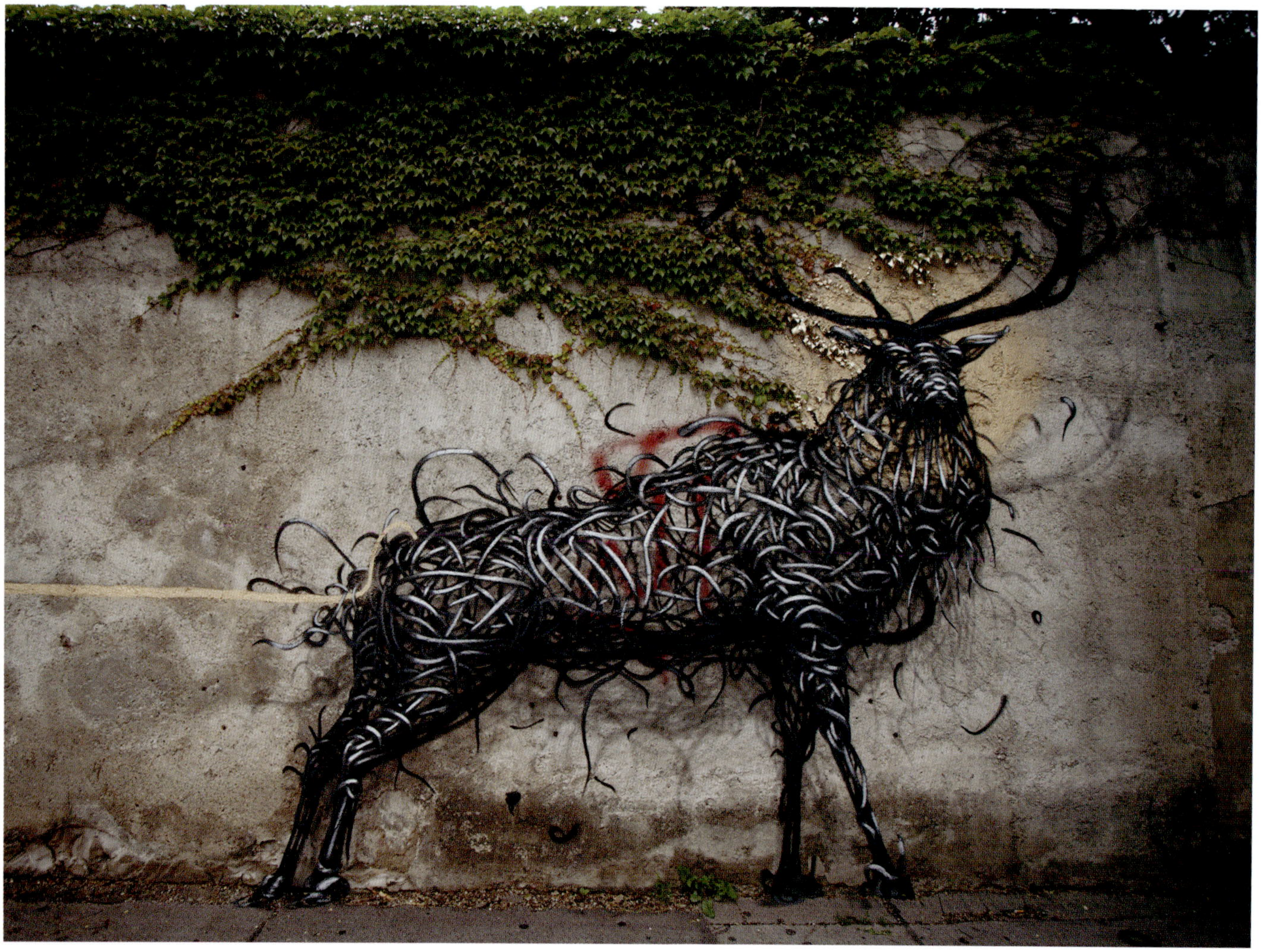

VIENNA, AUSTRIA

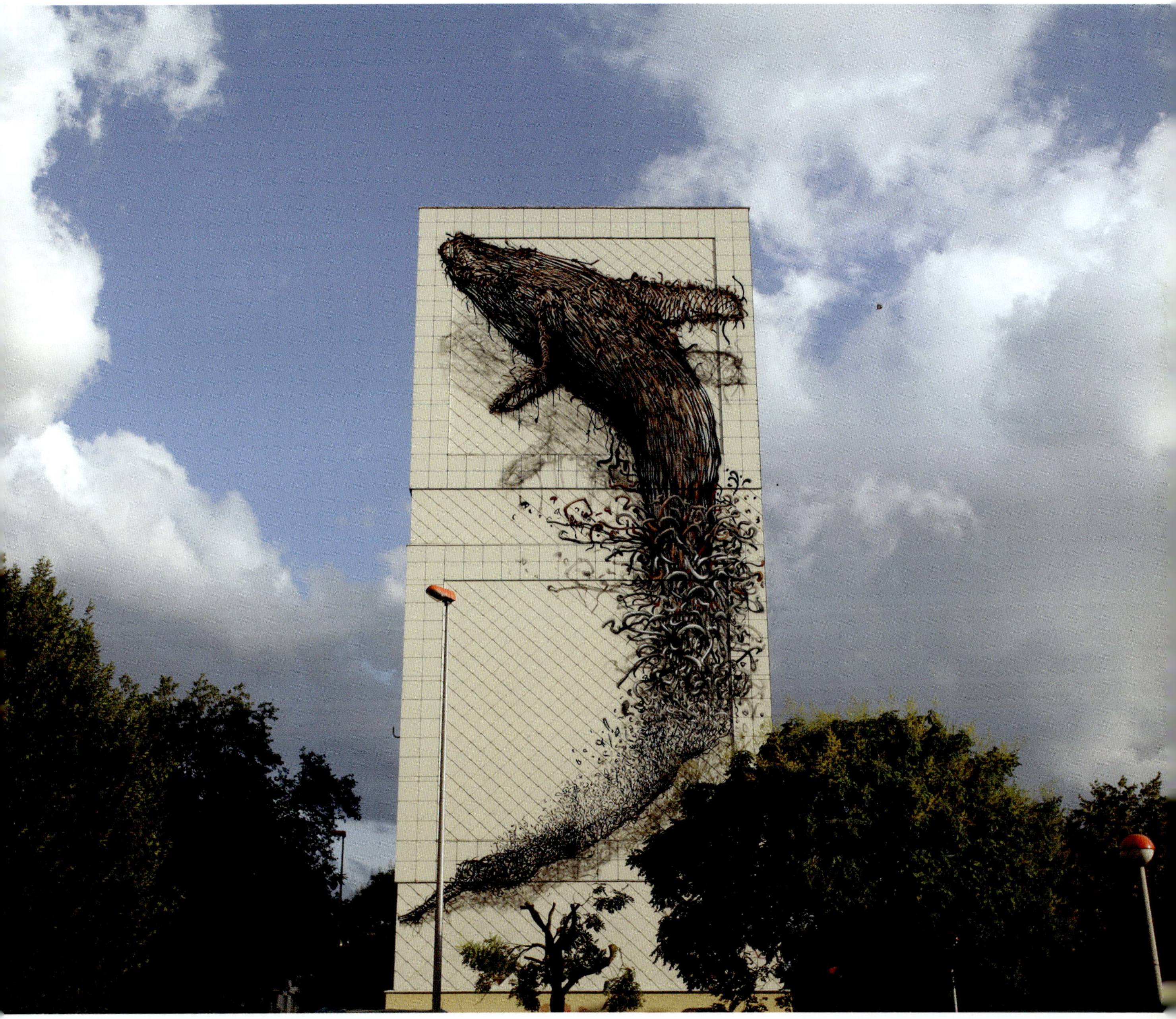

MELUN, FRANCE

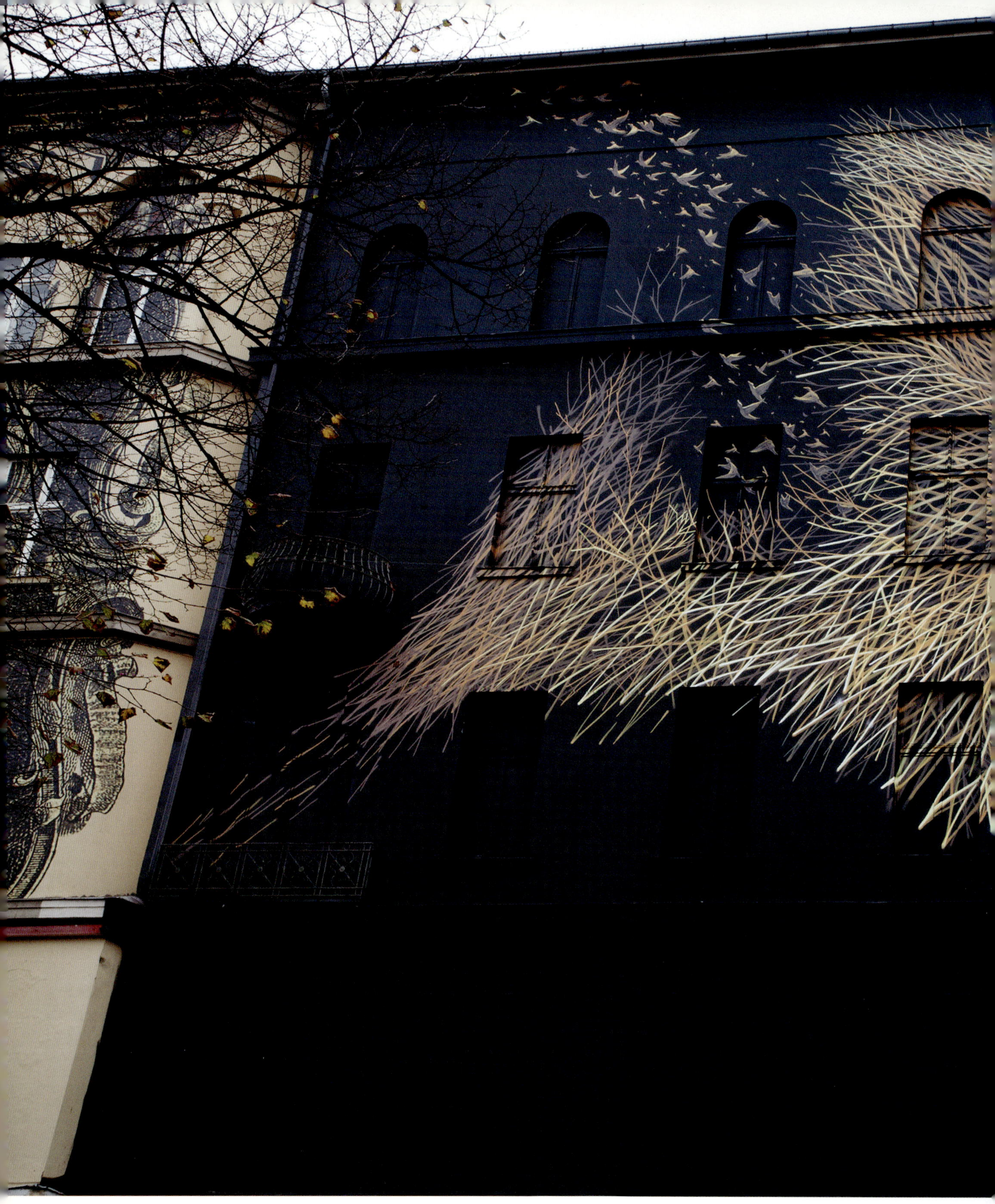

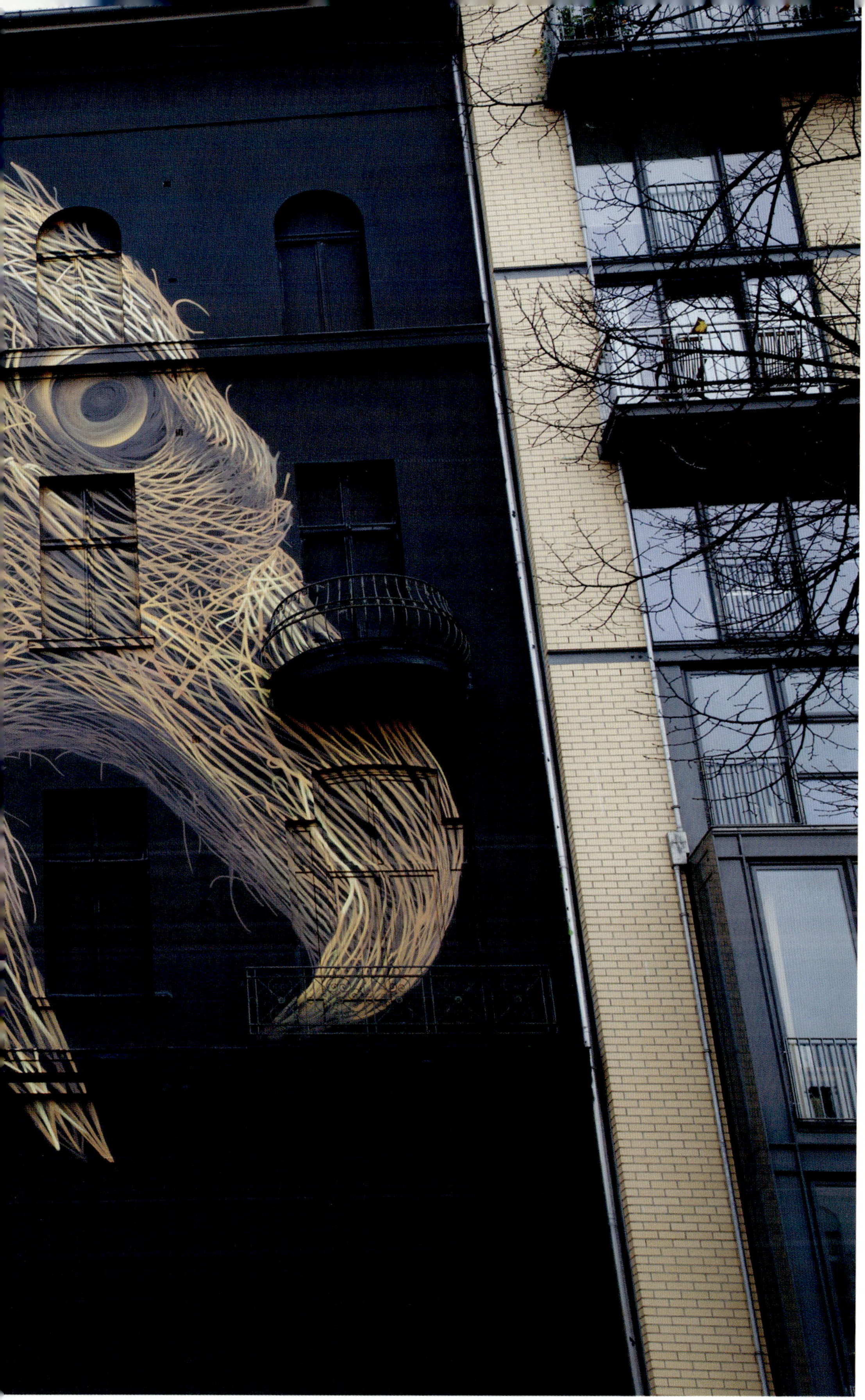

DEFOLIATION P,
BERLIN, GERMANY

JANE KIM

SAN FRANCISCO, CALIFORNIA

Science as a Way of Thinking

I'm always paying attention to environmental news. For instance, the government is currently considering putting the monarch butterfly on the endangered species list. Since the mid-'90s, their population in the US has dropped ninety percent. So, we're beginning to think about what a monarch *Migrating Mural* might look like and how it might bring attention to the issue. But what really drives my work isn't the news cycle, it's inspiration I get from science and biology that I think will drive people to appreciate and protect the natural world.

Animal Dreams

For as long as I can remember, I've represented my animal obsession through art, whether it was making stuffed teddy bears, or sculpting clay horses, or painting flowers. I used to draw animals on my bedroom walls as a little girl, so it's a joy to be able to draw animals on walls for a living today.

Flawed Philosophy

Climate change, ocean acidification, deforestation, these are all huge issues, but really they're just symptoms of a much larger problem—our flawed philosophy toward, and relationship with, the natural world. Art can't change the amount of carbon we're putting into the atmosphere, but it can challenge and inspire us to change the way we think and behave, which is the only way we can begin to solve these massive problems. I'm afraid that, as the world changes, I'll lose the things that most inspire me and allow us to enjoy life on this planet in the first place.

Humans are the audience. My focus is to connect people to everything else that is living on the planet.

Lives in the Balance

People try to ascribe value to different forms of life—a blue whale is worth more than brine shrimp—but the reality is that every life form plays a critical role in maintaining a livable planet. They're all equally powerful.

Defining "Environmental Artist"

What does that mean? Is it someone who draws trees and animals? Or is it an artist whose work is influenced by, or focuses on, the environment and surroundings? By the latter definition, we'd all be environmental artists.

Merger in a Mural

Politics, especially in this country, have become incredibly divisive. My hope is that public art can help people who may ordinarily disagree find common ground. Consider the *Migrating Mural.* In the Eastern Sierra, the issue of bighorn conservation is very political. Parties focusing on mountain lion protection and those focused on big horns have actually been at odds with each other. But when you put both animals in a mural together, representing the balance of life, it can become a unifying force. There's even a *Migrating Mural* on the Bishop Gun Club, a place where people who hunt other species of bighorns have target practice.

Where Trees Fall Into the Ocean

I've been fortunate enough to see rainforests, deserts, and oceans, but the place that brings me to tears is the Northern California coastline, where the redwoods fall into the Pacific Ocean. The size and beauty of that landscape makes me feel tiny, insignificant... and free.

MURAL AT THE NATIONAL AQUARIUM (DETAIL), BALTIMORE, MARYLAND

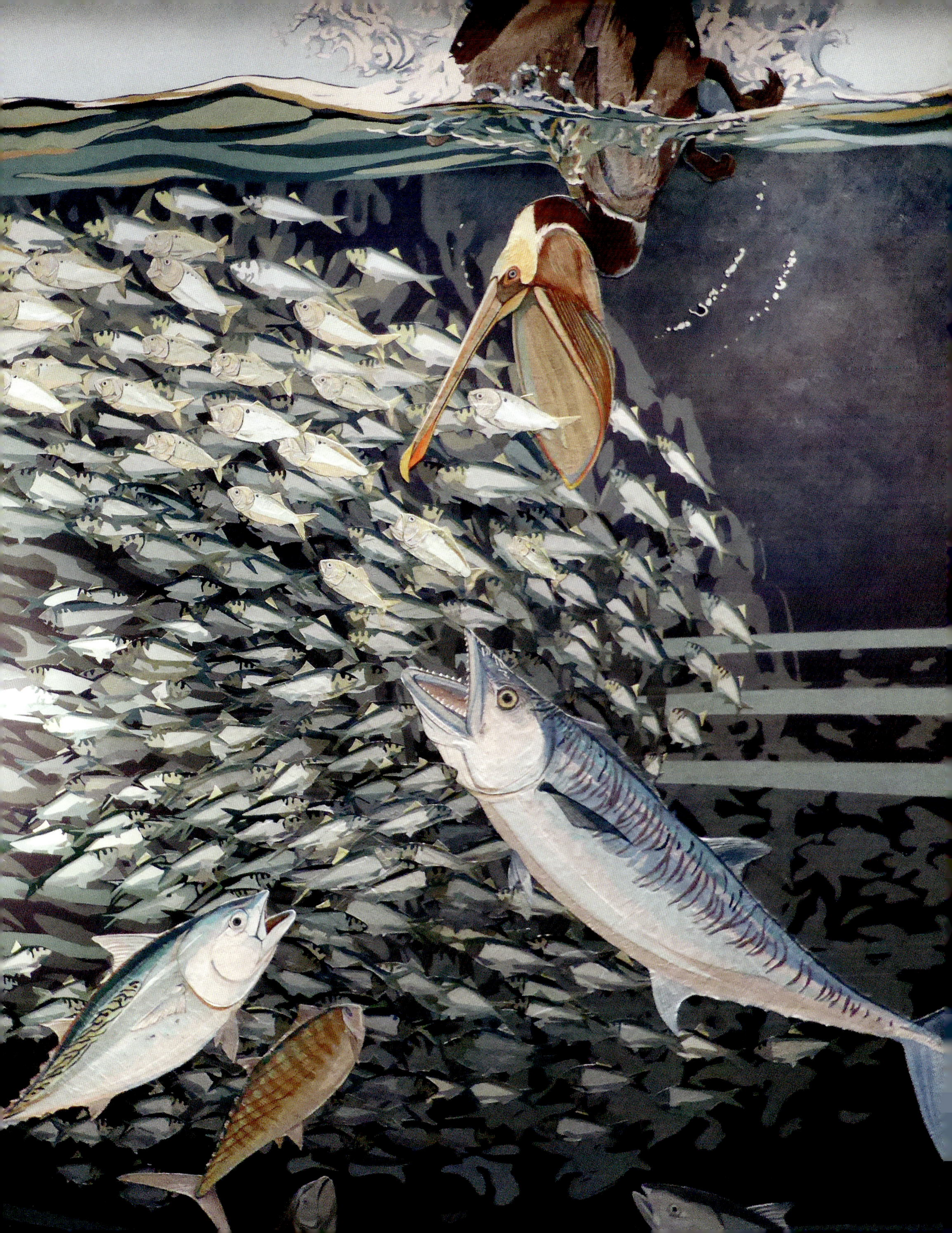

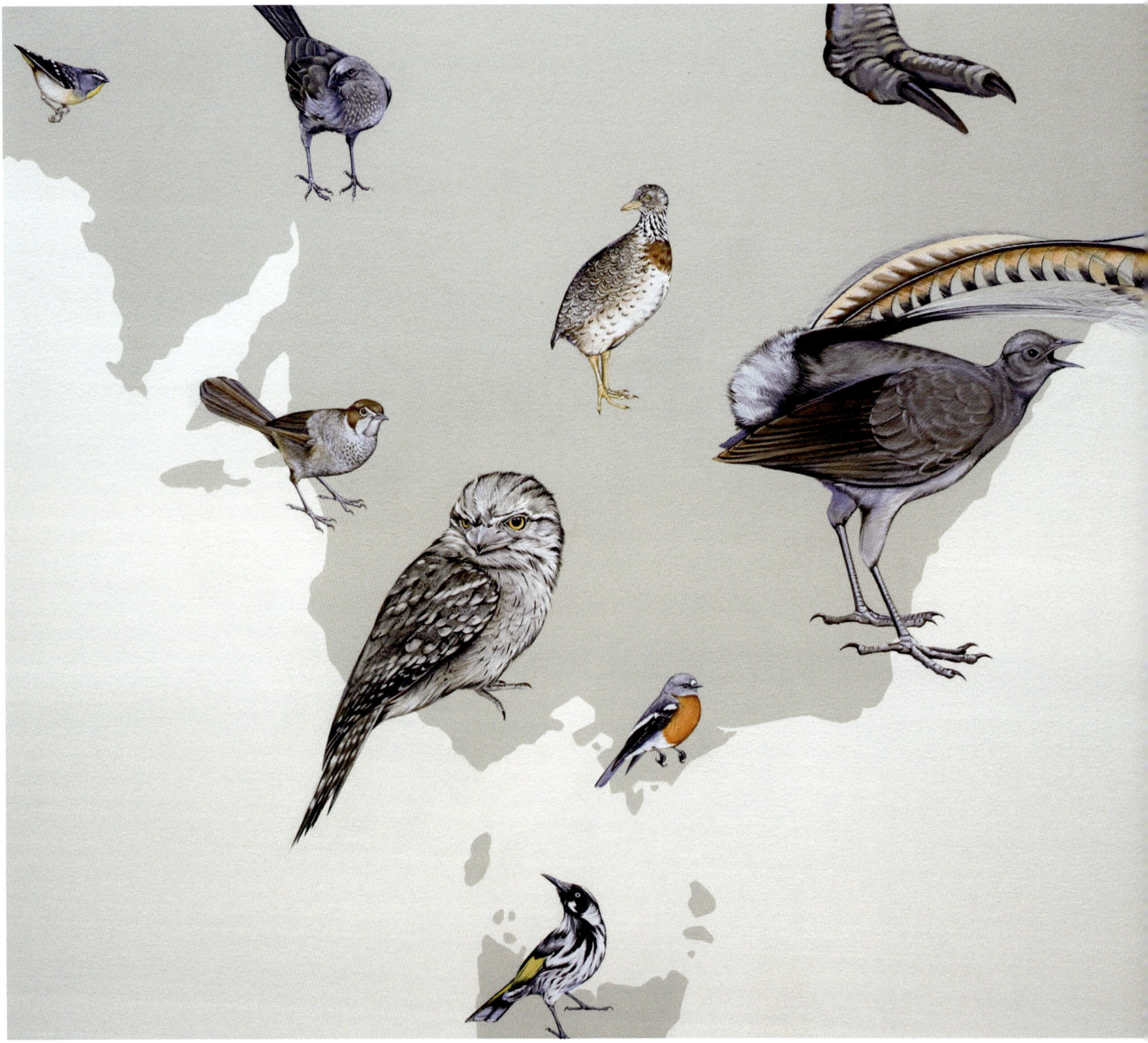

WALL OF BIRDS
CORNELL LAB OF ORNITHOLOGY
PHOTOS BY DANZA CHISHOLM-SIMS

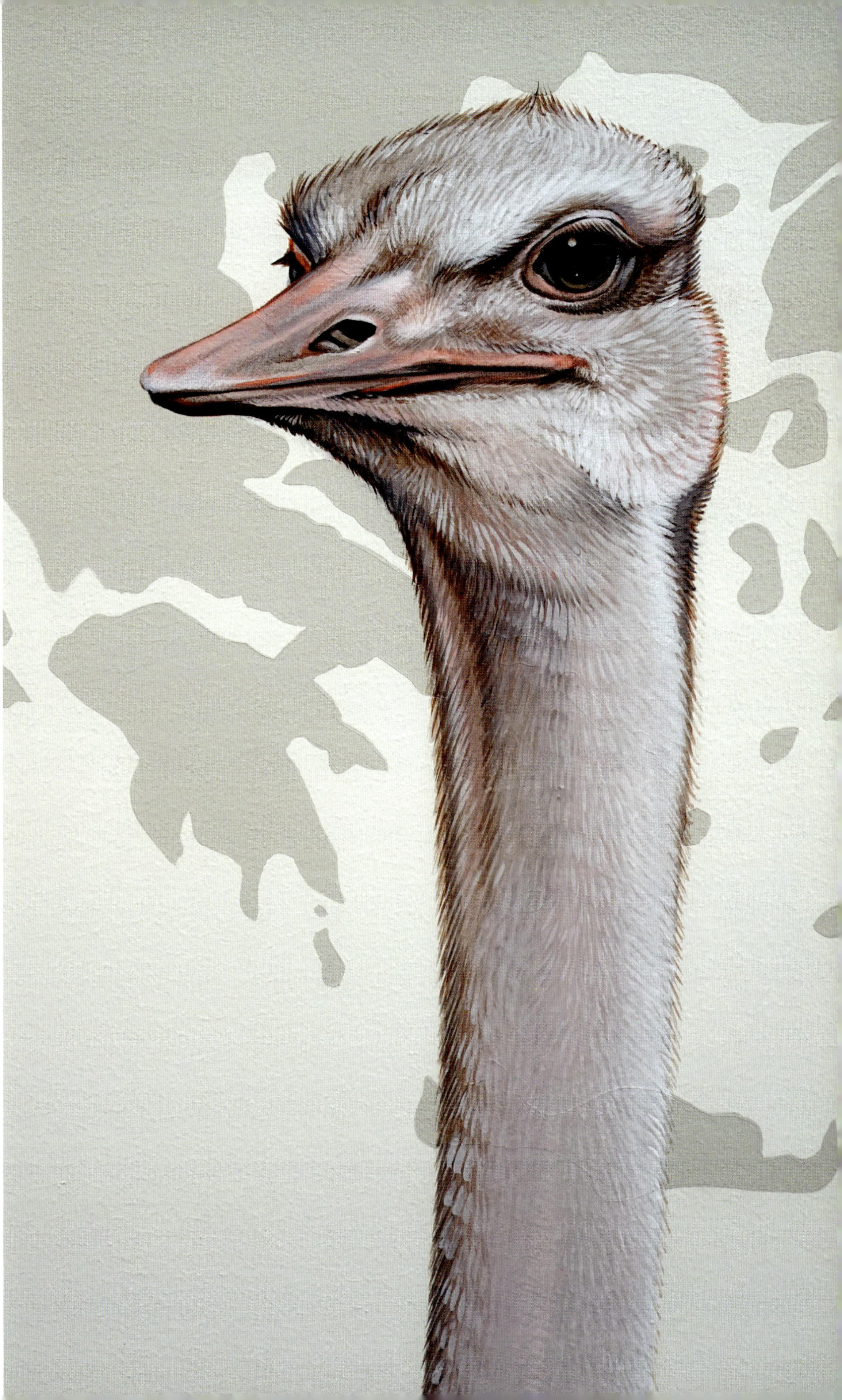

WALL OF BIRDS (OSTRICH BIRD)
CORNELL LAB OF ORNITHOLOGY
PHOTOS BY DANZA CHISHOLM-SIMS

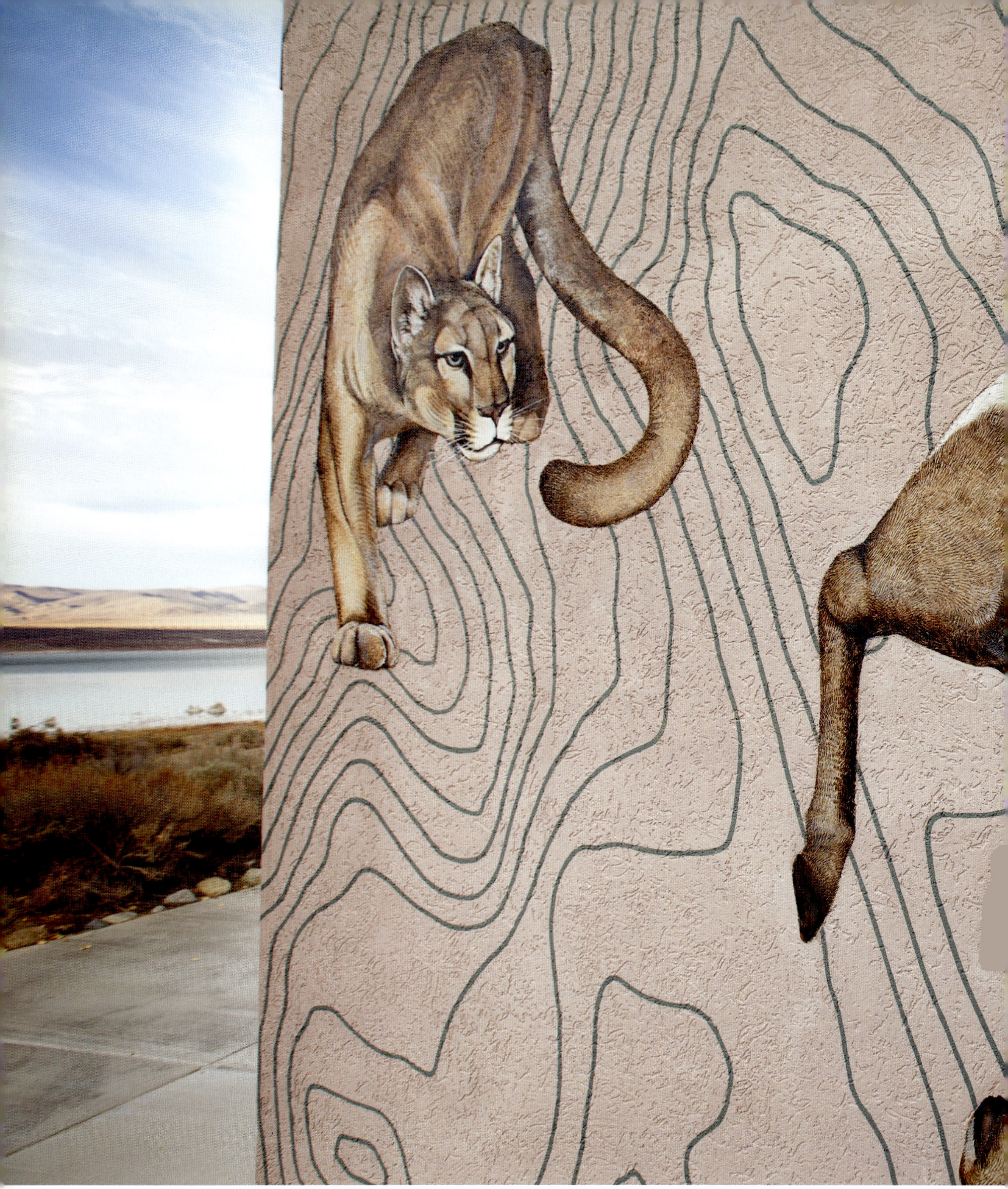

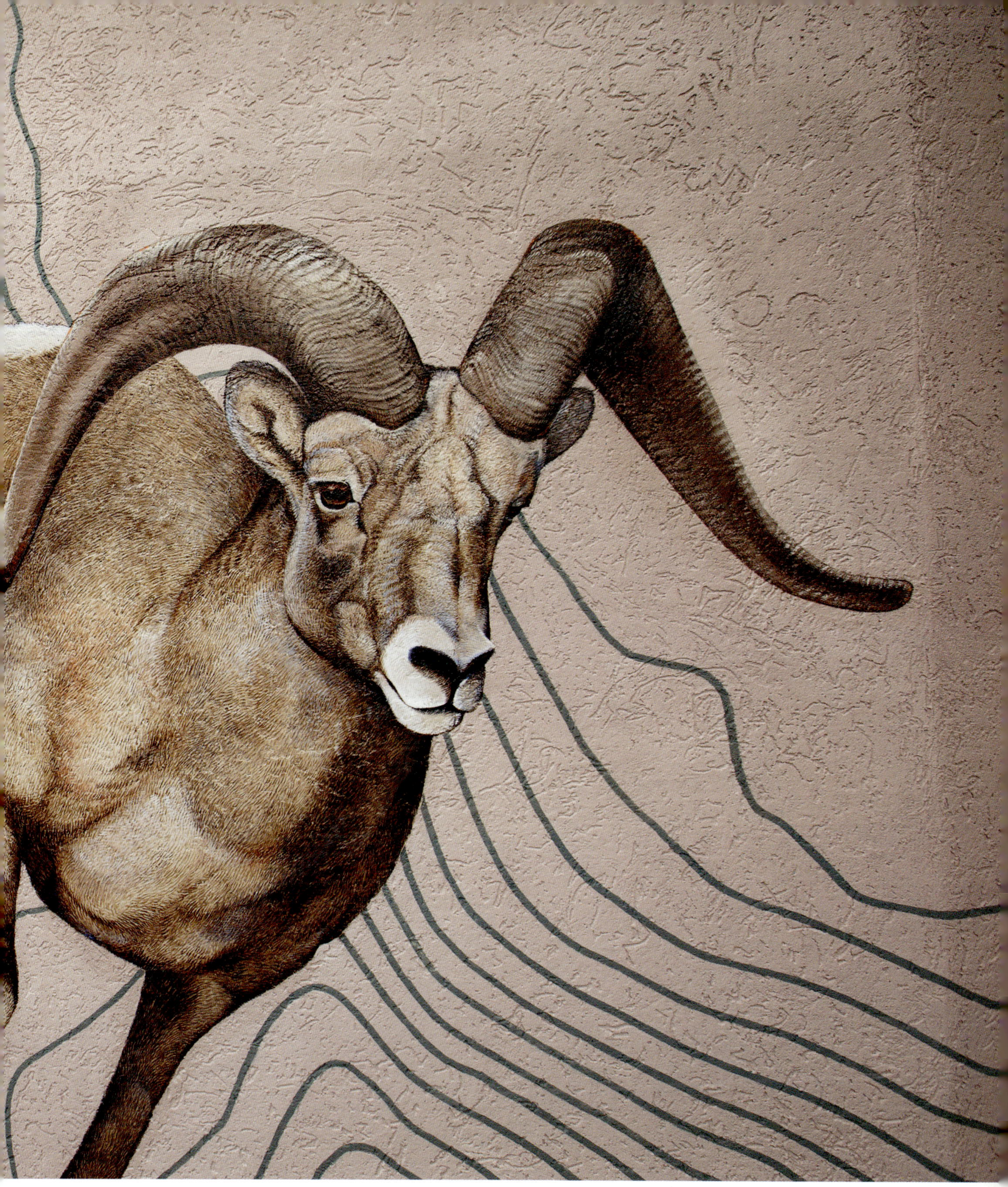

MIGRATING (MURAL DETAIL), MONO BASIN VISITOR CENTER, CALIFORNIA, PHOTO BY CODY TUTTLE

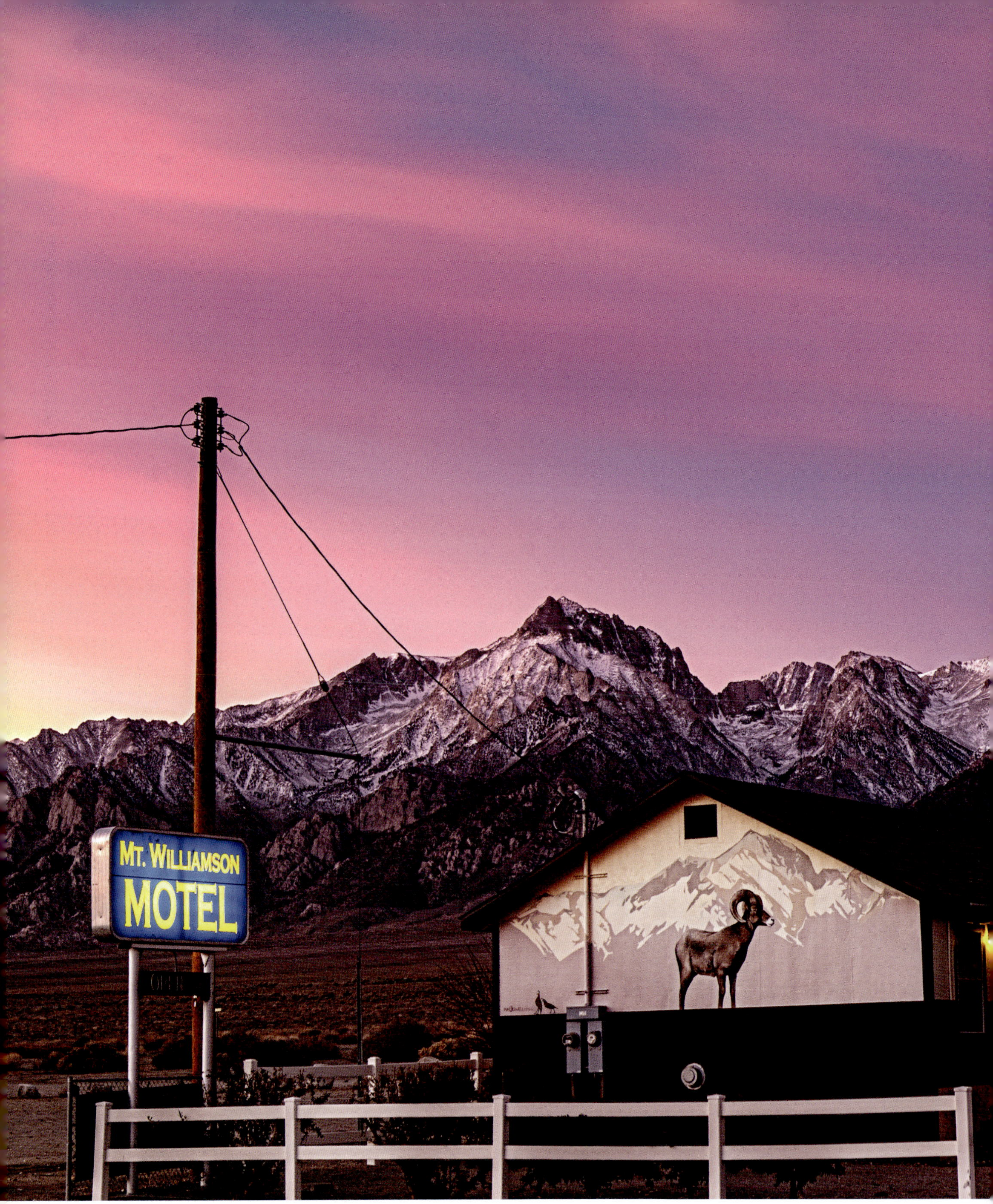

MIGRATING MURAL, MT WILLIAMSON MOTEL, INDEPENDENCE, CALIFORNIA, PHOTO BY CODY TUTTLE

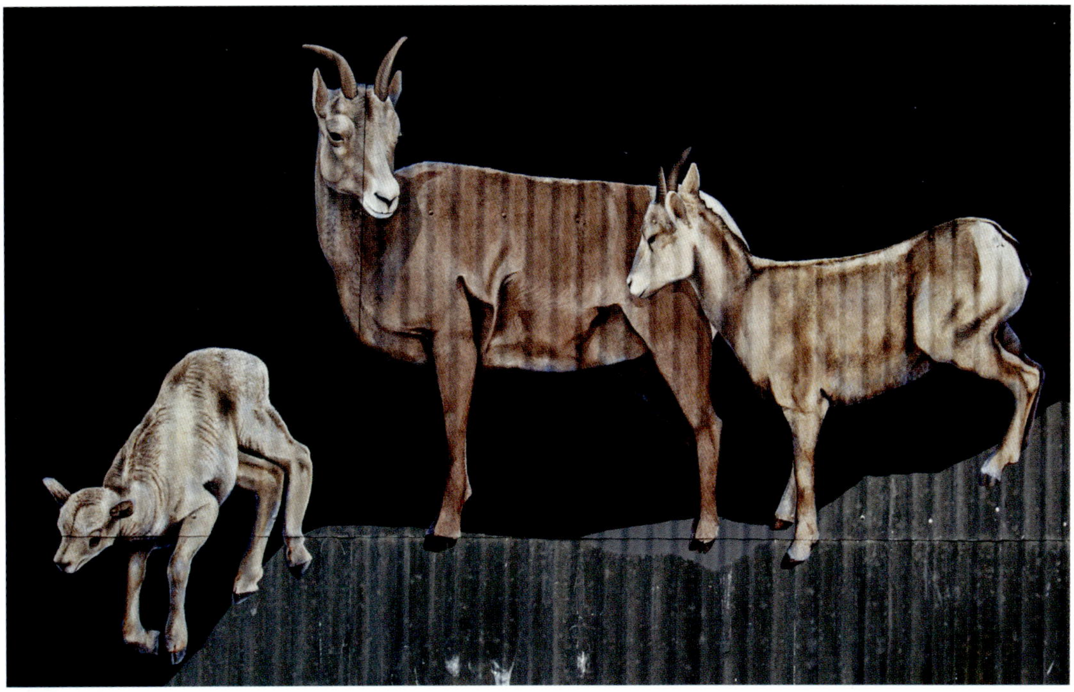

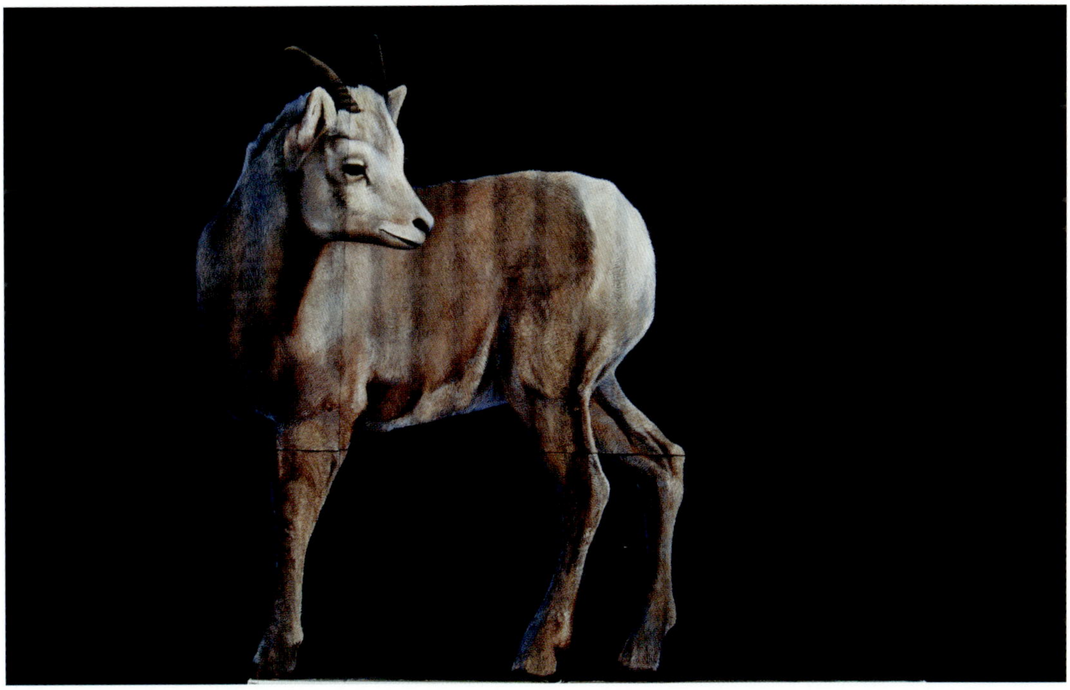

MIGRATING MURAL (DETAILS), LONE PINE REGIONAL AIRPORT, LONE PINE, CALIFORNIA, PHOTOS BY CODY TUTTLE

DENNIS McNETT

RICHMOND, VIRGINA

Something Ain't Right
Environmental issues, overpopulation and pollution really bothered me when I was a kid. I try not to follow the news or dwell on those things too much now. They are bleak and out of my immediate control. I do pay attention to what I see with my own eyes or digs into my guts, like animals species disappearing forever. I was in NYC for the hurricane. I was in Houston for the floods. I can't help but feel something is off.

Beasts of Burden
I've always been obsessed with animals and have drawn them ever since I can remember. I really started using them as characters to carry weight and to separate me from the equation around 2001.

Understanding the Wolfbat
The Wolfbat is a fictional character that is a cross between a Wolf called Fenris and a bat. I use this character to discuss historical issues, as content, to create mythology, ceremonies, etc.

The Others
I've painted people I care about or friends I've lost in the past years. Any people outside of that usually turn out as dark characters. Animals have more weight, are more expressive and are more fun to draw for me.

The Death Stare
The most powerful animal is definitely a wolf. I had a timber wolf when I was eighteen till I was about twenty. She was amazing. They are not dogs. They are very intelligent, pack is everything, and their expressions are intense. When she was pissed, she would throw her front feet down stiff, bristle all the hair up on her back, roll her lips up to expose her teeth, and be dead silent with a stare.

All Natural Artists
There's Andy Goldsworthy, who's using nature and natural things as his art. There is every artist that uses recycled materials. There are groups like Just Seeds that try to make people aware of environmental issues. Maybe engineers who have created cars, homes, self-sustaining gardens or anti-carbon-footprint hoobydoobs are the environmental artists.

One Last Do-Over
There are only a few times I've set out to be political, and I don't know that I would call what I do now political. Maybe everything is political in its own way. As I mentioned before, I've felt something was off, even as a kid. Maybe, in part, that is why I make up fictional stories and characters doing ceremonies to undo bad things or reset a way a thinking.

The Right Spots
Yellowstone, most shorelines, and the Badlands. I had a very strange and life-changing experience in the Badlands.

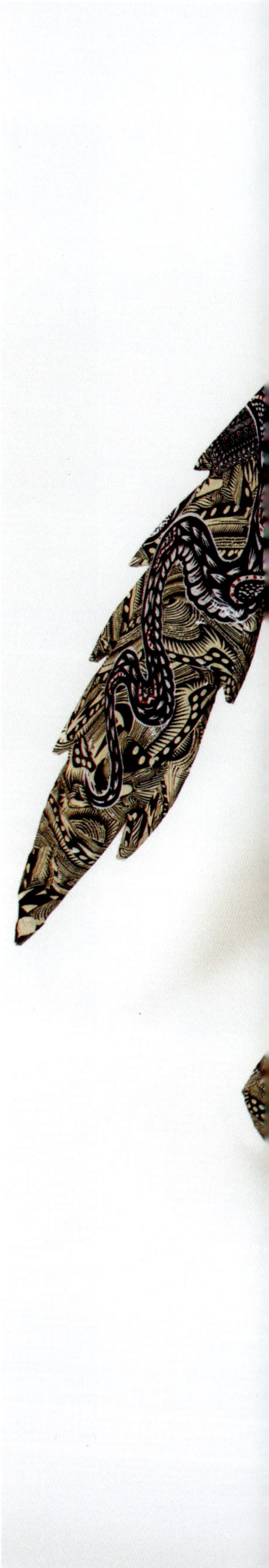

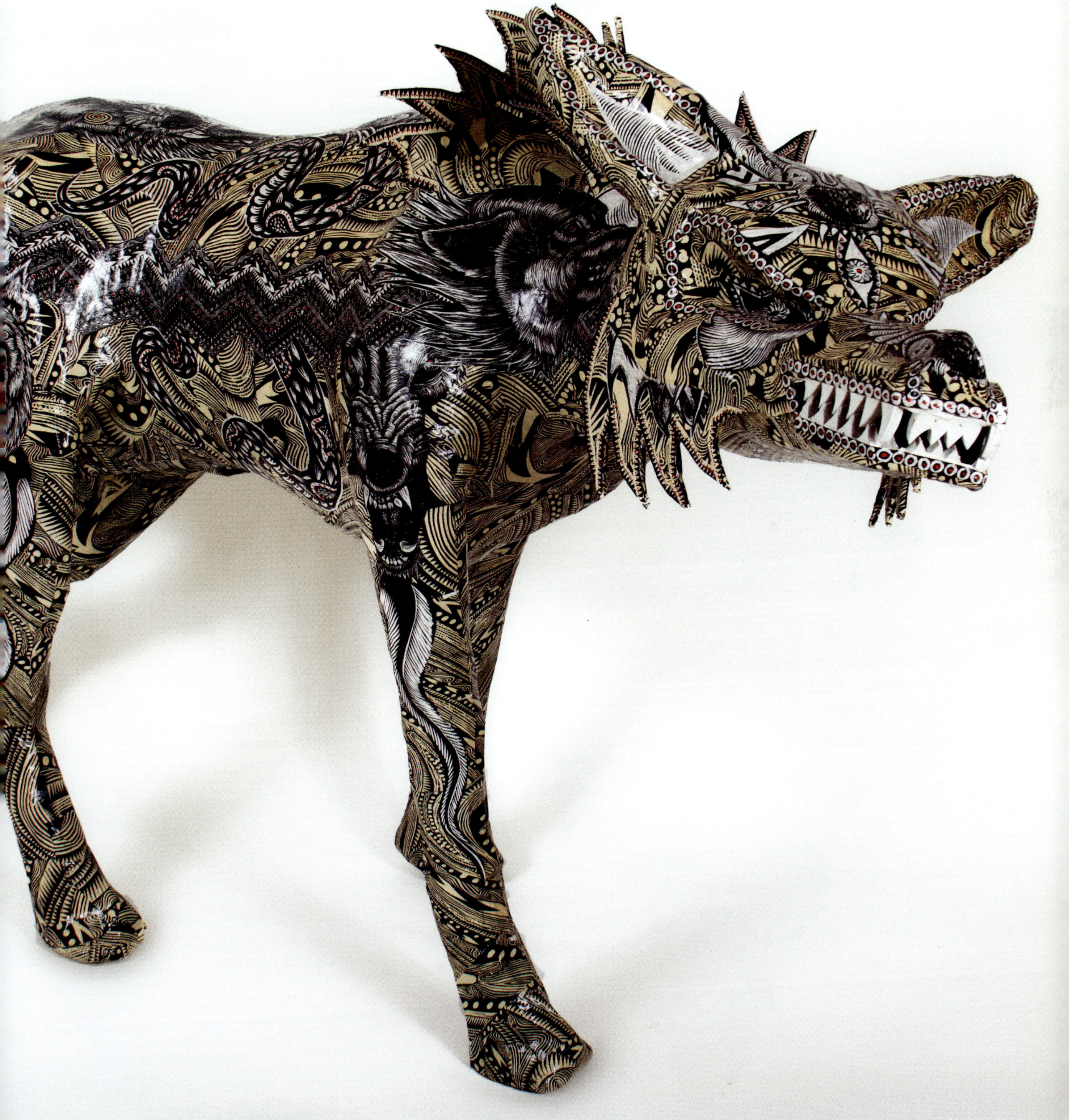

PSYCHIC WOLF, PAPER MACHE, WOOD AND WOODBLOCK PRINTS

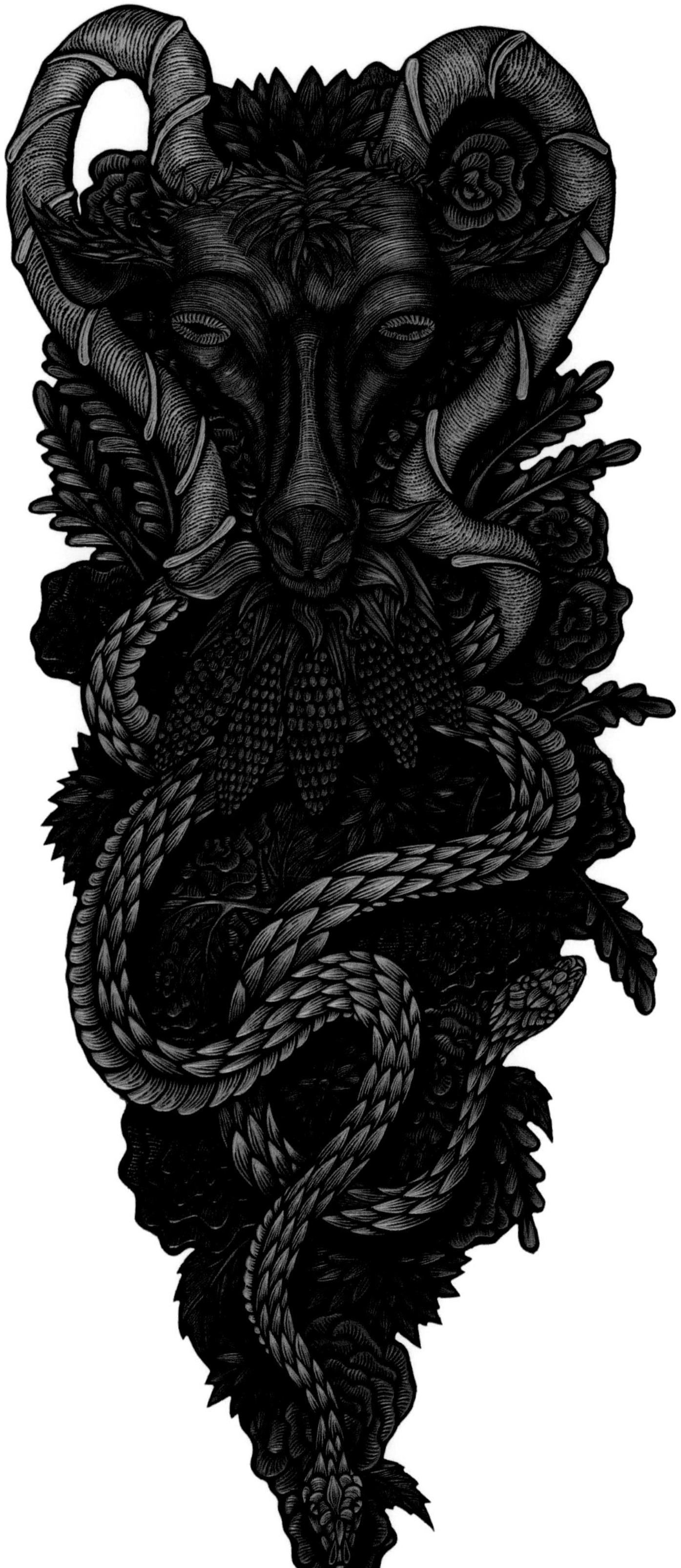

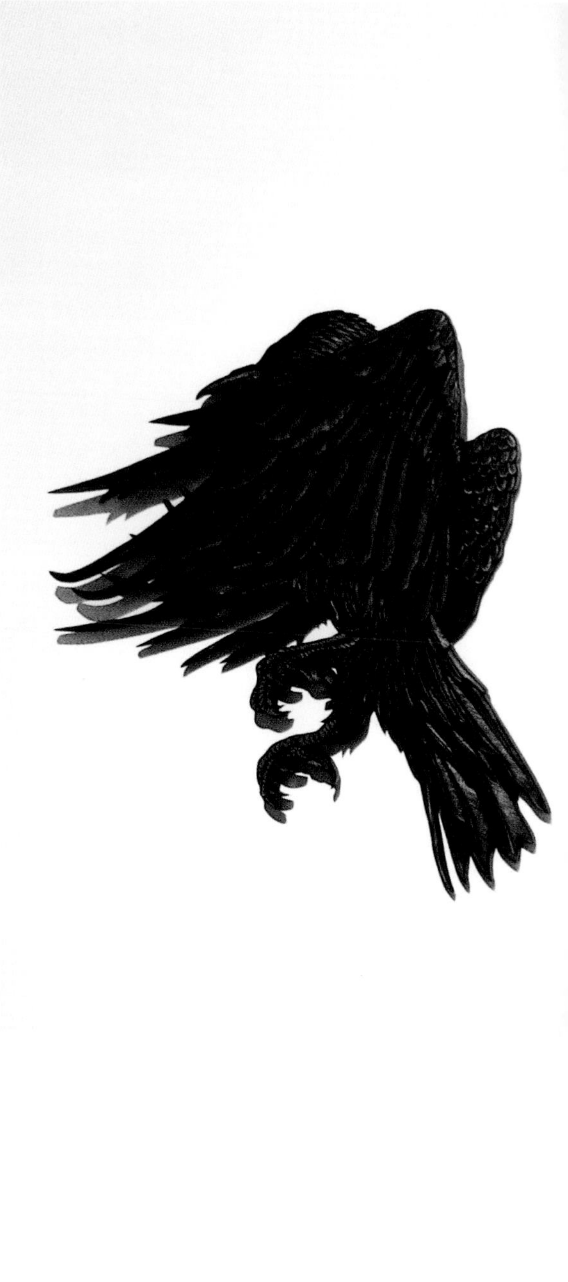

AUTUMN DEITY
WOODCARVING AND ACRYLIC

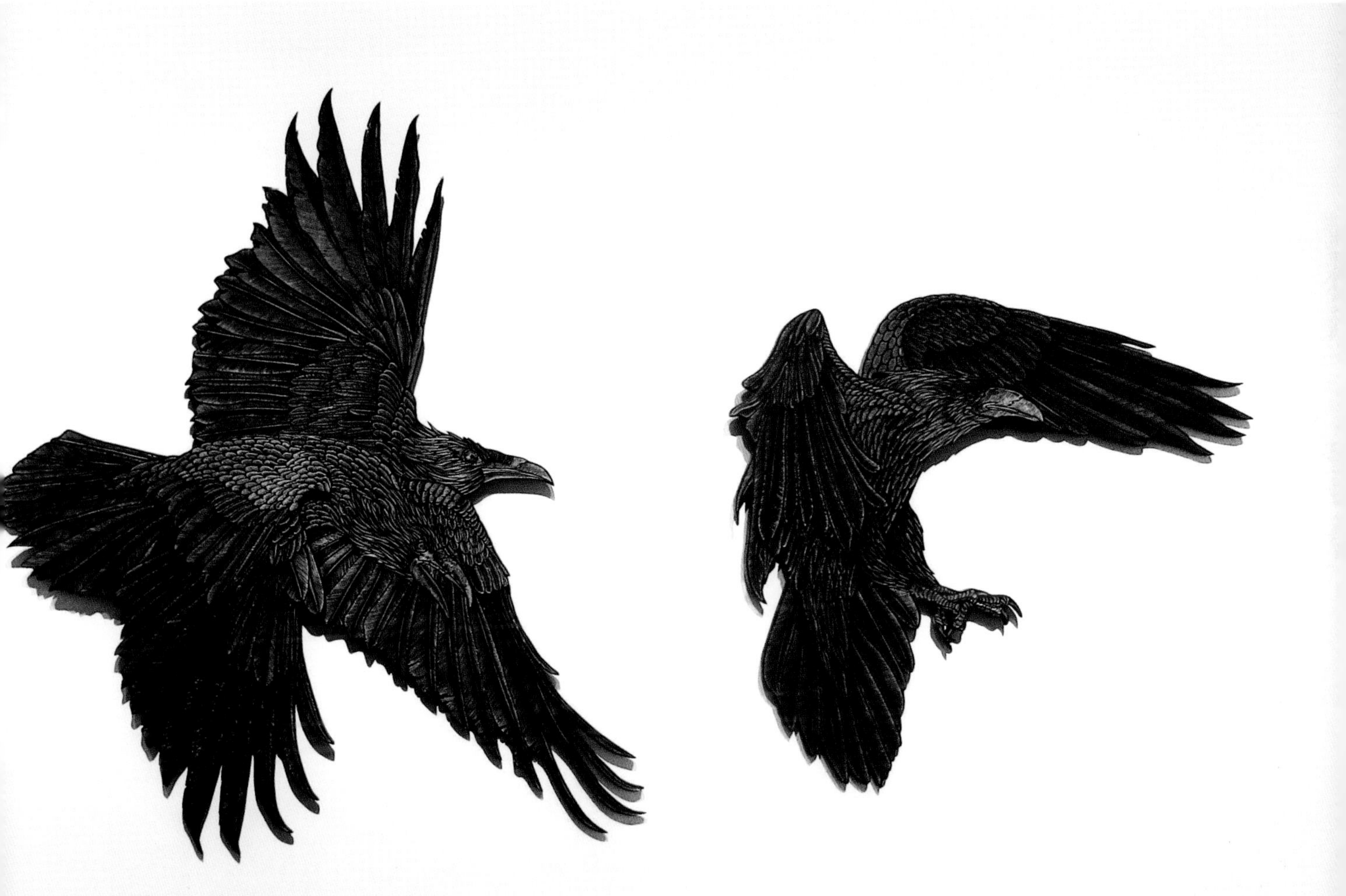

RAINBOW CROWS, WOODCARVING AND ACRYLIC

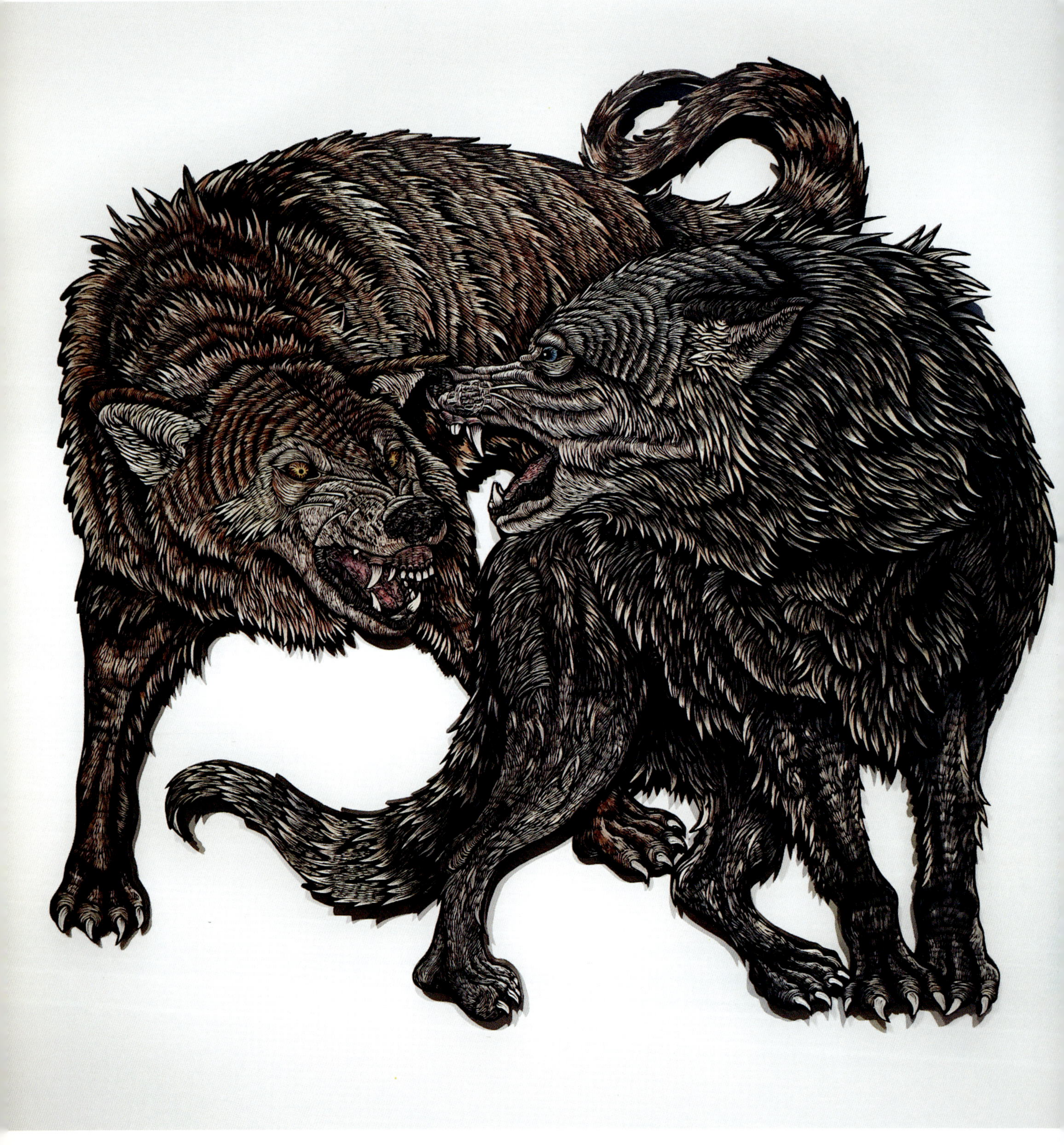

THE CHASE OF SKOL AND HATI, WOODCARVING AND ACRYLIC

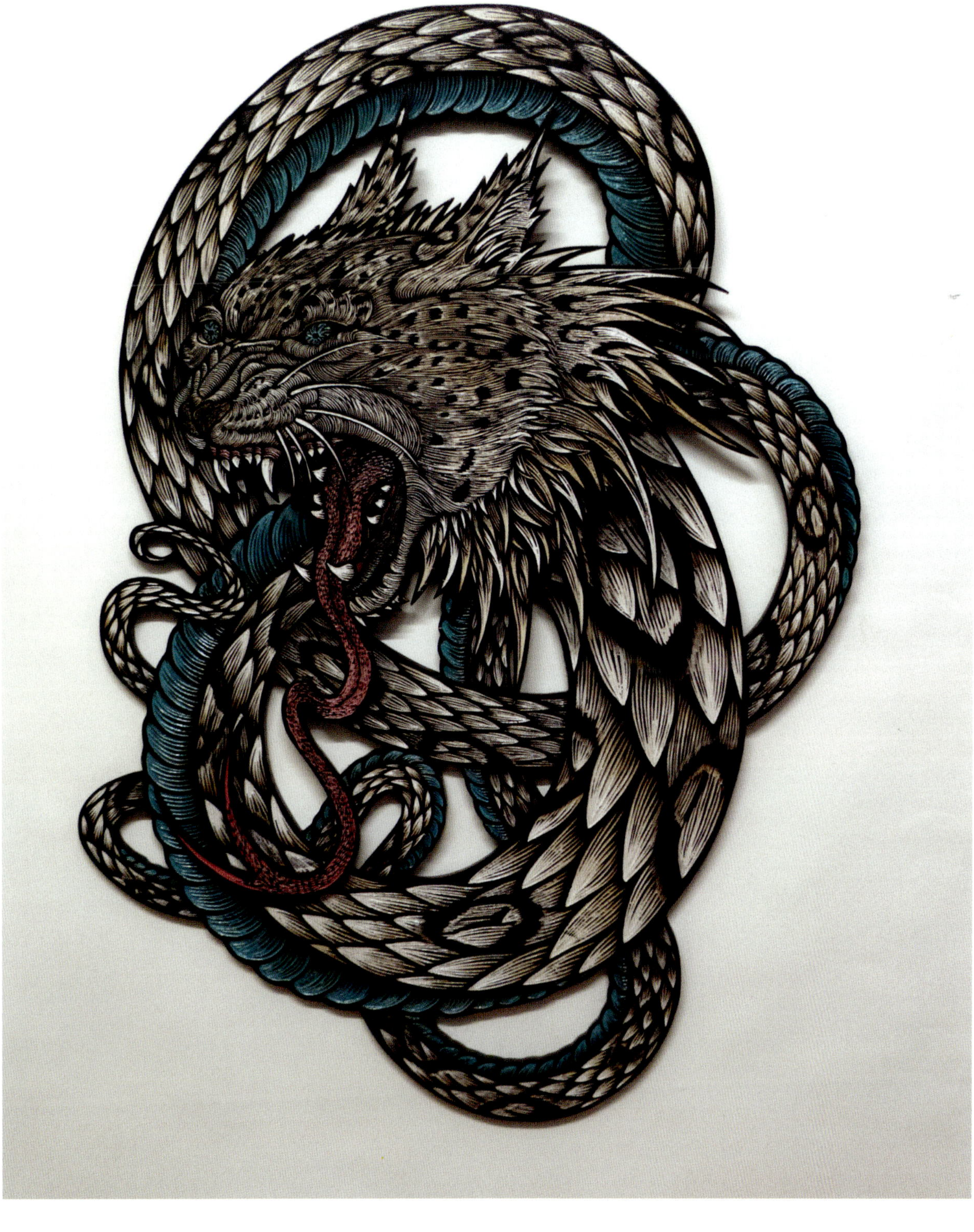

WOLFBAT LEOPARDSNAKE, WOODCARVING AND ACRYLIC

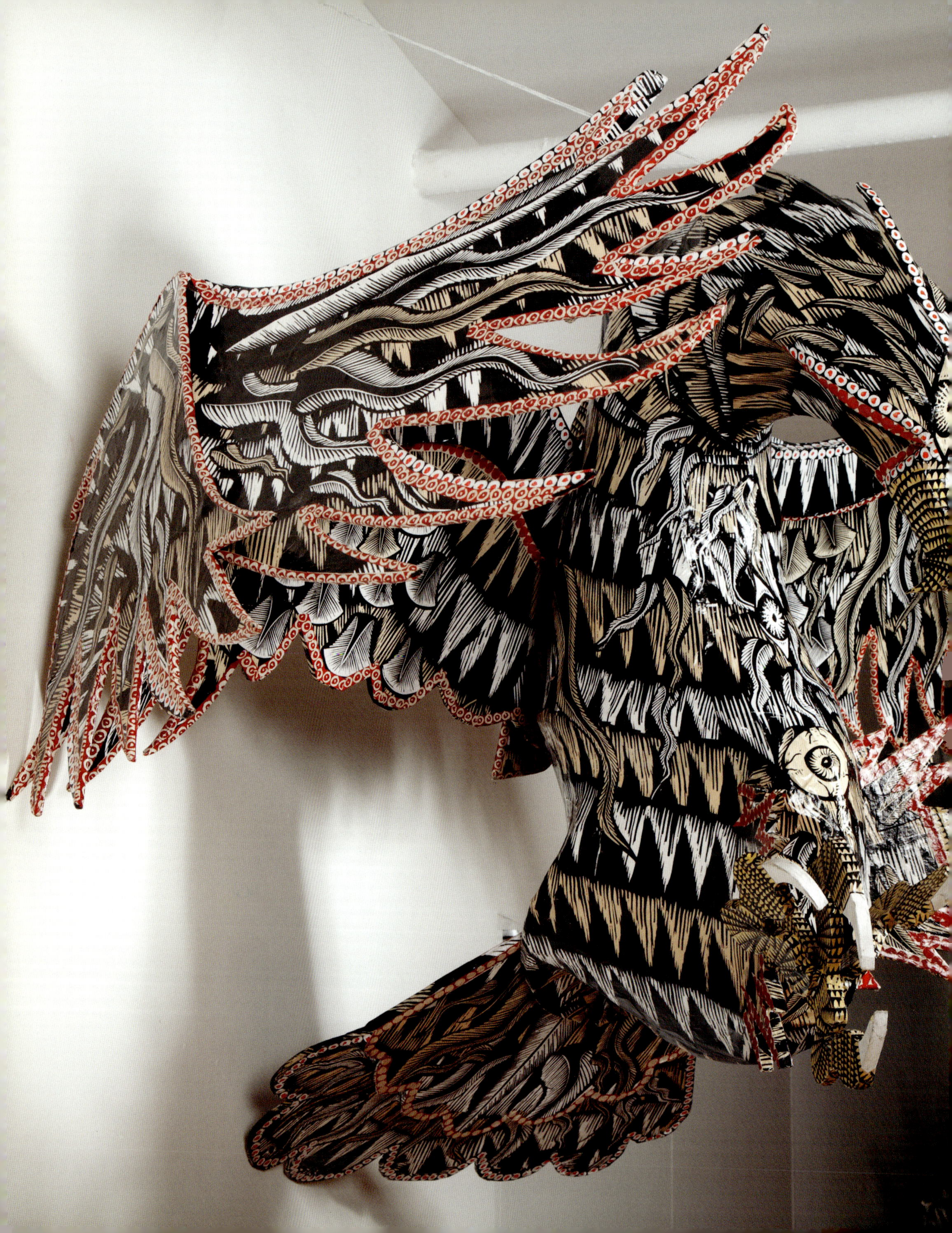

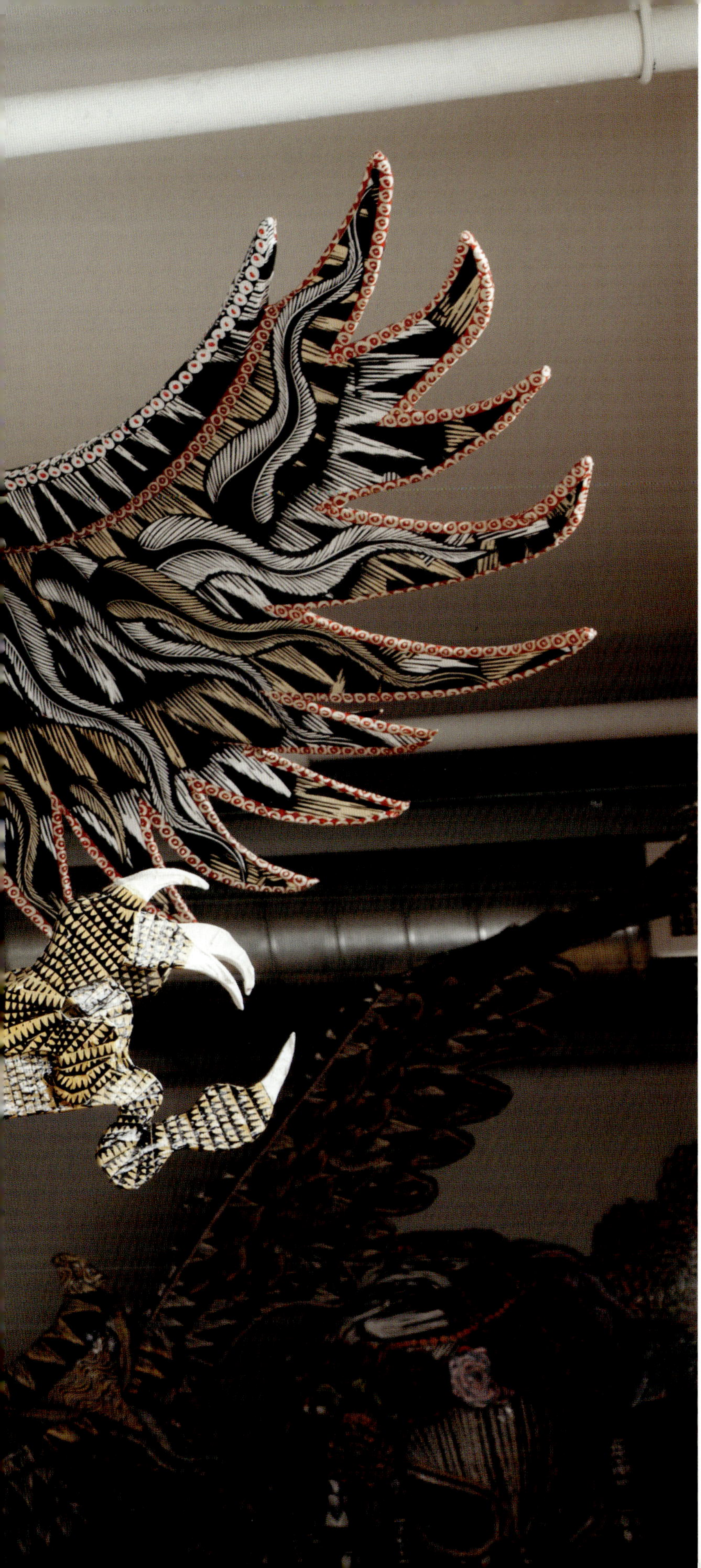

EAGLE SPIRIT
PAPER MACHE, WOOD AND WOODBLOCK PRINTS

DEEDEE CHERIEL

LOS ANGELES, CALIFORNIA

Pay Attention
It's easy to feel overwhelmed and powerless in the face of rapid environmental and climate changes, but I feel it is our duty to read, pay attention and do what we can to make positive change. A while back, I felt bad about how much plastic shit is floating in the ocean and how much plastic people buy every day without thought about where it will spend the rest of eternity on this planet. So my response was to make my *Care for this Garden* poster and wheat-paste it all over LA. It was my environmental poster campaign that was sort of like a public service announcement.

The Bird Girl
When I was much younger, I traveled to Santiago, Chile. I was reading a bunch of Latin American writers at the time, and some of the magical realism in the literature affected my painting. The first girl with a bird head I painted was a cartoonish portrait of the girlfriend of the guitarist in my band. I was hanging out with other bohemian-artist types, painting and playing music. My bandmate lived on the twenty-first floor of this building, and we would sit around and drink wine, and his skinny, model girlfriend would wander around the apartment talking in a little high-pitched voice. She was like this beautiful bird with long legs wearing ballet slippers in a cement cube cage, living up above the clouds of exhaust and the hum of the city.

Wild Inside
When I was spending more time in India with my family there, I was painting a lot of Indian iconography—women in Saris copied from the covers of matchbooks. I like to occasionally paint people in human form, but usually I am motivated to convey a stronger element of what that person is like by giving them a tiger head, or a tree-on-fire head, or a beard of leaves to depict their intrinsic nature.

Grizzly Woman
I paint a lot of bears. I was going through a tough time where I had to let go of something. I was meditating on the Buddhist idea that to desire is to suffer. My friend was working on Herzog's *Grizzly Man*, and I was thinking about bears' insatiable appetite to consume, how it aligns with the human appetite to consume things—food, cars, homes, etc. So I started painting a lot of bears—bears with human bodies, bears with ball gowns, bears screaming, crying, singing, and bears with their own language. I also did a public service campaign. I made a poster that read, "You Have Everything You Need," in western-style lettering, in an effort to get people to stop thinking they need more shit to be happy.

Animal Agency
I studied International and climate change politics, and grew up camping every summer in the Pacific Northwest with my family in Oregon. As a child, I was so saddened to see all the clearcutting, and then all the loggers out of work. There was a poster above our bathtub when I was a kid that said, "The Earth is our garden and we are its caretakers." It is amazing how an image from the popular culture of the '70s can stick in a kid's mind for their whole life. That is why I want to make prints that have simple messages that give people hope and that will stick with them, like advertising for animals and trees that can't afford the ad agency. It is our duty, as citizens of this planet, to use the voice we have to make the change we want to see.

The Oregon Trail
I love the Oregon coast because it is beautiful and dramatic. I love Yosemite, Fall Creek in Eugene, Oregon, and the McKenzie River, near where I grew up.

THE SOURCE OF EVERYTHING IS PROFOUND (DETAIL), 36" X 24", MIXED MEDIA AND ACRYLIC ON WOOD

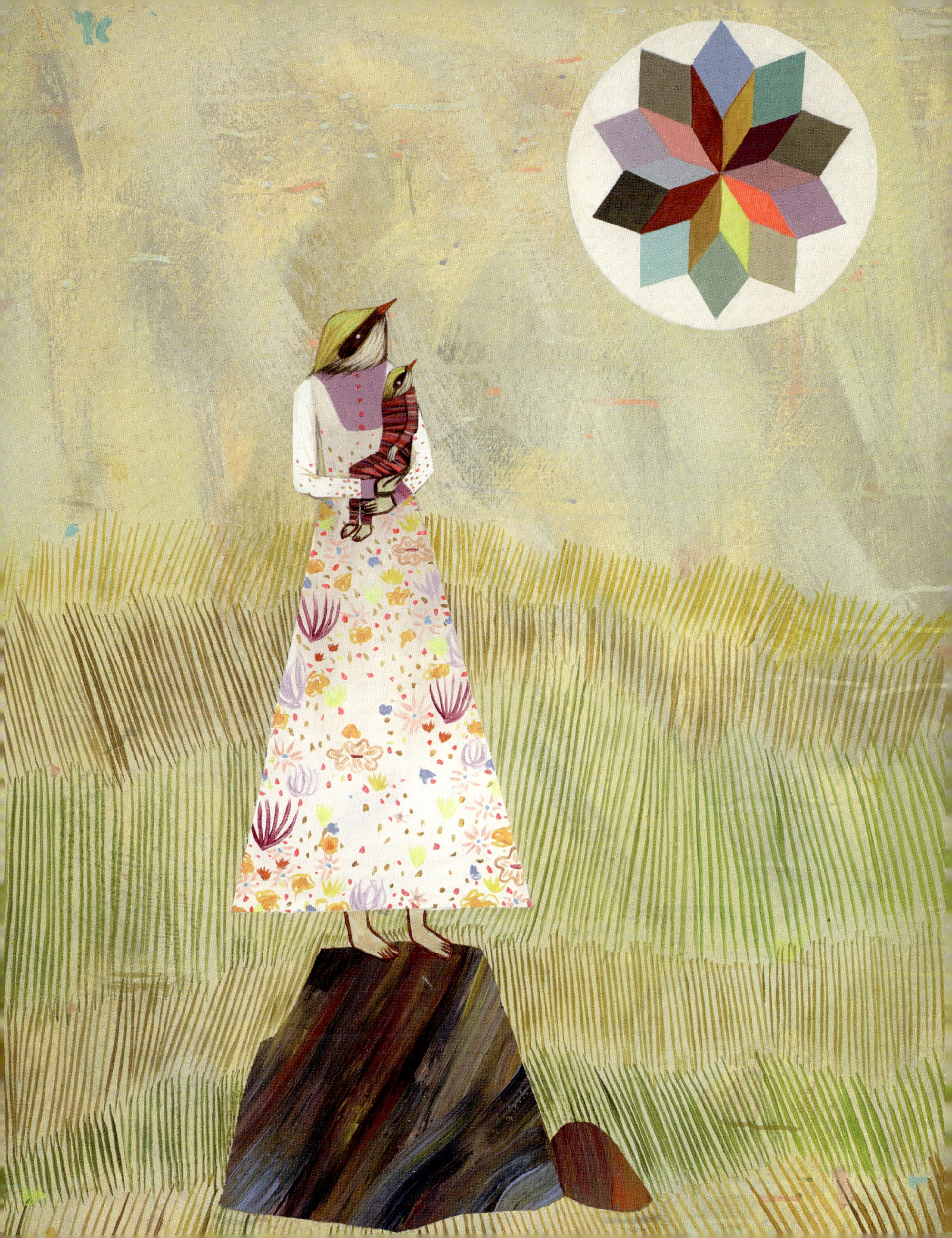

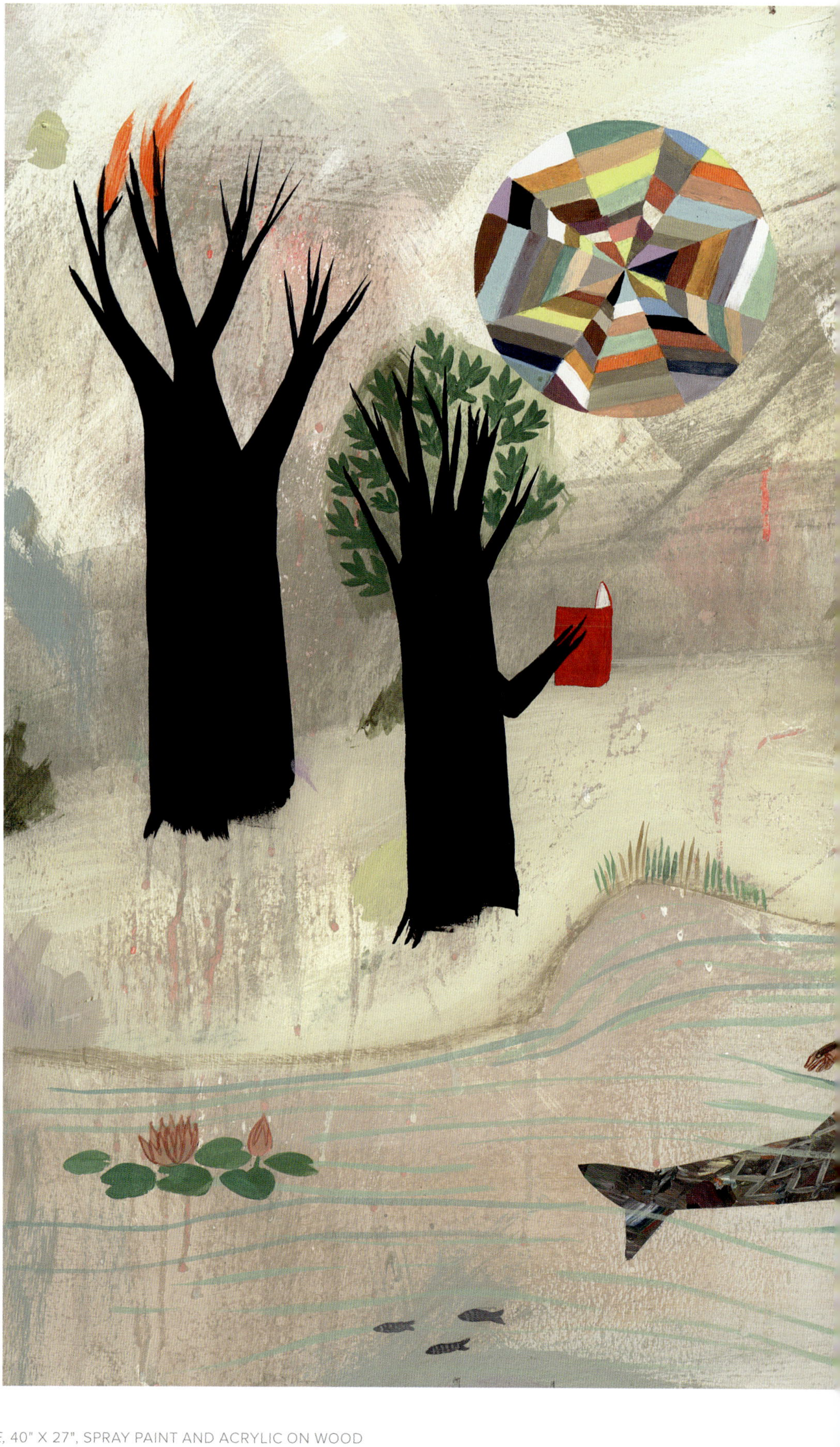

TRADING FOR POWER AND AQUIESENCE, 40" X 27", SPRAY PAINT AND ACRYLIC ON WOOD

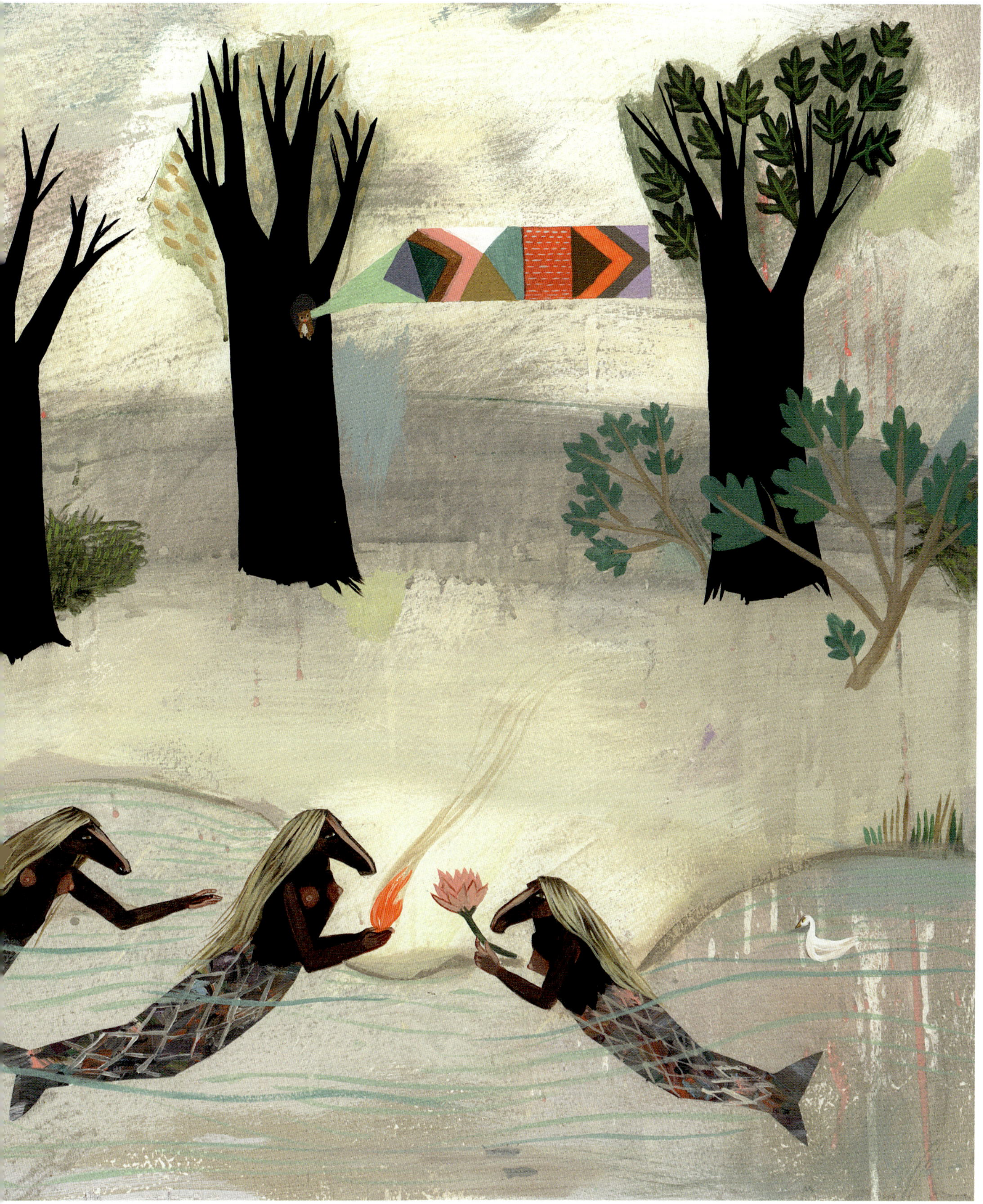

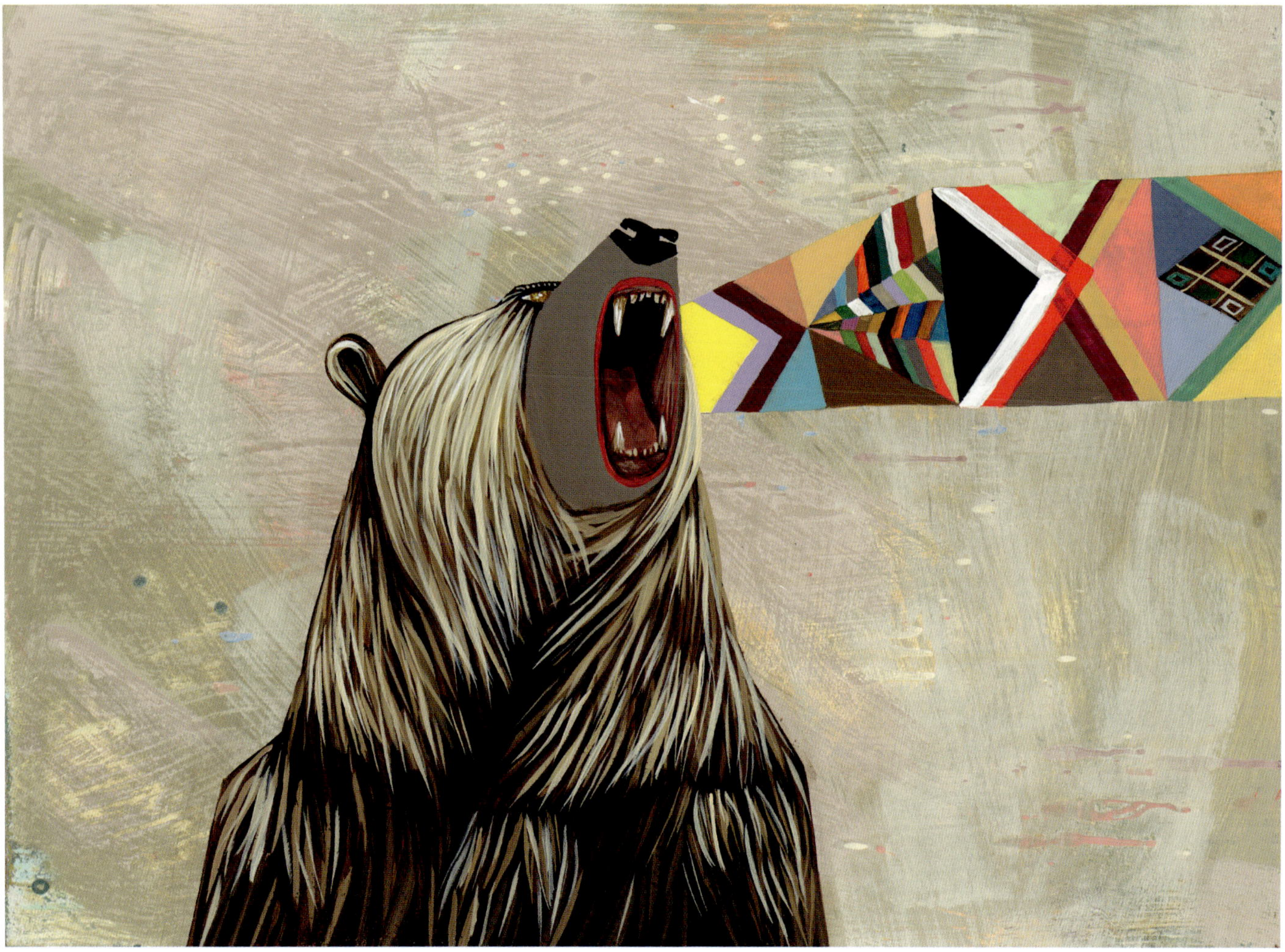

TO DESIRE IS TO SUFFER, 18" X 24", MIXED MEDIA AND ACRYLIC ON WOOD

TAMING THE TIGER: IT'S EASIER TO SEE ME ANGRY THAN TO GRIEVE WITH ME
18" X 24"
SPRAY PAINT AND ACRYLIC ON WOOD

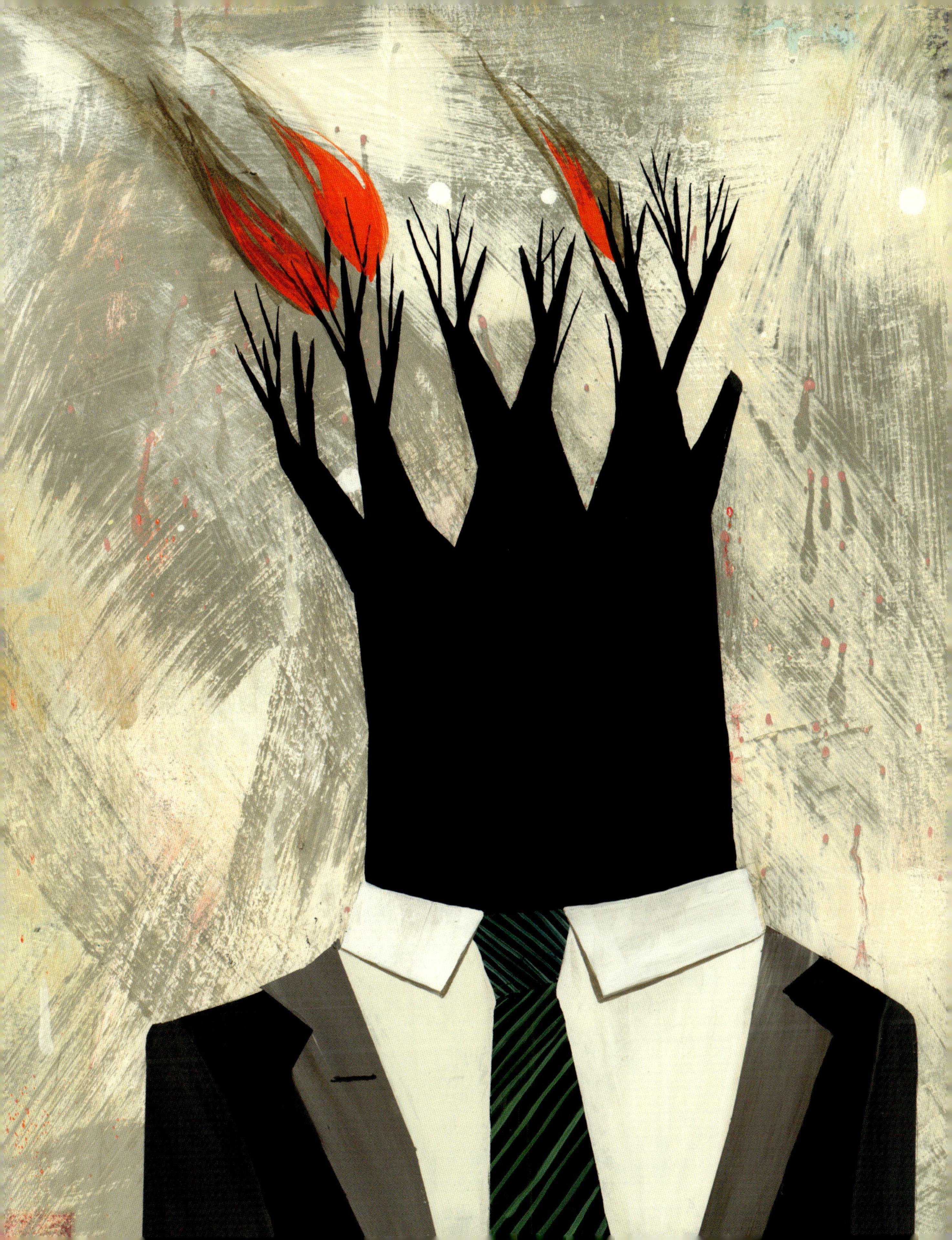

CALEB BROWN

BROOKLYN, NEW YORK

Parallel Evolution
The animals in my paintings serve as proxies for the natural world as they appear distorted and displaced from their natural state, such as otters being the size of buildings, or sharks falling through the sky. They are positioned in opposition to the urban settings and human figures. Sometimes they're pretty menacing, but even when they seem more benign, as in the *Otter City* paintings, they're always at odds with the rest of the scene. In the *Red Panda City* paintings that I've been working on most recently, the animals, though large and imposing, are often being overwhelmed and alarmed by humans, while the people are interested but unafraid.

I have a theory that the Internet's obsession with animals is a subconscious attempt to fill the void normally occupied by our natural relationship with them. Humans have, after all, evolved over millions of years alongside wild and domesticated animals, hunting them, fearing them, and forming symbiotic relationships with them. Now, for the first time, modern humankind is estranged from almost all of their natural relationships with animals, but they still preoccupy our minds in increasingly inexplicable ways. In my more recent paintings, the human figures are always photographing the animal components, reflecting this detached fascination.

From the Beach to the City
I grew up on the beach of the Strait of Juan de Fuca on the border of the Hoh Rainforest in Washington, which must be one of the most unique natural environments in the US, although it seemed pretty ordinary at the time. My work could be seen as an almost literal collision of my childhood surrounded by nature, and my adulthood living in the epicenter of urban America. I suppose that any artists who are making the work that they truly want to make end up producing thinly-veiled self-portraits. In more practical terms, my artistic beginnings are definitely rooted in a childhood spent in relative isolation and near-constant rain. My work has definitely also benefitted from the intense creative energy of New York City and of all of my friends and peers living and working here.

Human Impact
My paintings have become more and more about the way in which we've drastically changed the environment. I try not to approach these themes from a preachy or lecturing perspective, but rather from the point of view that the state of our environment, and our relationship to the natural world is so rapidly changing, and changing is such unpredictable ways, that it drowns out nearly all of my other concerns. I definitely think that environmentalist advocacy is important, and that in a perfect world, a vast majority of humankind's energy and resources should be devoted to preserving and repairing the natural environment. However, as a pragmatist, I believe that we've passed the point of no return, and that the best we can hope for is a new, strange and dangerous world shaped by strength of human ingenuity and the resiliency of nature.

View From the Top
My favorite kind of natural space has always been a deserted West Coast beach, however, in my daily life, my favorite spaces have to be Brooklyn rooftops on summer nights.

What the Animals Would Say
"You people are weird and terrifying."

A Cute Threat
I've been enjoying painting red pandas lately because they're so expressive and adorable. I love trying to find the perfect size to paint them so that they teeter on the border of cute and menacing. To be honest, though, painting fur can drive me crazy after a while. I love the act of painting sharks, but they lack conceptual ambiguity.

BUG CITY, 25" X 30", OIL ON LINEN

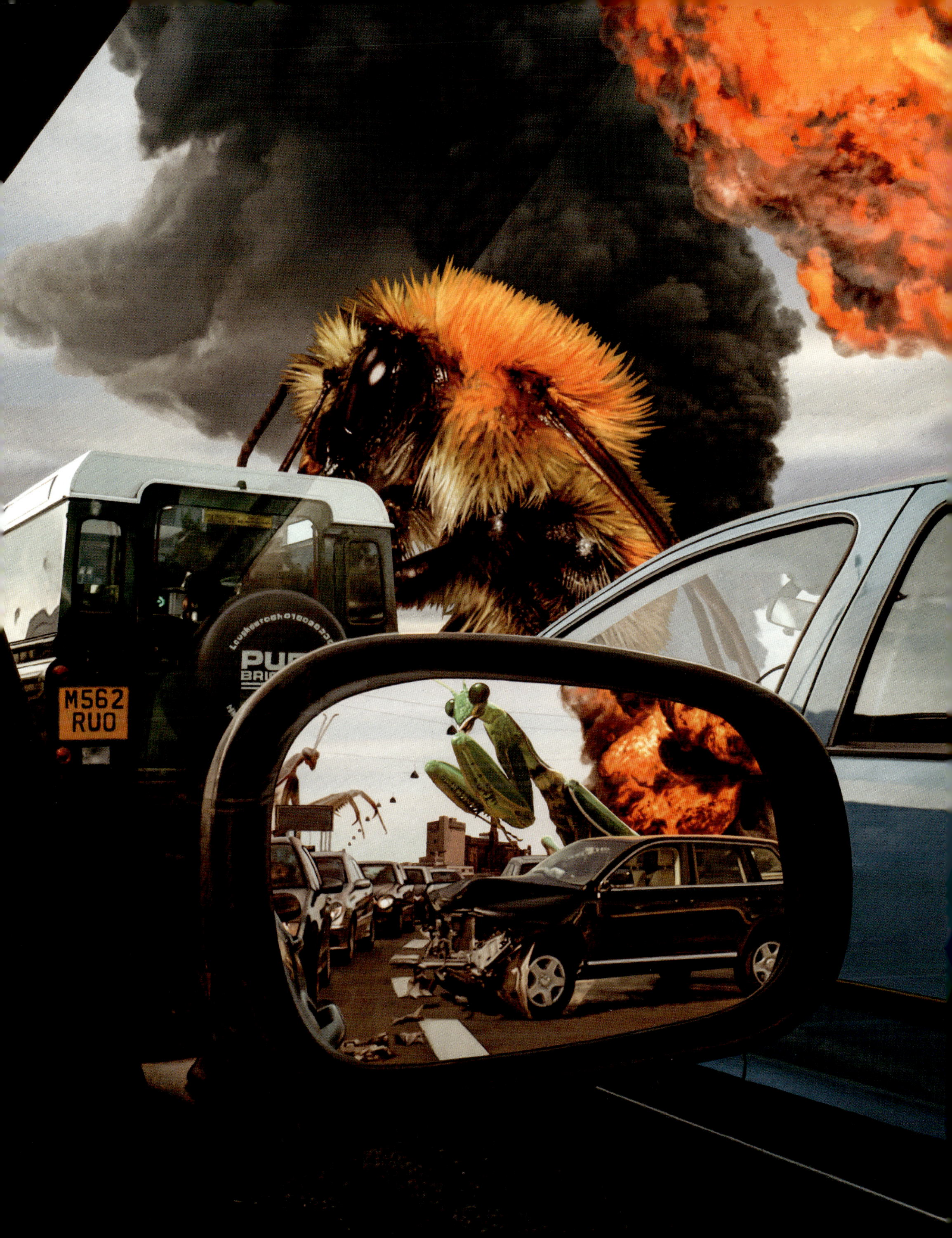
M562
RUO

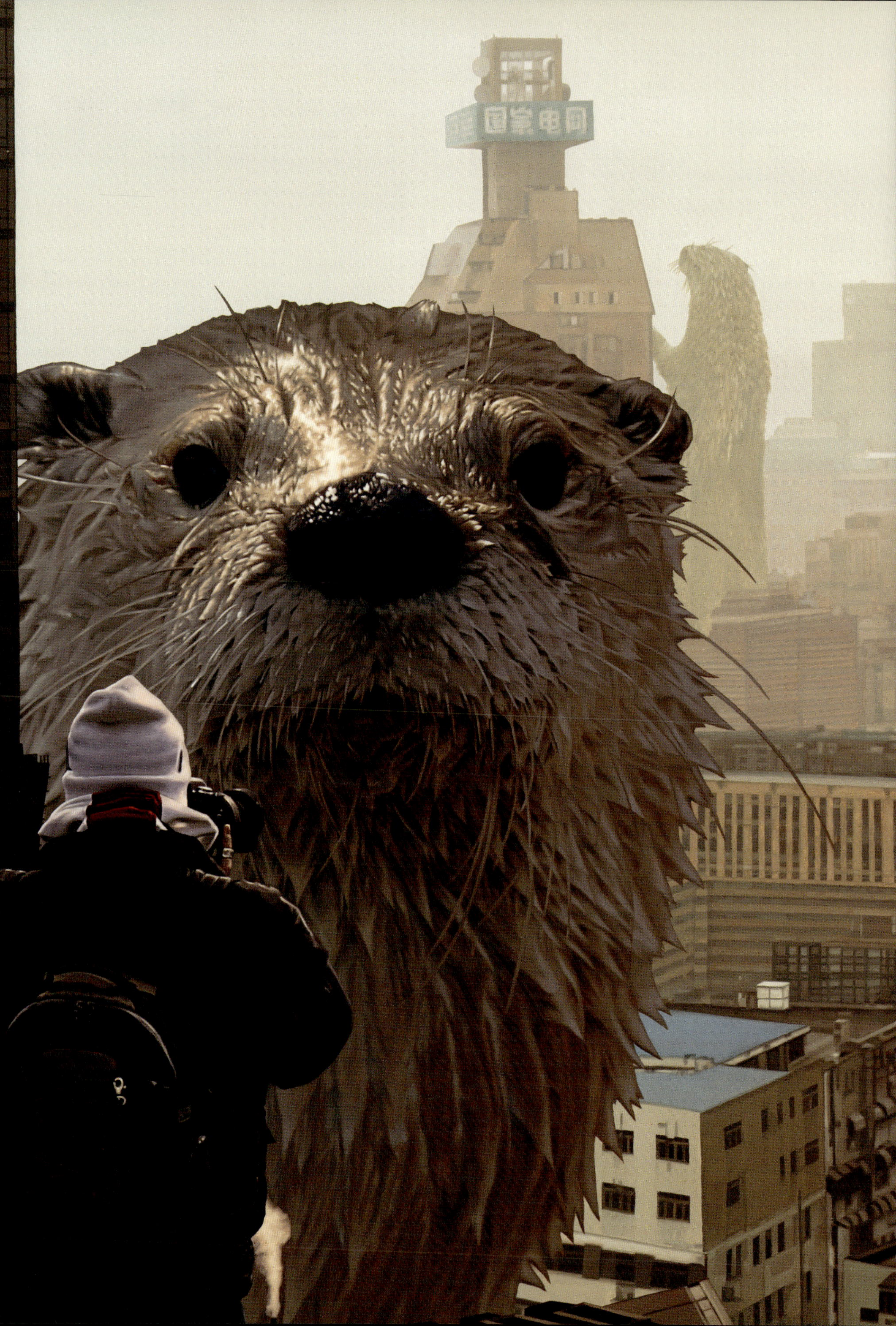

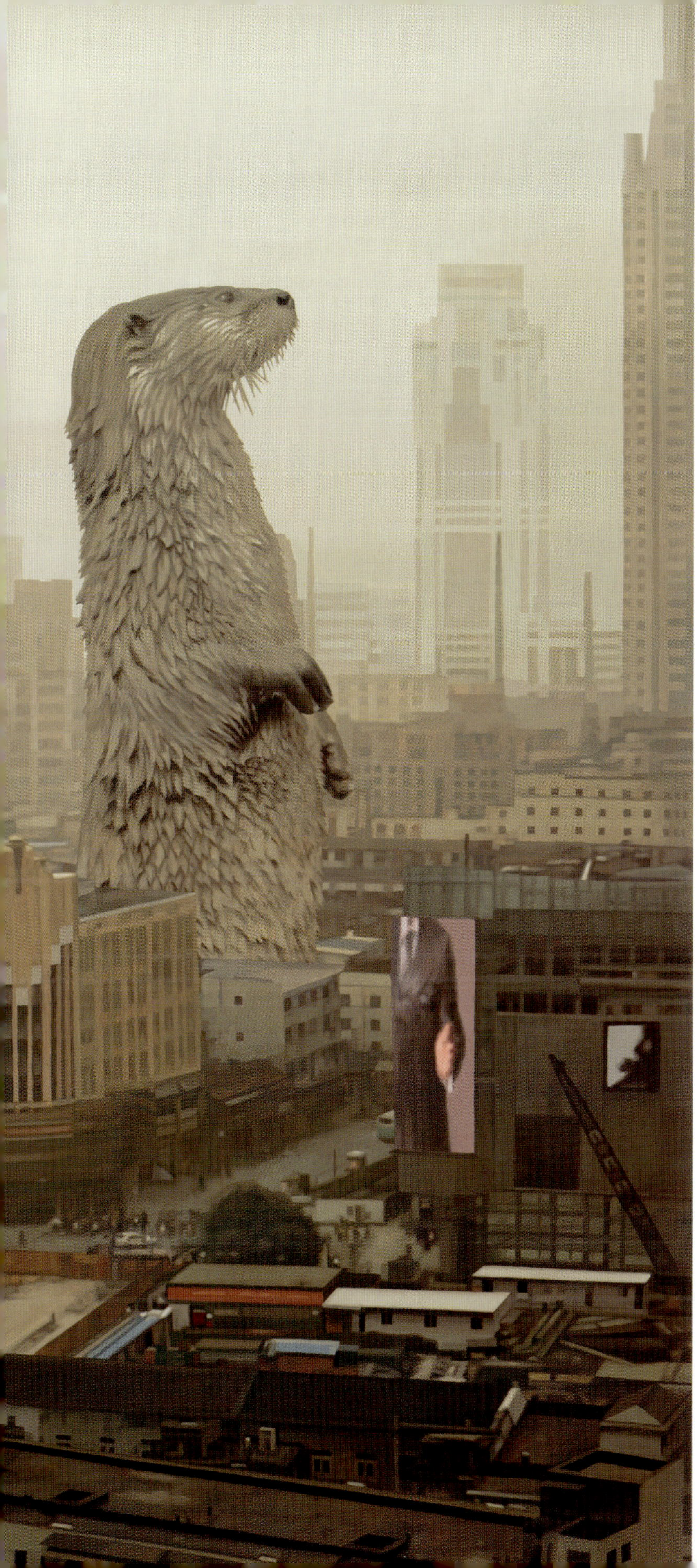

OTTER CITY 2
35" X 28"
OIL ON CANVAS

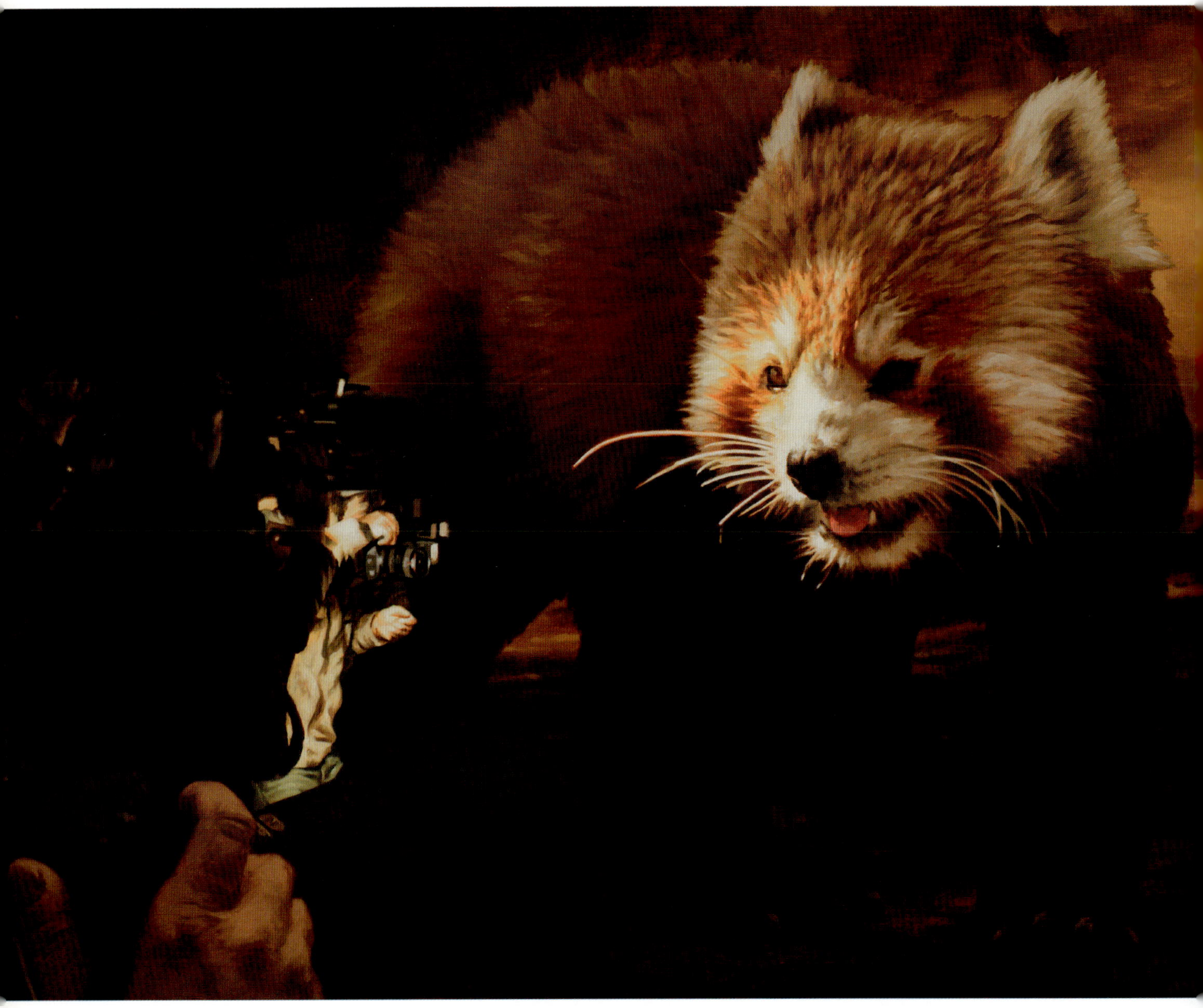

RED PANDA CITY 2, 11" X 14", OIL ON PANEL

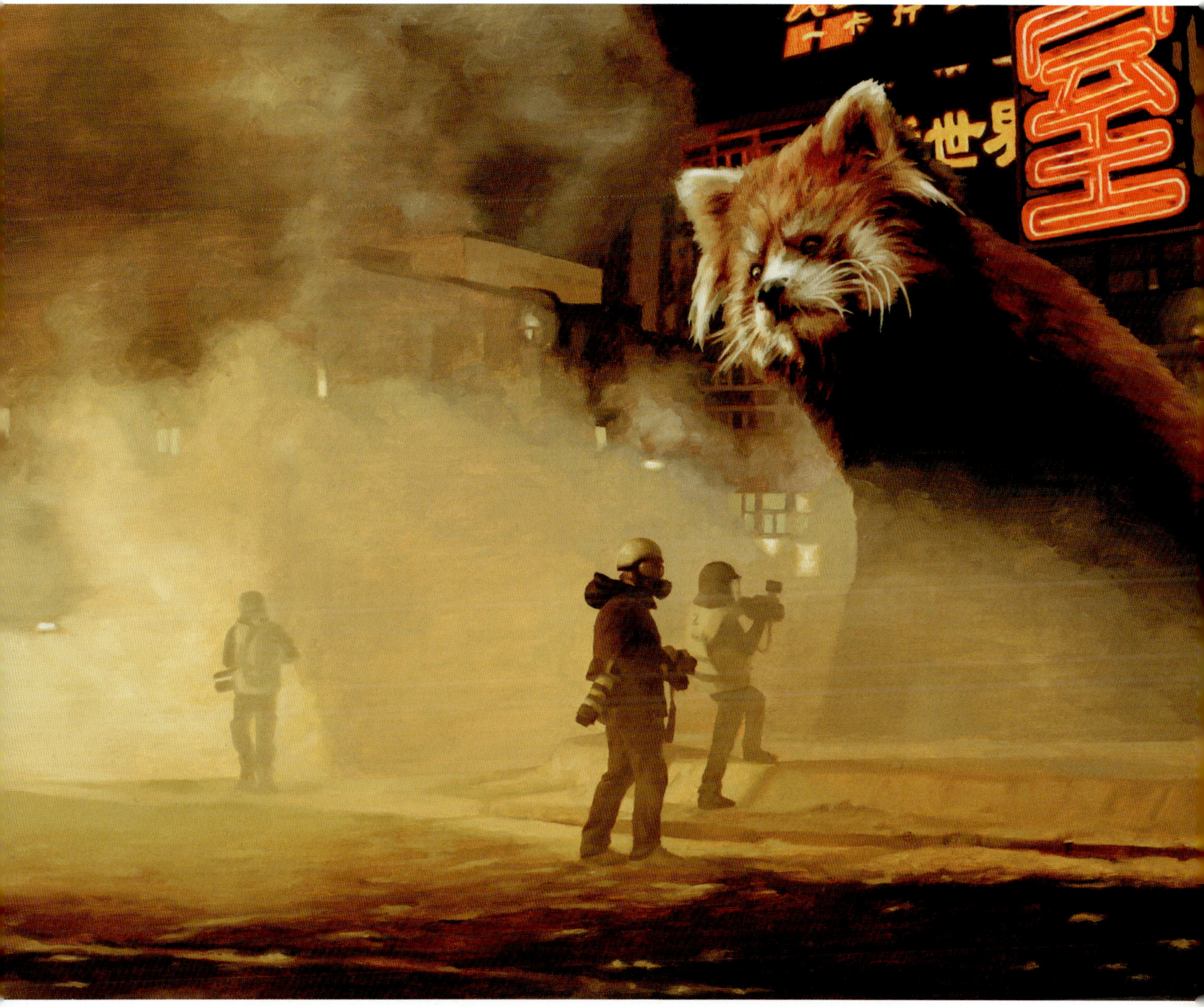

RED PANDA CITY 1, 11" X 14", OIL ON PANEL

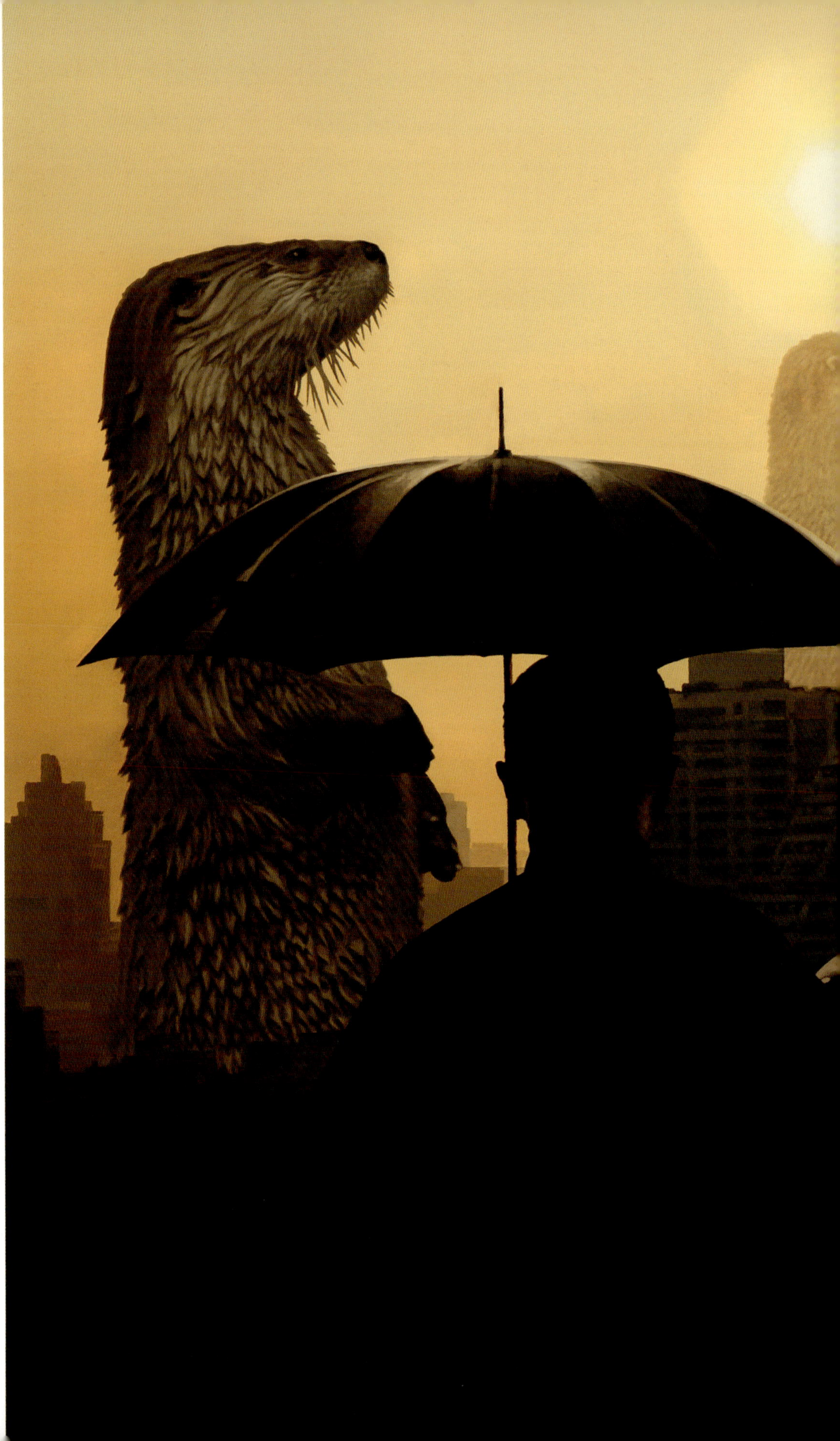

OTTER CITY 1
35" X 28"
OIL ON CANVAS

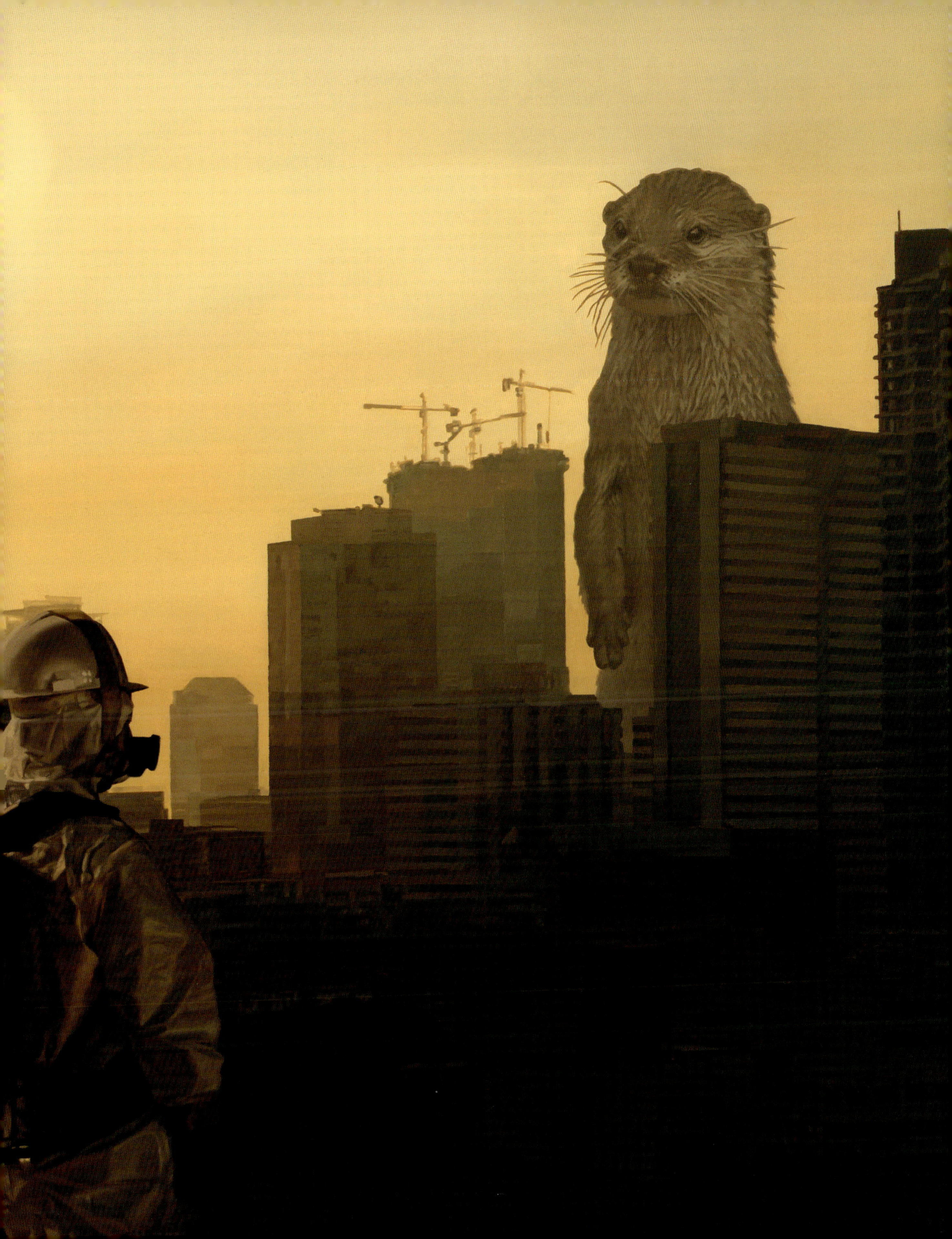

TARA TUCKER

BERKELEY, CALIFORNIA

Staying Wild
I haven't ever put humans in my work. Mostly, I think that there are enough representations of humankind out there that are brilliant, but I don't see enough spectacular animal and nature art being produced. I want to try and represent nature as best I can, even if it's through my slightly skewed vision of what nature is.

The truth is that I'm afraid I might destroy the whole feeling of intimacy between the viewer and my animal subjects, kind of like having a third person along on your hot date. It feels invasive. I often try to include eye contact between the viewer and my animal main character. There are human elements in my subject's eyes, posture and body stance. An actual human body could be something for me to explore at a future time. It just doesn't feel right for me yet. Nothing, however, is written in stone.

The Old World
Spider Monkeys really speak to me. I like the Old World monkeys best out of all of the primates. Psychologically, monkeys used to be very hard for me to draw. They kind of freaked me out with their human-like fingers and the nearly human interactions with one another. Now, I kind of like to be freaked out. Portrayed as both the token "wise man" and the "trickster," monkeys get typecast a lot. They make great characters in my many stories that I secretly assign to them as I draw. Perhaps it was too obvious of a choice for me to use in the past, and now I've given in? I am always wanting to tell human stories with animal bodies, and monkeys often fit the part.

An Uneasy Approach
Leonard Baskin was a huge inspiration to me when I started out as an artist. For me, Baskin could easily be regarded as an environmental artist. His drawings, paintings and sculptures of animals, in particular, speak to the world around him. He most often portrayed local animals and insects. Baskin's natural history illustrations show his emotional connection to his subject. As a sculptor, printmaker, illustrator, and painter, Baskin also concentrated on the human condition. Many of his works united both subjects. Particularly with his Raptors series, Baskin's art straddled that uneasy space between what it is to be human and also an animal, merging the two forms into one.

Julie Heffernan's exquisite self-portrait paintings create landscapes that, at first look, are complex worlds of huge floral arrangements or topiary. Then one notices the unnaturally shaped, surreal composition melding into a pictorial collection of rooms. Each room holds a very human situation, like a tenement building with its walls stripped away, but it's Heffernan's mind that is laid open for all to see. Each room is a blaring examination of Julie's own mental environment. It is scary and so beautiful that I can't take my eyes off her paintings. Her work is a fragile environment and a mirror of what is inside of all of us.

A Migration
My stepfather's driveway in Santa Barbara, California is the best place to experience nature. His house is on the cliffs leading to the beach, and his driveway could be considered an out-of-the-way country road. It isn't fancy; it's rustic and old. In the early morning, or at dusk, there are bobcats, coyotes, red-tailed hawks and skunks to be seen. Part of the driveway is lined with fifty or so old eucalyptus trees. For as long as I can remember, the monarch butterflies have migrated to these trees each year. Twenty years ago, the sky was thick with them—an orange and black cloud. Now, with the change in our climate, there are just a fraction of monarchs left. It is still amazing to see, but I find it sad to see them disappear. I love it there, on that driveway. It's still the place I like to walk and think.

MODEL WEARING ORCHID SHRUG, 25" X 18", ACRYLIC PAINT ON HANDWOVEN LINEN MATERIAL

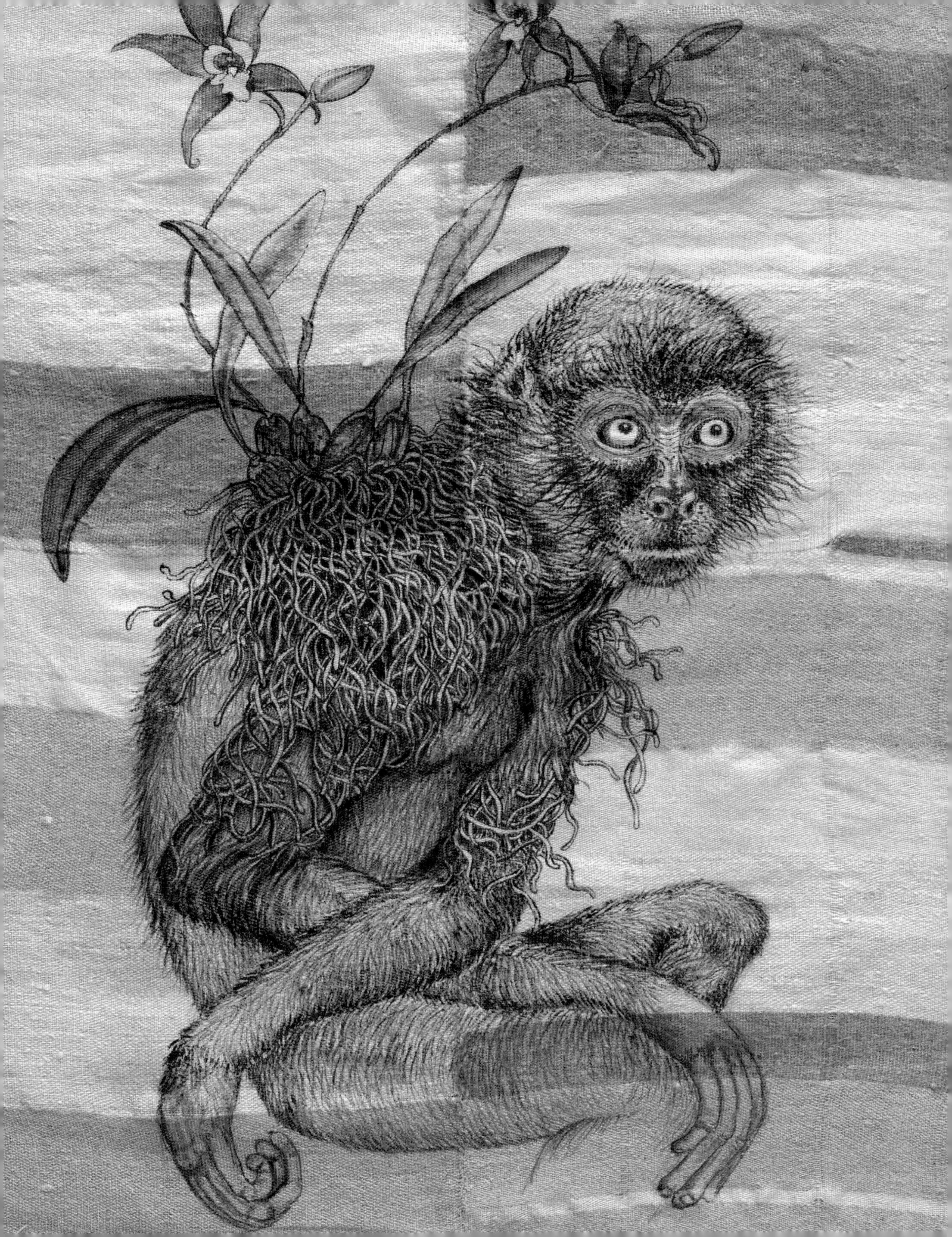

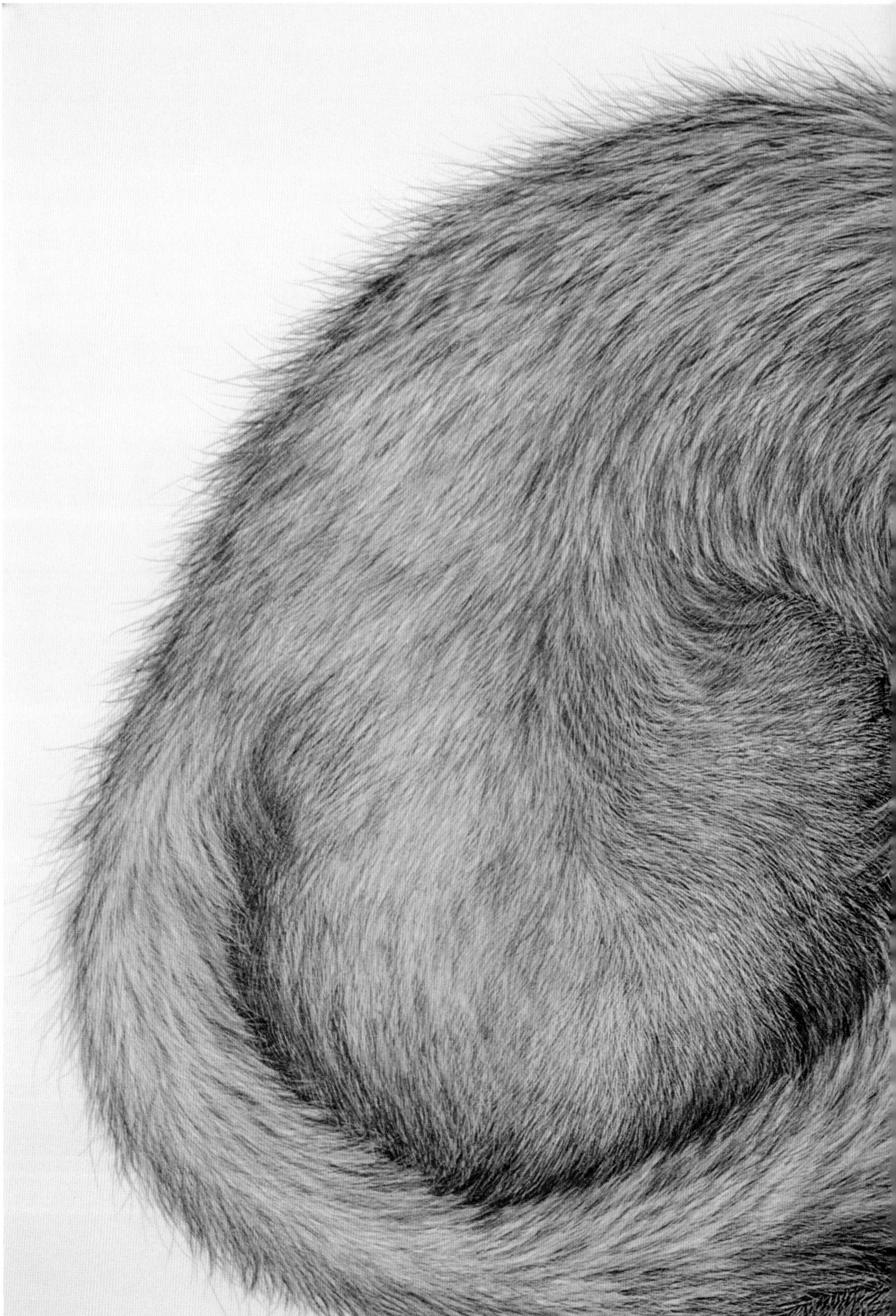

I'M THE ONE YOU TELL YOUR FEARS TO, 11" X 17", GRAPHITE ON PAPER

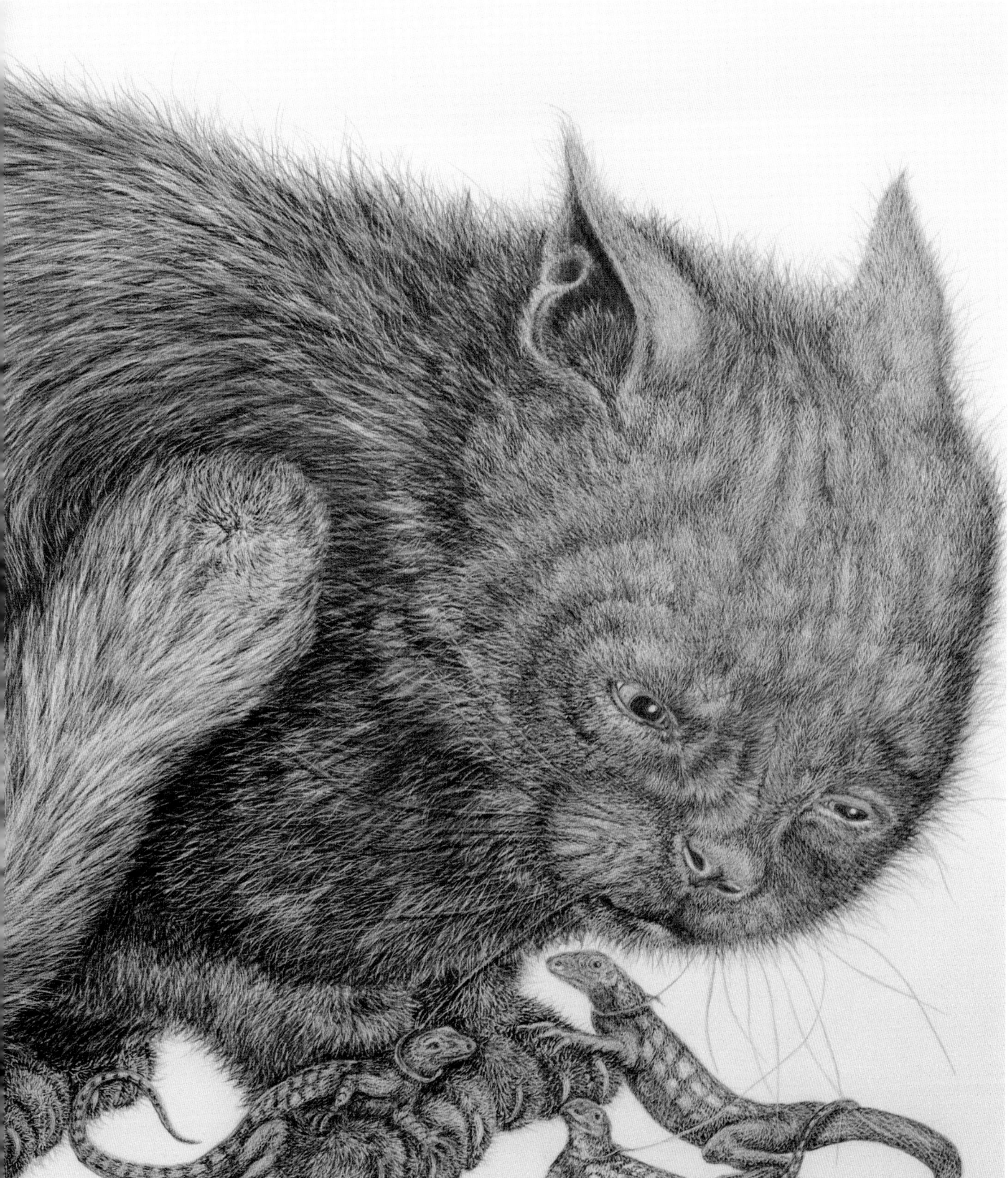

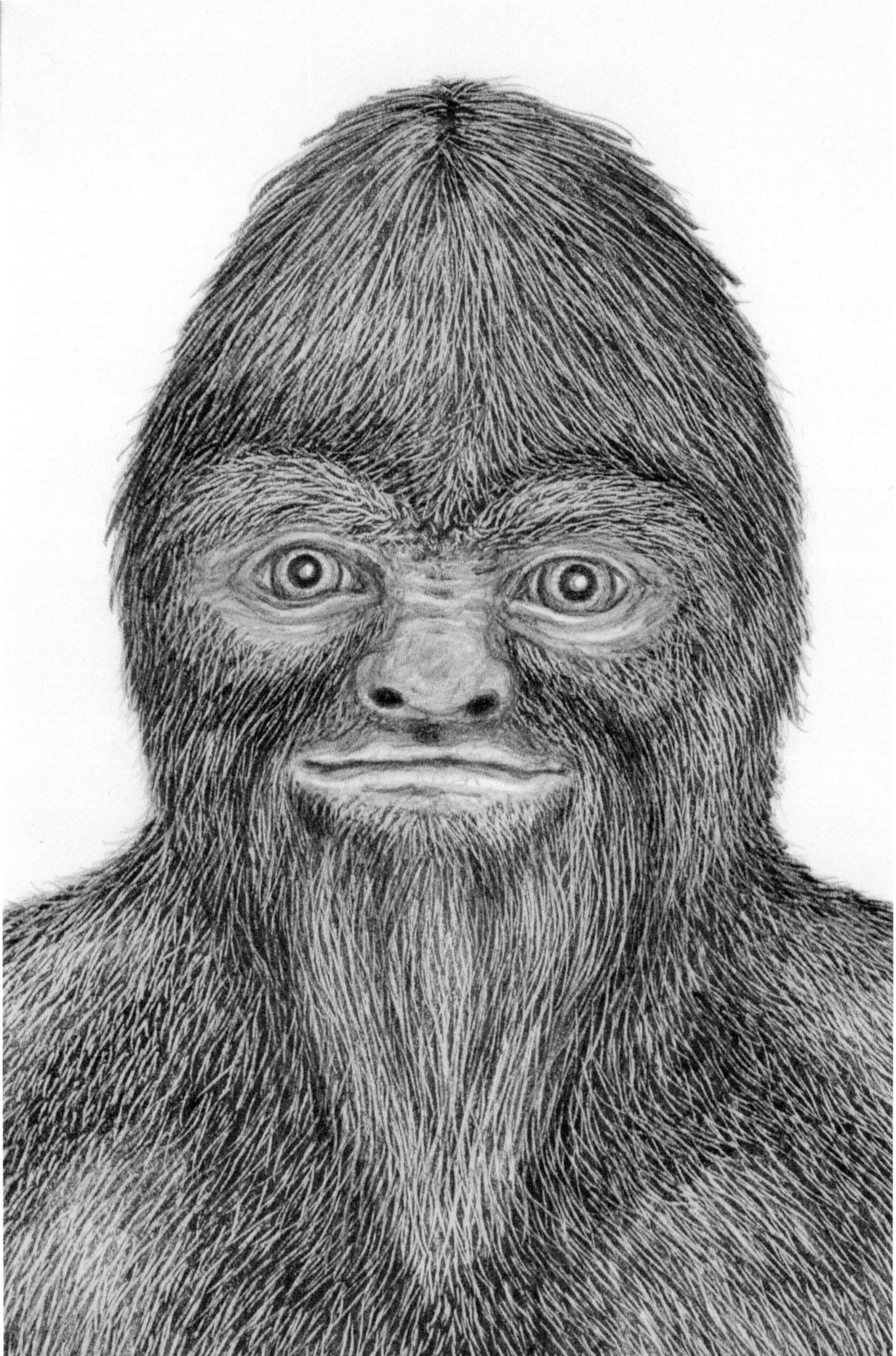

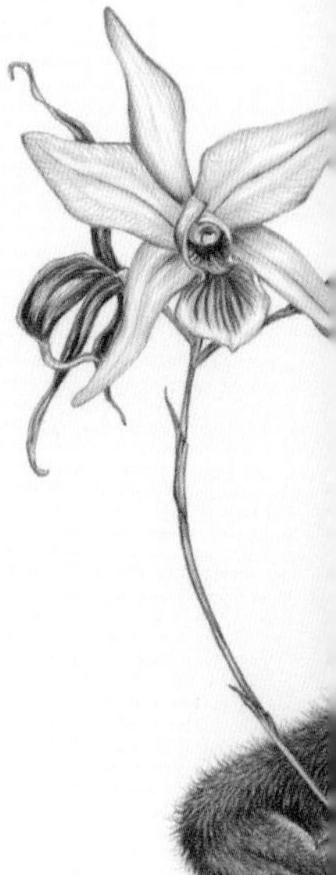

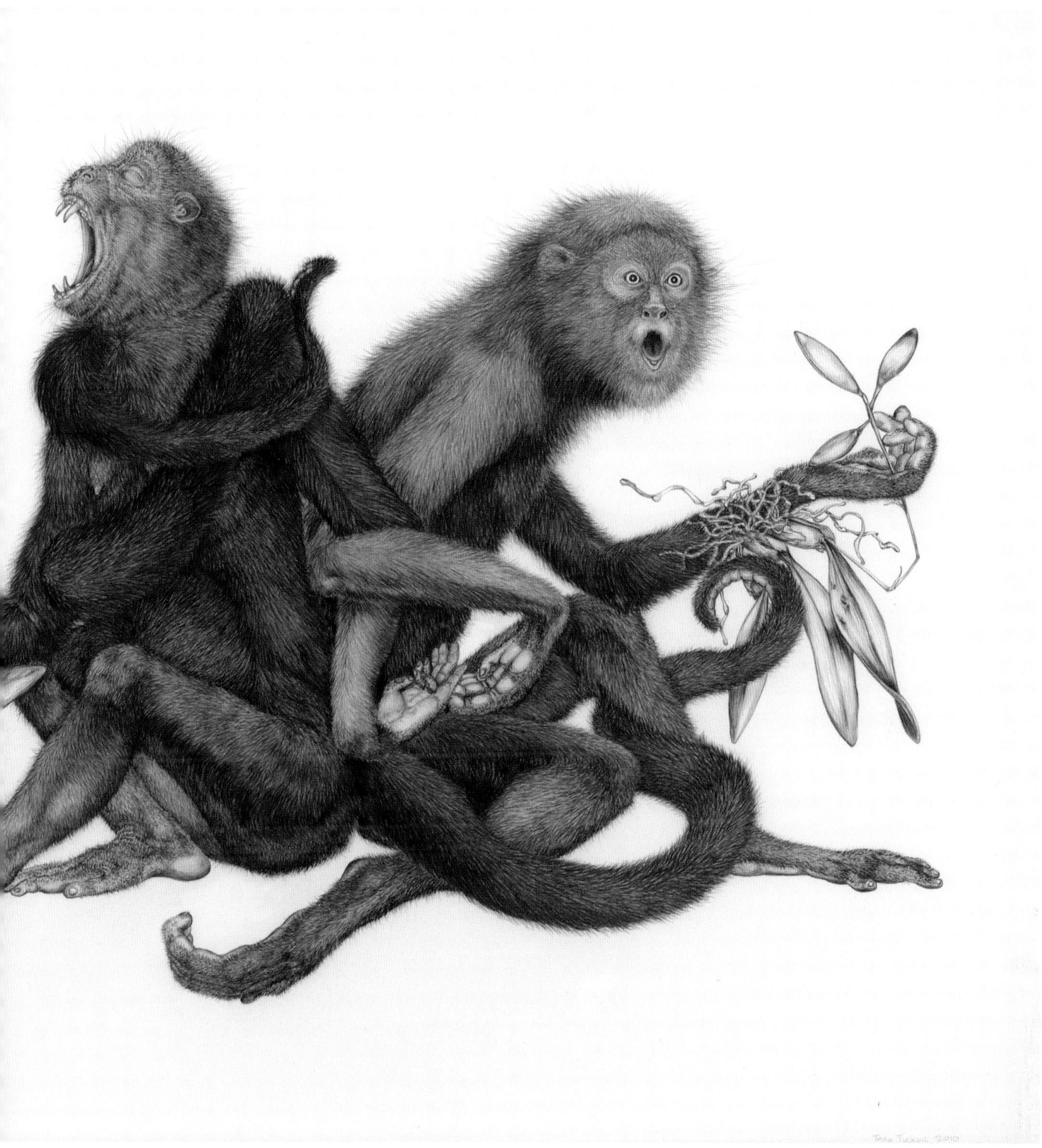

FROM LEFT:

NORTH AMERICAN SASQUATCH
13 3/8" X 20"
GRAPHITE ON PAPER

WHEN YOUR HANDS ARE BROKEN. WHEN YOUR WORDS ARE SLIPPING. PUT YOUR ARMS AROUND HER
23" X 28"
GRAPHITE ON PAPER

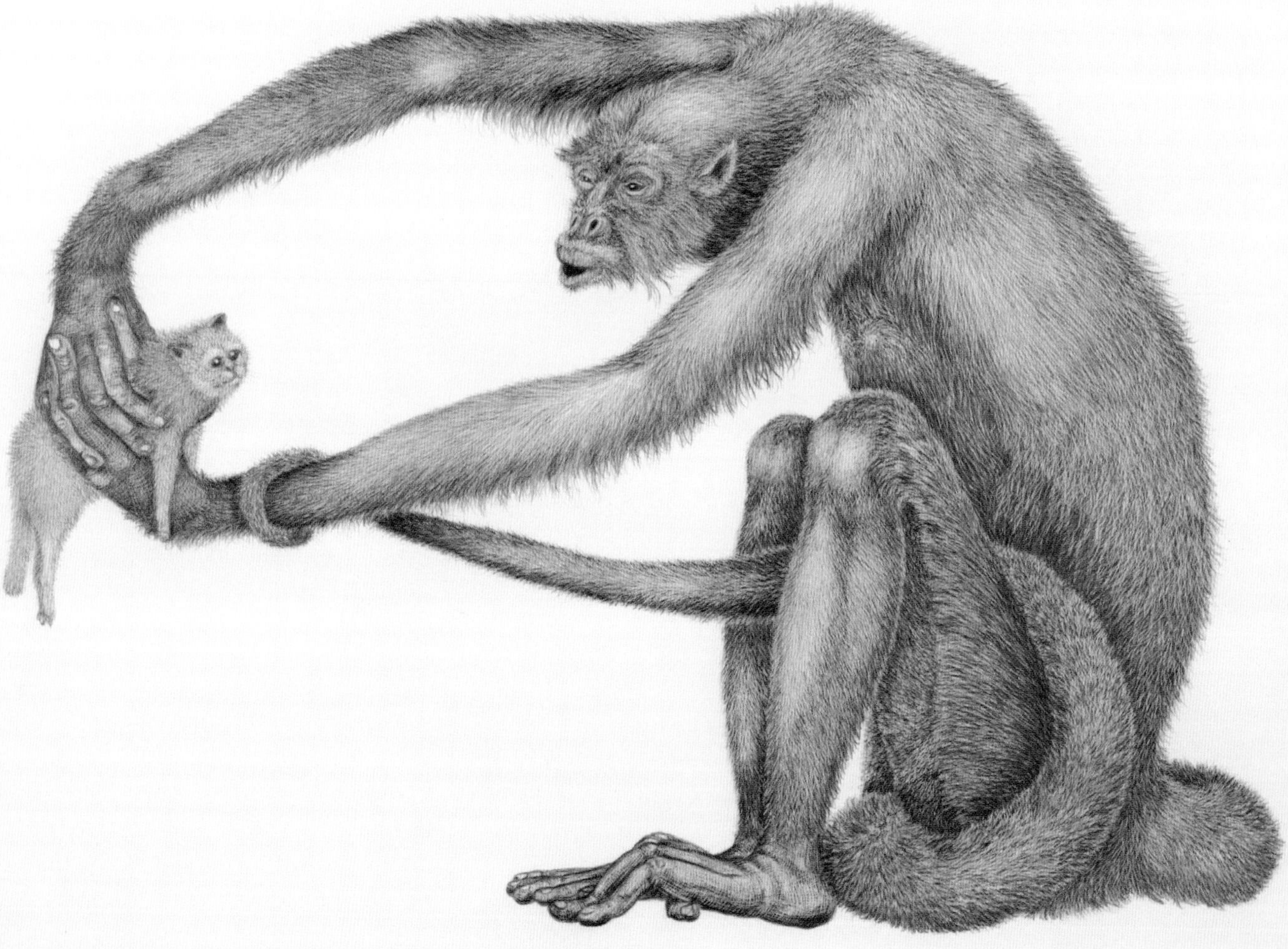

YOU BE THE CLASS CLOWN, I'LL BE THE BEAUTY QUEEN, 11" X 17", GRAPHITE ON PAPER

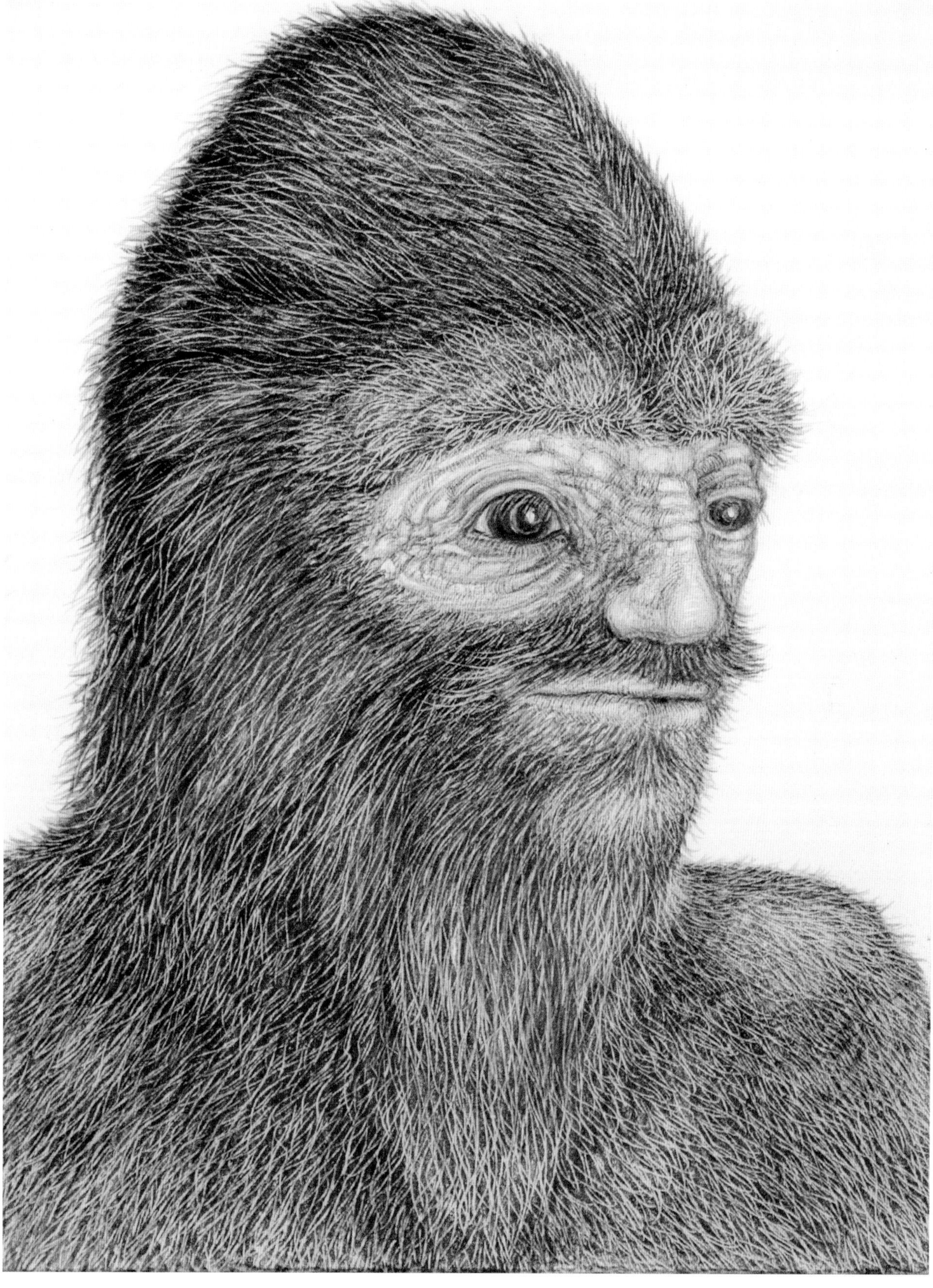

AUSTRALIAN YOWIE, 5" X 7", GRAPHITE ON PAPER

LARASSA KABEL

DES MOINES, IOWA

A Hazardous Love

I love drawing animals. They allow me to talk about issues that would be difficult for viewers if I used a person in the composition. Take the *Hazards of Love* series, for example. After becoming a mother, I became acutely aware of how devastated I would be if my son died. I have a lot of people in my life that I would be terribly sad to see die, but having a child put that fear on a whole new level. When you open yourself up for that kind of love, you become incredibly vulnerable. I used the fawns in the *Hazards of Love* series as symbols of child mortality. I felt they drew a person in with their beauty and then revealed themselves as something heartbreaking.

Horse Girls

When I was two years old, I became enamored with horses. Total horse girl right from the start—obsessed! Some people try to ascribe some sort of erotic connotation to horse girls, but it is really such a pure thing. I used to have horses and rode all the time until I went off to college. Now I live in the city and have dogs instead.

Into The Woods

I'm a sucker for a forest. Throw in a stream or lake, and I'm in heaven.

A Dark and Stormy Day

A couple of years ago, I had a very strange day. It felt like I was on a spirit walk or had been dumped into a fable. I was walking my dog around a lake where I go nearly every day, and as we were walking, we came upon a baby bird that had fallen out of its nest. It was really newly hatched, raw looking, bald, and covered with ants, and it was still alive and moving around. I looked everywhere for the nest and couldn't see where it could have possibly come from, and I realized that the kind thing to do would be to kill it. It was just a horror show. But I couldn't do it. The idea of killing it paralyzed me, and I felt like a coward walking away. I hadn't gone thirty feet before I came upon a fish on the ground. And it was alive and gasping. I picked it up and ran all the way to the lake, which was at least forty feet away, and threw it in. The strange thing about it was that I couldn't figure out how it got there. It was completely uninjured, so I didn't see how it could have been caught by a bird, and there wasn't anyone else around, so it couldn't have flipped out of a fisherman's bucket. And it couldn't have been there long because it was still alive. It made me feel a little better after the bad experience with the baby bird. As I was driving home at the end of the day, we got a very heavy rainstorm. It was just pouring. I was getting close to home when I saw a young boy crouched on the ground next to a yellow lab that was lying on its side and not moving at all. I stopped to see if he needed help, and he said his dad was coming and that he was all right, but I could see that the dog was too still. When I added it all up, I had found something that belonged to the air stuck on the ground, something that belonged in the water drowning on dry land, and something that needed air that looked like it was drowning on the land. Each encounter felt staged somehow.

Swimming With The Fishes

I would love to see whales up close. The more I learn about their intelligence, the more curious I become about what their experience of the world would be like. And it would be amazing to be near something so large. That's as close to dinosaur size as I can get.

RELENTLESS, 22" X 18", COLORED PENCIL ON PAPER

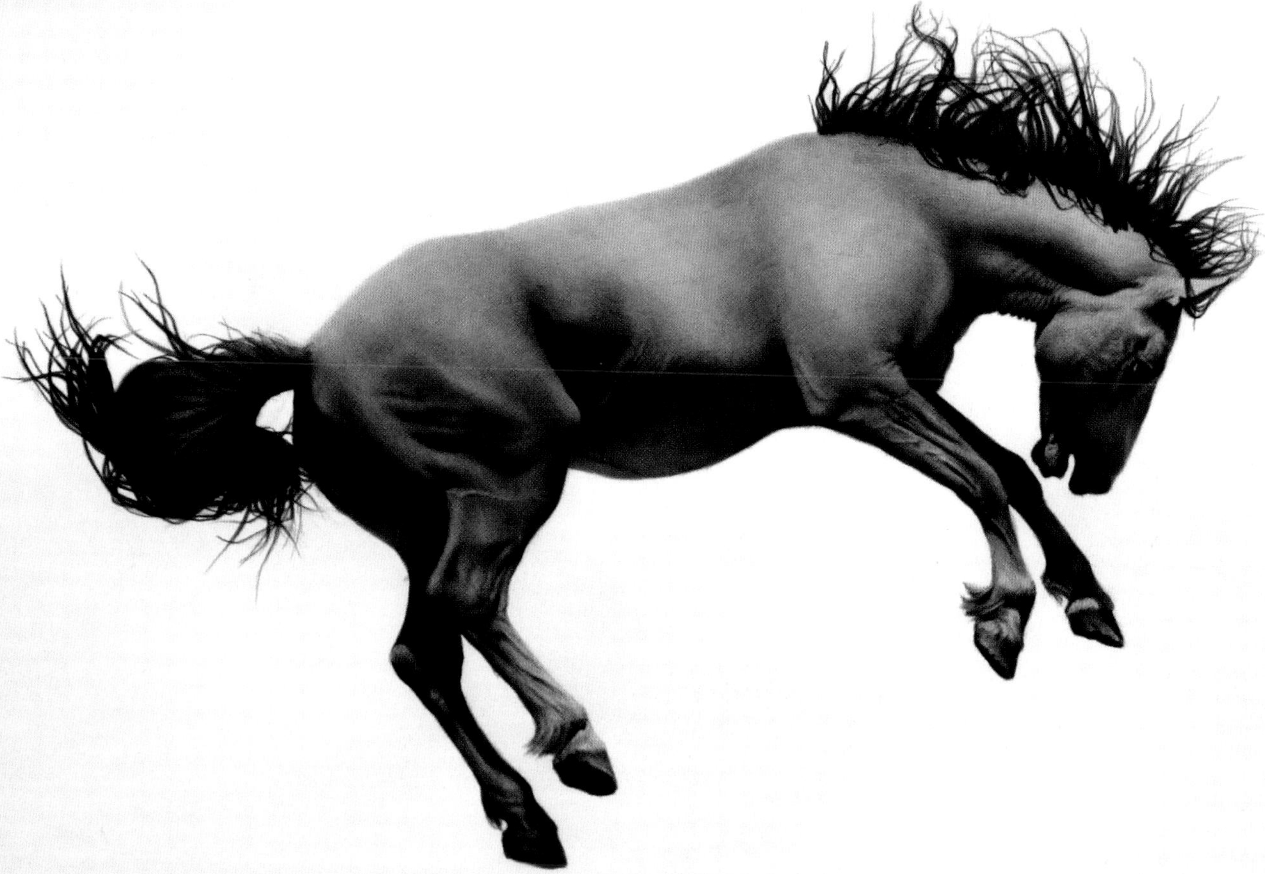

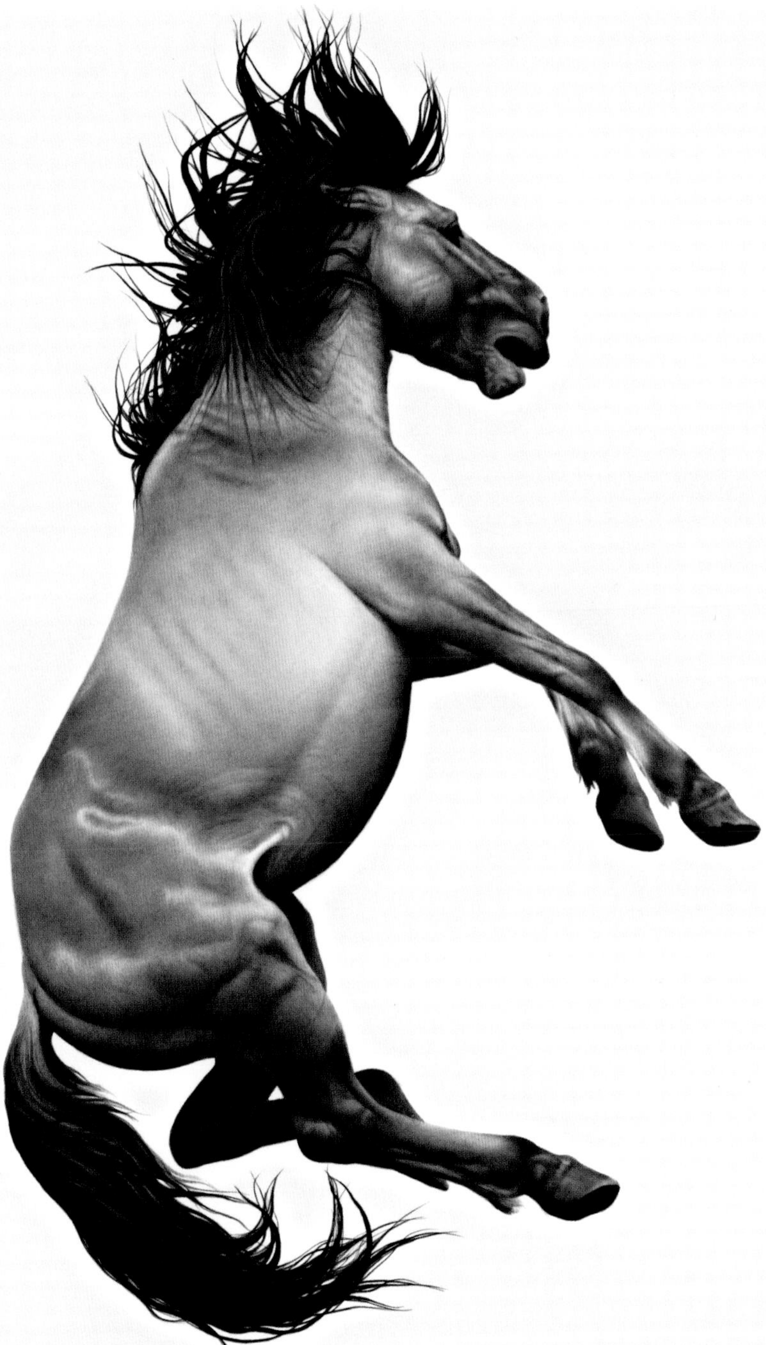

THE FALL, 48" X 48", COLORED PENCIL ON PAPER

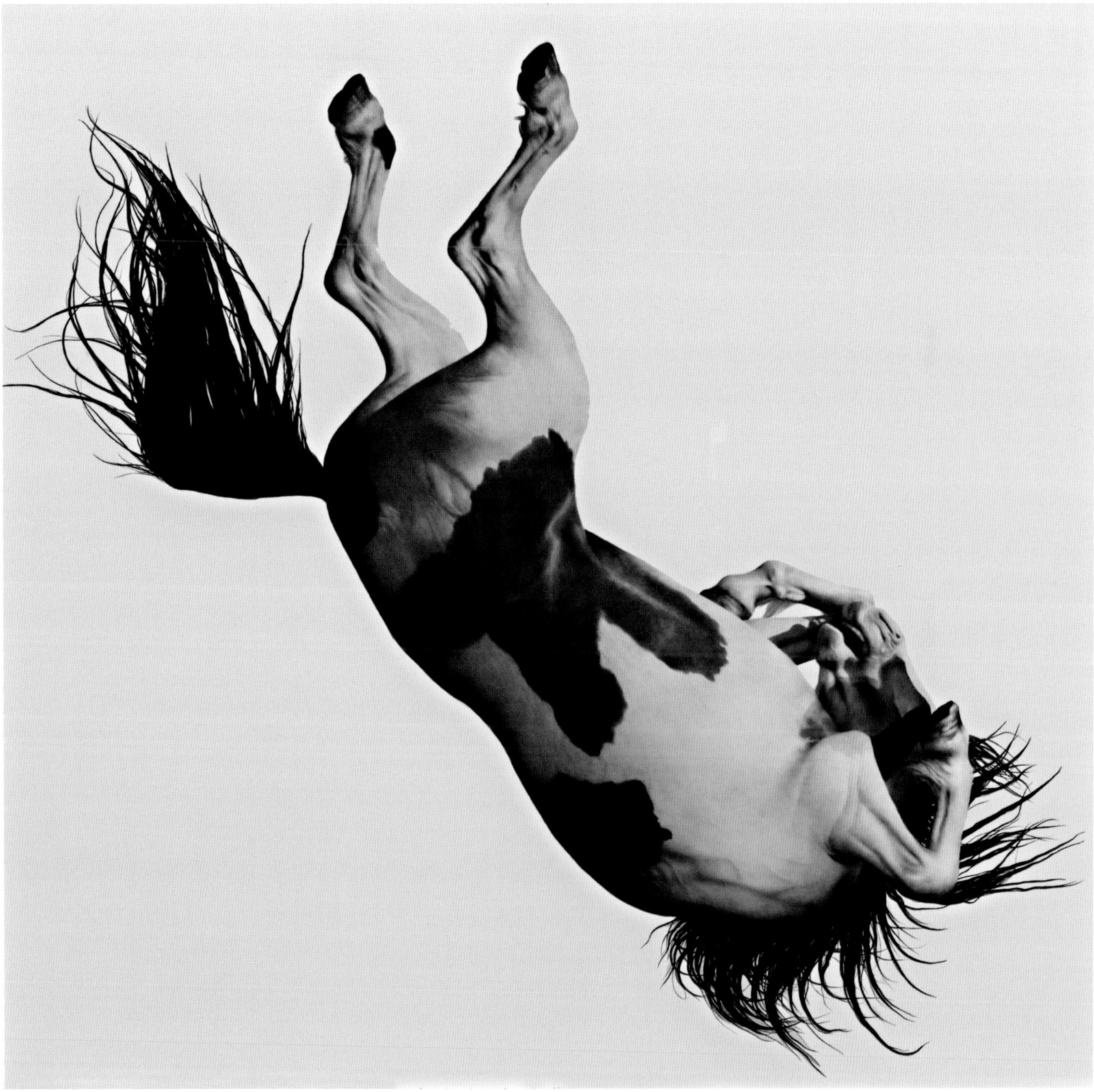

ANY MINUTE NOW, 96" X 96", COLORED PENCIL ON PAPER

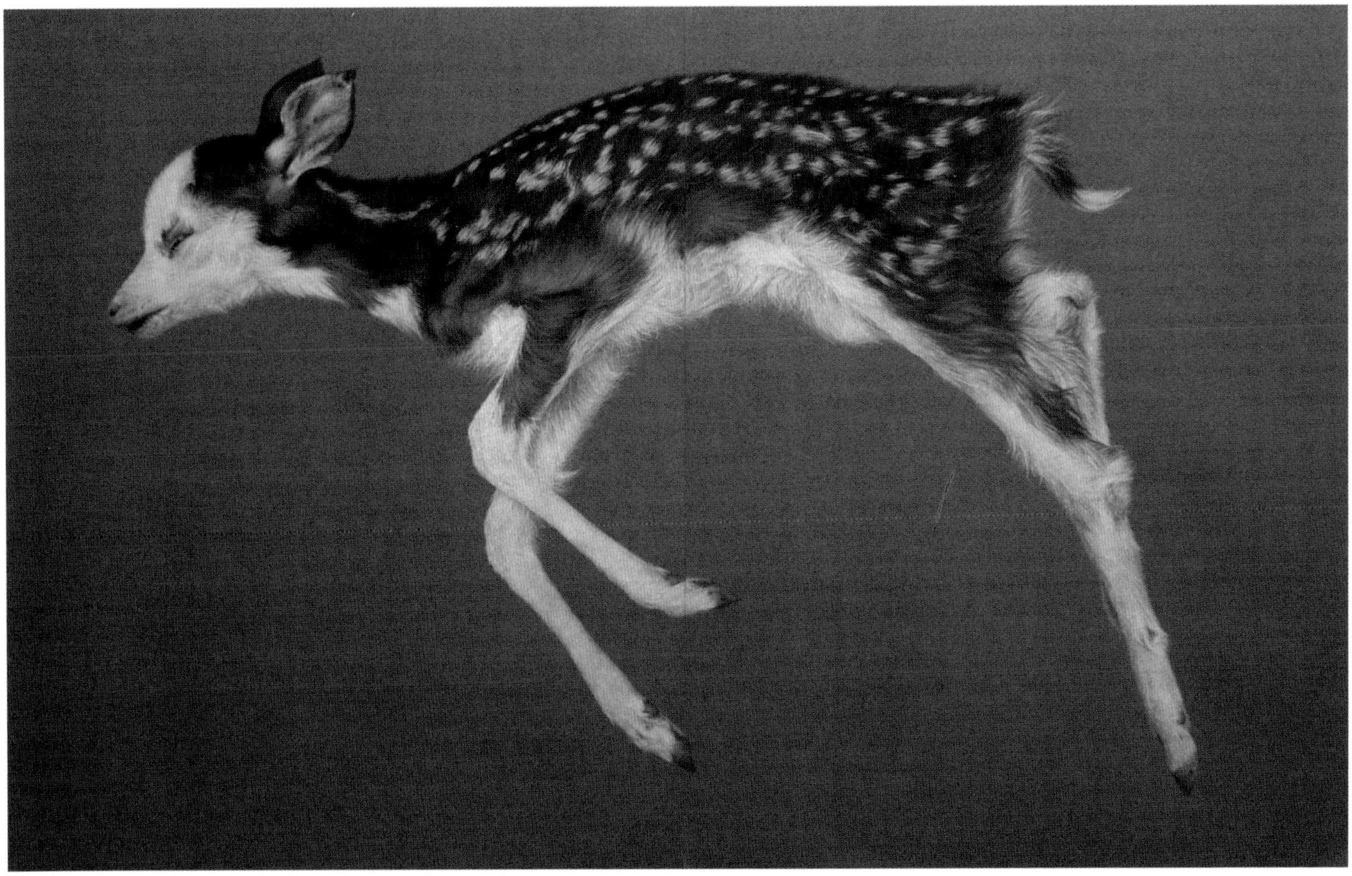

THE HAZARDS OF LOVE - PRICE, 25.5" X 38.5", COLORED PENCIL ON TONED PAPER

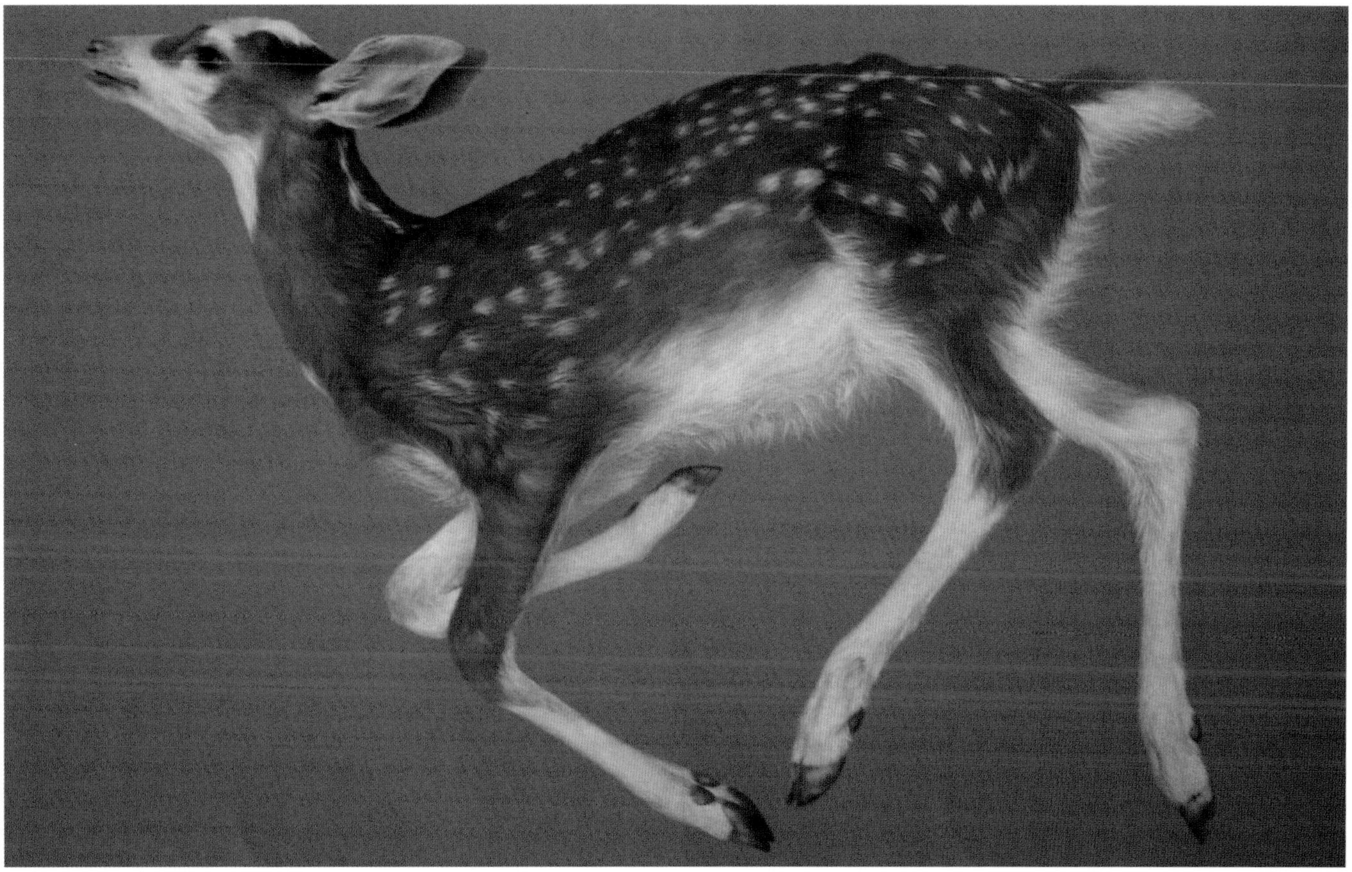

THE HAZARDS OF LOVE - TRINA, 25.5" X 38.5", COLORED PENCIL ON TONED PAPER

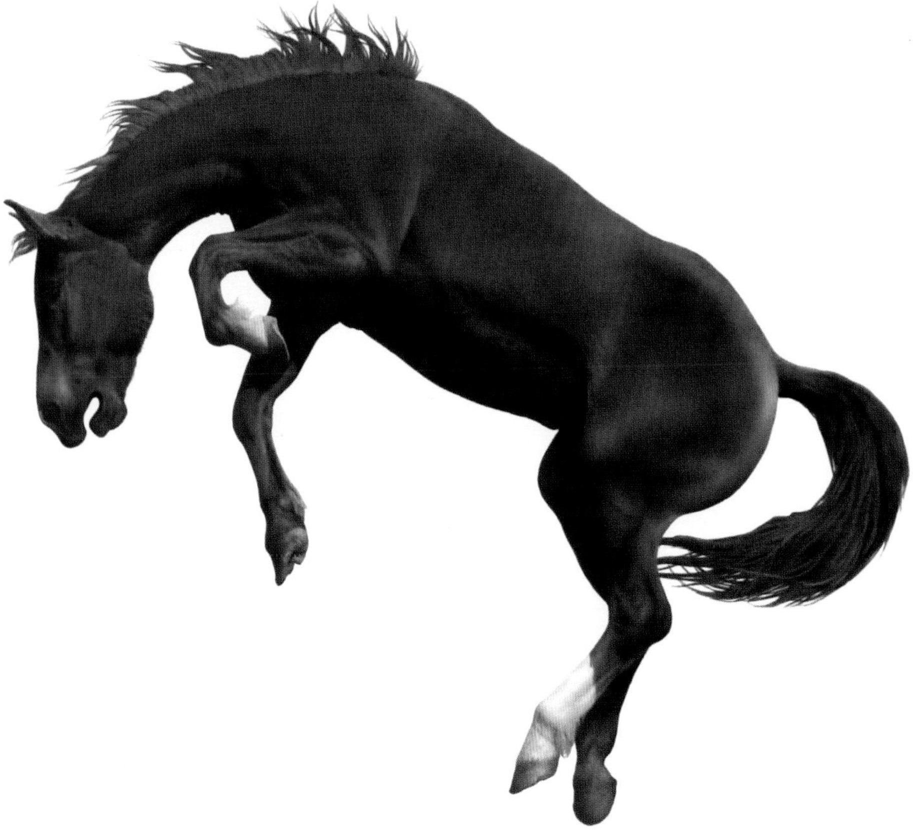

ANGEL BABY
60" X 52 1/2"
COLORED PENCIL ON PAPER

SONOMA
45" X 36"
COLORED PENCIL ON TONED PAPER

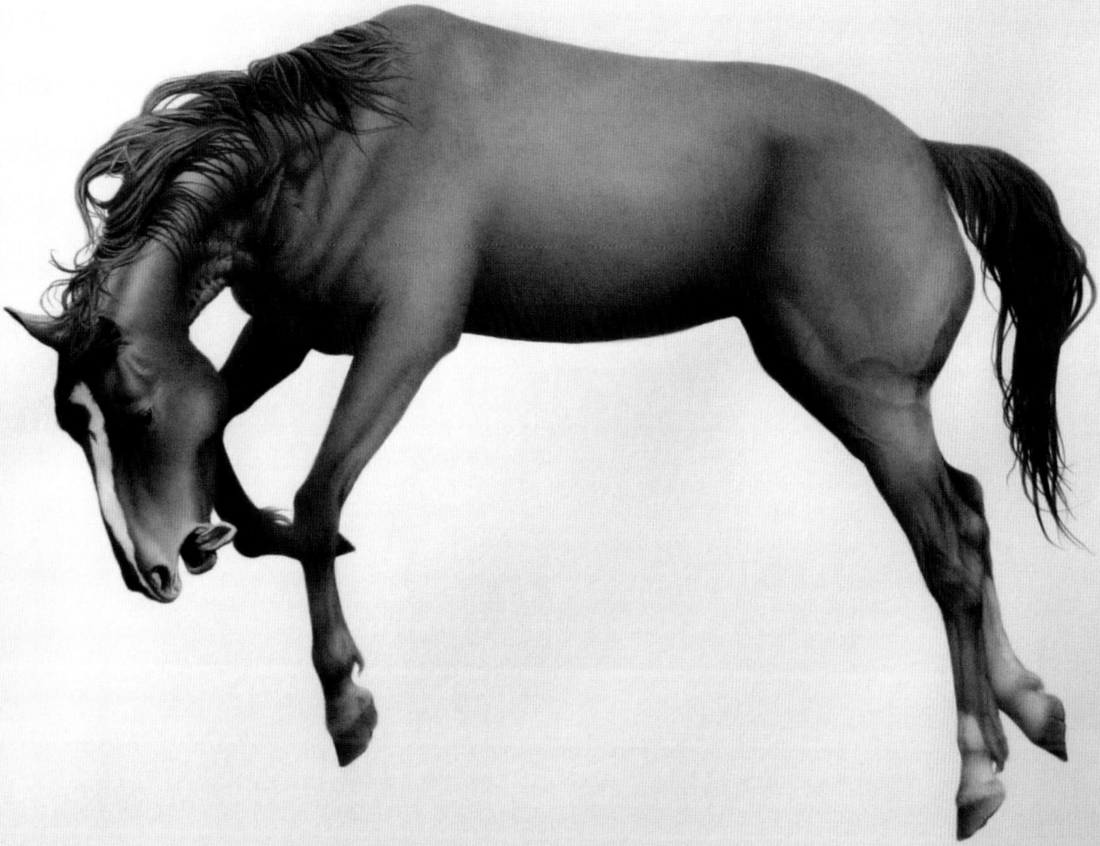

LINDSEY CARR

GLASGOW, SCOTLAND

Crisis and Conflict
Climate effects are shown over decades, politicians are in power for short periods. Telling voters and businesses that they need to make enormous cutbacks in order to stop something which might happen in a few decades is not going to be the popular vote. The problem with people is that we typically don't act unless there's a crisis, and regarding runaway climate effect theory, it will be too late by then. Climate activist James Hansen suggests political changes are too slow, and social revolution is probably necessary, which typically also only takes place under crisis conditions. On the other hand, five-day weather forecasts are so tricky to predict that climate change is going to be incredibly difficult to predict accurately. It's a vast, sprawling topic with unpredictability at its center. I'm interested to see what happens, to be honest.

Finding the Animals
Herons turned up in my work because I loved their obvious reptilian looks. Primates were always there because my grandad had a monkey when he was a child and he drew them all the time, it was my first introduction to drawing. Foxes, because I lived on a piece of land where they raised birds for hunting, which involves culling foxes. I was brought a dead vixen once by the groundskeeper. He heard I painted animals and thought I'd appreciate it. Animals live in a complicated relationship alongside us, are a lot like us, and we've had very different ideas about them over the centuries.

Making Ourselves Scarce
It's not common for people to show up in my work. Generally, the animals are there to talk about humans, so it seems a bit odd to put us in the mix as well.

On Audubon
I'm not sure most people would call Audubon an environmental artist these days, but I massively respect his obsessional drive to represent the animal as it is. I love all of the printmakers, really. I respect the mix of craft and draftsmanship.

Social Politics
I wouldn't say any of my work is concerned with current environmental politics, except pieces specifically produced for organizations like PangeaSeed. I'm more interested in human social and historical politics.

Revenge of the Wild
One of the places I like a lot is Benmore Botanic Garden on the west coast of Scotland. The thing that always cheers me up, though, is seeing weeds growing out of the cracks in buildings. It feels like a silent revolt, sticking it to the man.

GARDEN (DETAIL), 14" X 21", WATERCOLOR ON PAPER

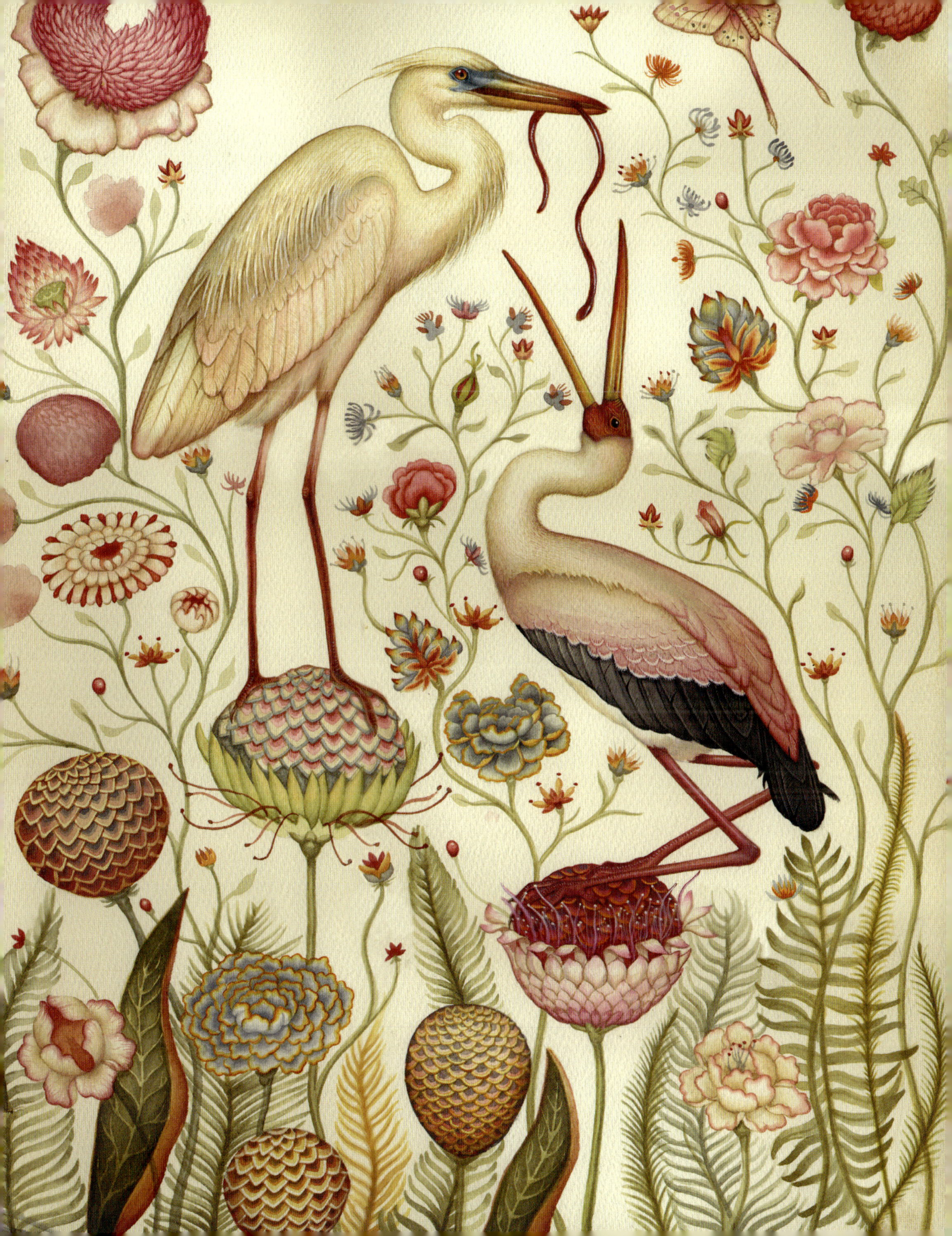

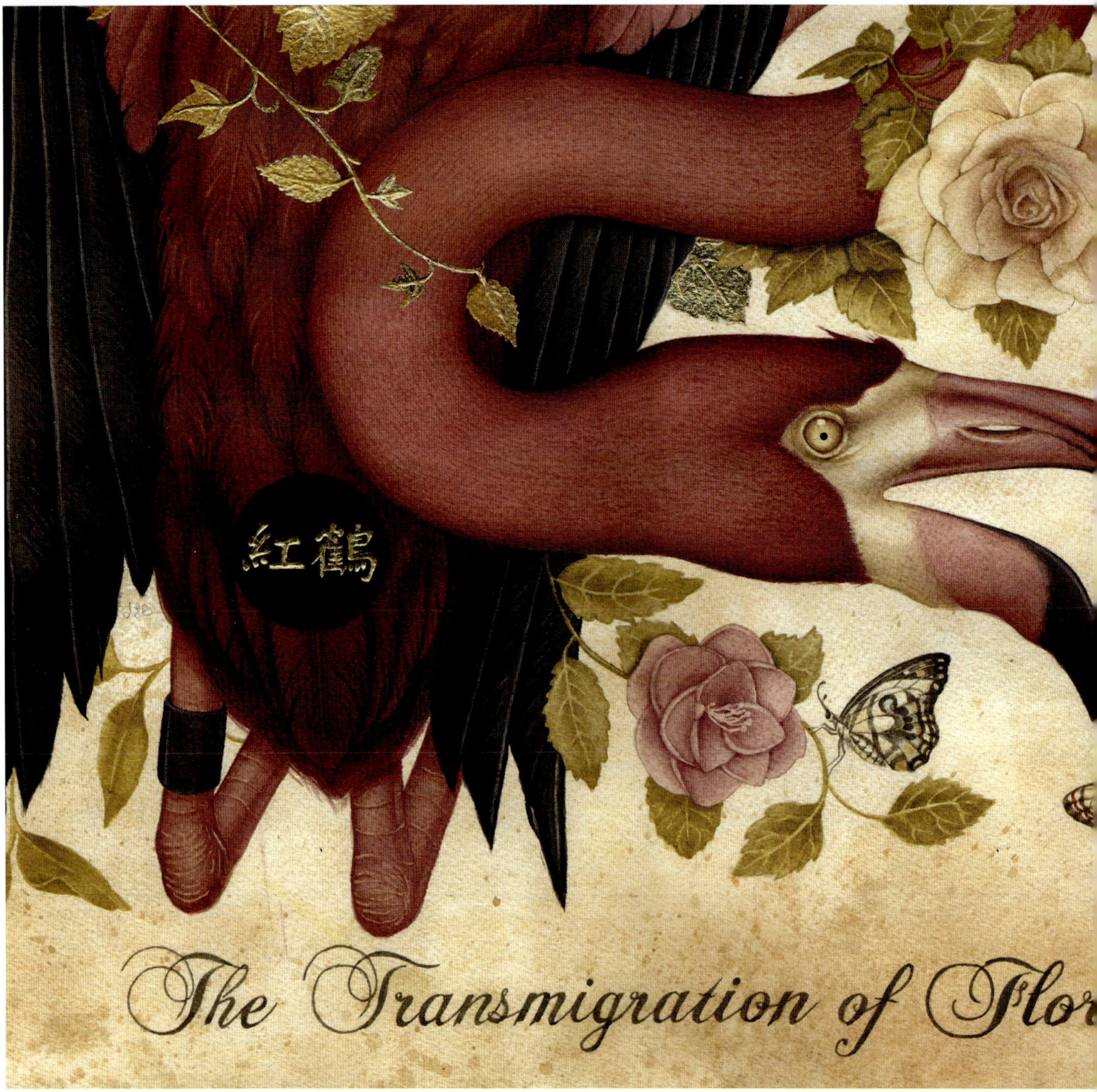

TRANSMIGRATION OF FLORA, 16" X 12", WATERCOLOR AND INK AND GOLD LEAF ON PAPER

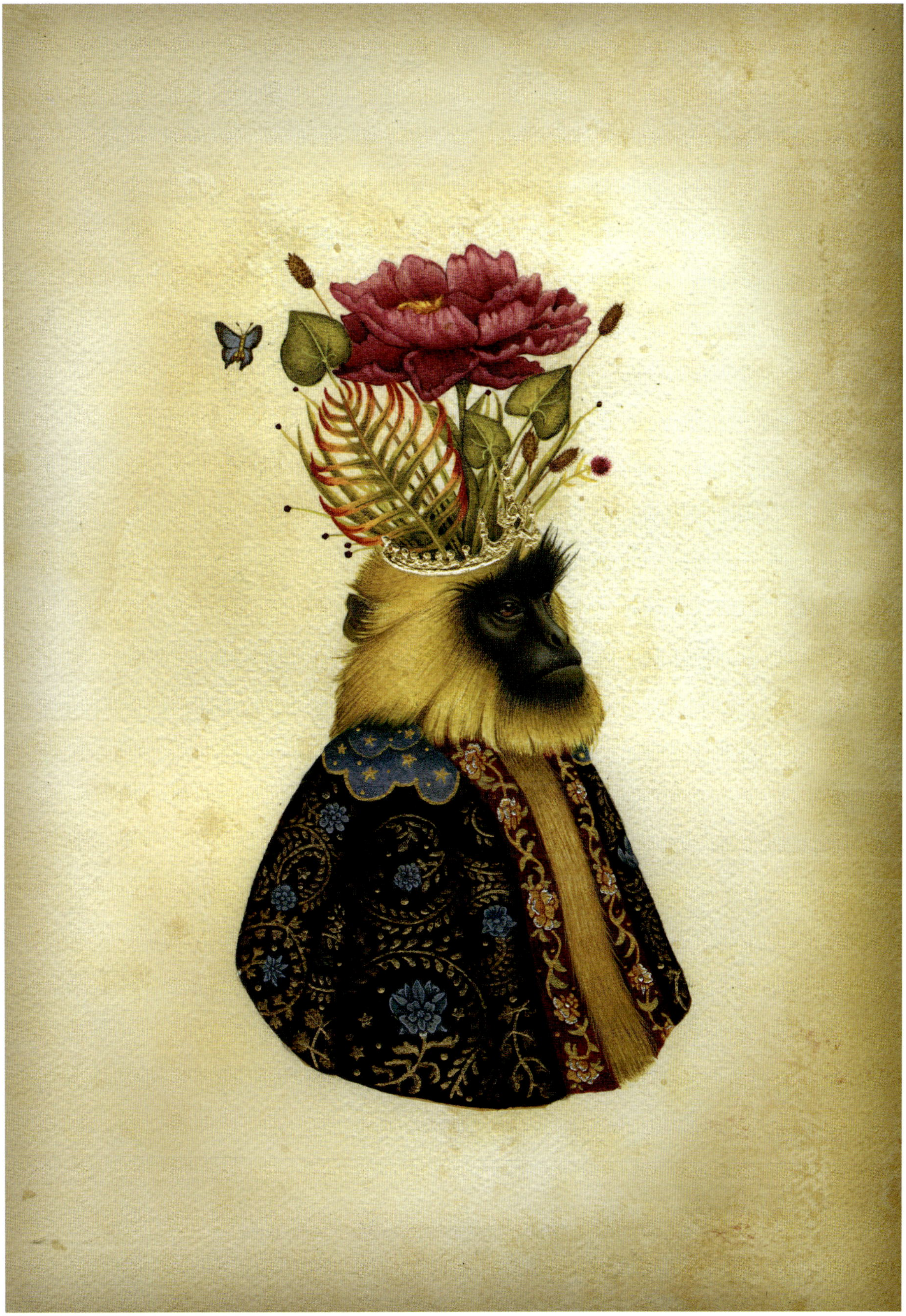

THOUGHTS OF FUTURE, 8" X 11", WATERCOLOR AND INK ON PAPER

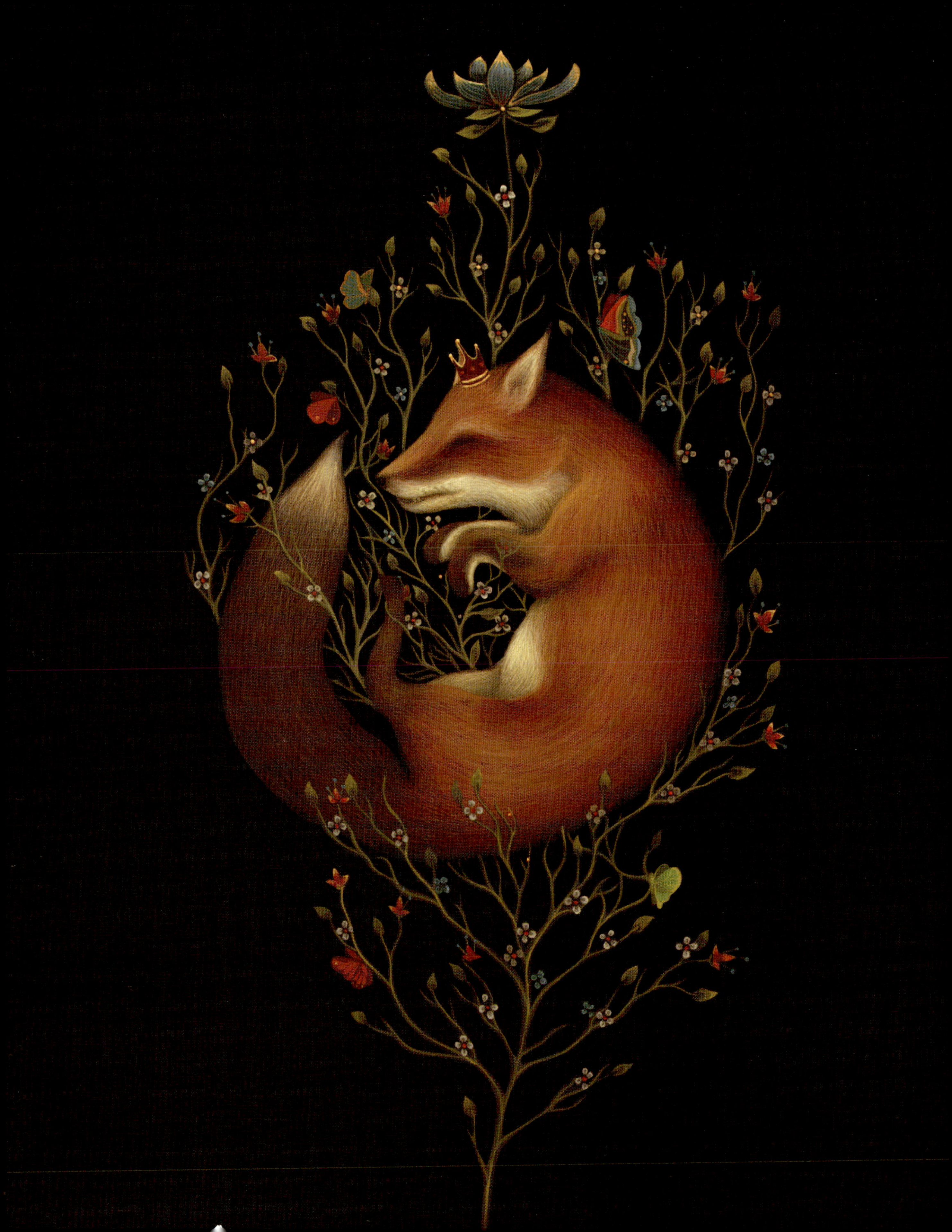

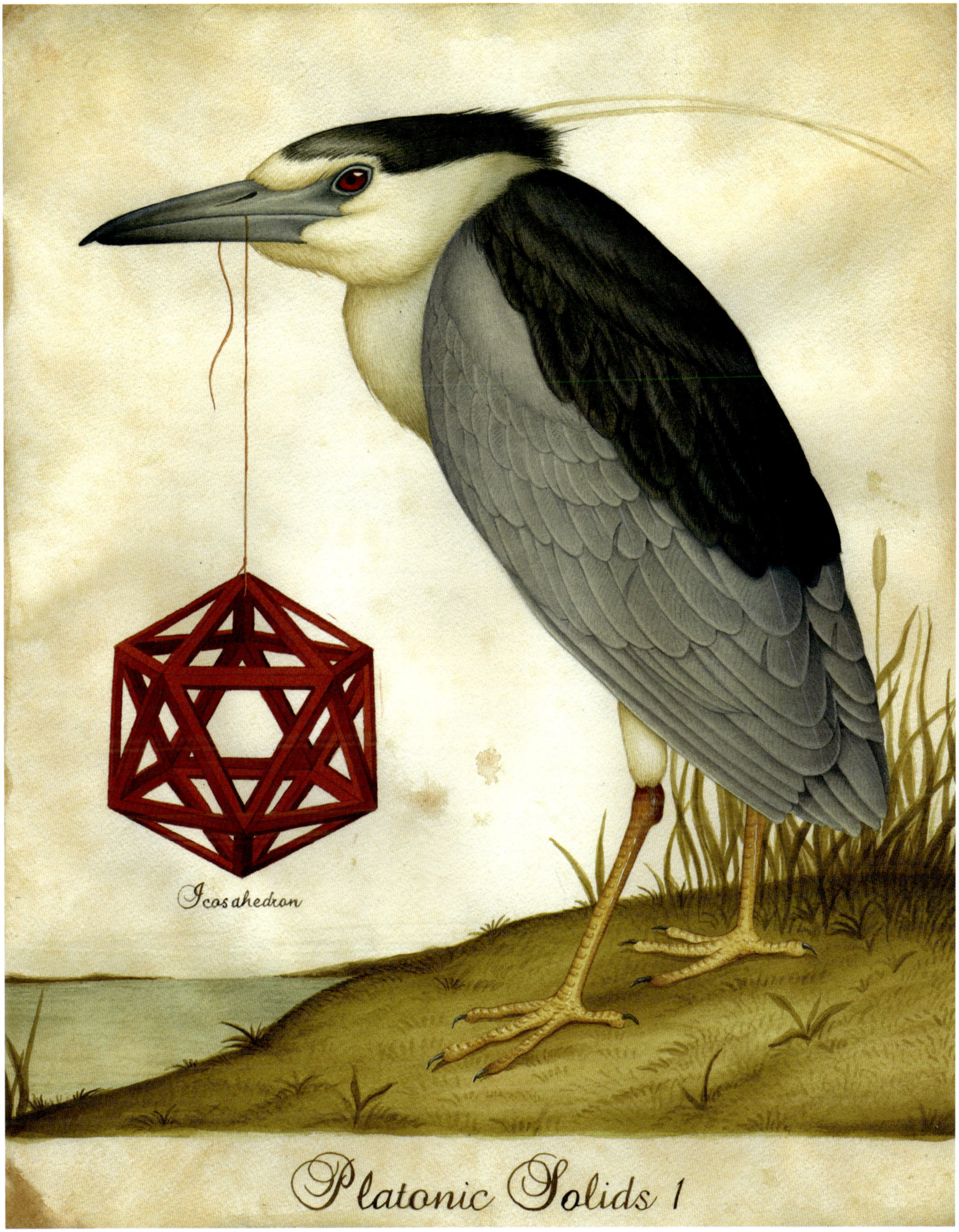

LEFT: *MORPHEUS*, 8" X 11", OIL ON WOOD PANEL

ABOVE: *PLATONIC SOLIDS*, 14" X 18", WATERCOLOR & INK ON PAPER

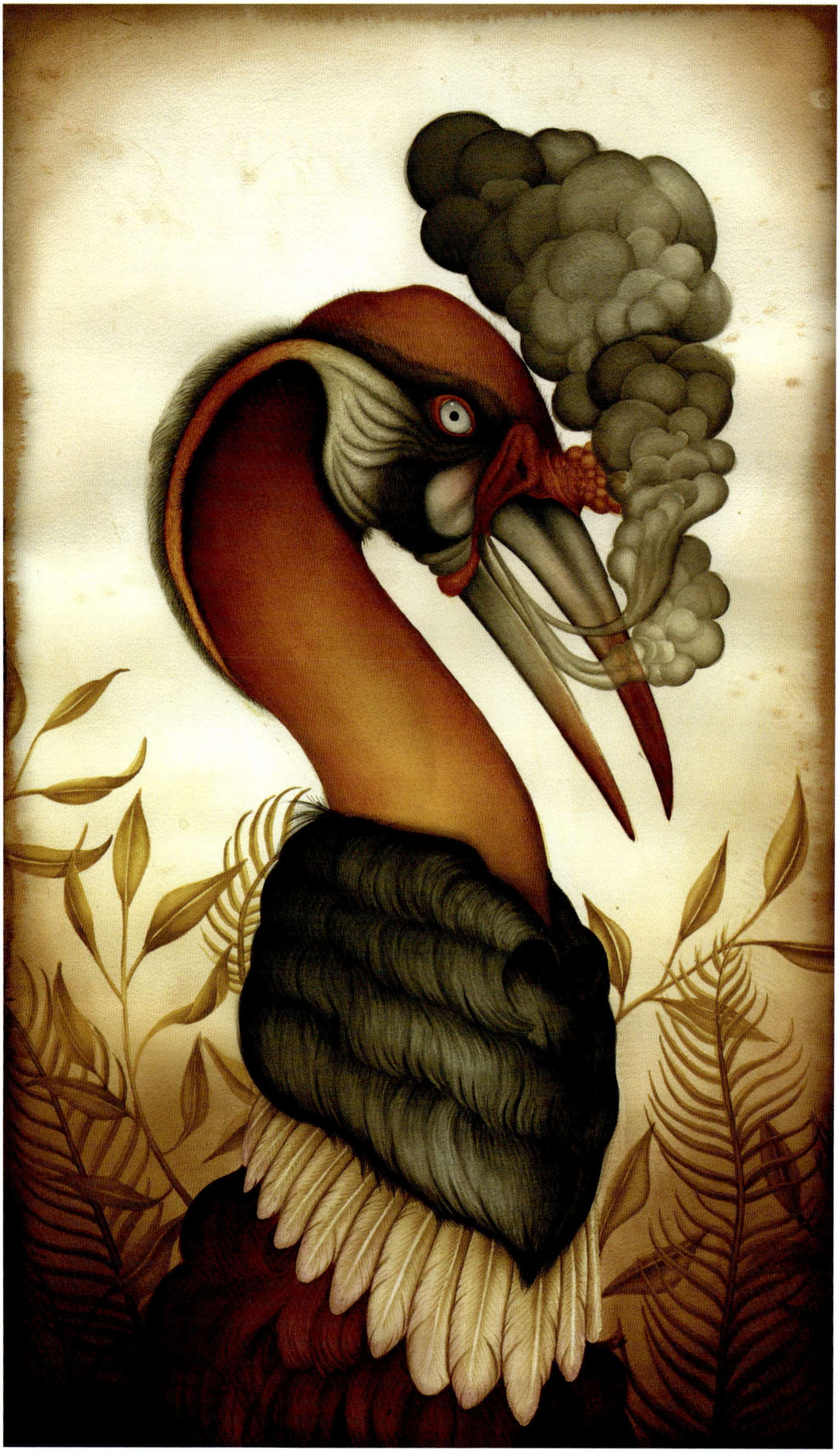

AUGMENTATION 1, 16" X 30", WATERCOLOR AND INK ON PAPER

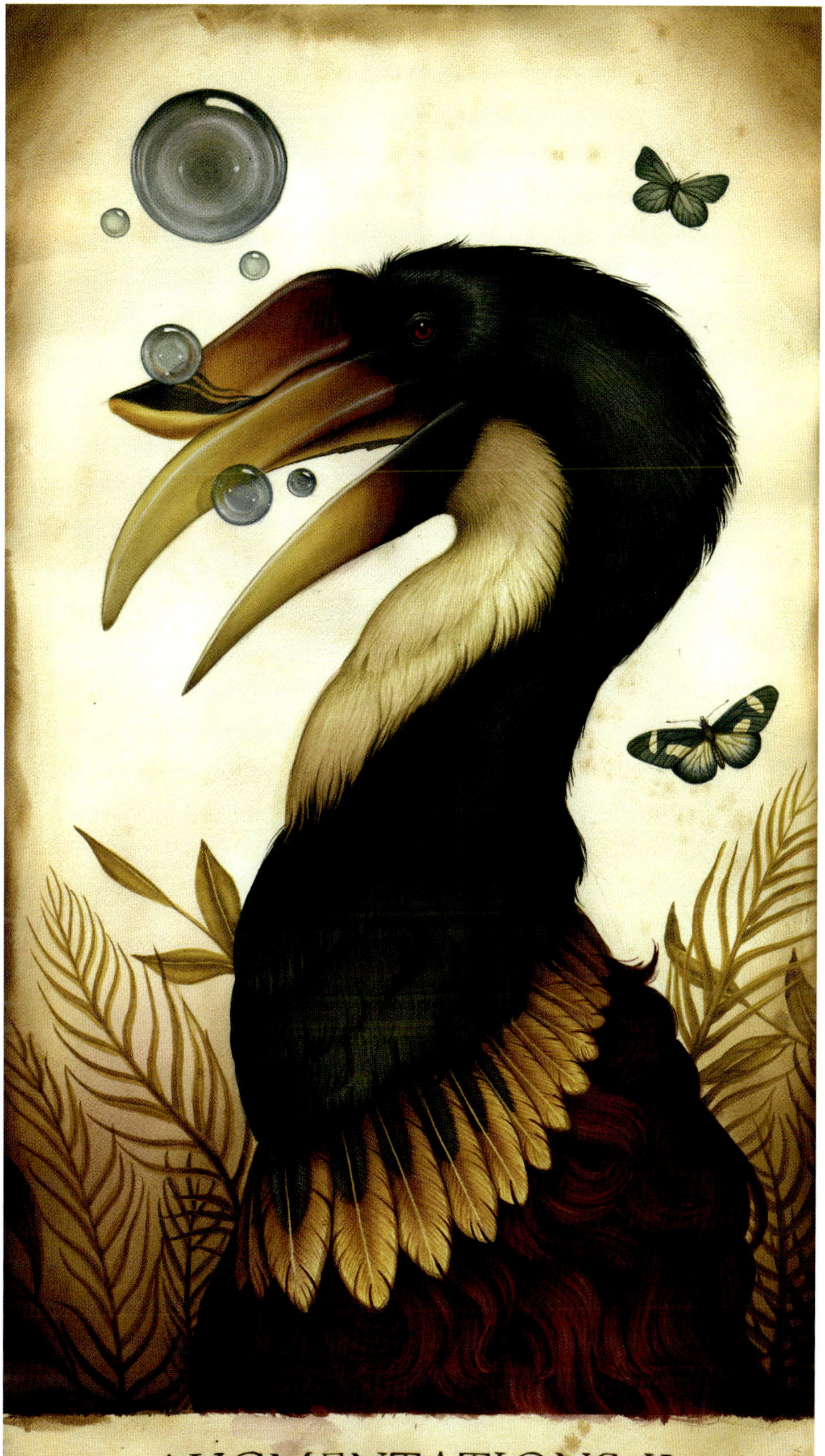

AUGMENTATION 2, 16" X 30", WATERCOLOR AND INK ON PAPER

CAITLIN HACKETT

OAKLAND, CALIFORNIA

Creature Features
I have always loved animals. My earliest sketches were of winged horses, ghost cats and parades of rainbow-colored creatures. I was always attracted to the animal form, and wished desperately to be an animal myself when I was little. My twin sister and I would gallop about on all fours pretending to be cats, wolves or horses. We were never very interested in dolls or other toys. It was always creatures that attracted us.

Growing up in rural northern California, I spent my time camping, hiking, swimming in rivers and running on beaches, so nature was always a big part of my life. Although I had originally planned on studying wildlife biology, I ended up going into the arts.

Childhood Menagerie
My family had two cats, and my sister and I each had a pet rat. My little brother had a gecko and a hamster. We lived in the woods, so we were surrounded by deer, raccoons, grey foxes, black bears, otters, mountain lions, seals, sea lions, herons, ravens, hummingbirds and so many more remarkable creatures.

Fantastical Roots
My art is often inspired by mythology and fairytales. I always loved mythical beasts as a child and was fascinated by the transformations and mutations that are often represented in those stories. Talking animals, enchanted stags, animal gods, fairies and sprites who would ferret away human babies and leave changelings in their places—these darkly magical tropes definitely played a role in the formation of my artistic style. I often combine human and animal forms as a way of alluding to our shared bond as living creatures, and as a way of diffusing the differences between us.

Power Symbols of the Wild
The symbolic power of any given animal varies from culture to culture, and many would probably say it is the lions and big cats that I paint that are the most powerful, since traditionally they are animals of considerable physical and symbolic strength across many cultural divides. For me personally, it is the deer and the hummingbirds that are most symbolically potent.

Fawns and stags have always been symbolic of the forest for me, and the love of forests is deeply embedded in my identity because of where and how I grew up. Hummingbirds are often symbolic of time, and of the ability to control it, because they fly both backwards and forwards, and hover in place. I am fascinated, enchanted and vaguely horrified by the irrevocable passage of time, and so hummingbirds are often included in my work as a symbol of our efforts and failures to capture or stop time.

The Animalier Influence
James Audubon was always an inspiration, although in reality, the man was something of a monster, killing thousands upon thousands of birds in his lifetime in order to paint his scenes, always searching for the perfect specimens. I also feel I owe a debt to countless other illustrators and artists whose names I can never recollect, because I collected illustrated encyclopedias of animals and bones as a child. Also, a show at the Brooklyn Museum of Walton Ford's remarkable work that I saw during my time in school at Pratt set me on the path to where I am today. Seeing his work made me realize that my childhood love of sketching animals was something that could be more than a hobby.

At One With The Trees
Walking alone through the Lady Bird Johnson Old Growth Redwood grove is my version of heaven. The trees there are two thousand years old, with trunks so wide you could drive a car through them, and bark as thick and gnarled as stone. To walk through those ancient trees is to feel truly mortal, more real than I feel anywhere else, and truly whole.

THE DODO'S WIDOW (DETAIL), 22" X 30", WATERCOLOR, BALLPOINT PEN, COLORED PENCIL ON PAPER

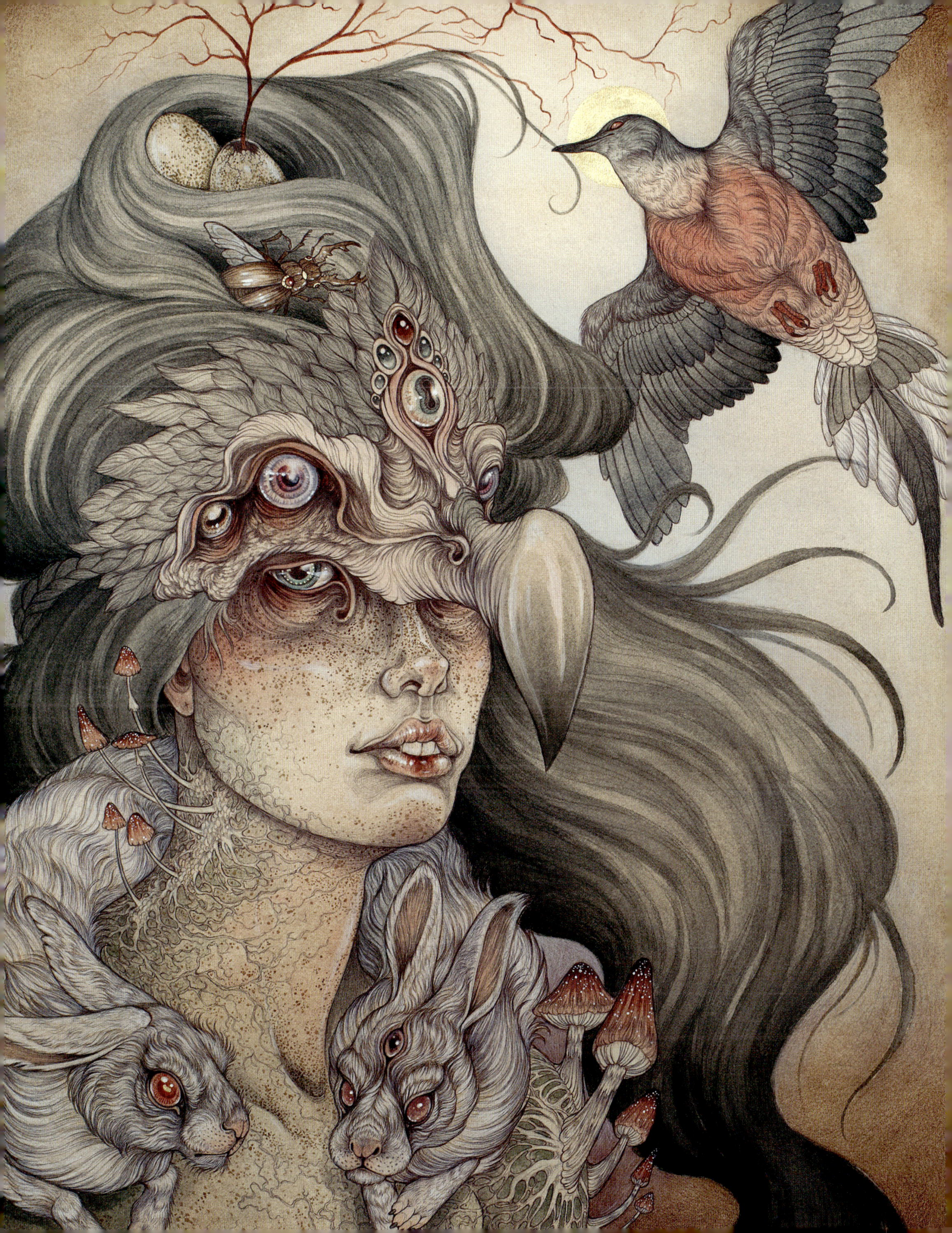

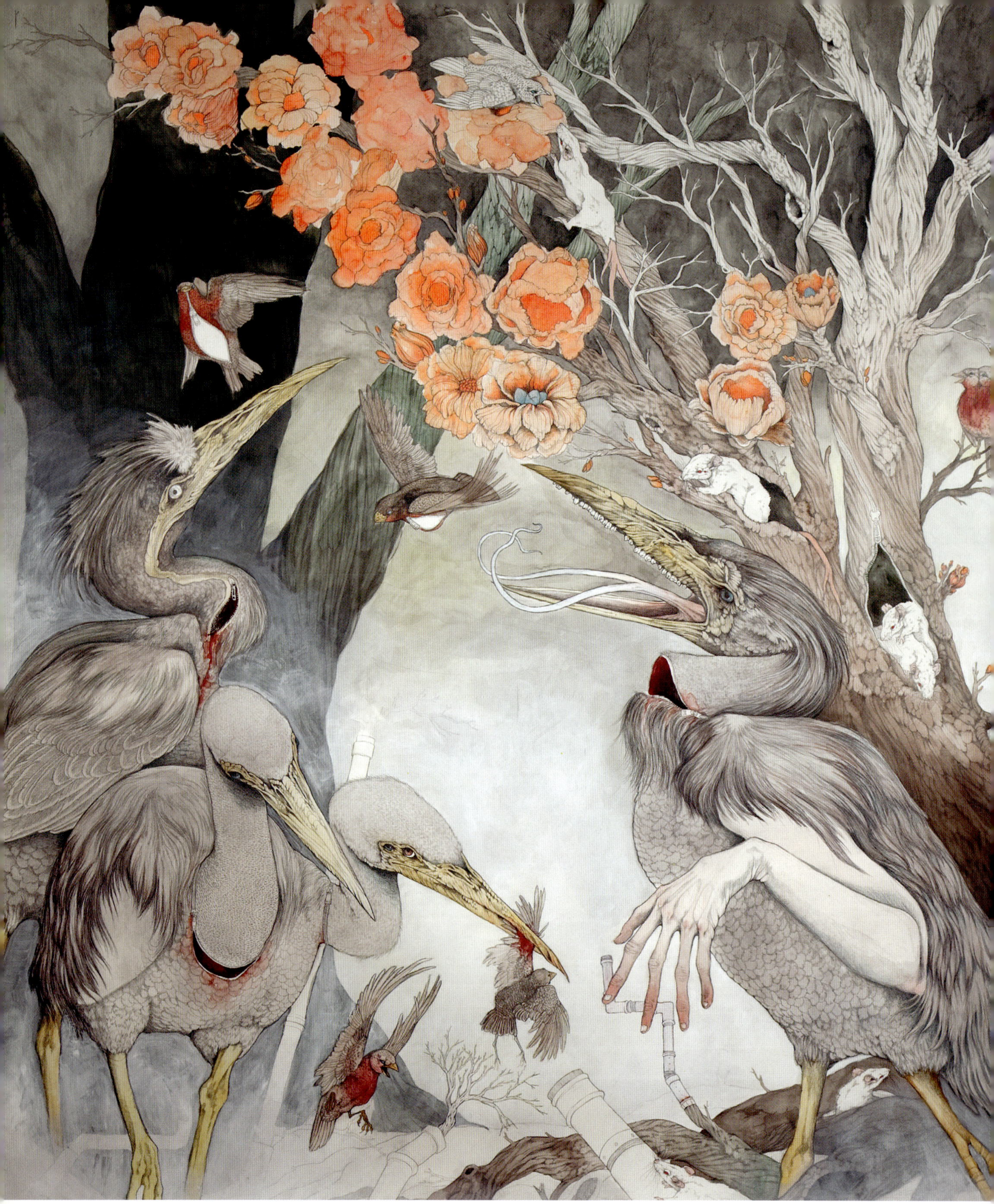

IN THE AFTERMATH, 54" X 63", WATERCOLOR, ACRYLIC, BALLPOINT PEN, GRAPHITE AND COLORED PENCIL ON PAPER

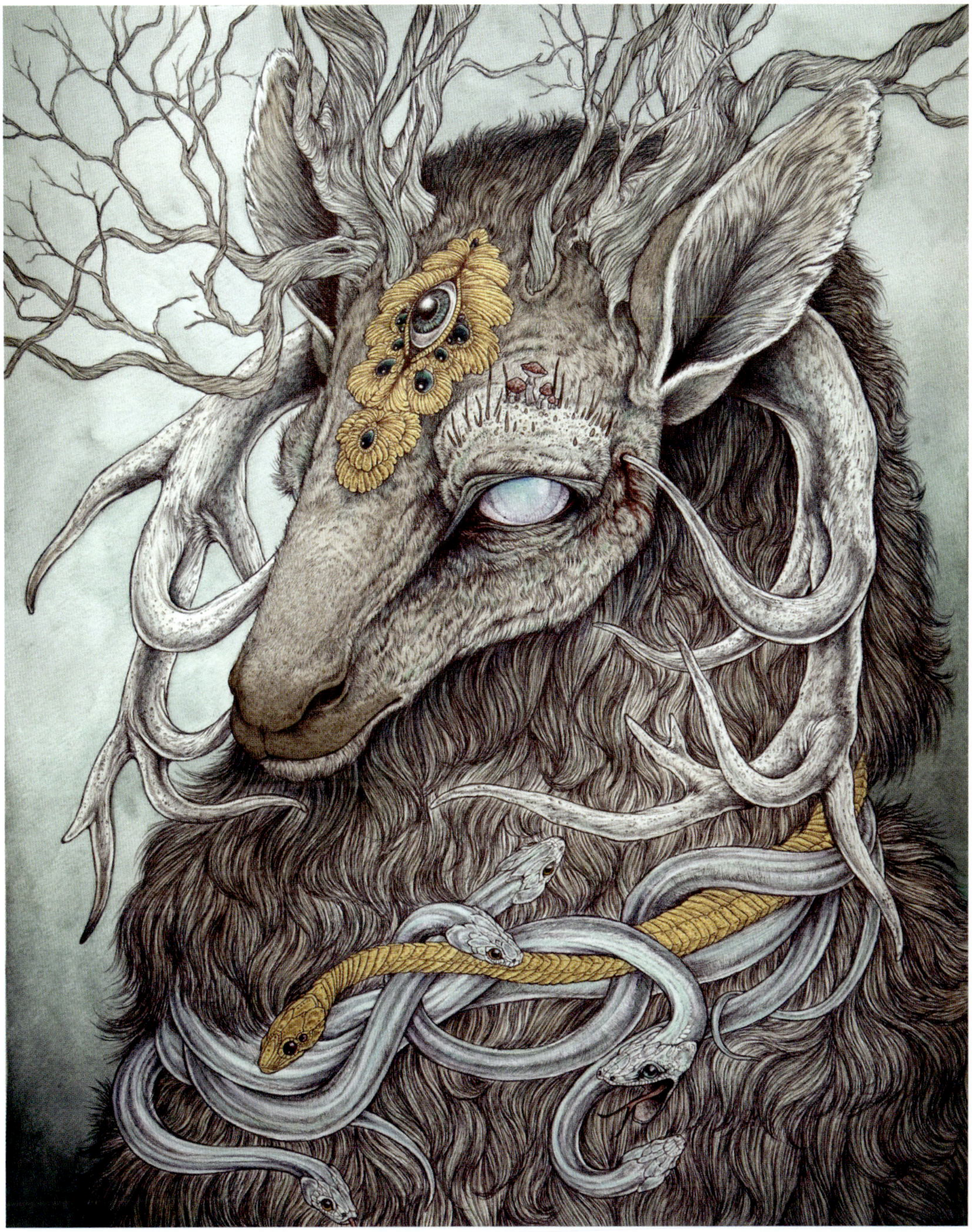

IN MEMORY, 18" X 24", WATERCOLOR, BALLPOINT PEN, COLORED PENCIL ON PAPER

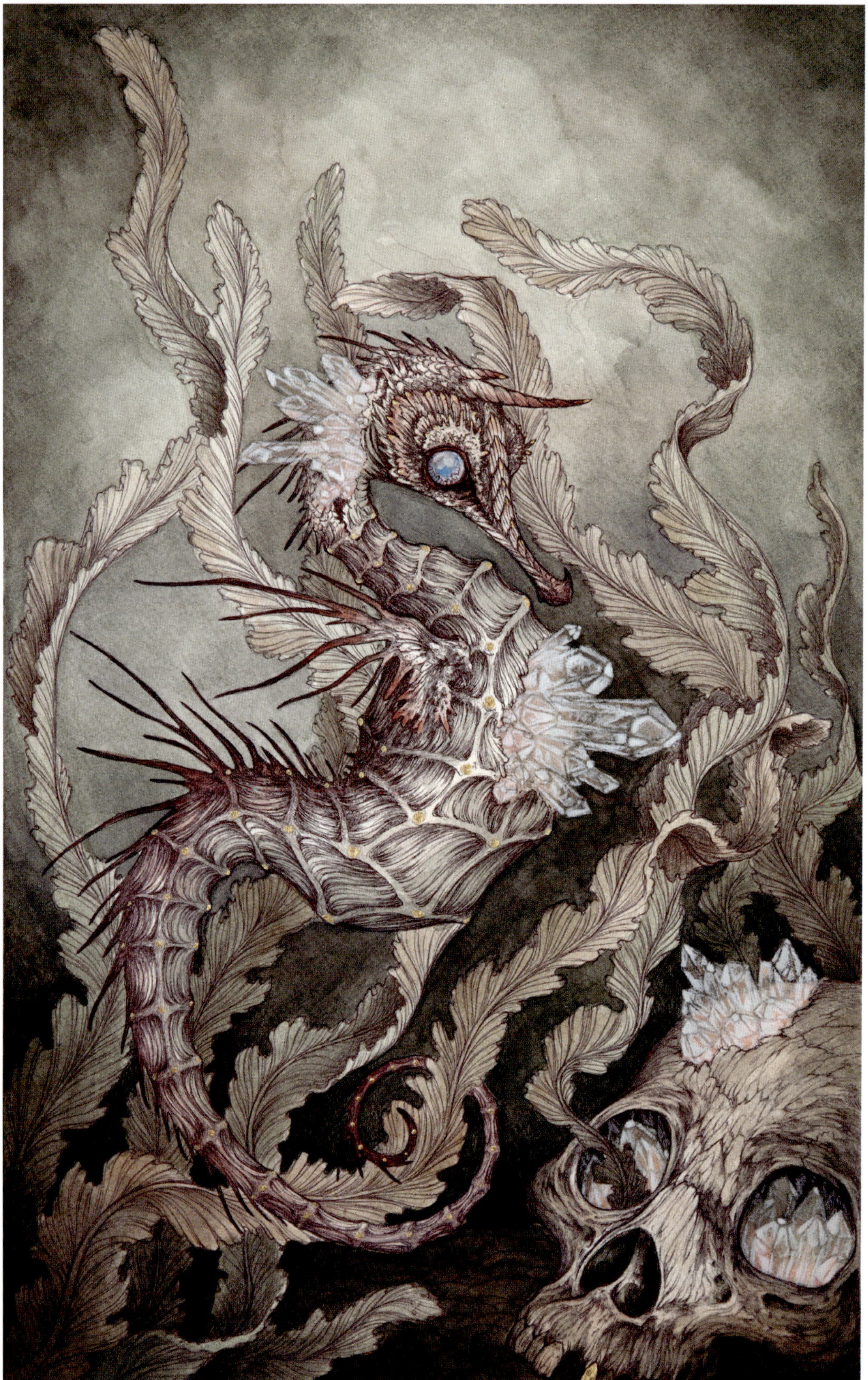

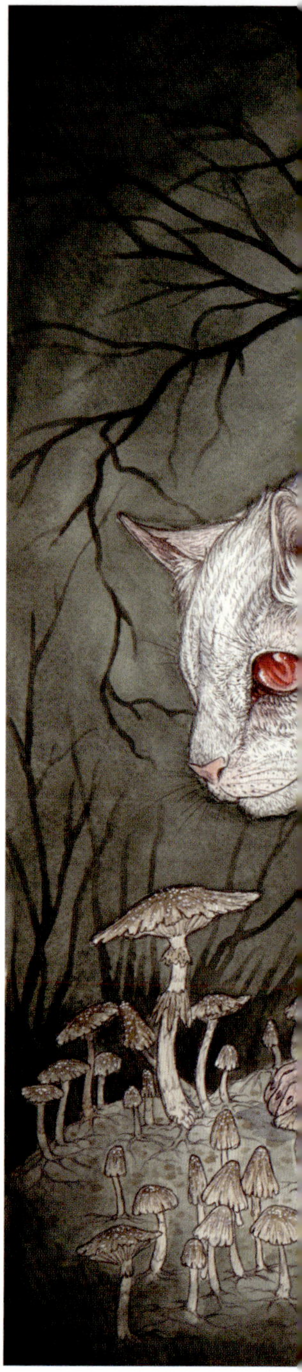

WHEN THE SEAS RISE, 12" X 16", BALLPOINT PEN, WATERCOLOR, COLORED PENCIL ON PAPER

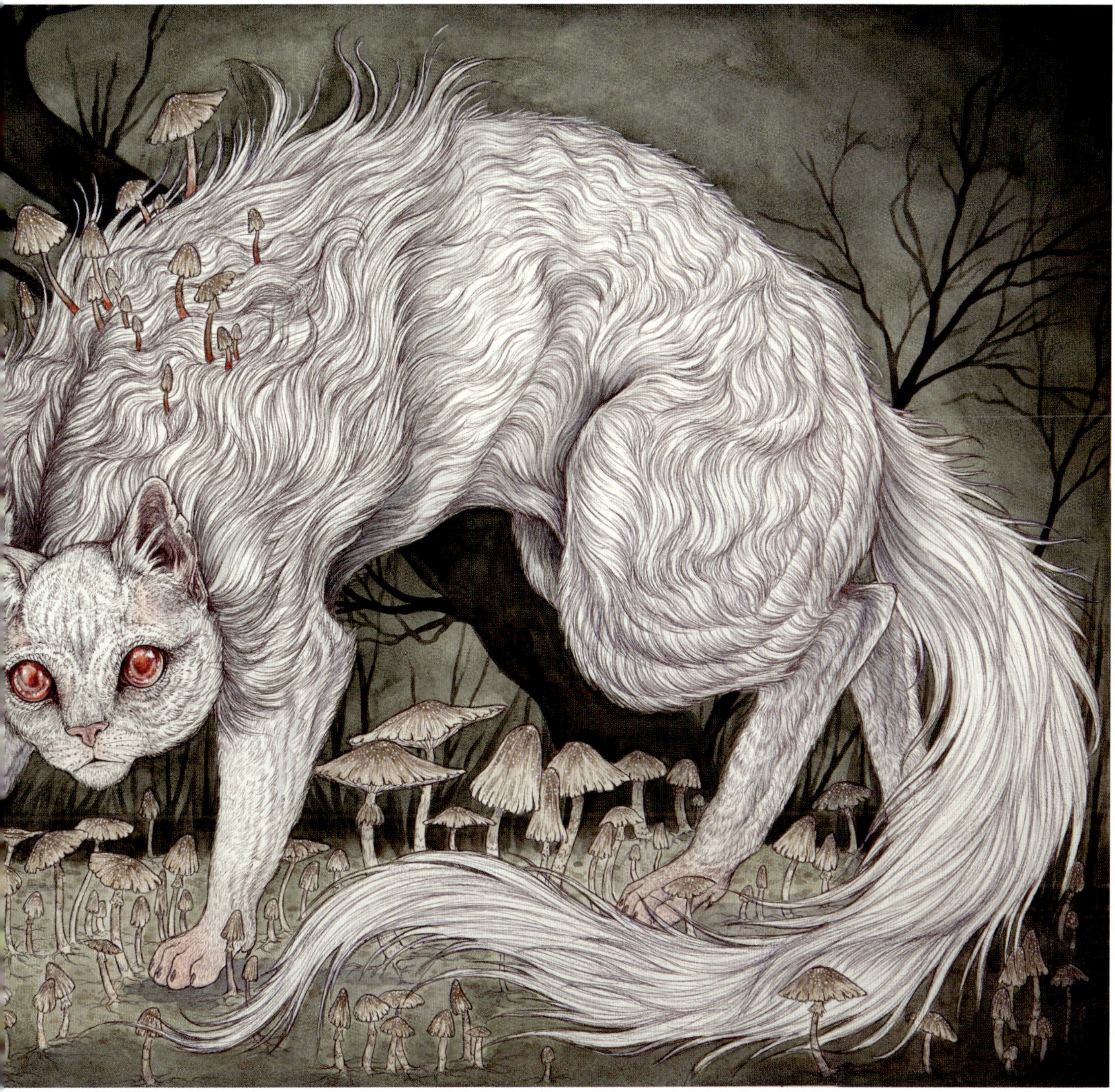

EIGHTEEN LIVES, 18" X 24", BALLPOINT PEN, WATERCOLOR, COLORED PENCIL ON PAPER

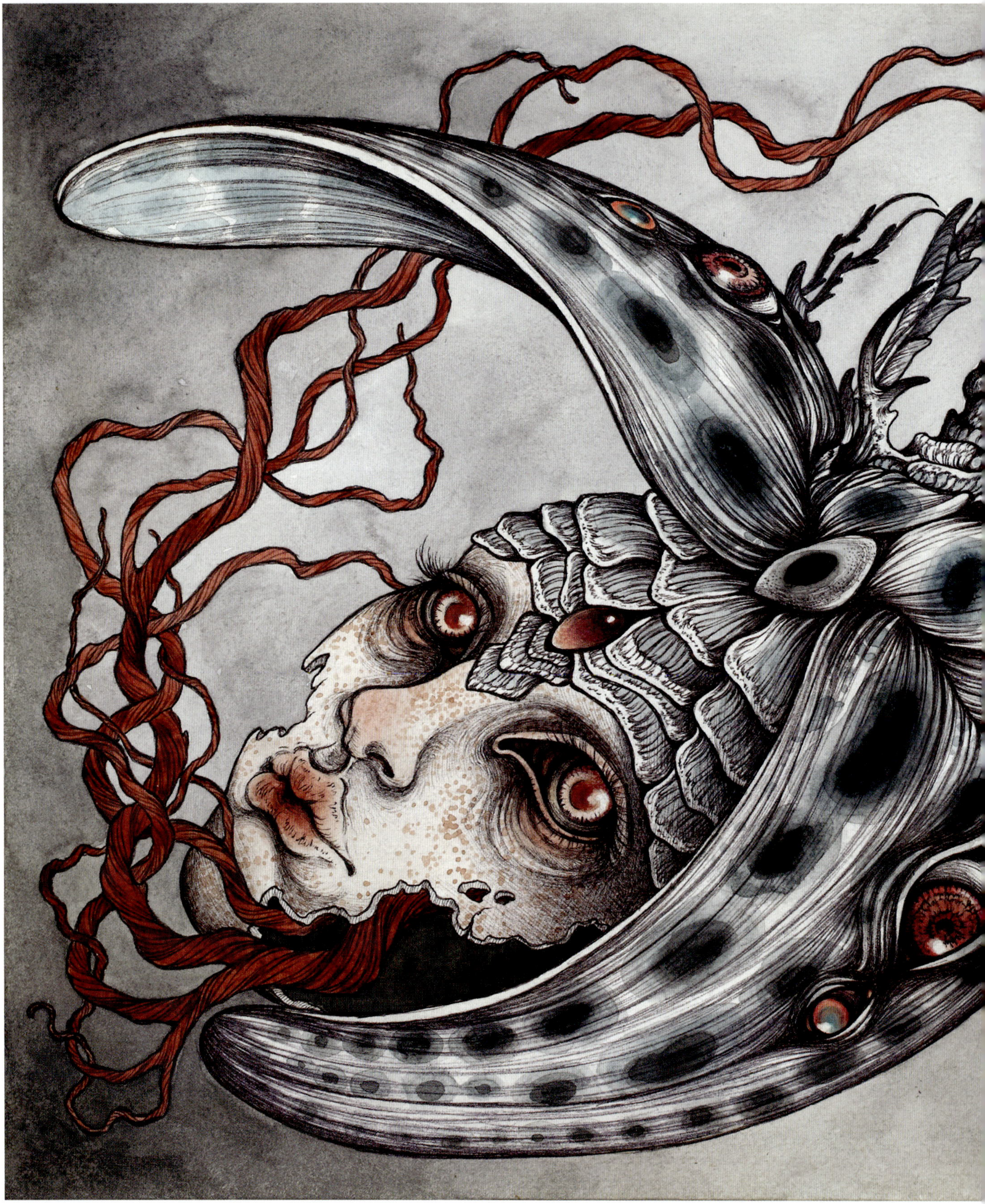

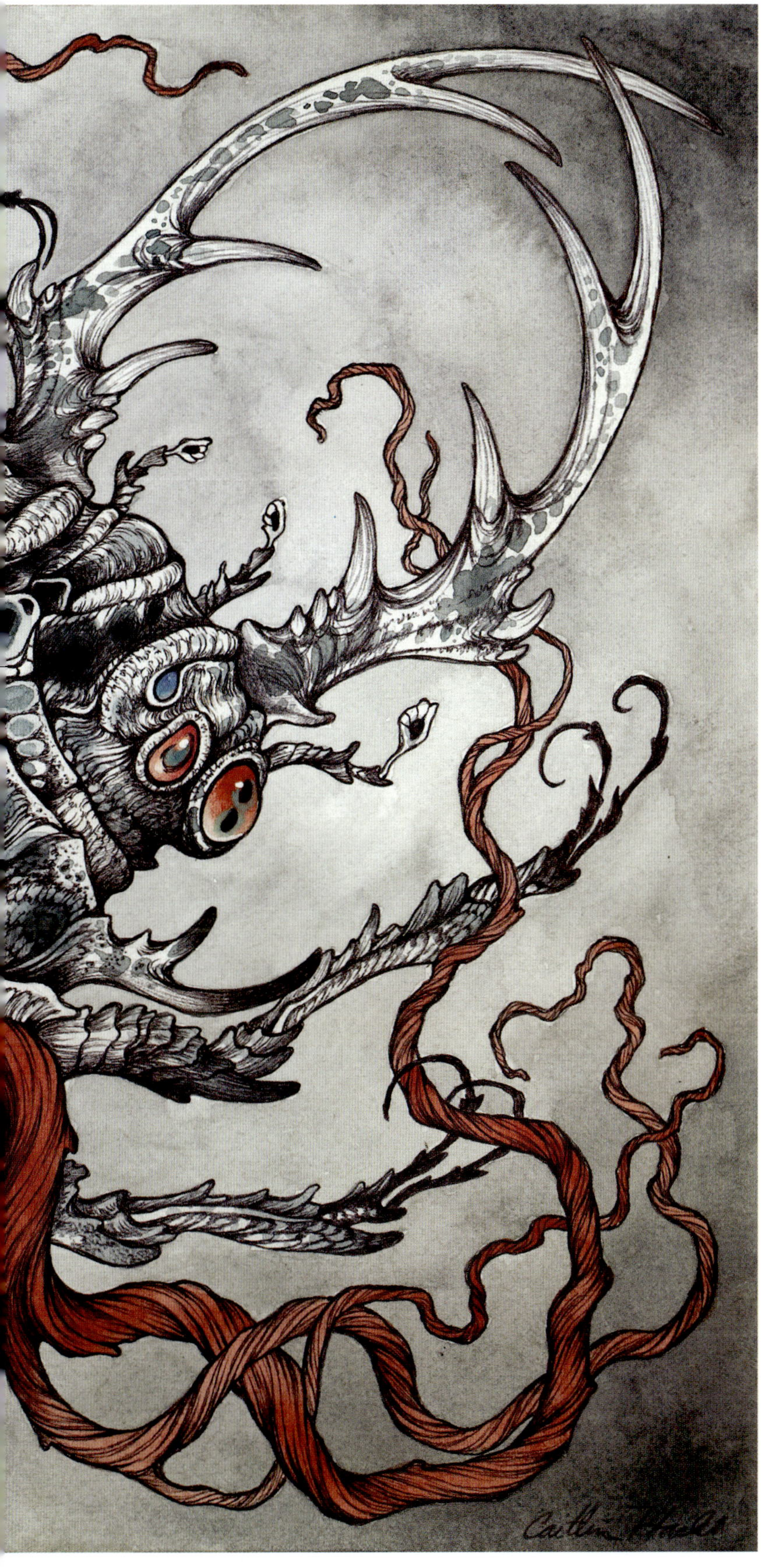

ILLUSIONS OF SEPARATION
11" X 14"
WATERCOLOR, BALLPOINT PEN,
COLORED PENCIL ON PAPER

DAVID HEVEL

OAKLAND, CALIFORNIA

Jewels on a Giraffe
I was making artwork that was pretty serious and introspective. When my first child was born, life became much more complicated, so I wanted to make work that made me laugh, yet maintained a critical eye on American culture. When my second was born, I became obsessed with plastic grapes and monkeys, maybe because life had become so full, like bunches of grapes. I bought every plastic grape I could find for an entire year and started building a ten-foot explosion of fruit. It needed monkeys, of course. That's when I discovered that you can buy practically any taxidermy form on the Internet. I titled that piece, *Paris Hilton Says That's Hot*. I continued to explore a wide variety of animal forms, juxtaposing them with pop culture iconography. Looking back, I think I've created a contemporary *Alice in Wonderland*-esque fairytale about American consumerism.

Taxidermy Toys
There is something very toy-like about working with taxidermy forms. I don't like the idea of working with real taxidermy animals, just the hint of reality. I alter the forms into different poses, then flock and paint them, giving them a cheap texture like carnival toys, which were my favorite objects as a child. The animals are often surrounded by a jungle of flora from the craft store and bejeweled with all kinds of gems, sometimes cheap jewels that are a hundred years old. We've been making this junk for centuries. Like the plastic grapes I was obsessed with a decade ago, I can't help but keep adding more and more junk to a work of art. I think a world so abundant with junk needs artwork that reflects the detritus we're all consuming. Putting jewels on a giraffe just seems logical.

Martha Stewart Covered in Bugs
At first glance, I want people to think the work is beautiful. Sometimes I actually think about how Martha Stewart might make a flower arrangement, coming right up to the edge of beauty, but then I'll hide teeth inside, or drip plastic over it, or cover the sculpture in bugs. Beauty is a seductress that draws you in, but when you get too close, beauty can be ugly, disgusting, and truth-telling.

The Superior Species
Animals are neutral. Animals don't lie, they don't live outside their means, and they don't waste. In many ways, animals are a blank canvas or an empty vial for us to project our own image onto. Humans have been doing this for centuries. Whether it be the image of the dancing pig at Carnaval, or Meissen porcelain monkey bands from Germany, or the classic novel *Animal Farm*, we've been creating animals in our own image to help tell our stories. Right now, Americans are consumed by one thing: pop culture. What better way to tell a story about America than turning Mariah Carey into an old goat?

I move back and forth between wild and domesticated animals. I'll get stuck on a species and obsess for a while and then switch to another one. For a show about Britney Spears and her family, I used all baboons and monkeys because their eyes are so human-like, eliciting empathy, and perhaps guilt.

Dogs can be simultaneously lovable and vicious. They protect and they are our domestic companions, but they can be wild, rabid killers. Lately I've been thinking about pigs, swine, hogs, runts and boars. Each conjures up different feelings of repulsion. I think it's about time to repurpose this animal into a pop culture world.

Amber Waves of Grain
Hiking in the mountains of eastern Oregon, or in the redwoods of Northern California on a foggy day, or standing in a wheat field in Missouri at the beginning of harvest—I enjoy places with no people, noise, or TV!

ADORATION OF BRAD PITT, 102" X 48" X 48", TAXIDERMY FORM, HAIR EXTENSIONS, MIXED MEDIA

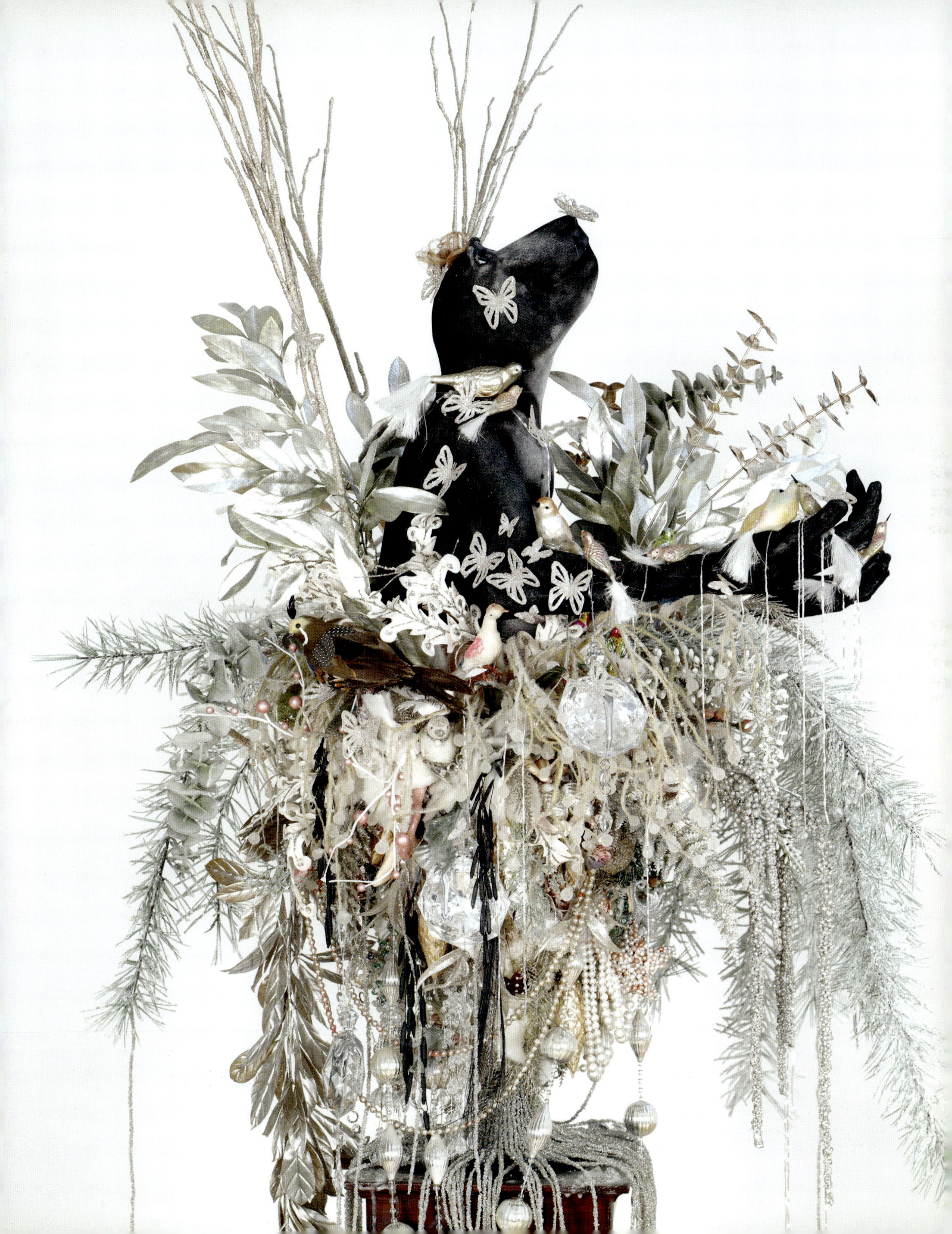

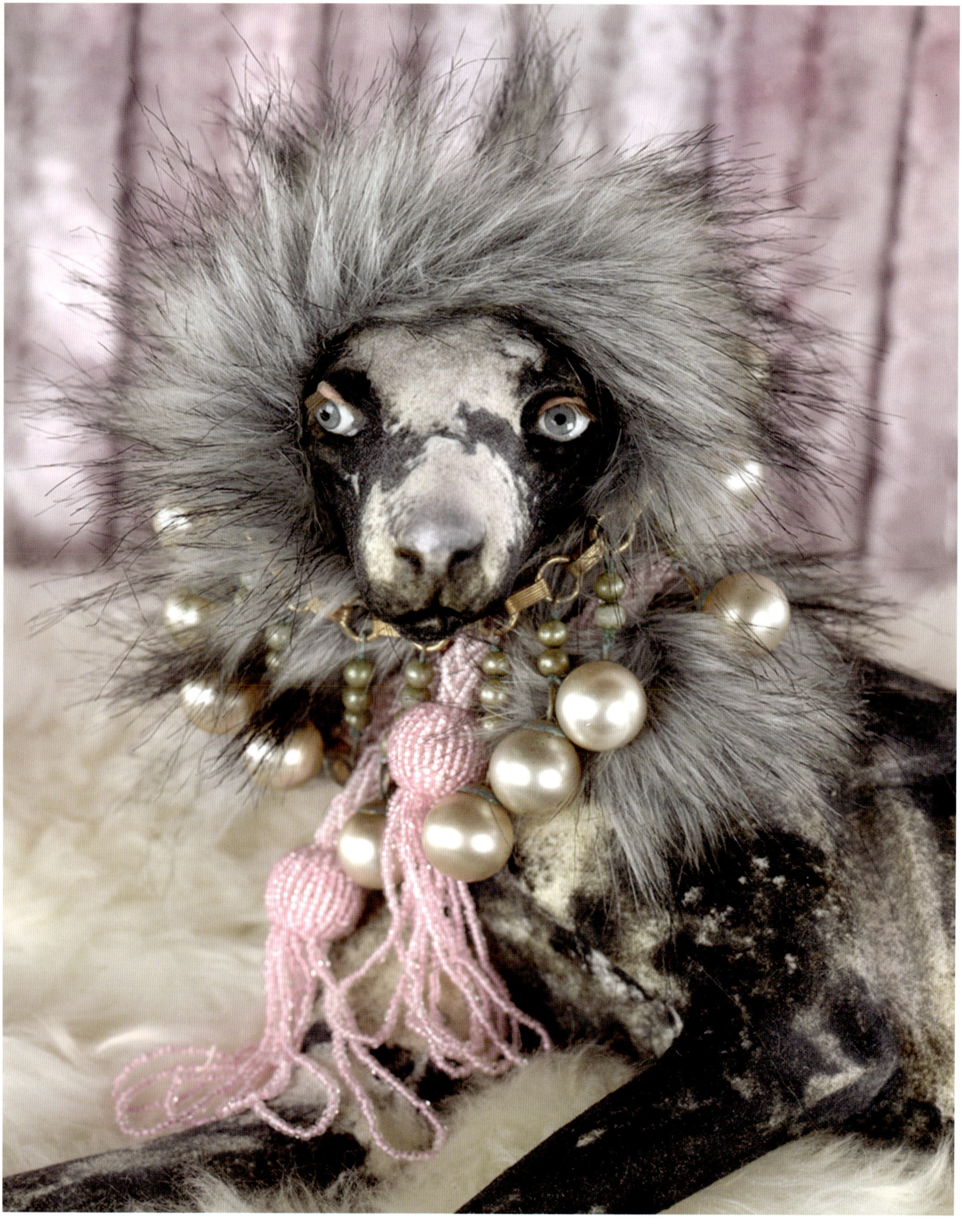

ABOVE: *BIG ANNA*, ARCHIVAL DIGITAL PRINT

RIGHT: *BRITNEY'S BEAVER*, 84" X 44" X 40", TAXIDERMY FORM AND MIXED MEDIA

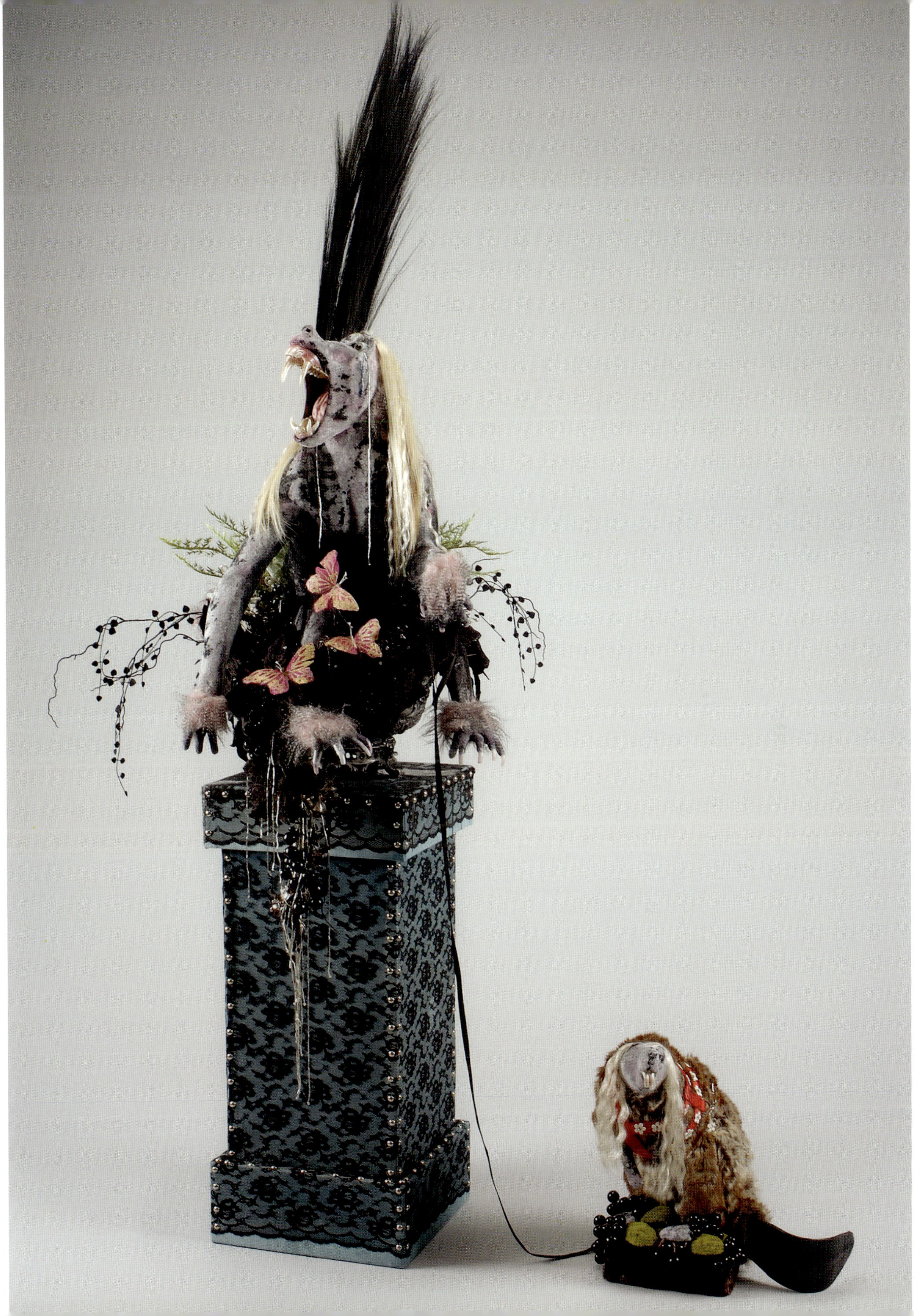

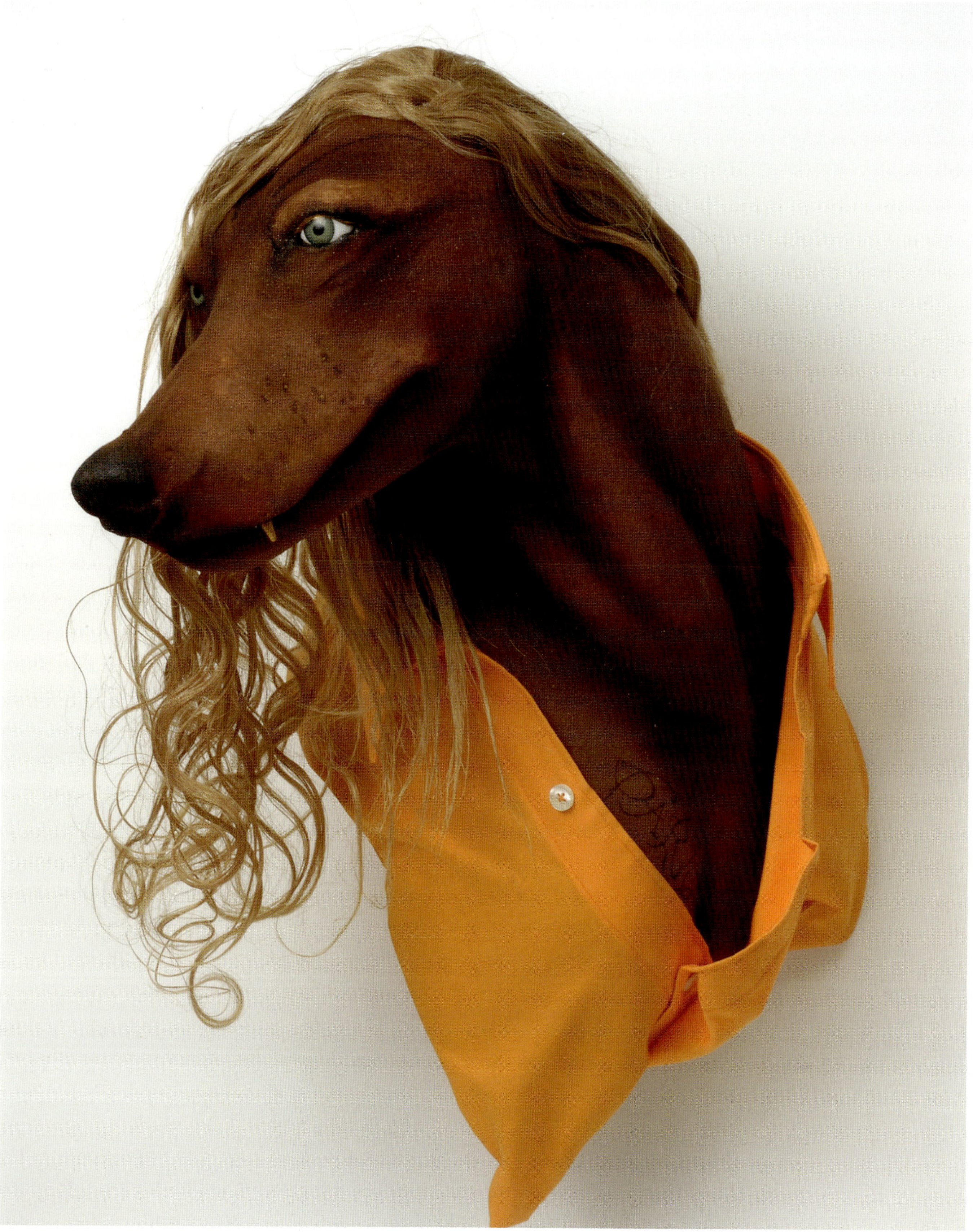

PARIS HILTON WAS MY BITCH, 16" X 12" X 12", TAXIDERMY FORM, HAIR EXTENSIONS, CLOTH AND MIXED MEDIA

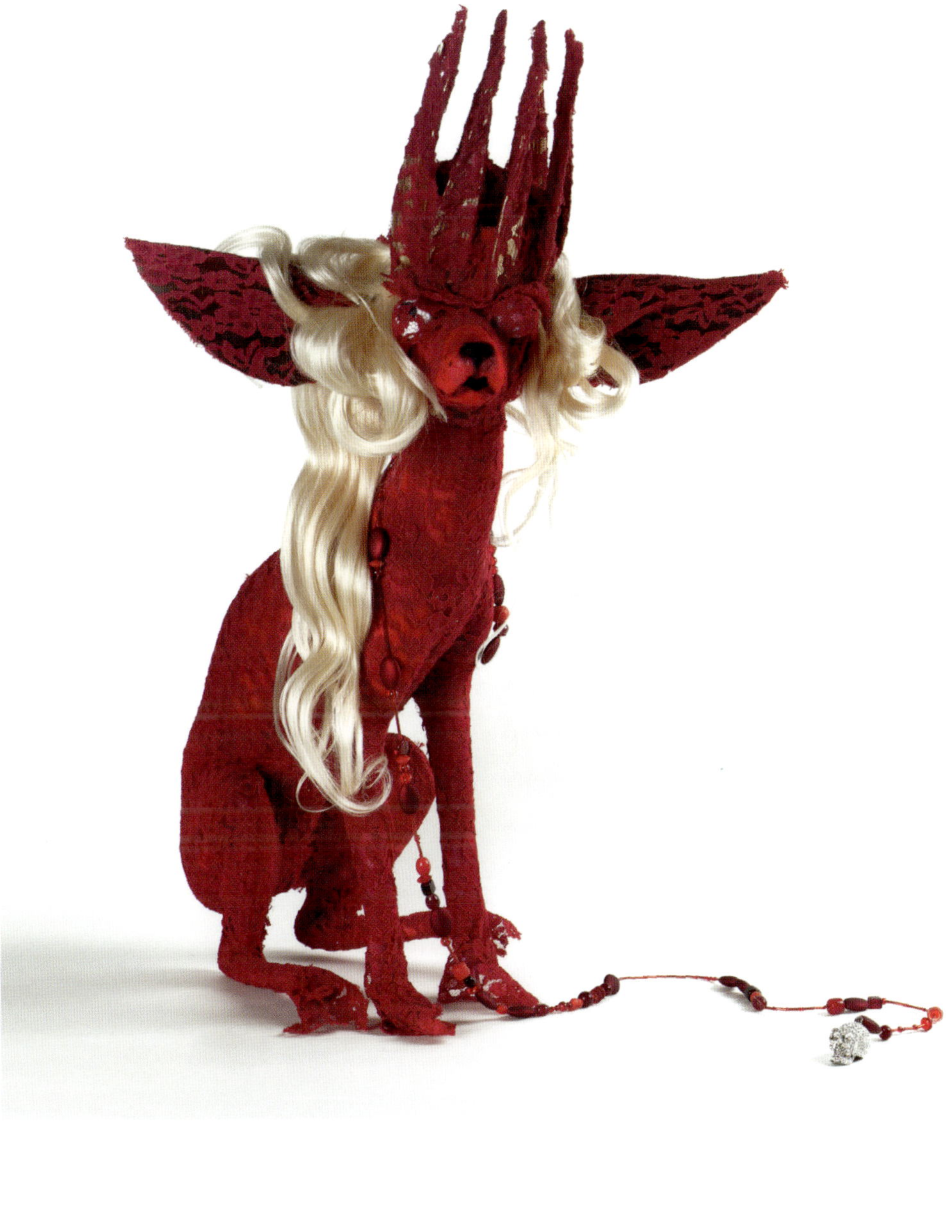

LIL' MONSTER, 18" X 18" X 18", DOG TAXIDERMY FORM, MIXED MEDIA

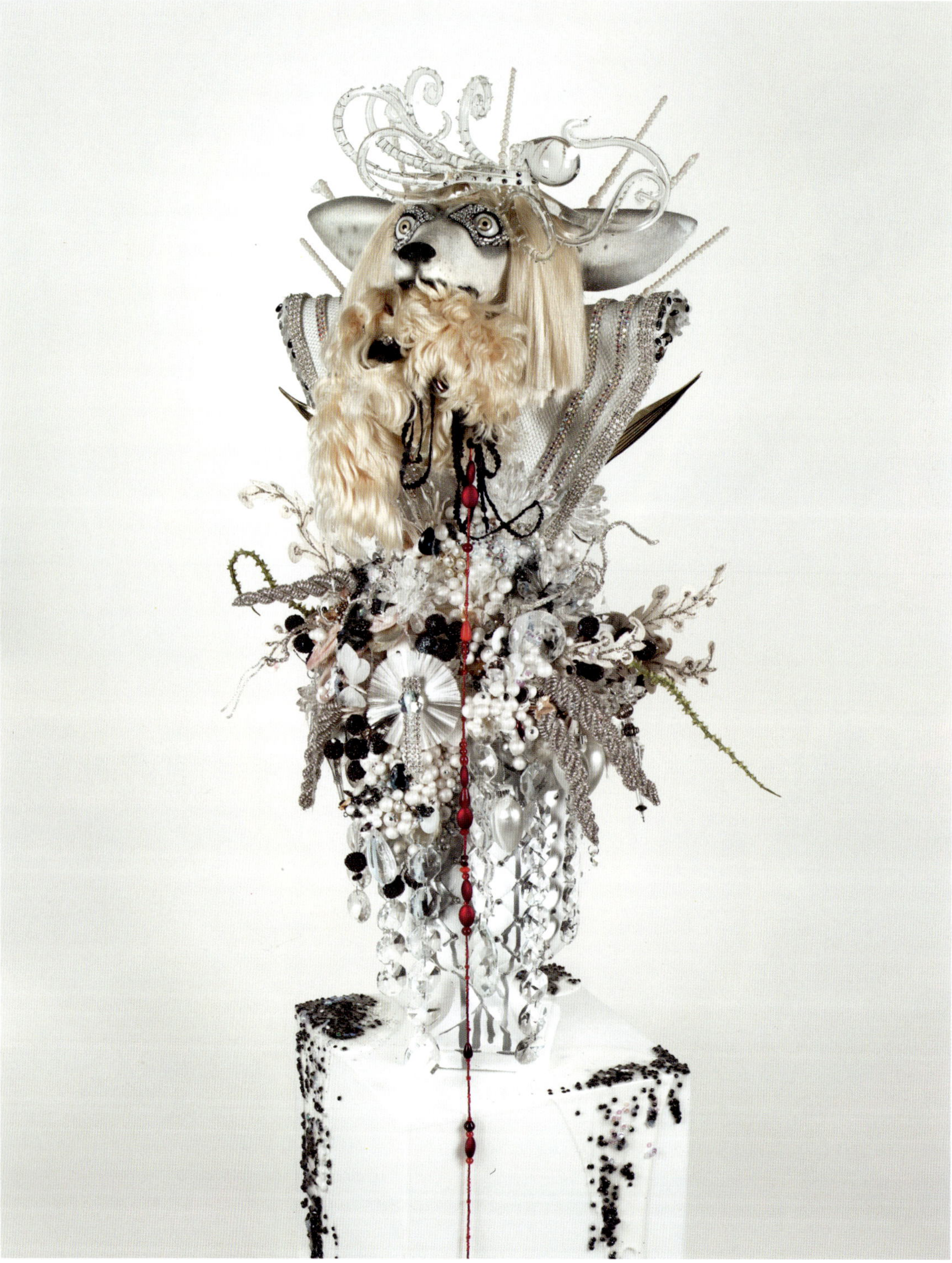

ABOVE:
FAME MONSTER
75" X 20" X 21"
TAXIDERMY FORM AND MIXED MEDIA

RIGHT:
HEAVEN CAN'T WAIT
66" X 36" X 21"
TAXIDERMY FORM AND MIXED MEDIA

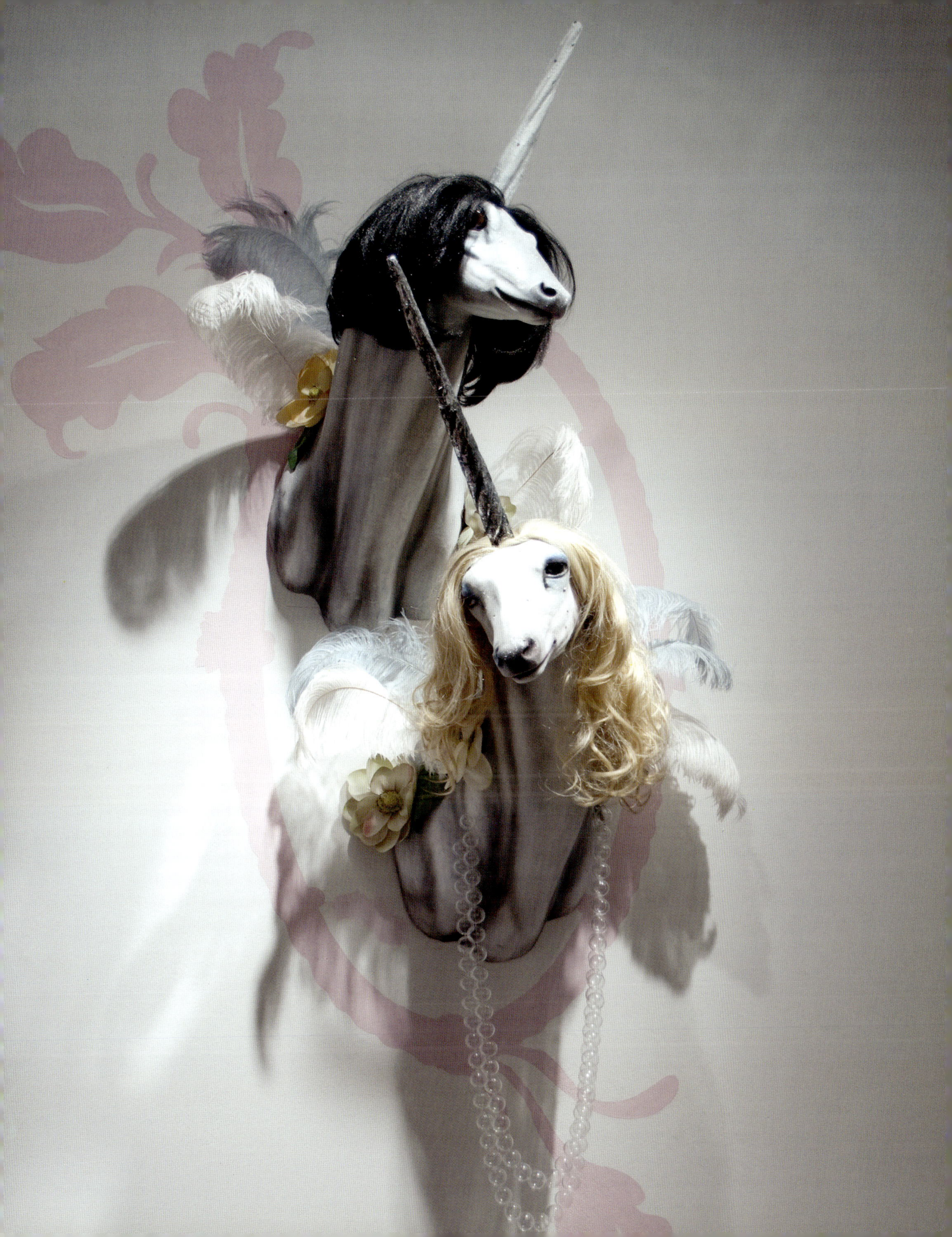

FAITH47

CAPE TOWN, SOUTH AFRICA

Softening the Chaos
We, as a species, have become so distanced from nature, we arrogantly exploit the planet with no care of the impact we are having on the intricate and fragile eco-systems in place. Archetypally, symbolically and spiritually, animals can teach us deeper truths. Our attitude towards them is counter intuitive, essentially self- destructive, reflective of our own inner turmoil and chaos. The animal paintings are intended to subtly reconnect us to the natural world, softening the harsh city architecture with gracefulness and a spirit-like presence. I want to state their presence, to allow them space, nostalgically reflecting on the lands that were once theirs to share.

Talking to a Wall
The textures of the walls speak to me. I look for decay, for history etched and fallen. I can work with that. I can create a dialogue between what has been and what is; what will fade and what will eventually fall to dust.

Remember the Rhinoceros
The rhinos that I painted in China are special to me. There are unending reports of rhinos being ruthlessly killed for their horns. During 2014, in South Africa alone, a staggering 1,215 rhinos were killed by poachers. That's one every eight hours. It has reached a crisis point but very little is being done about it. I wanted to bring the ghosts of these rhinos to Asia, where the demand for rhino horn is causing this situation. I chose to paint the rhinos on the "nail houses" in Shanghai. The nail houses are the stubborn houses that people refuse to leave when the government pushes for the demolition of certain sections in order for high- rises to be built. They demolish the houses around the nail house and make life unbearable for that family until they eventually leave. I felt the relationship between this architectural space and the inevitable destruction of one of the planet's most ancient and strongest animals was something that resonated.

Where to Find Me
Under the night stars.

Universal Energy
My work is extremely personal. I don't hold any agenda to transform or impact the world, but I do believe in the power of each person's consciousness radiating and affecting each other, so this I embrace fully.

SOLAR LOGOS, LONDON, ENGLAND

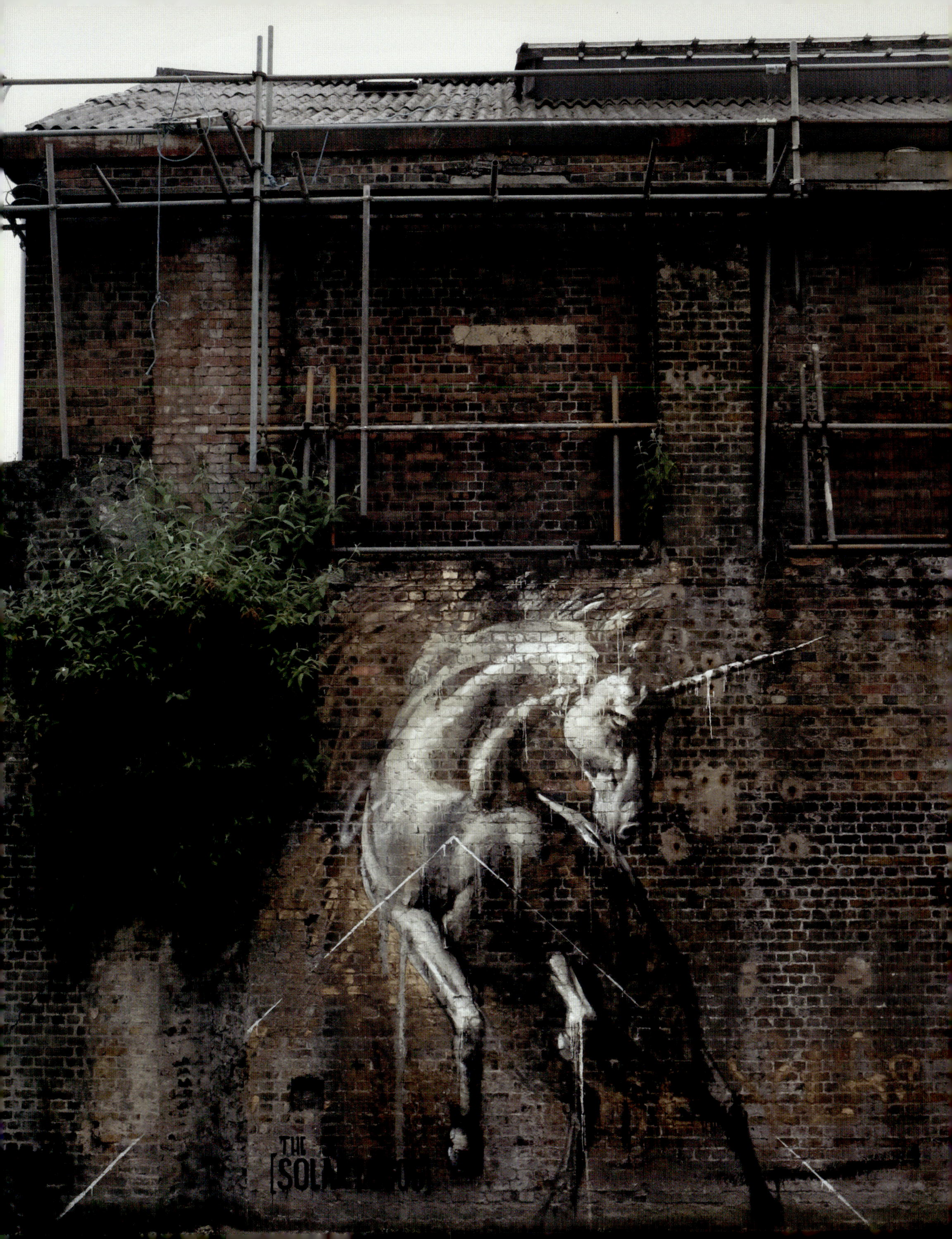
THE

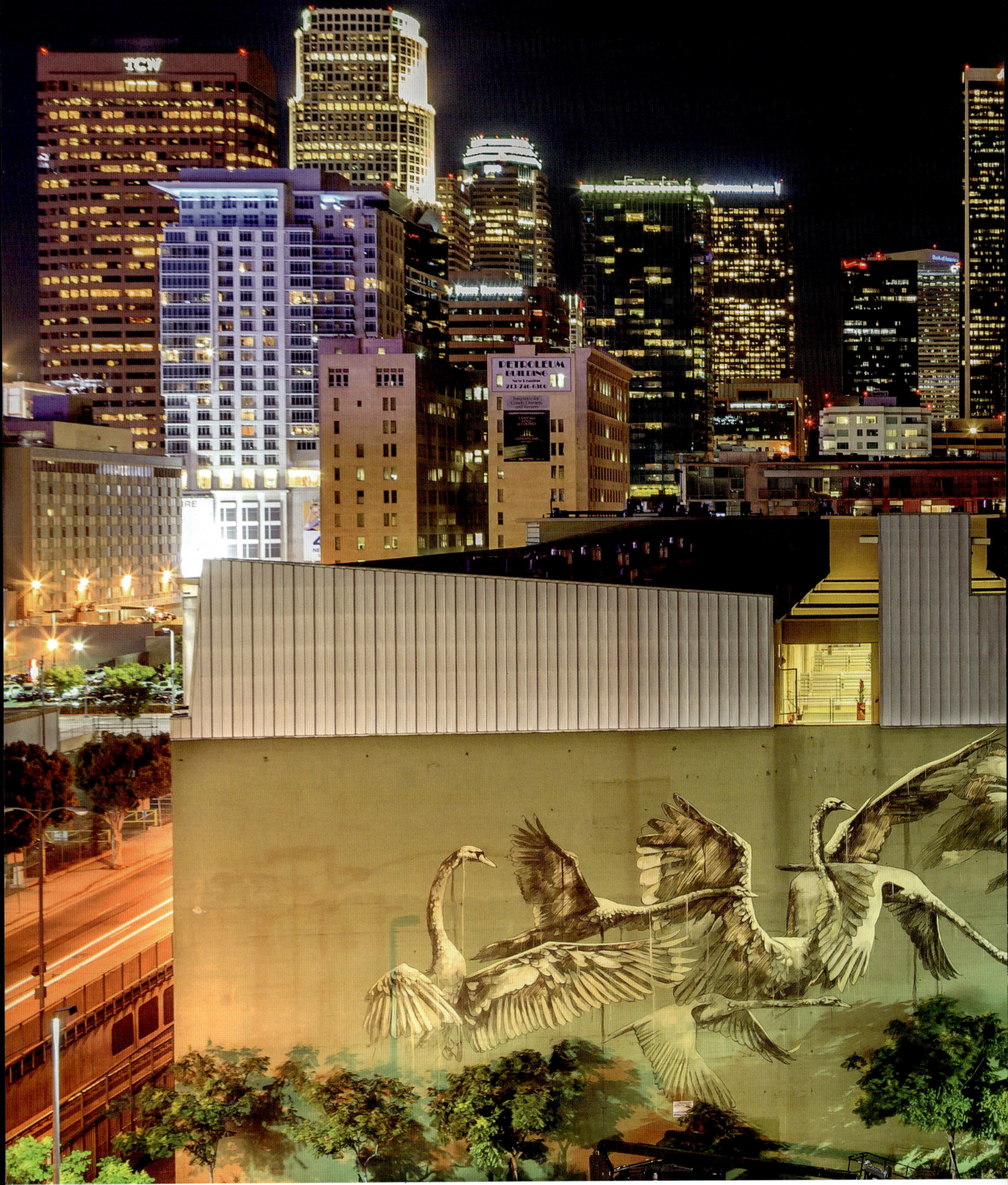

THE PRECIOUSNESS OF THE HUNT, LOS ANGELES, CALIFORNIA

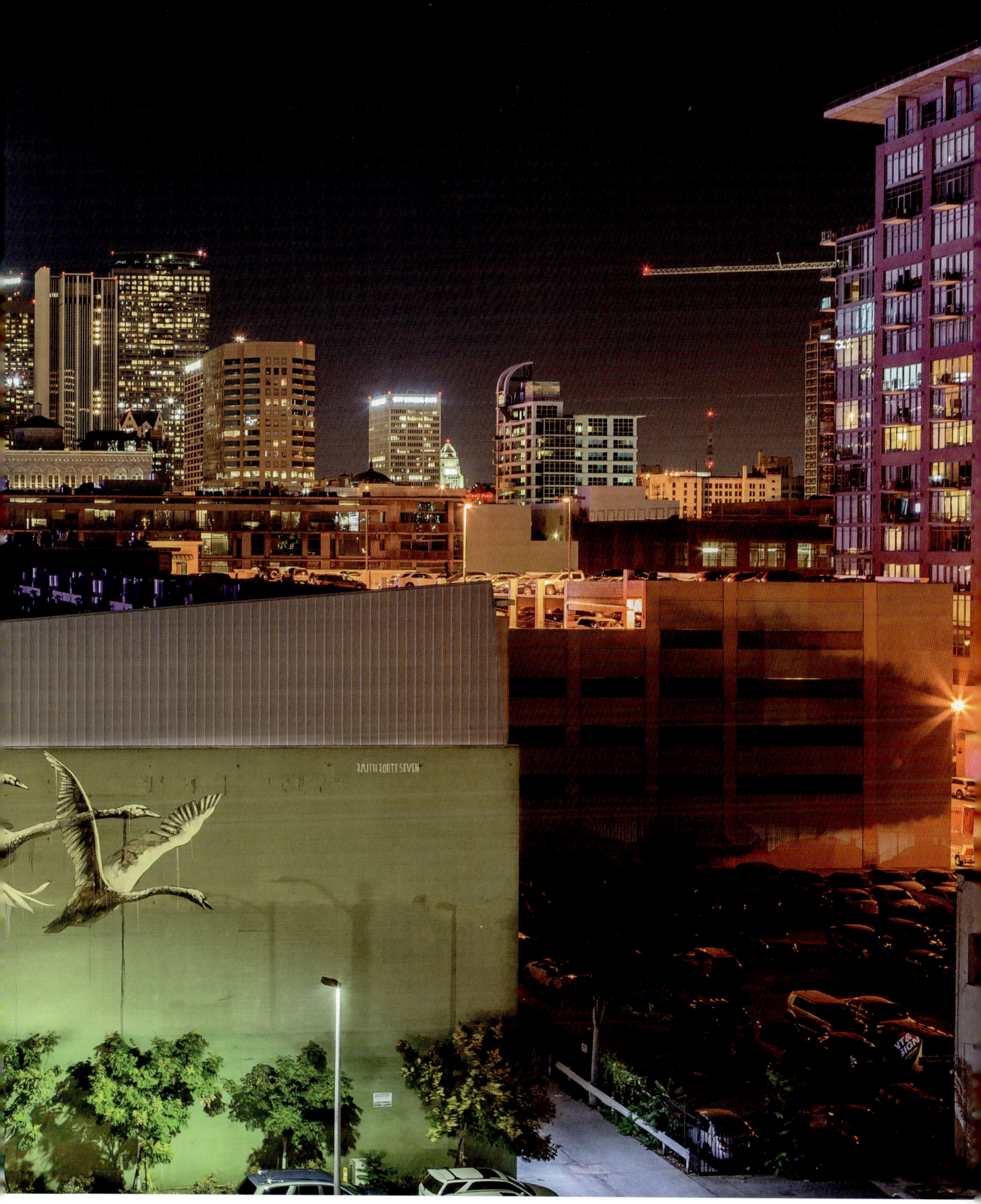
FAITH FORTY SEVEN

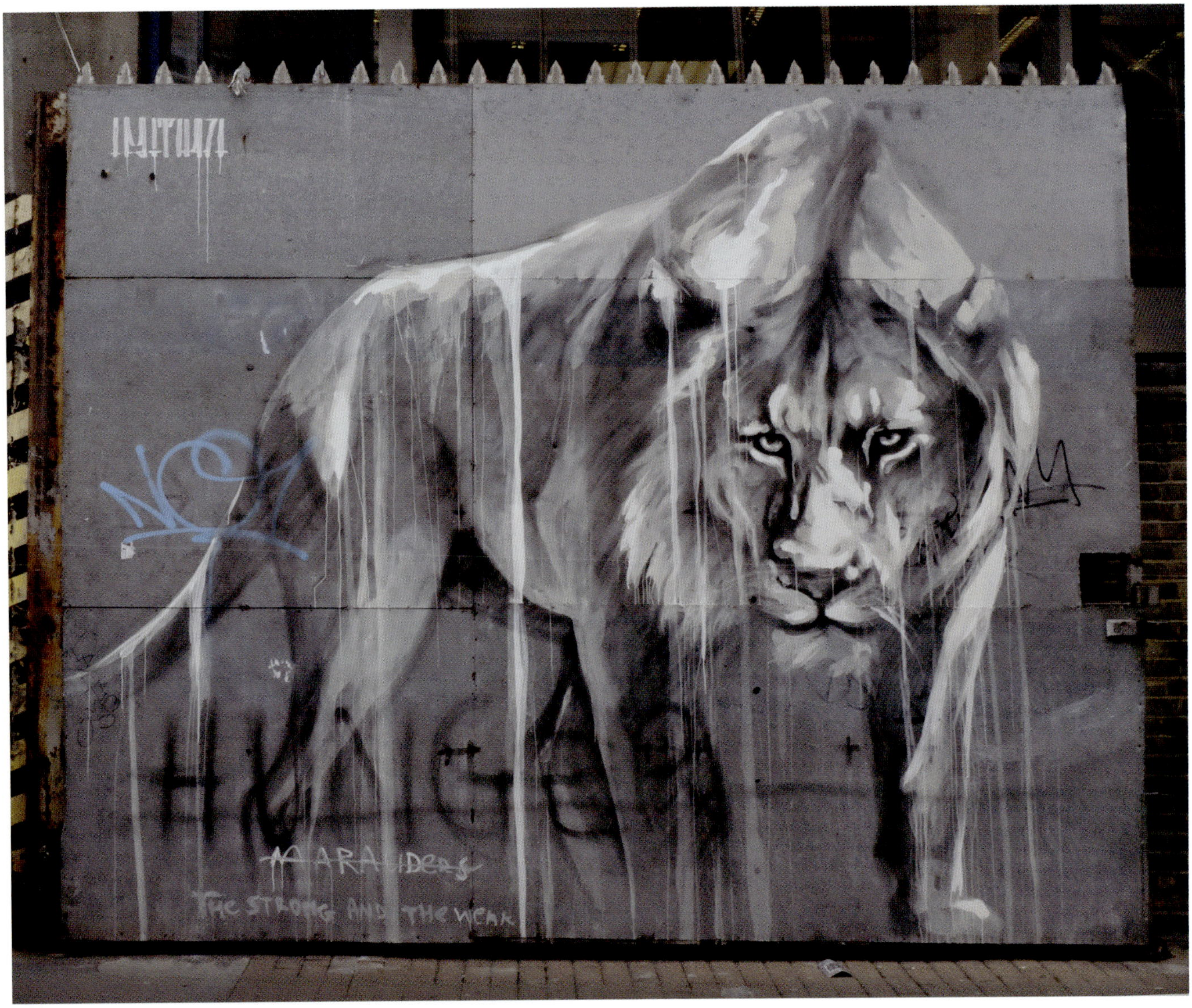

HUNGER, LONDON, ENGLAND

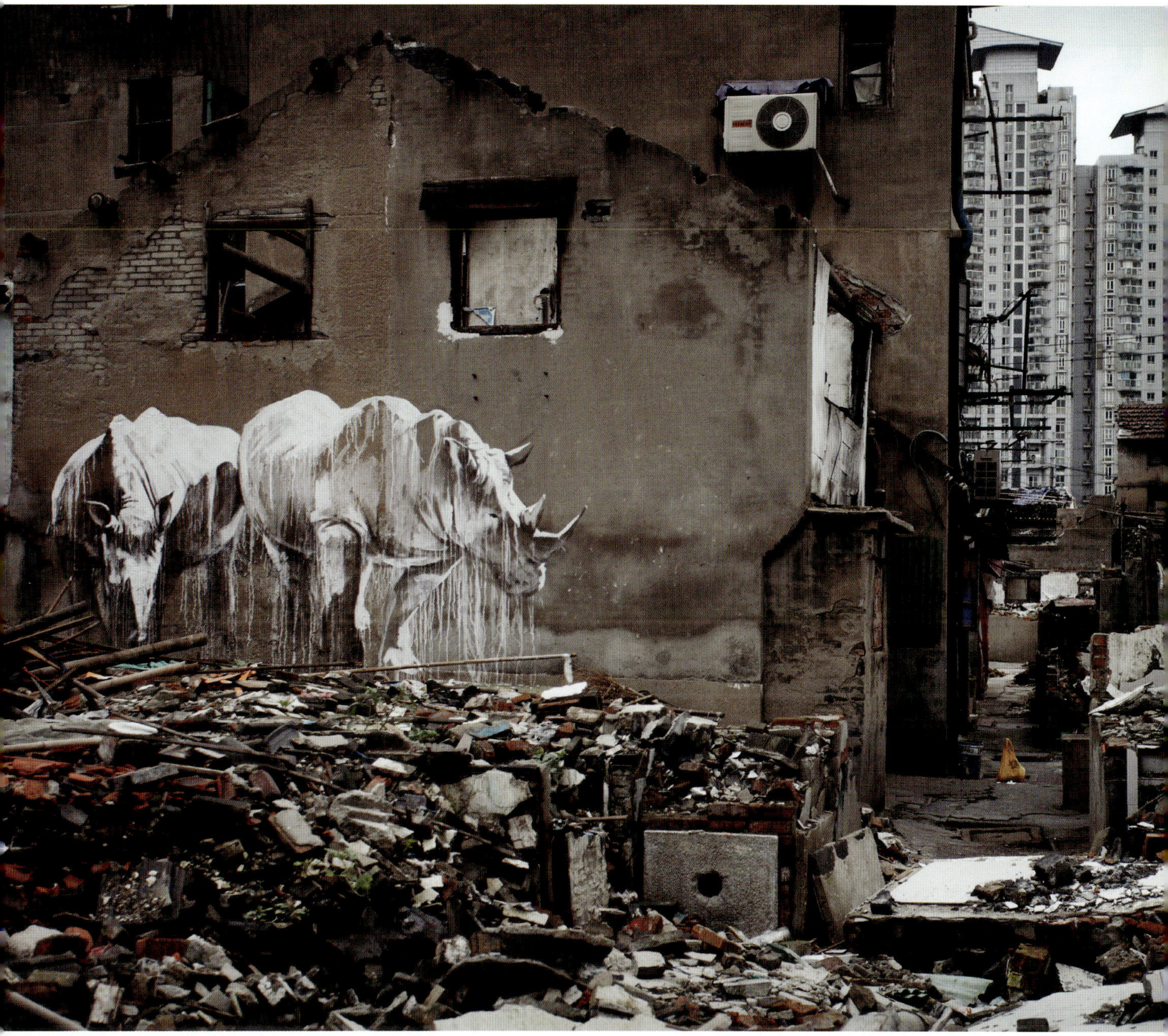

THE TAMING OF THE BEASTS, SHANGHAI, CHINA

FOLLOWING SPREAD:
UNA SALUS VICTUS NULLAM SPERARE SALUTEM, JOHANNESBURG, SOUTH AFRICA

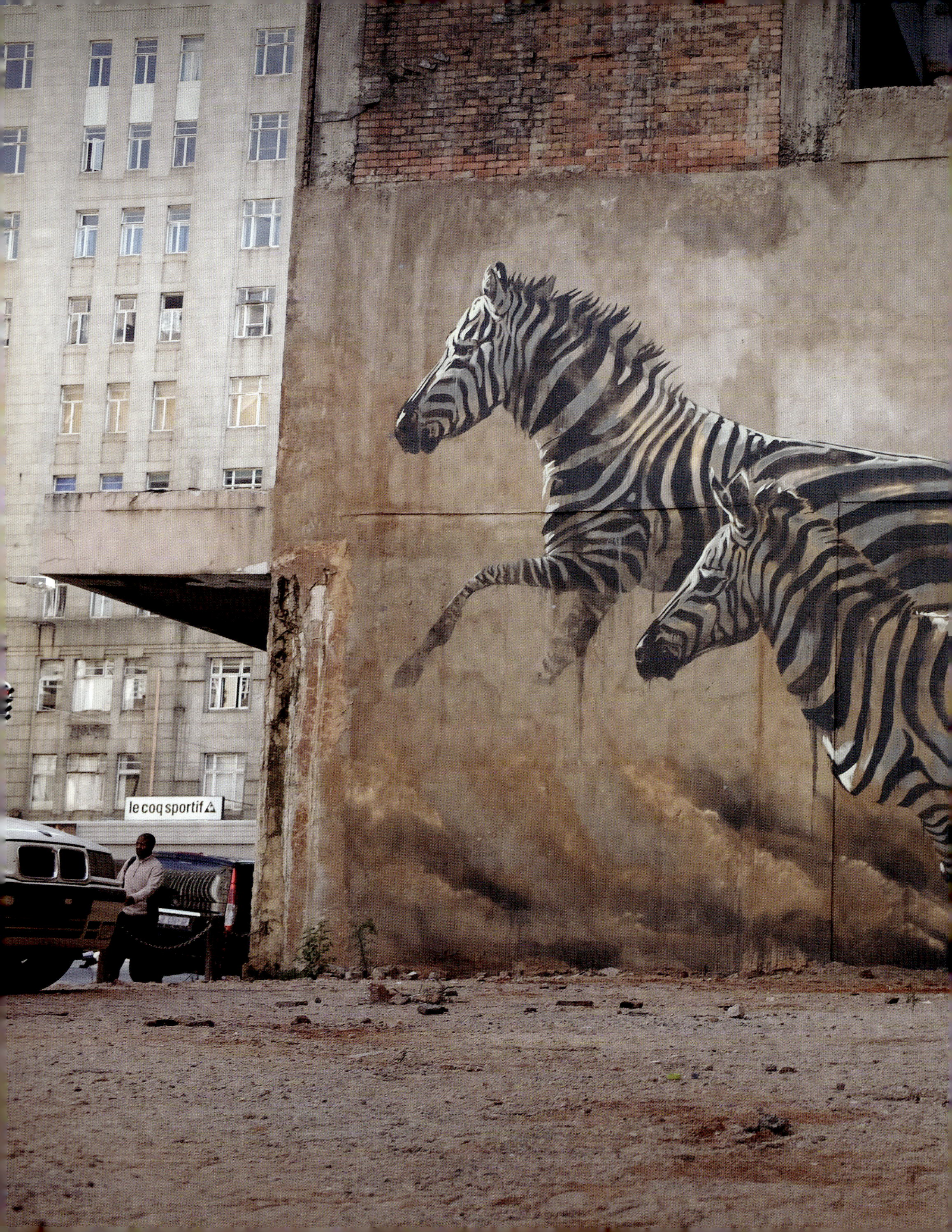
le coq sportif

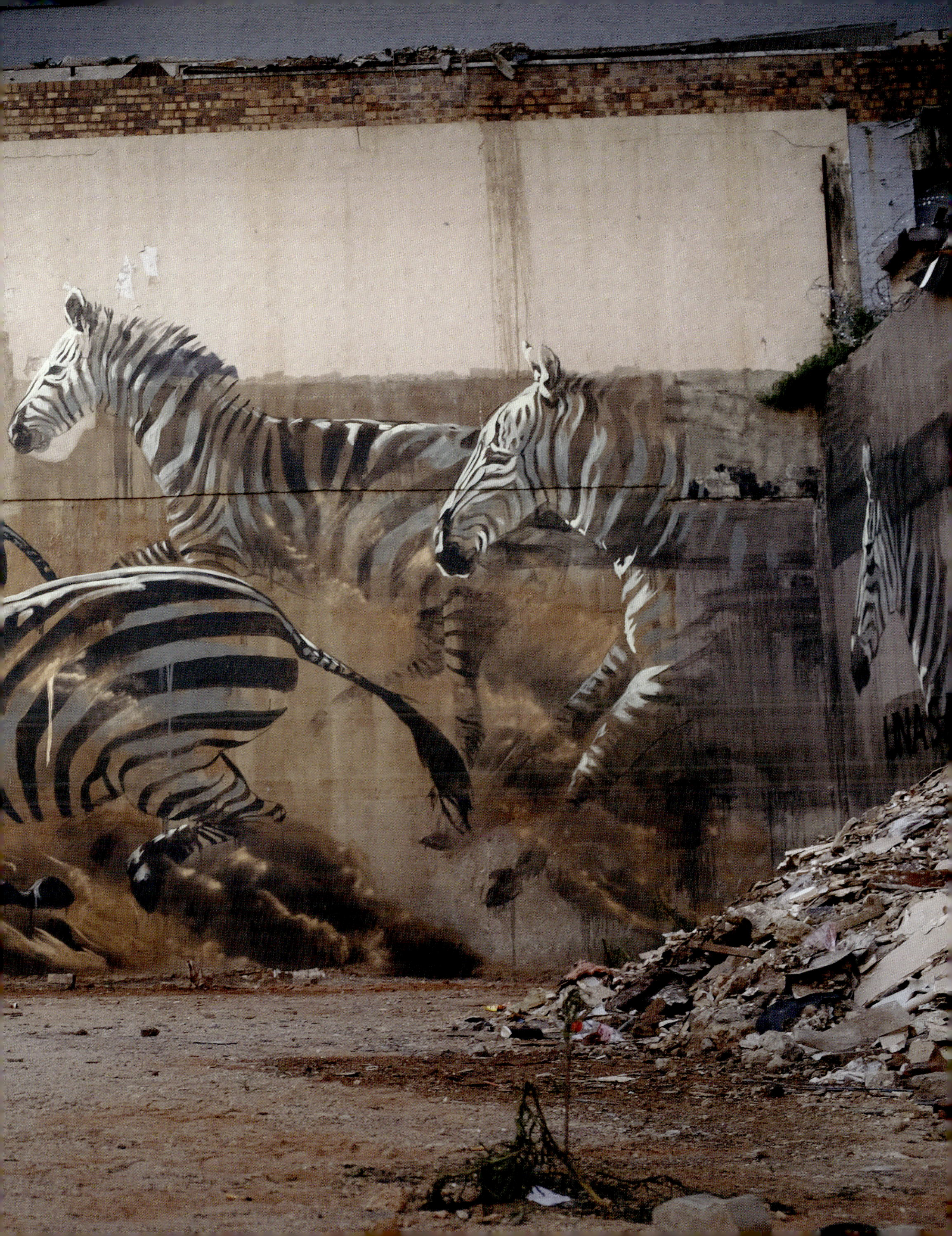

CHAD HASEGAWA

SAN FRANCISCO, CALIFORNIA

Bear Roots

The bear came about totally on its own. I wanted to paint something for everyone to enjoy that also made sense for the environment where I was painting, San Francisco. I was really into backpacking in California National Parks. It was great not really knowing what to do, or how to do it; just myself and nature. The only problem was my fear of getting attacked or encountering the animal on the California state flag, the Grizzly bear. At night, during the pitch-black, I would be afraid of using a flashlight in case of getting the attention from unwanted company. I would sharpen the toughest stick I could find, like *Lord of the Flies*. I would go through so much to be prepared for an encounter, but like seeing a shark in the ocean, it never happened. Finally, I see a sign with a legend on it, and I read that there haven't been any Grizzlies in the area for a hundred years. The greatest part was that it said San Francisco used to have a population of ten thousand Grizzly bears. I was blown away by that, so I wanted to bring them back and paint them where they belong. I try to make them a part of the neighborhood. I want them to make you feel like you are sharing the space together. In a way, they will protect you or look out for you. Personally, sometimes they represent my passed-away relatives, or other family and friends.

I paint them in places where people don't mind having a little bit of a mess around, and getting paint on the ground ain't so bad compared to real problems. Those are the types of places where the art is really appreciated. I want folks in the neighborhood to have a place to go and look at something wild and full of energy, or just take a break and stare at colors. I paint them as if they are that beast scaring away unwanted things. I feel like I should be putting them everywhere in San Francisco right now.

Meeting a Bear in Person

I never have. Always wondering when that will happen. I've wondered what sort of personality they really have. Are they smart like dogs?

The Messengers

Before I did the bears, I painted Hawaiian fish and an ostrich. I recently painted a cow for the first time. The aggressive bears are the protectors, but the cow is the giver. They give a lot in many ways and have many uses—Earth's gift.

The Museum of Modern Bears

There is a reason for everything I hang on the wall in a gallery. One time, I ripped off the Abstract Expressionism room at SFMOMA. I recreated all the paintings and sculptures but turned them into bears. Then I hung them in the same exact order on the wall and named everything after the original artist.

Bear Friends Forever

The sculptures in my last show were named after friends I grew up with. The postures reminded me of theirs. I positioned them staring at the paintings; hopefully it got the people who came to the show to do the same thing.

Aloha Fresh

A wall I painted in Honolulu is located across a main street from the biggest homeless camp I have ever seen. My friend Keola Morse collaborated with me and painted the letters that read, "Aloha Fresh," and I painted a bear for each letter. That wall mimics the repetition of the blue-tarp shelters in paradise. I wanted to give the people something to look at on their way home, and art was all I had to offer.

BIG JOURDAN, 72" X 72", LATEX ON CANVAS

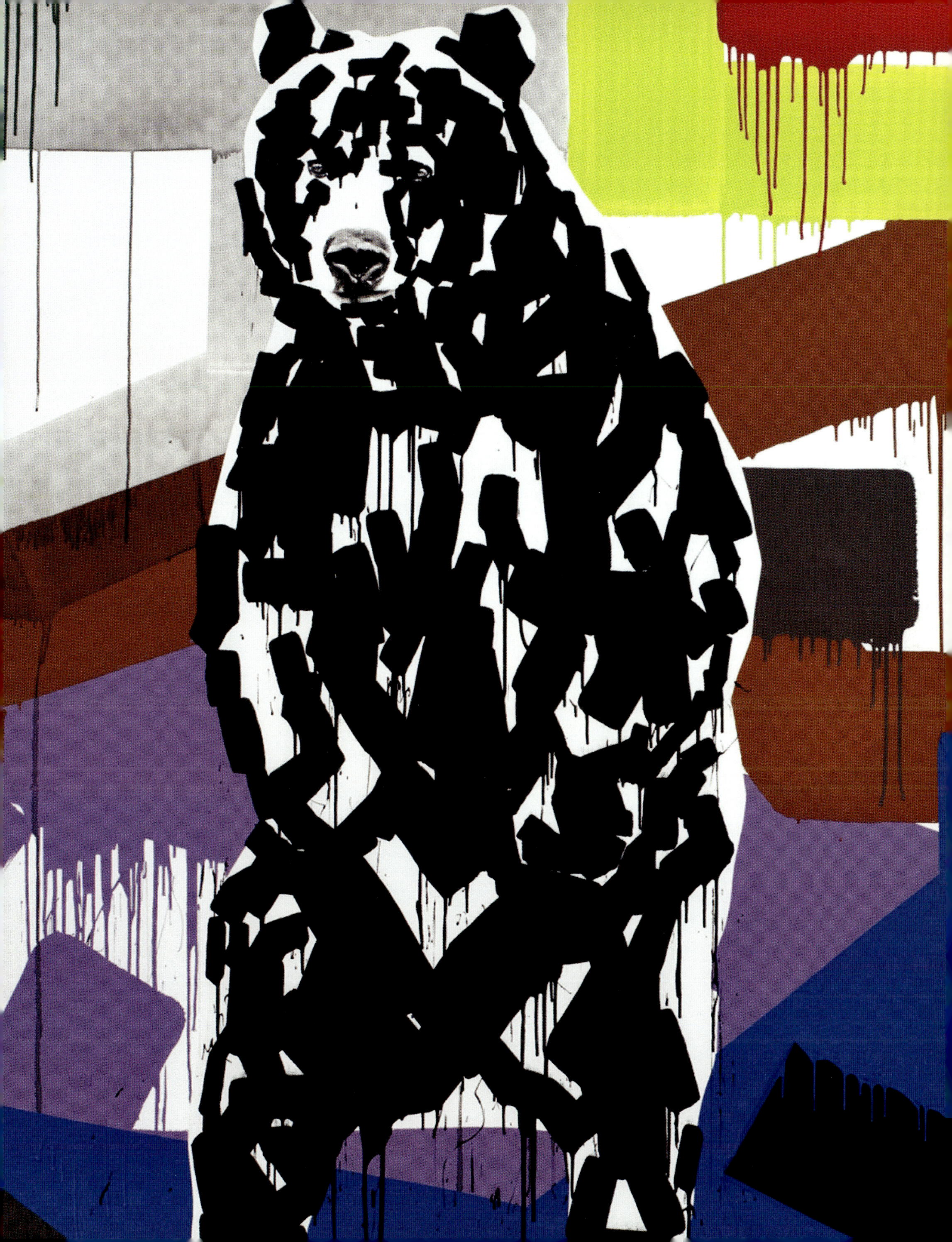

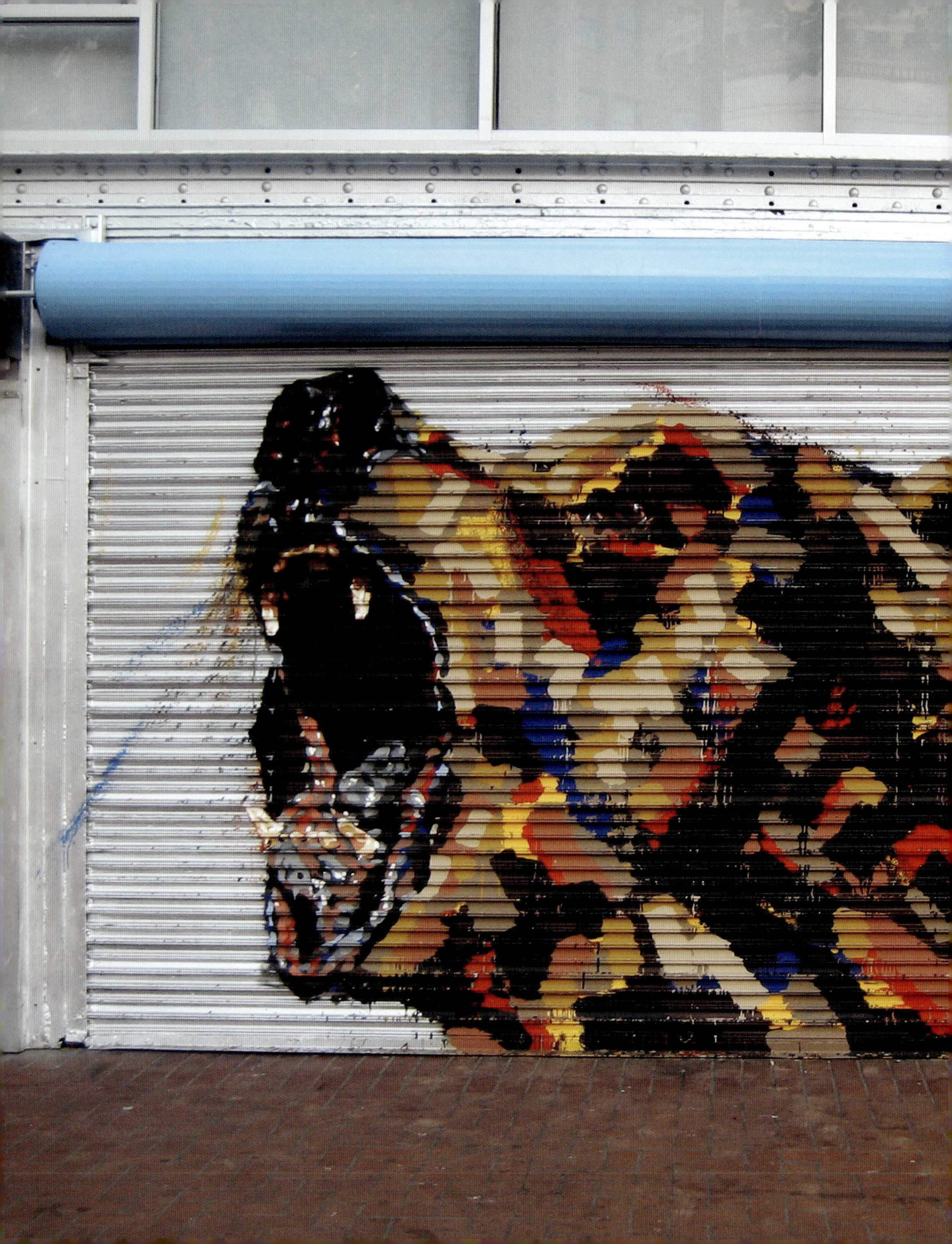

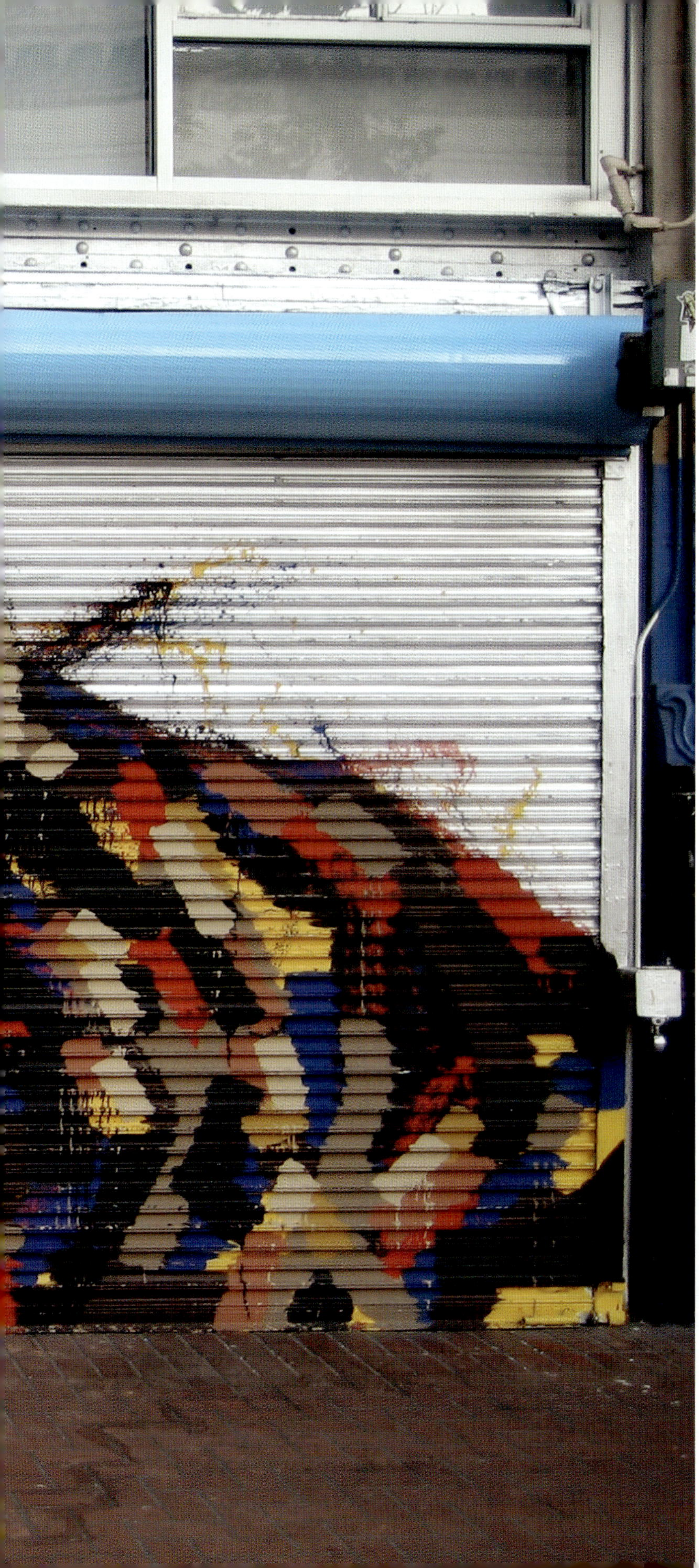

MOTHER MARKET
16' X 9'
LATEX ON METAL

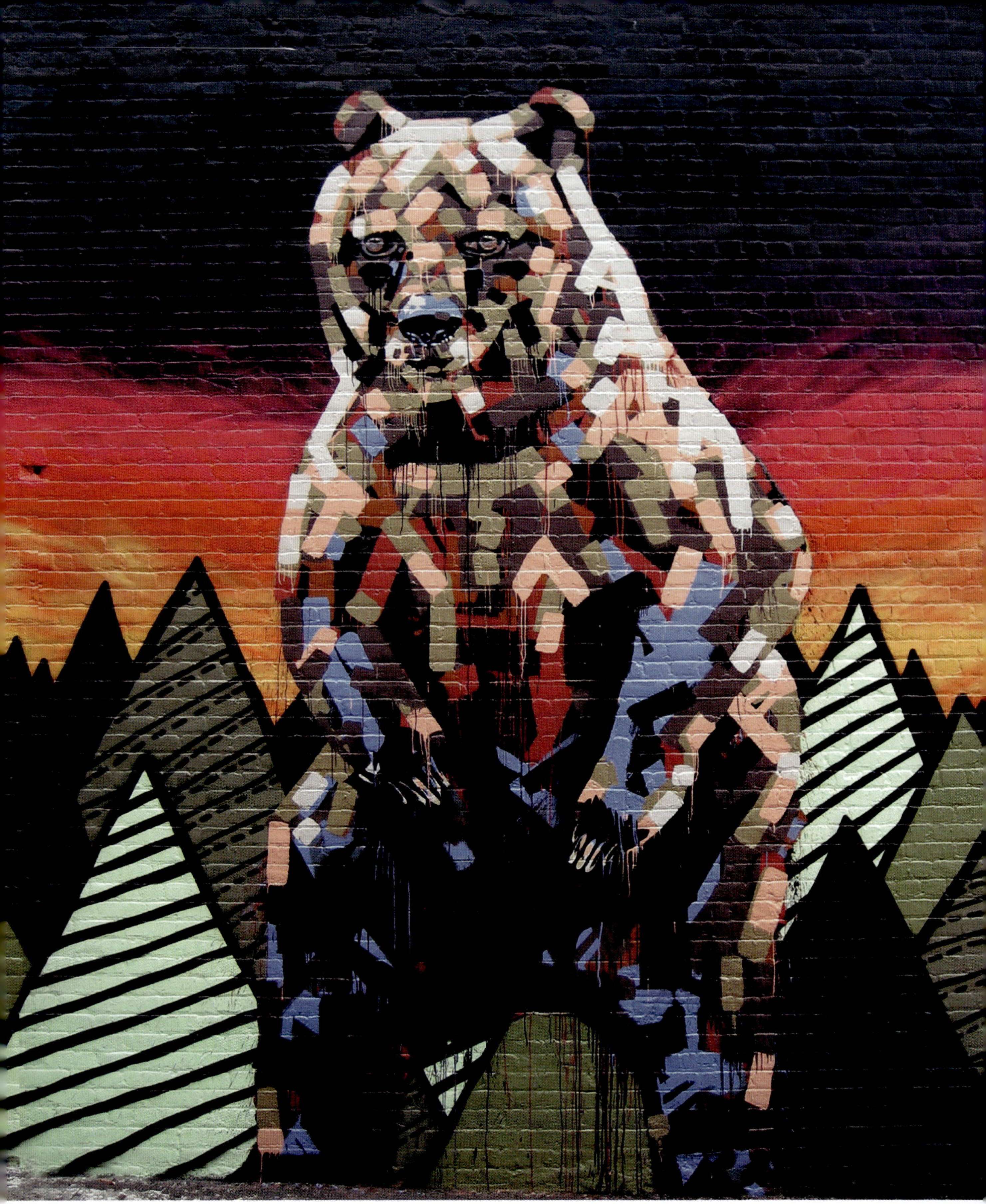

DREAM BIG, 17' X 18', LATEX ON BRICK

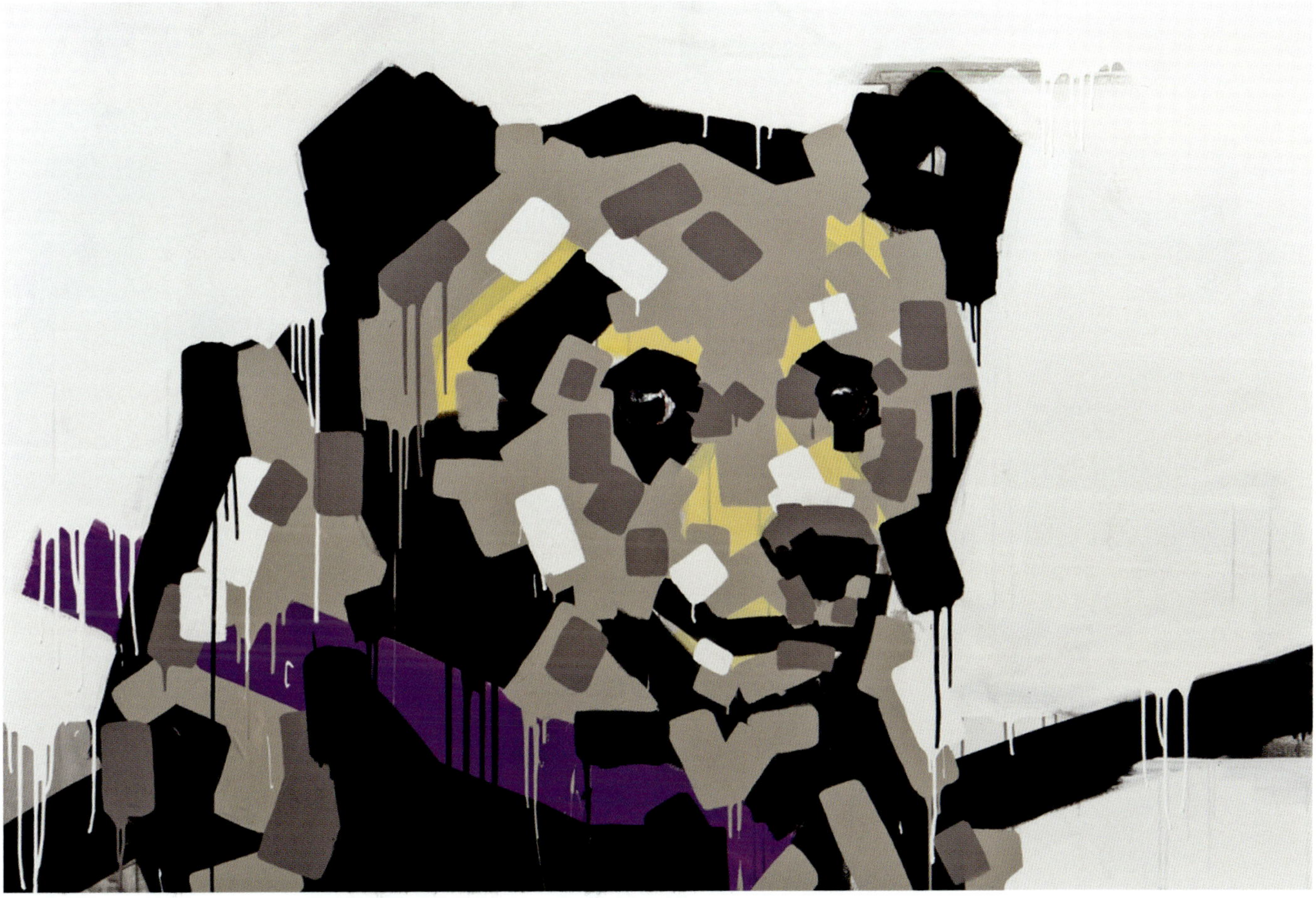

KLINE, 76' X 52', LATEX ON CANVAS

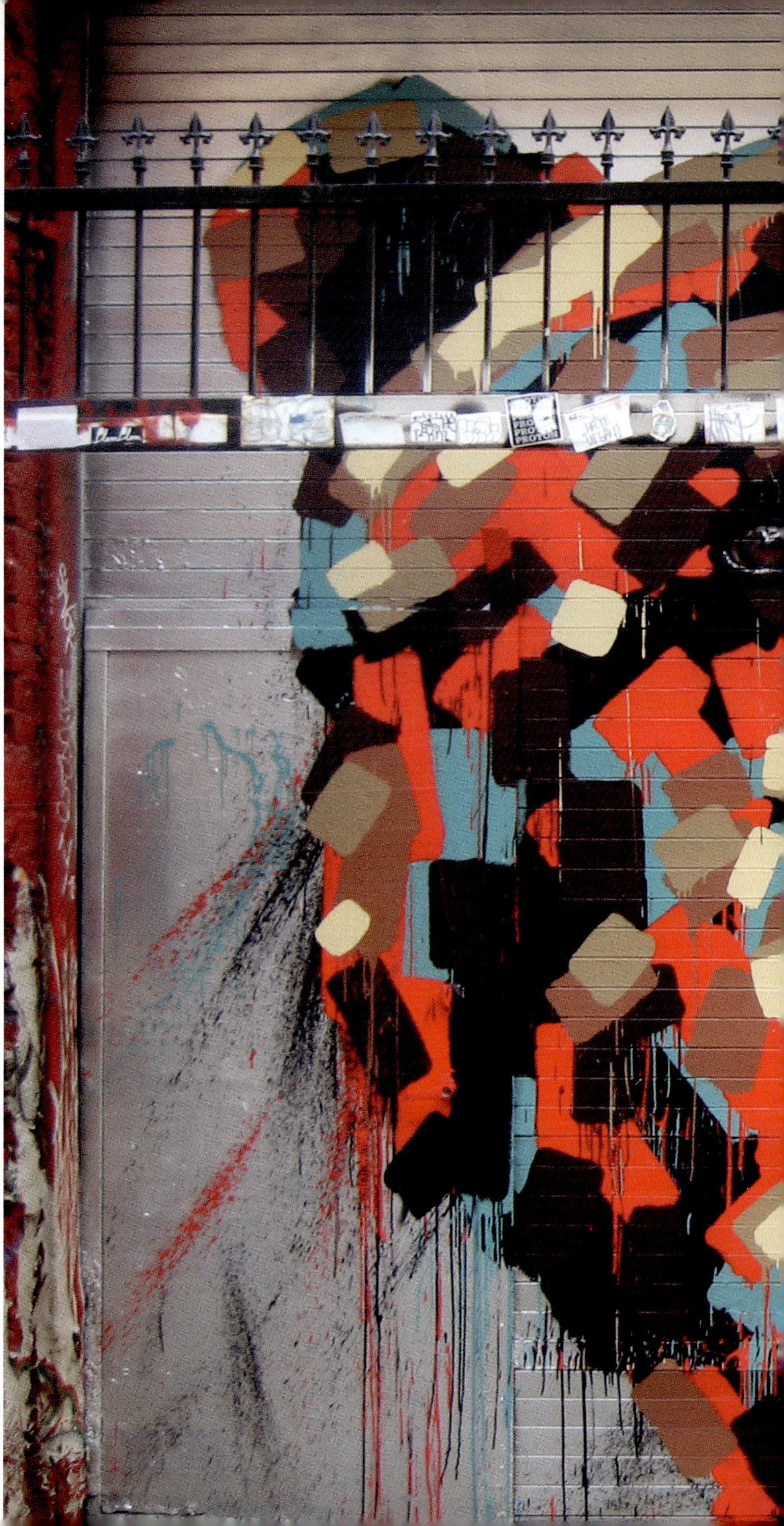

ZOOED
13' X 12'
LATEX ON METAL

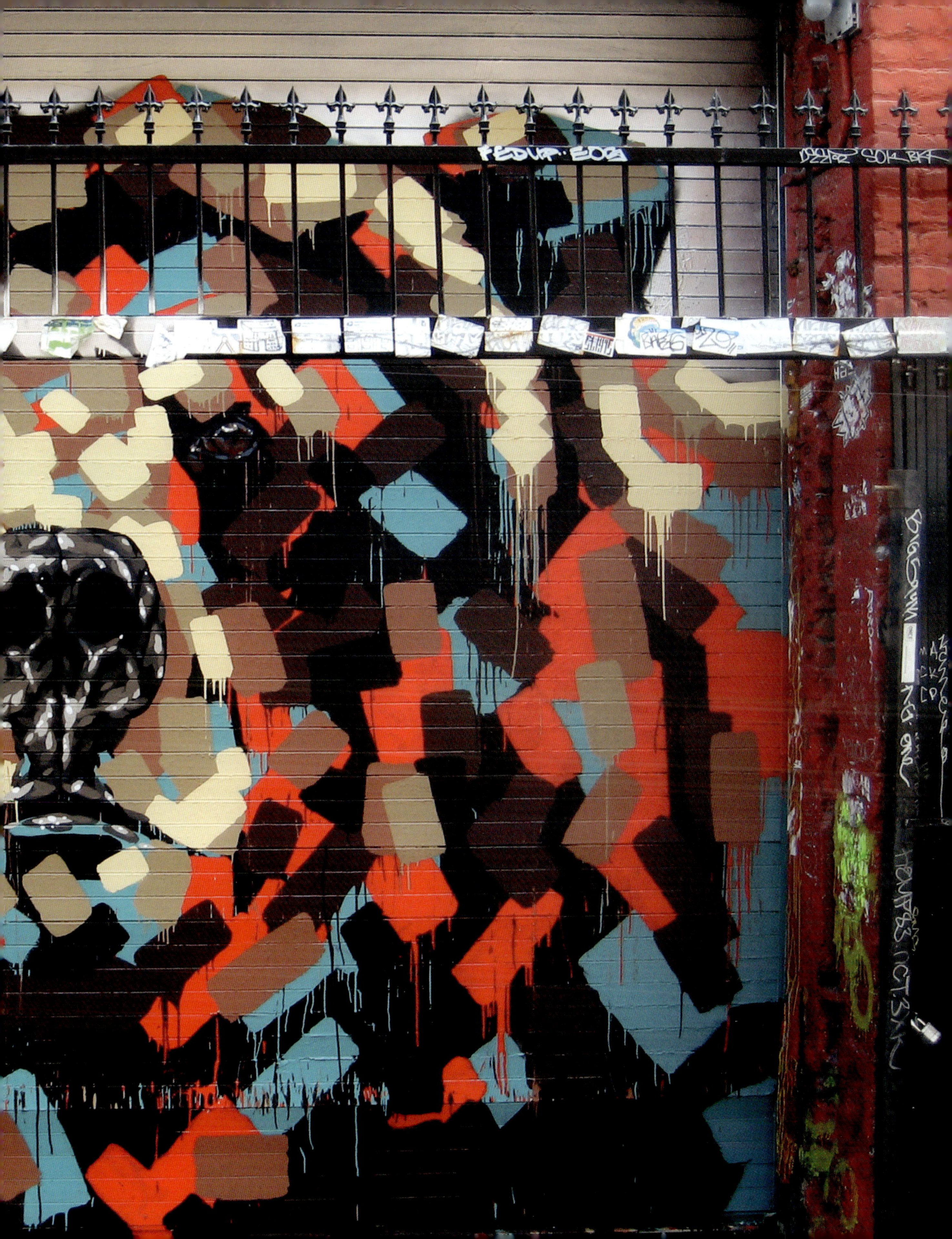

JUXTAPOZ